ASPECTS OF PEACEKEEPING

Edited by

D. S. GORDON

Senior Lecturer
Department of Defence and International Affairs,
Royal Military Academy Sandhurst

and

F. H. TOASE

Head of Department
Department of Defence and International Affairs,
Royal Military Academy Sandhurst

THE SANDHURST CONFERENCE SERIES

General Editor
Matthew Midlane

FRANK CASS
LONDON • PORTLAND, OR

First published in 2001 in Great Britain by
FRANK CASS PUBLISHERS
Newbury House, 900 Eastern Avenue
London IG2 7HH

and in the United States of America by
FRANK CASS PUBLISHERS
5824 N.E. Hassalo Street
Portland, Oregon, 97213-3644

Website: www.frankcass.com

British Library Cataloguing in Publication Data
Aspects of peacekeeping. – (The Sandhurst Conference series
; no. 2)
1. United Nations 2. Peace 3. Security, International
I. Gordon, D. S. II. Toase, F. H.
327.1'72

ISBN 0-7146-5040-4 (cloth)
ISBN 0-7146-8101-6 (paper)
ISSN 1468-1153

Library of Congress Cataloging-in-Publication Data
Aspects of peacekeeping / edited by D.S. Gordon and F.H. Toase.
    p. cm. – (The Sandhurst conference series, ISSN 1483-1153)
Includes bibliographical references and index.
ISBN 0-7146-5040-4 (cloth) – ISBN 0-7146-8101-6 (pbk.)
    1. Peacekeeping forces. 2. Humanitarian intervention. I. Gordon, D. S. (D. Stuart)
II. Toase, F. H. III. Series.

JZ6374 .A85 2000
341.5'84–dc21   00-043217

Typeset by Vitaset, Paddock Wood, Kent
Printed in Great Britain by
MPG Books Ltd, Bodmin, Cornwall

ASPECTS OF PEACEKEEPING

THE SANDHURST CONFERENCE SERIES
ISSN 1468-1153
Series Editor: Matthew Midlane

Thank you, as always, Amanda
for your special patience and boundless support.
Thank you also Elloise and Evelyn
for all your smiles. S.G.

To the Department of International Politics,
UCW Aberystwyth, where my interest in the
United Nations was aroused;
to Catherine, who sustained me through my PhD
on a related subject; and to Emily, Jennifer, Timothy
and Andrew who saw rather less of me than they
deserved while this book was under way. F.T.

Contents

Tables

Series Editor's Preface

This is the second in a series of three books charting important themes for the British Army, and perhaps every Army, in the post-Cold War era. The first book in the series, *The Media and International Security* edited by Stephen Badsey, explores the impact of the media on conflict and military operations. This, the second volume, begins to unpack many of the features of contemporary peace support operations. While it is not intended to provide an exhaustive survey of every debate surrounding such operations, it does endeavour to provide the reader with a flavour of many of the themes impacting upon the broad array of organisations thrown together in response-complex emergencies. We have made a conscious effort to reflect the diversity of actors working alongside one another and to begin an exploration of the nature of the relationships which can and do form among organisations and institutions. For an institution such as the Royal Military Academy Sandhurst seeking to understand such relationships, particularly – although not exclusively – at the tactical and operational levels, is of obvious importance. For any academic institution seeking to explore the issues that bind and divide the diplomatic, humanitarian and military communities this book provides an exceptionally useful multidisciplinary introduction.

The third book in this series, edited by Paul Latawski and Stephen Badsey, examines the broad impact of the dissolution of the Former Yugoslavia. While it is not intended to act as a primer on the Balkans, it will provide a survey of issues ranging from the historical roots of conflict in the region and the impact of the Second World War through to humanitarian–military relationships during the course of NATO's Kosovo campaign.

For the British Army the dissolution of the Former Yugoslavia has been a formative experience. It has affected doctrine, attitudes to the use of force, relationships with the humanitarian community, the UN and other government departments. Ultimately, the experiences of the United Nations Protection Force and the NATO-led Peace Implementation and Stabilisation forces (IFOR and SFOR) underpinned the Strategic Defence Review and the emergence of the British expeditionary strategy. It has also stimulated changes within the transatlantic alliance both in terms of relationships between allies and the force structures themselves. In short, it has served to define our attitudes and responses to a vast range of operations below the threshold of general or regional war.

We hope you enjoy reading the series.

Matthew Midlane
Director of Studies
Royal Military Academy Sandhurst

Preface

This volume draws largely on a series of diverse presentations delivered at the Royal Military Academy Sandhurst. The rationale behind the book was to capture at least some of the diversity and complexity of activity within contemporary peace support missions. It is not intended to be a comprehensive exploration of all of the issues facing and impacting upon practitioners, but it is a means of bringing together aspects of several disciplines which contribute to a broader understanding of the nature of peace support operations. We sincerely hope that this book adds to an already lively interdisciplinary debate.

The editors would like to thank the Royal Military Academy, particularly the Director of Studies, Matthew Midlane, for supporting the project. Any opinions expressed in the book, however, are those of the contributing authors only; any errors are those of the 'team' and not those of the many persons who have helped us in this project.

SG, FT
RMA Sandhurst
Summer 1999

Notes on Contributors

Koenraad Van Brabant is currently a Research Fellow at the Overseas Development Institute in London. He trained as an anthropologist and in development studies and, for eight years, managed aid programmes in Afghanistan, Ethiopia and Sri Lanka. Recently he has been actively involved in various initiatives to improve policy and practice for the security of aid agencies, including a contribution to the development of a training course on security management in violent conflict.

Richard Connaughton was, until recently, Colonel Defence Studies for the British Army. He is now a freelance consultant on defence issues.

Christopher Dandeker is Professor of War Studies at the Department of War Studies, King's College, London.

Rosemary Durward is a Senior Lecturer in the Department of Defence and International Affairs at the Royal Military Academy Sandhurst. She has published in the areas of international and European security.

Edward Flint is a Senior Lecturer in the Department of Defence and International Affairs at the Royal Military Academy Sandhurst. He contributed a chapter on the defence industry to F. H. Toase and E. J. Yorke (eds), *The New South Africa* (Macmillan, 1998). He has a research interest in civil affairs.

Stuart Gordon is a Senior Lecturer in the Department of Defence and International Affairs at the Royal Military Academy Sandhurst. He has also taught at the United Kingdom Joint Services Command and Staff College, Bracknell. A former Royal Air Force officer, his current research focuses upon civil–military relations in complex emergencies. His doctoral thesis is on the United Nations Protection Force in Bosnia-Herzegovina.

James Gow is Reader in War Studies in the Department of War Studies, King's College, London.

Ian Johnstone is a senior official in the United Nations, working in the Executive Office of the Secretary-General. Previously he has served as a Senior Associate of the International Peace Academy as well as a legal officer in the United Nations' Office of Legal Affairs. He has written widely on the United Nations and his publications include *Rights and Reconciliation: UN Strategies in El Salvador* (Lynne Reinner, 1995) and *Aftermath of the Gulf War: An Assessment of UN Action* (Lynne Reinner, 1994).

Paul Latawski is a Senior Lecturer in the Defence and International Affairs Department at the Royal Military Academy Sandhurst. He is also an Associate Fellow in the European Security Programme at the Royal United Services Institute for Defence Studies and an Honorary Visiting Fellow at the School of Slavonic and East European Studies, University of London. His research interests concern security and defence issues in the former communist states of Central and Eastern Europe. He has published widely on these topics.

Sergio Vieria de Mello is Under Secretary-General for Humanitarian Affairs and Emergency Relief Coordinator at the United Nations.

Paul B. Rich is joint editor of *Small Wars and Insurgencies*. He has degrees from the Universities of Sussex, York and Warwick and has taught at the Universities of Bristol, Luton and Melbourne. He is currently teaching at the University of Cambridge. He has written extensively on international relations and African issues and has published *State Power and Black Politics in South Africa* (St Martin's Press, 1996) and co-edited *The Counter Insurgent State* (Macmillan, 1997) and *Warlords in International Relations* (Macmillan, forthcoming).

Hugo Slim is a Senior Lecturer in International Humanitarianism at Oxford Brookes University.

Shashi Tharoor is Director of Communications for the United Nations.

Francis Toase is Head of the Defence and International Affairs Department at the Royal Military Academy Sandhurst. He gained his BSc (Econ) in International Politics and History, his MSc (Econ) in International Politics and his PhD in International Politics from the University College of Wales, Aberystwyth. He has written extensively on political and military affairs, his most recent work being *The New South Africa* (Macmillan, 1998), co-edited with E. J. Yorke.

Jim Whitman was formerly at the Faculty of Social and Political Sciences, Cambridge University. He is now a Senior Lecturer in the Department of Peace Studies at Bradford University.

Edmund Yorke is a Senior Lecturer in the Department of Defence and International Affairs at the Royal Military Academy Sandhurst. He has a doctorate in Central African History from Cambridge University. His most recent publication is *The New South Africa* (Macmillan, 1998), co-edited with Francis Toase.

Abbreviations

ACMI	African Crisis Management Initiative
ACRF	African Crisis Response Force
ACRI	African Crisis Response Initiative
ADFL	Alliance of Democratic Forces for the Liberation of Congo-Zaire
AFCENT	Allied Forces Central Europe Command (NATO)
AFL	Armed Forces of Liberia
ANC	African National Congress (South Africa)
AOR	area of responsibility
ARRC	Allied Rapid Reaction Corps (NATO)
BALTBAT	Joint Baltic Peacekeeping Battalion
BALTDEFCOL	Baltic Defence College
BALTNET	Baltic Airspace Surveillance Network
BALTRON	Joint Baltic Naval Squadron
BDF	Botswana Defence Force
BH	Bosnia-Herzegovina
BHC	Bosnia-Herzegovina Command (UNPROFOR)
BiH	Bosnian Army
BSA	Bosnian Serb Army
CA	civil affairs
CAO	civil affairs officer
CAP	combat air patrol
CAS	close air support
CEE	Central and Eastern Europe
CENCOOP	Central European Nations Cooperation in Peace Support
CFSP	Common Foreign and Security Policy (EU)
CIMIC	civil–military cooperation
CIMICTF	CIMIC Task Force

CIS	Commonwealth of Independent States
CJTF	Combined Joint Task Force (NATO)
CMOC	Civil–Military Operations Centre
CMTF	Civil–Military Task Force
CRUA	Revolutionary Committee of Unity and Action (Algeria)
CSCE	Conference on Security and Cooperation in Europe
DAM	Department of Administration and Management (UN)
DFID	Department for International Development (UK)
DFOR	Dissuasion Force (projected NATO-led force in Bosnia)
DHA	Department of Humanitarian Affairs (UN)
DPA	Department of Political Affairs (UN)
DPKO	Department of Peacekeeping Operations (UN)
EAPC	European-Atlantic Partnership Council
EC	European Community
ECOMOG	Economic Community of West African States Monitoring Group
ECOWAS	Economic Community of West African States
EMU	European Monetary Union
ESDI	European Security and Defence Identity
ESTCOY	Estonian Company
ETS	Educational and Training Services (British Army)
EU	European Union
FAC	forward air control
FAO	Food and Agriculture Organisation (UN)
FCO	Foreign and Commonwealth Office (UK)
FLN	Front de Libération Nationale (Algeria)
FRELIMO	Frente de Libertação de Moçambique
FRY	Former Republic of Yugoslavia
FSU	Former Soviet Union
FYROM	Former Yugoslav Republic of Macedonia
G5	Military headquarters branch responsible for CIMIC
GFAP	General Framework Agreement for Peace (Dayton Accords)
GMOs	gratis military officers
GUAM	Georgia, Ukraine, Azerbaijan and Moldova
HAC	Humanitarian Affairs Centre (Haiti)
HIC	high-intensity conflict
HOC	Humanitarian Operations Centre
HV	Hrvatska Vojska (Croatian Army)
HVO	Hrvatsko Vijece Odbrane (Bosnian Croat Army)

IASC	Inter-Agency Standing Committee (UN)
ICFY	International Commission on the Former Yugoslavia
ICRC	International Committee of the Red Cross
ICVA	International Consortium of Voluntary Agencies
IFAD	International Fund for Agricultural Development
IFOR	Implementation Force (NATO-led force in Bosnia)
IMF	International Monetary Fund
IMG	International Management Group (UN)
INPFL	Independent National Patriotic Front of Liberia
IPA	International Peace Academy
IPFL	Independent Patriotic Front of Liberia
JDISS	Joint Deployable Intelligence Support System
JNA	Jugoslav (Yugoslav) National Army
KLA	Kosovo Liberation Army
KVM	Kosovo Verification Mission
LATCOY	Latvian Company
LIC	low-intensity conflict
LITCOY	Lithuanian Company
LITPOLBAT	Lithuanian–Polish Peacekeeping Battalion
LTTE	Liberation Tigers of Tamil Eelam
MCRMP	Mechanism for Conflict Resolution, Management and Prevention (OAU)
MIC	mid-intensity conflict
MISAB	Mission to Monitor the Implementation of the Bangui Agreement
MMWG	Mixed Military Working Group
MNARDPF	Multinational African Rapid Deployment Peace Force
MNF	Multinational Force (UN authorised force proposed for Great Lakes)
MOU	Memorandum of Understanding
MPF	Multinational Protection Force
MPFSEE	Multinational Peace Force South-Eastern Europe
MSF	Médecins sans Frontières
NAC	North Atlantic Council
NACC	North Atlantic Cooperation Council
NATO	North Atlantic Treaty Organisation
NCCNI	NGO Coordinating Committee for Northern Iraq
NGO	non-governmental organisation
NLF	National Liberation Front (Vietnam)
NMOG	Neutral Military Observer Group (OAU)
NPFL	National Patriotic Front of Liberia
NSS	National Security Strategy (USA)

OAU	Organisation of African Unity
OCHA	Office for the Coordination of Humanitarian Affairs
ODA	Overseas Development Administration (UK)
OECD	Organisation for Economic Cooperation and Development
OFDA	Office of Foreign Disaster Assistance (USA)
OHR	Office of the High Representative (in Bosnia)
OLS	Operation Lifeline Sudan
OMIB	OAU Mission in Burundi
ONUMOZ	United Nations Operation in Mozambique
ONUSAL	United Nations Observer Mission in El Salvador
OOTW	operations other than war
OSCE	Organisation for Security and Cooperation in Europe
OSOCC	On-site Operation Coordination Centre (Rwanda)
PE	peace enforcement
PfP	Partnership for Peace
PGM	precision-guided munition
PJHQ	Permanent Joint Headquarters (UK)
PK	peacekeeping
POLUKRBAT	Polish–Ukrainian Peacekeeping Battalion
PSO	peace-support operation
PSYOPS	psychological operations
RDMHQ	Rapid Deployable Mission Headquarters
RENAMO	Resistãnçia Nacional Moçambicana
ROE	rules of engagement
RUF	Revolutionary United Front
SACEUR	Supreme Allied Commander Europe (NATO)
SADC	Southern African Development Community
SAM	surface-to-air missile
SANDF	South African National Defence Force
SCNS	Supervisory Commission of Neutral States in Korea
SCSI	Strategic and Combat Studies Institute (UK)
SDR	Strategic Defence Review (UK)
SEAD	suppression of enemy air defences
SEEBRIG	South-Eastern European Brigade
SFOR	Stabilisation Force (NATO-led force in Bosnia)
SHIRBRIG	Stand-by Forces High Readiness Brigade (UN Multi-national)
SNM	Somali National Movement
SPM	Somalia Patriotic Movement
SRSG	Special Representative of the (UN) Secretary-General
SSDF	Somali Salvation Democratic Front

TA	Territorial Army (UK)
UK	United Kingdom
UN	United Nations
UNAMIR	United Nations Assistance Mission for Rwanda
UNAVEM	United Nations Angola Verification Mission
UNDP	United Nations Development Programme
UNHCR	United Nations High Commissioner for Refugees
UNICEF	United Nations International Children's Emergency Fund
UNITAF	Unified Task Force
UNMIH	United Nations Mission in Haiti
UNOMIL	United Nations Observer Mission in Liberia
UNOSOM	United Nations Operation in Somalia
UNPREDEP	United Nations Preventive Deployment Force
UNPROFOR	United Nations Protection Force (in Bosnia-Herzegovina)
UNSAS	United Nations Standby Arrangement System
UNTAC	United Nations Transitional Authority in Cambodia
UNTAG	United Nations Transition Assistance Group (in Namibia)
USA	United States of America
USAID	US Agency for International Development
USAR	United States Army Reserve
USC	United Somali Congress
VOPP	Vance–Owen Peace Plan
WEU	Western European Union
WFP	World Food Programme
ZANU-PF	Zimbabwe African National Union-Patriotic Front
ZNA	Zimbabwe National Army

Introduction

STUART GORDON AND FRANCIS TOASE

The nature of United Nations (UN) operational involvement in the practical management of conflict has evolved dramatically. There are a variety of reasons for this. Until the ill-fated operations in Bosnia and Somalia the UN Security Council showed itself to be increasingly willing to deploy troops into situations where the consent of the belligerent factions was no longer the absolute that it once was. Furthermore, the dilution of the concept of sovereignty as a prohibition on intervention, as well as a more collaborative approach to diplomacy on the part of the members of the Security Council, has led to involvement where once there would not have been an operational role for UN troops.

The purpose of peacekeeping also appeared to expand. While there was a clear and continuing requirement for traditional interpositionary and observer operations, a new implicit purpose appeared to be evolving. Traditionally peacekeeping forces were a means for simply containing regional conflict *after* a political and military hiatus had been reached in the conflict dynamic. Such 'traditional' operations were a product of a diplomatic process already engaged in drawing the military conflict to its end. However, particularly with the UN Protection Force (UNPROFOR) deployment to Bosnia-Herzegovina, the Security Council deployed troops into situations where, perhaps, they could create the conditions for a ceasefire and a viable political process. They were, implicitly, a 'causal' factor in the movement toward an end to active fighting rather than a simple catalyst for a process already under way at the time of their deployment. In other words, UN troops were deployed into a situation where they might generate the conditions for a peace process rather than reflecting a pre-existing process. This was the birth of the, arguably still-born, concept of 'strategic peacekeeping'.

There has also been a process of evolution within the (broadly defined) humanitarian community. The expansion in the numbers of humanitarian non-governmental organisations (NGOs) and an evolution in the concepts underpinning humanitarian action have accompanied the increasing salience of the right of humanitarian intervention.

The consequences of these changes have been enormous. This book, drawing on a conference held at the Royal Military Academy Sandhurst, attempts to explore a number of these operational issues.

From a military perspective perhaps the critical change that this new environment has brought is its impact upon the nature and utility of military force itself. Military force has developed a dual nature: it is simultaneously both 'protective' – a means of self-defence – and potentially 'escalatory' – a means of pursuing what are, in essence, political objectives. This was seen most clearly in the case of the UNPROFOR and the Unified Task Force (UNITAF) missions.

The inability to use limited force in a precise way that is clearly linked to achievable and well-defined political objectives has, to a significant extent, diluted the enthusiasm of the international community to harness military tools for humanitarian objectives. There has been an increased acceptance that, where force is used, it should be significantly greater than that provided to uphold, for example, the Bosnian safe areas or the consent-based, humanitarian access regime that prevailed in that war-stricken country until late 1995. These two factors also stimulated a vigorous debate on the nature of peace-support operations (PSOs). Whilst identifying the characteristics and operating principles which define both peacekeeping and war fighting is a relatively straightforward task, performing the same task for the activities which seem to lie between these categories has proven to be a far more difficult task for politicians. The mixing of consent-based and coercion-based mandates in Bosnia and Somalia clearly leads to a theoretical and practical illogicality: making war and peace against the same people, at the same time, on the same territory. UNPROFOR's operations in Bosnia also challenged the belief that the difference between the actions required of the belligerents by the international community and those concessions made freely by them could be bridged by the precise and limited use of air-strikes in a 'compellent' role. It was also recognised that troop deployments designed to promote a consent-based mandate provided a degree of vulnerability to reprisals that short circuited the 'compellence' elements of a coercive approach to generating consent. In effect, the Security Council confused consent by coercion and consent that was given freely.

This realisation challenged those who formulate military doctrine as they, unlike the academic community, had to provide a body of advice to commanders deployed operationally. This new environment challenged many of the certainties which had characterised warfare, at least in

Western minds, since the ending of World War II. It was an environment that few had a clear understanding of, let alone a capacity to provide effective guidance to military practitioners. Bearing this in mind, one can perhaps begin to understand the way in which several peace-support doctrines emerged. Fathered by necessity, they lacked the degree of reflection that would provide them with a capacity to endure. This was seen, perhaps most clearly, with the British Army doctrine of Wider Peacekeeping. This has now been subsumed into the more conventional peacekeeping doctrine but was only ever issued as an interim document reflecting, perhaps, the understandable haste with which it was constructed. This has, subsequently, been superseded as a result of experiences in Bosnia between 1992 and 1995. Essentially, it encouraged an overextension of the principles of peacekeeping into an environment to which they were ill suited.

To some extent, the removal of Wider Peacekeeping as a separate doctrine is unfair. Designed as 'tactical' doctrine, a guide to low-level commanders, it provided guidance on how to function in a challenging and volatile new environment where consent was not uniform. It was not designed to, nor is there any evidence to suggest that it did, guide the deliberations of the Security Council. Far from being hamstrung by low-level British Army doctrine, the Security Council remained as much a prisoner of national interest and the vagaries of international diplomacy as ever. However, the doctrine gave clear guidance to commanders on how to maintain and develop 'consent' for a mission that was generally accepted by the principal power brokers within a conflict, but which was not accepted by limited numbers of lower level commanders. In some ways the doctrine provided a benchmark of where action could and could not take place and gave guidance on the levels of troop numbers, their deployment patterns and required capabilities. In many ways, far from reflecting the failure of UNPROFOR, correct application of the implicit criteria for action contained in the Wider Peacekeeping doctrine would have encouraged inaction or wider enforcement action, not the half measures which characterised UNPROFOR.

Furthermore, despite the perceived failure of the (now deceased) doctrine in the UNPROFOR mission, one can still argue that the principles themselves remain valid. One needs to be careful not simply to draw the lesson of their failure from an environment that, in terms of consent for a UN presence, never met even the basic conditions for the deployment of a Wider Peacekeeping type of mission. Wider Peacekeeping doctrine, therefore, died not so much as a result of a failure of its core principles, but as a product of its application to an environment which was entirely inappropriate. In some ways, therefore, the extinction of the British doctrine of Wider Peacekeeping represents something of an overreaction to the failures encountered during UNPROFOR's mission.

These failures were, themselves, the product of numerous and diverse factors: a paucity of military resources; a confused and incrementally emerging mandate; technical and political limitations upon the utility of air-power; and a critical lack of consensus on objectives among the members of the Security Council. In other words, the problems of UNPROFOR were not a straightforward product of the failings of the principles underlying Wider Peacekeeping doctrine.

The nature of PSOs has changed in other ways. Solution-based military, humanitarian and political programmes, at least in terms of the declared aspirations, have led to the harnessing of these components of the UN machine in an attempt to develop synergies which will help to facilitate a convergence on a 'solution' to the conflict. These lines of action, as described in *An Agenda for Peace* (UN: New York, 1992), represent the 'silver bullet' intended to slay the social, political and economic forces which generate violence. Furthermore, such efforts, designed to undermine the processes which may also regenerate and perpetuate violence, potentially take PSOs beyond the containment strategies of the Cold War. Clearly, the evolution of such a 'peacebuilding' strategy has been somewhat suffocated by bureaucratic obstruction, a lack of resources and a paucity of political will, but it has contributed to an enormous institutional diversity in terms of the agencies which take action designed to resolve conflict within a given state.

This has created an unprecedented degree of inter- and intra-institutional 'multifunctionality'. Consequently, those who study PSOs have been challenged to understand the limits on coordination and cooperation between, and even within, the several actors. What, for example, are the limitations on the degree to which UN forces can provide security for humanitarian agencies of all types? What considerations drive emergency relief-based organisations, working in conflict, to request that security is provided by a peacekeeping force? How can they improve their own security? Such questions are not simply limited to issues of security. How, for example, can the limited quantities of resources – financial and material – be harnessed so as to provide the most effective emergency response to a humanitarian catastrophe? What factors limit the degree of cooperation between the community of NGOs and why do they take radically different stances on issues? Such questions are at the heart of a process which has led political, military and humanitarian actors, in the context of a UN intervention in a complex emergency, to examine what amounts to the nature of the 'division of labour' and relative organisational precedence.

For the humanitarian community the questions have not simply been restricted to those regarding coordination and a division of responsibilities. Humanitarian organisations have been particularly challenged to respond to what could be described as an evolving operational environment. Diluted prohibitions on encroachments upon state sovereignty, the increasing intentional, rather than incidental, targeting of civilians and the consequent increased salience of human rights issues have forced the humanitarian community to reassess the relevance of their operating principles. There has been a clear tension between the pragmatic imperative to secure access to beleaguered populations and the moral imperative to challenge and remedy the source of their misery. While it is improbable that this dilemma can be resolved entirely, it is likely that the dilemma will have a direct bearing on both the effectiveness of the operational programmes and the security of humanitarian agencies. What this new environment represents, more than anything else, is the increasing political and strategic salience of humanitarian action. Such action has become a potentially greater part of the conflict dynamic than has hitherto been the case.

The resulting debate within the humanitarian community as to the validity of operating principles has had a direct bearing on the nature of relationships between organisations. It has also stimulated a debate on the nature of the 'humanitarian space' when working in the context of conflict. Such a new environment has also forced an evolution in the way in which military forces deployed on PSOs deal with the civilian population and humanitarian community.

While civilian population movements have always had an enormous impact upon military operations (often restricting a commander's freedom of movement and action), the amelioration of the impact of such events was a product of military necessity rather than pure altruism or humanitarianism. Increasingly, Western militaries, in particular, have recognised that managing the humanitarian–military and the civilian–military interfaces have become essential aspects of operations. The former is a self-evident necessity when deployed on what amount to humanitarian support missions. The latter, however, has a variety of purposes. It provides a means of ensuring that the military fill 'gaps' where humanitarian agencies, as a result of the speed of the onset of a crisis or the volatility of the security environment, are unable to operate. However, it also represents a means of building the consent for the deployment of military formations. This may reduce the reliance upon 'hard' security for defence, replacing what is effectively 'military deterrence' or even 'compellence', with a more freely given form of consent. Such activities also offer a means of overcoming, to some extent, the dual nature of the peacekeeping force's use of force: transforming it back into its defensive, rather than retaliatory, punitive and, consequently, escalatory guise.

Military involvement in forms of activity which have traditionally been the preserve of humanitarian agencies, whilst obviously not problem-free, has provided a potential means of 'operationalising' the concept of peace-building. It potentially ensures a transition between building a peace through activities designed to promote a ceasefire and undercutting the military sources of tension, to the creation of an agenda which increasingly ensures that the less tangible, but equally substantive, social, economic and political issues are dealt with. It offers, therefore, a mechanism for managing the transition from a purely military agenda to an essentially 'civilian' one. It constitutes part of the 'end state' of military operations, in effect, both a means of withdrawal and of transition to a 'civilian' dynamic which offers some hope of resolving a crisis.

However, military activity in emergency, and then rehabilitation, humanitarian activity is not cost-free. It reinforces confusion in the minds of the belligerents by conflating categories such as 'humanitarian actor' and 'PSO troops'. This has clear implications for the concept of 'humanitarian space', which is the principal means by which many humanitarian agencies provide for their own security. Potentially it also places the PSO military in competition with humanitarian organisations for control of the humanitarian effort and introduces a political agenda into humanitarian programmes which will be resented and is potentially counter-productive.

The broader institutional architecture involved in the conduct and management of PSOs has also changed noticeably. Increasingly, regional structures and bodies, in Eastern Europe and Africa in particular, have been created. Why has this happened? Is this simply a product of the enthusiasm for peacekeeping which emerged at the end of the Cold War? The reality is far more complex and diverse.

In the case of many of the European peacekeeping structures their popularity with governments relates to the reorganisation of Central and Eastern European security provision. Several of the Central and Eastern European multinational peacekeeping formations are part of the efforts to reorientate political, economic and military processes towards the West. They have become a mechanism through which regional stability is maintained and aspirations to join the Western European economic and security structures are pursued.

In Africa the creation of peacekeeping capacities represents a dual-natured process. In part they represents the emergence of African inter-state regional structures; they are a part of a limited African renaissance, a struggle for identity and the evolution of African states in the post-

Introduction

colonial and post-Cold War world. However, they also represent a means for Western disengagement: a means of facilitating the emergence of African capacity to intervene in African problems. In the aftermath of Somalia, American politicians, rarely enamoured of the UN at the best of times, and fearful of incurring casualties in places where national interests were not self-evident, have attempted to create a policy of intervention avoidance. A key element of this is to delegate responsibility for interventions. However, in order to effect such a policy, a regional capacity in Africa for limited intervention operations needs to be created. Clearly, such capacities need to be established in some form of multilateral structure if the legitimacy of the intervention is to be retained. However, such a process of capability creation has, in itself, become enmeshed in inter-state competition, both on a regional basis and between former colonial powers.

Such a focus upon regional capacity-building has also been stimulated by the institutional shortcomings of the UN system. However, the failure to address radically these failings raises the danger that a focus upon regionalism will lead to what amounts to a competitive, rather than complementary, relationship between the UN system and regional bodies, at least in terms of the management of peace-support operations.

SECTION I
The United Nations and the International System:
Evolution and Change

The Humanitarian Security Dilemma in International Peacekeeping

SHASHI THAROOR AND IAN JOHNSTONE

INTRODUCTION

Modern peacekeeping is defined by complexity and insecurity. Never a simple exercise, peacekeeping has always depended for its success on the creativity and improvisational skills of its practitioners. But, in the early days, it was a technique of conflict control that assumed the consent and the cooperation of the hostile parties. Traditional operations, normally deployed in situations of inter-state conflict, were designed to monitor a truce, troop withdrawal and/or buffer zone while political negotiations were allowed to go forward. The notion of using unarmed or lightly armed soldiers to make peace rather than war – a 'sublime' concept in the words of Sir Brian Urquhart – presented its share of challenges, but those challenges were to be met through negotiation rather than coercion. Where the voluntary cooperation of the parties was not reliable, it was understood that peacekeeping was not the appropriate instrument and peacekeepers would not be deployed.

Most conflicts since the end of the Cold War have been within (intra) rather than between (inter) states. Typically fought between regular armies and irregular forces or among regular forces, they often involve more than two parties with shifting allegiances and alliances, and, in many cases, are accompanied by humanitarian emergencies, human rights abuses and the breakdown of law and order. In extreme cases, as the United Nations High Commissioner for Refugees has noted, effective government structures have been replaced by warlords whose activities blur the distinction between the struggle for political power, social banditry and organised crime.[1] These sorts of conflicts, as Secretary-General Kofi Annan has pointed out, do not lend themselves to the traditional peacekeeping treatment.[2] The demands upon, and the dangers to, the peacekeepers are greater than those faced by military personnel deployed along a well-defined front line between two states. When the United Nations (UN) deploys a mission in these circumstances, the tasks it is asked to perform are extensive and complex, combining military, police and civilian elements.[3]

Even in consent-based multidimensional operations, in which the UN monitors and helps to implement comprehensive peace agreements, the security of international personnel is an issue. A significant step beyond traditional peacekeeping, the nature of the consent granted and purposes for which the parties accept an international presence in these cases are qualitatively different from traditional operations.[4] Because the peace agreements go to the roots of the conflict and are designed to bring about a substantial political and social transformation of the state, they cannot provide for every contingency that may arise in the life of the operation. The UN must, necessarily, exercise a degree of independence in carrying out its mandated tasks. It faces challenges and dilemmas that cannot be resolved simply by referring to the terms of the agreement or the explicit consent of the parties. One of the parties may deliberately violate the written agreement or circumstances may arise that are not covered by it and cannot be settled by new negotiations. Even more troubling, the parties may – as a peace process unfolds – strike deals that contravene the terms of the original agreement and possibly run foul of international norms. In the circumstances, should the UN always defer to the stated will of the parties? What if, for example, the parties – all of whom may have a chequered history – unexpectedly agree to a blanket amnesty for all past human rights violations? What is the UN's appropriate role in these circumstances?

The dilemmas go deeper still in operations where there is no comprehensive peace agreement. The lessons of Somalia, Bosnia and Rwanda have taught us the perils of peacekeeping when there is no peace to keep. They have raised, in often painful terms, difficult conceptual questions about the nature of impartiality and the implications of intervention. The UN has been asked in recent years to assume tasks without being given the resources or political backing to carry out those tasks properly. Too often, when global opinion called for the world to 'do something', the UN became the 'doer', whether it was given the tools or not.[5] Lacking the political will to address the root causes of a conflict, the salve of humanitarian action was applied to soothe the conscience of the international community. To relieve human suffering, of course, is at the heart of the mission of the UN. But what if, in providing relief to besieged populations, the international community inadvertently fuels the conflict that causes their suffering? Can force, or its threat, be used to protect the delivery of that relief, without also protecting its recipients? What if, in caring for refugees and displaced persons, the care-providers inadvertently facilitate the work of ethnic cleansers? What if humanitarian action serves as a surrogate for the political or military action that the situation calls for? Even knowing all of this, does the UN ever really have the option of standing aside?

The perils of intervention are real and painful choices must be made. If nothing else, the experience of recent years has taught us that we cannot hide behind vague mandates to avoid confronting the dilemmas of peace-keeping and humanitarian action. The aim of this chapter is to examine one aspect of that recent experience – namely, efforts to provide security for humanitarian activity – which brings these dilemmas into sharp relief. In so-doing, we hope to shed light on some of the conceptual issues arising and to offer some practical suggestions on a way forward.

THE HUMANITARIAN DILEMMA

In the post-Cold War world humanitarian workers must often operate in an environment of profound insecurity. Whereas in the past aid agencies were 'protected' by their reputation for impartiality and neutrality, today the actors with whom they must deal often have little respect for humani-tarian credentials. Attacks on relief convoys, hostage-taking, the theft of aid and the manipulation of its distribution by belligerents, including its diversion to combatants, have become all too common. 'It is more dangerous', a close observer of the UN has observed, 'to be a United Nations humanitarian worker handing out food to the starving or helping refugees than to be a soldier on peacekeeping duty in a war zone'.[6] As High Commissioner Ogata recently told a journalist:

> Today there are very few international wars where the rules of engagement are clear; you mostly have internal wars between various political factions, ethnic groups and even mafias. The human costs are so high that ... humanitarian agencies are encouraged to take it on. In today's age, you cannot just leave children, women, old people to their fate.[7]

Many humanitarian organisations have sought armed protection for their activities, though not without considerable hesitation and soul-searching. The hesitation derives largely from concern that links with the military, especially where the latter engages in coercive action, would undermine the impartiality of the humanitarian workers. The essence of humanitarian action is its non-partisan character: providing relief to victims, regardless of who they are or which side they may be on. Military escorts, it is feared, will tarnish that image and could, in fact, increase the danger humanitarian organisations face by making them targets. The fear is not unfounded; in the midst of a war action that may seem impartial to those engaged in it may be perceived differently by the local actors. Providing relief under armed escort to the inhabitants of a besieged town, for example, will not be seen as neutral if the inhabitants are thought to be supporters of the enemy. Whether justified or not, humanitarian workers must live with the reality that for them, combatants' perceptions of neutrality become the practical measure of neutrality.[8]

Seventeen civilian relief workers were killed in the first seven months of 1998, and serious questions are being raised about whether the UN can continue to deploy staff, as it has always done, wherever there is a need. Secretary-General Kofi Annan told a news conference in the summer of 1998:

> I'm really concerned about the level of casualties we're taking. We should be able to say that it has become too dangerous for us to operate and to be effective, that it has become too dangerous for us to risk that many staff.[9]

The humanitarian dilemma then is real: the lifeblood of humanitarian action is its impartial character, yet such action is sometimes not possible without armed protection – the very fact of which can compromise that impartiality (at least in the eyes of those who matter) and therefore can increase the prevailing dangers. There is no magic formula for avoiding this vicious circle, but recent experience has taught some important lessons.

FORMS OF HUMANITARIAN ACTION

There are at least three areas in which armed forces have been used to provide security for humanitarian activities in recent years: in the delivery of humanitarian relief; in establishing safety zones or 'safe areas'; and in refugee camps.

Protecting the Delivery of Humanitarian Relief

The difficulties that humanitarian workers faced in Somalia during the terrible famine of 1992 were a turning point in terms of the perceived need for armed protection. Despite the best efforts of UN system pro-grammes, funds and agencies, the International Committee of the Red Cross (ICRC) and non-governmental organisations (NGOs) – all sup-ported by an extraordinary emergency airlift operation – the conditions in the country were simply too insecure to ensure a reliable flow of food and other aid. Every step forward in one part of the country was met by a resurgence in fighting and threats to the aid programme in another. Looting was rife and, because the aid had become a major source of income in the country, UN and voluntary agencies became targets of extortion and armed attacks – prompting some to pay for 'protection' by Somali gunmen. Despite some major successes, the quantity of food aid reaching the people eventually slowed to a trickle, causing the Secretary-General to conclude in late 1992 that the humanitarian emergency would not end unless the problem of protection and security were solved. In a more general vein, the then Under Secretary-General for Humanitarian Affairs, Jan Eliasson, stated in a speech delivered in February 1993:

> Additional measures for respect of humanitarian aid and for pro-tection of relief personnel are now necessary. The blue ensign of the United Nations and the symbols of the International Red Cross and Red Crescent, and other relief agencies, no longer provide adequate protection.

The result in Somalia was UNITAF (Unified Task Force) – a US-led force with a mandate 'to establish a secure environment for humanitarian relief operations'. Reaching some 37,000 troops at its peak, UNITAF took control of significant parts of the country, permitting the UN and NGOs to move about safely. Within a matter of months, the back of the famine was broken.

Few questioned Under Secretary-General Eliasson's conclusion that humanitarian credentials were no longer enough to guarantee the safety of those providing the aid, although not everyone agreed with the UNITAF prescription. This and subsequent cases where military force was used to deliver aid have been met with uneasiness, on both sides of the equation. For the military, protecting convoys and aid depots can put them in vulnerable and exposed positions, subject to risks they would not normally face in traditional peacekeeping or military operations. It can also generate unrealistic expectations if the mandate and resources of the military force are more limited than local or international public opinion is willing to countenance. Thus, in Bosnia, the United Nations Protection Force (UNPROFOR) was initially deployed to provide support for the delivery of humanitarian aid, but was soon criticised for failing to protect

besieged civilians, halt atrocities and impose peace on warring groups
that had no interest in making peace. Indeed, UNPROFOR's presence
prompted an accretion of non-humanitarian mandates without a change
in the underlying political will that had determined the limits of its
mission.

For the aid agencies, the main problem relates to the need for impartiality: using military escorts to force aid through to the intended recipients is bound to put them on the wrong side of the belligerents. In extreme
cases, it can make the humanitarian agencies feel *less* secure, because the
aid becomes a target for those who oppose the military presence.[10] Thus,
in Somalia, when United Nations Operation in Somalia II (UNOSOM II)
and the US Rangers became involved in efforts to disarm one of the
factions and arrest General Aideed, some of the humanitarian agencies
sought to distance themselves from the military. Indeed, in the end, the
military action led to the UN forces being perceived as one more warring
tribe – a part of the problem rather than a part of the solution.

Moreover, the cost of military protection sometimes exceeds the value
of the aid. In Somalia, the aid protectors at one point outnumbered the
aid-givers by ten to one and, in the view of informed Western observers,
mostly ended up protecting only themselves. Critics pointed out that the
size of the military presence meant that the international community was
spending four dollars to protect every dollar's worth of aid it was sending
in. (Of course, the sums came from different budgets that were not
fungible, but the numbers are still dismaying.)

But there are incidental advantages that humanitarian organisations
derive from cooperating with armed forces: the military can provide
logistic support, airlift capability and other assets that permit the speedy
delivery of large quantities of aid. The Sarajevo airlift is a case in point.
In the longest-running humanitarian airbridge in history, hundreds of
thousands of metric tons of food and medical supplies were delivered to
the 440,000 people trapped in the city over a period of three years. The
military also has intelligence capabilities which are helpful in identifying
populations most in need of aid and developing strategies for ensuring
that the aid actually reaches them. And finally, the presence of soldiers
can raise international awareness of the magnitude of the humanitarian
problem.

Safety Zones

An even more basic mandate for peacekeepers than protecting relief
delivery is to protect the recipients of that relief – the victims of human
rights and humanitarian violations. Peacekeepers have long viewed the

protecting of civilians as part of their job, although they typically try to do so through good offices, negotiation, and persuasion rather than force.[11] As the Security Council became more willing to authorise relief missions under Chapter VII of the UN Charter, it became increasingly difficult – and morally untenable – to deny protection to the innocent civilians caught up in conflict.

Moreover, the viability of humanitarian relief operations has, in some places, been so tenuous that the only option seemed to be to carve out safe areas or havens where the recipients were relatively free from intimidation and abuse. These efforts have met with mixed results and some commentators have questioned the validity of the concept altogether.

In Bosnia, the Security Council decided in the spring of 1993 to declare Srebrenica, Sarajevo and four other towns 'safe areas'. The implications of this decision, and the manner in which it was implemented, are still being felt today. 'Safe areas' have their roots in an older international humanitarian law concept of 'safe havens' or 'safety zones', but with two important distinctions: safety zones in humanitarian law are based on consent and they must be completely demilitarised.[12] UNPROFOR's mandate in the safe areas did not qualify on either count: it was adopted under Chapter VII of the Charter and it allowed the Bosnian government to maintain troops, paramilitary units and military equipment within the towns. Though not based on consent, UNPROFOR's mandate was not coercive: it had neither the authority nor the means to protect or defend the civilians in the safe areas and indeed the words 'protect' and 'defend' do not occur in the relevant Security Council resolutions. Rather, UNPROFOR was expected by its presence to deter attacks and, if necessary, to use force (including the right to call in NATO air-strikes) – 'acting in self-defence' – in reply to bombardments, armed incursion or obstruction of freedom of movement of UNPROFOR or humanitarian convoys. The resolution is a masterpiece of diplomatic drafting, but largely unimplementable as an operational directive.[13] Moreover, of the 34,000 troops the Secretary-General's military advisers initially assessed the UN would need to fulfil the task of deterrence through strength, the Security Council authorised only 7,600 – and these took a year to arrive.

The establishment of the safe areas, therefore, did not signify that the Security Council had taken sides in the conflict. UNPROFOR was not relieved of its other responsibilities, including the responsibility to help deliver aid, which required deployment in several dispersed locations in highly visible white vehicles. To take sides in those circumstances would have exposed unarmed and lightly armed troops and aid workers to reprisal attacks and hostage-taking. To the extent that there was a strategy behind the safe-area concept, it was based on bluff – a bluff that was called when the Serbs overran Srebrenica in 1995. It was only then that the major powers collectively acknowledged that the situation of UNPROFOR had become untenable and a new approach was agreed upon. The fact that UNPROFOR troops had been driven from Srebrenica and Zepa, and forced to cease operations in other Serb-held areas, made them less vulnerable to retaliation: powerful air-strikes could be launched against the Bosnian Serbs without fear of reprisal. Meanwhile, the Krajina area fell to the Croatian Army causing a decisive shift in the balance of military power, and an assertive diplomatic effort led by the USA produced the Dayton Peace Agreement.

Obviously the safe areas in Bosnia were not safe. They conformed to neither the traditional humanitarian law concept based on consent and cooperation nor did they benefit from a credible threat of force to defend them in the absence of that cooperation. They were a compromise born of a desire to 'do something' in response to the humanitarian tragedy and an unwillingness to take decisive action to help bring an end to the conflict that gave rise to that tragedy. As such, the 'safe areas' may even have increased the level of insecurity of their inhabitants by serving as staging grounds for confrontation between the parties and convenient places to test the resolve of the international community. Such a safe area concept is, as the then Secretary-General of the UN, Boutros Boutros-Ghali, pointed out in several reports to the Security Council, fundamentally flawed. The international community (and in particular the Security Council) must decide in each case which of the above two conceptual models is appropriate for the circumstances and provide commensurate resources. To opt for the middle ground, as it did in Bosnia, is simply not tenable.

Refugee Camps

The issue of security in refugee camps was highlighted most acutely in Rwanda. Nearly one million refugees flowed across the border into eastern Zaire in the space of eight days in mid-July 1994, following the genocidal violence that seized the country. It was one of the largest refugee crises ever and it nearly overwhelmed the capacity of the international community to react. However, due in large measure to logistic and other support from American, French, Irish, Israeli, Japanese and Dutch troops, the immediate crisis was contained.

But among the refugees were large numbers of former Rwandan government officials, military forces and militia, many of whom had been involved in the genocide. They effectively took over the camps, controlled (or at least influenced) the distribution of food, and actively discouraged the refugees from returning to Rwanda, often with violence. It was believed that these elements were using the camps as cover for training and to conduct low-intensity operations across the border, perhaps even preparing for a full-scale invasion. The dilemma for the relief organisations was that they had to try to provide what relief they could to the innocent refugees, but in doing so they were compelled to operate among genocidal killers who were effectively holding the refugees hostage.

In the circumstances, some NGOs withdrew from the camps. The UN High Commissioner for Refugees (UNHCR) staff and other UN agencies, however, did not have that option. Instead, as the security situation deteriorated, the High Commissioner, Sadako Ogata, worked with Secretary-General Boutros-Ghali to prepare a report to the Security Council that proposed three options for addressing the problem: a UN peacekeeping operation to establish security progressively in the camps over a period of time; a UN force under Chapter VII to separate the former political leaders, military personnel and militia from the ordinary refugees; and a multinational force, under Chapter VII, for the same purpose.[14] The report also suggested, as an additional measure that could be associated with any of the three options, the possibility of providing foreign security experts to train and monitor the local forces.

As the political will for military action to separate the leaders and militia from the refugees was clearly lacking, the Secretary-General concluded that the first option was the most realistic – a peacekeeping operation whose mission was to provide security for the relief workers and the delivery of humanitarian assistance, and to escort to the border those refugees who wished to return. As might have been expected, the Security Council reacted cautiously by noting that the options required further elucidation. It requested that the Secretary-General, in the meantime, should consult potential contributors to a peacekeeping operation. Of the 60 countries consulted, only one had replied favourably by the time the Secretary-General reported back to the Council at the end of January 1995. Given this lack of interest, and as a stop-gap measure, the UNHCR reluctantly turned to the government of Zaire, which agreed to deploy 1,500 experienced military and police personnel to work alongside a smaller number of foreign advisers serving as a 'liaison support group'. The agreement was unprecedented for the UNHCR and it garnered criticism, the thrust of which was that the humanitarian agencies were protecting and feeding those who had committed genocide.[15] But the High Commissioner felt that she had no choice: the innocent and truly needy refugees could not be left to their fate. The Security Council ultimately agreed that this was the only realistic option, although it asked the Secretary-General to continue to explore others.

The security situation in the camps did improve for the refugees but cross-border tension increased. It came to a head when the forces of the Alliance of Democratic Forces for the Liberation of Congo-Zaire (ADFL) led by Laurent Kabila swept across eastern Zaire in late 1996, prompting new calls for intervention to assist in the repatriation of refugees and to protect relief operations. Canada volunteered to lead a military coalition and the Security Council authorised it, although it would not have had a mandate to separate the military elements from the refugees. As it happened, however, the force was never deployed, largely because thousands of refugees returned spontaneously before it was assembled.

MODES OF HUMANITARIAN ACTION

The real choice for the UN in its humanitarian activities is often not whether it should seek military protection, but whether it should engage in humanitarian action at all. In the midst of ongoing conflicts the option of delivering aid without protection is not always available. The danger to workers is too great, the loss of aid to combatants too conspicuous and its distribution too easily subject to abuse. Often the civilian populations face such grave security risks that the delivery of aid is simply not the issue. Humanitarian action in those conditions is at best, a stopgap measure and, at worst, a substitute for political engagement, which not only forestalls a political solution but may even add to the misery by enabling the combatants to fight on, well fed. Some would argue that it is better for aid agencies to abstain in these circumstances than to get caught in what has been called 'the humanitarian trap'.[16]

For NGOs and some governments, abstention may be an option. But it is difficult for the UN simply to withdraw from the field in times of crisis – to allow lives that could be saved to be lost while conflicts burn. Moreover, while Somalia and Bosnia have taught us that there are risks and costs to action, Rwanda and the failure to launch an operation in Congo-Brazzaville in 1996 demonstrate that inaction may also have severe consequences.

To accomplish their mission, therefore, humanitarian operations must sometimes rely on military protection. Neutrality and impartiality risk being compromised, but it would be ironic if those principles, invoked in the name of humanitarianism, served to prevent humanitarian action altogether. Moreover, the delivery of aid in the midst of an internal conflict may be seen as taking sides whether the military is involved or not. Because these conflicts are often fought among and with civilians, denial of aid to them is a common war tactic and providing relief is seen as aiding in the war effort of the other side. The use of military escorts may compound the problem, but it does not create it.

There is no simple answer to the humanitarian dilemma, but the key to a solution might lie in not trying to do two things at once. One of the basic lessons learned by the UN in Bosnia is that you cannot make peace and war with the same people on the same territory at the same time. It is never wise to try to coerce people with whom you must also cooperate, within the same set of circumstances. If force is to be used to deliver relief, protect civilians or provide law and order in refugee camps, then those using the force should not also be trying to negotiate with its targets.

The tidiest solution would be to insist that the protection force has no mandate in relation to the conflict other than the humanitarian one.[17] The relative humanitarian success of Operation Provide Comfort in northern Iraq and Operation Turquoise in Rwanda offers support for this proposition. The intervening forces (US-led in the former and French-led in the latter) carved out a piece of territory within which they had almost complete control and were able to minister to needy populations largely unfettered.[18] This is not to suggest that these operations did not have political implications or a political impact – clearly they did for the status of the Kurdish rebellion in northern Iraq and the conflict between the Hutus and Tutsis in Rwanda. But the humanitarian achievements of the two interventions are real.[19]

Less ambitious operations along those lines can be imagined. A 'humanitarian corridor', for example, could be established to allow relief to flow to a besieged town, with a military force deployed to protect the corridor. The force should have the authority and resources to take on all challenges to its narrowly defined mission. It should react in the same way to all violations, regardless of their source.[20] However, if it is going to have to use force, it should not also be deployed to far-flung locations, in fewer numbers and with lighter arms, and engaged in activities that require the cooperation of the protagonists. This mixture of mandates, like the mixture of peace enforcement and peacekeeping, is a recipe for disaster.[21]

But carving out an exclusive humanitarian mandate is not always feasible, especially in complex crises when humanitarian, political and military objectives tend to be intertwined. In these circumstances, it may be worth thinking in terms of a division of labour – a well-coordinated confederation of players, operating in concert but not completely integrated. It is impossible to conceive of a single mode of humanitarian protection to suit all circumstances. Ideally, the symbolic presence of UN civilians, police or unarmed soldiers would be enough. In Iraq, a contingent of 500 UN guards (under the umbrella of a US/British/French-enforced no-fly zone) allowed the humanitarian operation there to go

13

forward. At one point it was suggested that 'white helmets' could perform a protection function, although the conception ultimately endorsed by the General Assembly gave them more of a supportive than protective role in emergency relief and rehabilitation operations.[22]

Rapidly deployed peacekeeping troops can make an enormous difference to the success of a humanitarian operation and indeed can be much more effective – and less expensive – than a larger force that arrives after a situation gets out of hand.[23] The UN Department of Peacekeeping Operations (DPKO) is continuing to develop this capability through the stand-by arrangements system and the envisaged creation of a 'rapidly deployable mission headquarters'.[24] But member states are often not prepared to put their troops on the line for purely humanitarian purposes. Moreover, it is not clear that the military is the best form of protection in all cases. Not only does the presence of troops threaten the impartiality and neutrality of humanitarian assistance, difficulties can also arise in the management of these operations. As the High Commissioner for Refugees asks:

> Who decides how much relief should be delivered and in what location, particularly in situations where there is insufficient assistance available to meet all needs? And who is responsible for determining when a situation is so hazardous that a relief operation should be suspended?[25]

Sir Brian Urquhart has argued that what was needed in the camps in eastern Zaire throughout the crisis was not a military force but an international 'police, anti-violence operation'.[26] It was an argument he had made earlier with Erskine Childers in calling for an armed United Nations Humanitarian Security Police, with specially established rules of engagement and able to act with or without the presence of military forces.[27] The security force deployed in Goma was a variant of this theme – not an ideal arrangement by any means, but an improvement over the early days in Somalia when aid agencies had to hire local gunmen for protection.

Indeed, in his report to the Security Council and General Assembly on the causes of conflict in Africa issued in April 1998, the Secretary-General urged the establishment of an international mechanism to assist host governments in maintaining the security and neutrality of refugee camps and settlements. He said that such a mechanism might encompass 'training, logistics, financial support, the provision of security personnel and the monitoring of national security arrangements'. At a regional meeting on refugee issues in the Great Lakes region in May 1998, this concept was discussed among the UNHCR, the Organisation for African Unity

(OAU) and governments of the region. Proposals for stand-by law enforcement mechanisms were considered, ranging from support measures to host governments to the deployment of regional or international military forces.[28]

The merit of a dedicated humanitarian security force is that, with a carefully circumscribed mission, it would not fall prey to political entanglements and could better preserve its impartiality. Moreover, the problem of unrealistic expectations would be alleviated as would the risk of 'mission creep', by which military forces deployed for humanitarian purposes get drawn into a more active role in the conflict than was intended – or is helpful. That it was not meant for broader political and military engagement would be patent, and therefore the humanitarian action would be less easily used as an alibi for political inaction. The political will to establish a standing UN security force does not exist, but the principle of creating a distinct humanitarian protection element to provide security is worth careful consideration.

CONCLUSION

Humanitarian emergencies will continue and humanitarian actors will continue to heed the call. The UN cannot turn its back when the moral consequences of abandonment are so extreme that conscience rebels.[29] The dilemmas confronted by UN staff deployed in circumstances where they are as vulnerable as those they have been sent to help should also not be underestimated. Attempts to train local police in areas where relief workers are assigned, or simply to hire armed security guards for humanitarian workers, are under active consideration, though each raises additional concerns. Efforts to have attacks on humanitarian personnel treated as a war crime and subject to prosecution by an International Criminal Court still face an uncertain future. The overall context of humanitarian efforts is also crucial. Undoubtedly, the record is mixed in how we have responded to humanitarian crises, but the results, as Brian Urquhart recently noted in *The New York Review of Books*, have not been so poor as to force us to reject the possibility of devising mechanisms that will ensure 'peace, security and human survival'.[30]

We cannot hide from the fact that armed humanitarian action – humanitarian intervention – is bound to have political consequences: as the current Secretary-General, Kofi Annan, said about Somalia when he was Under-Secretary-General for Peacekeeping, there is no such thing as an 'immaculate intervention'. The well-known cliché tells us that you cannot make an omelette without breaking eggs, and here too eggs are broken; but the omelettes may become scrambled. Similarly, intervention in eastern Zaire on behalf of the refugees in late 1996 could have had the unintended consequence of slowing Kabila's drive across the country and thereby maintaining Mobutu in power. Military involvement in someone else's war always has consequences for the course of that war and involves risks for the intervenors. The question is, how much risk are they prepared to take? The level of political will required to prosecute a war is different from that required for peacekeeping and for humanitarian intervention. Knowing what the objective of the intervention is, and being very clear about the extent of the political commitment involved and the limits of the risks one is prepared to take, help establish the yardstick for a humanitarian intervention. Muddling through may be the best we can do for now, but the current lack of enthusiasm for new multilateral projects cannot be allowed to distract us from the long-term goal of equipping the international community, practically and conceptually, for effective humanitarian action.

NOTES

1. Sadako Ogata, 'Humanitarian Responses to International Emergencies', in Otunnu and Doyle (eds), *Peacemaking and Peacekeeping for the New Century* (Lanham, MD: Rowman and Littlefield, 1998), p. 217. See also 'Dealing with Obstructionist Leaders', an unpublished paper by Don Daniel and Bradd Hayes of the US Naval War College, 1998.
2. Kofi A. Annan, 'Peacekeeping, military intervention and national sovereignty in internal armed conflict', in *The Moral Dilemmas of Humanitarian Intervention in Internal Conflicts* (forthcoming, ICRC book), p. 1.
3. M. Doyle, I. Johnstone and R. Orr, 'Introduction', p. 4 in M. Doyle, I. Johnstone and R. Orr (eds), *Keeping the Peace: Multidimensional UN Operations in Cambodia and El Salvador* (Cambridge: Cambridge University Press, 1997).
4. Ibid., p. 7.
5. Kofi A. Annan, 'War, Peace and the United Nations', Address to the University of California at Berkeley School of International and Area Studies, 20 April 1998, p. 5.
6. Craig Turner, 'Humanitarian UN work is risky business', *Los Angeles Times*, 2 August 1998.
7. Ibid., p. 2.
8. Adam Roberts, 'Humanitarian Action in War', *Adelphi Paper* 305, pp. 51–2.
9. Craig Turner, 'Humanitarian UN work'.
10. Refugee Policy Group, 'Civilian and Military Means of Providing and Supporting Humanitarian Assistance During Conflict: A Comparative Analysis', March 1997, p. 9.
11. Marrack Goulding, 'The Use of Force by the United Nations', Mountbatten-Tata Memorial Lecture at the University of Southampton, 23 November 1995, p. 10.

12. Karen Landgren, 'Safety Zones and International Protection: A Dark Grey Area', *International Journal of Refugee Law*, 7, 1995, pp. 438–40. On safe areas in Bosnia, see Gordon, Chapter 13 in this volume.

13. Shashi Tharoor, 'Should UN Peacekeeping Go "Back to Basics"?', *Survival*, 37, 4, Winter 1995–96, p. 60.

14. S/1994/1308.

15. Sadako Ogata, 'Peace, Security and Humanitarian Action', The Alastair Buchan Memorial Lecture, International Institute for Strategic Studies, London, 3 April 1997, p. 5.

16. David Rieff, 'The Humanitarian Trap', *World Policy Journal*, Winter 1995–96, p. 8. Mr Rieff cites Jean-Christopher Rufin's discussion of the concept.

17. See Goulding, 'The Use of Force', p. 17.

18. Richard Betts, 'The Delusion of Impartial Intervention', *Foreign Affairs*, November/December 1994, pp. 32–3.

19. Sadako Ogata, 'Humanitarian Responses', p. 223.

20. In claiming that peacekeeping troops must sometimes act forcefully in the exercise of self-defence, former Under-Secretary-General for Humanitarian Affairs Jan Eliasson argues that a firm stance will not be seen as partial as long as peacekeepers react in the same way to all those who violate the mandate. Jan Eliasson, 'Humanitarian Action and Peacekeeping', in Otunnu and Doyle (eds), *Peacemaking and Peacekeeping*, p. 210. Impartiality in the execution of a mandate, as the Secretary-General has written, does not mean unthinking neutrality between the parties. Kofi A. Annan, 'Peacekeeping, military intervention and national sovereignty', p. 1.

21. S. Tharoor, 'Should UN Peacekeeping', pp. 56–7.

22. General Assembly Resolution A/RES/49/139 B, December 1994.

23. Brian Urquhart, 'Prospects for a Rapid Response Capability: A Dialogue', in Otunnu and Doyle (eds), *Peacemaking and Peacekeeping*, p. 190. General Romeo Dallaire, former Force Commander of the United Nations Assistance Mission in Rwanda, has said that a force of 5,000 deployed in the early weeks of the April 1994 genocide could have saved as many as 500,000 lives. See also, *Preventing Deadly Conflict*, Final Report of the Carnegie Commission on Preventing Deadly Conflict, 1997, Box P. 1 at p. 6.

24. The impetus for this effort came from a study by the Canadian government called *Towards a Rapid Reaction Capability for the UN* (September 1995). Similar studies were conducted by the governments of Denmark and the Netherlands.

25. S. Ogata, 'Humanitarian Responses', in Otunu and Doyle (eds), *Peacemaking and Peacekeeping*, p. 223.

26. B. Urquhart, interview published in *The Nation*, 'Saving the World and the Limits of Humanitarianism', 19 May 1997, pp. 15–16.

27. E. Childers with B. Urquhart, *Renewing the United Nations System* (Dag Hammarskjöld Foundation, 1994), p. 204.

28. Frustration with the non-response to calls by the Secretary-General and High Commissioner for Refugees for an international force to separate the combatants and criminals from the refugees in the camps in then-Zaire has provoked greater interest in the possibility of relying on regional forces in the circumstances. The achievements of NATO in Bosnia and the Economic Community of West African States Monitoring Group (ECOMOG) in

Liberia and Sierra Leone have been noted in this connection.
29. This proposition was the subject of an exchange between Shashi Tharoor and William Durch in *Survival*, Spring 1996, pp. 182–3. See also M. Doyle, I. Johnstone and R. Orr (eds), *Keeping the Peace*, p. 385.
30. Brian Urquhart, 'Looking for the Sheriff', *The New York Review of Books*, 16 July 1998, p. 9.

2

Icarus Rising and Falling: The Evolution of UN Command and Control Structures

STUART GORDON

INTRODUCTION

In recent years United Nations military forces have found themselves involved in complex and volatile environments, both in terms of the nature of the conflict into which they have been deployed and the institutional arrangements that have prevailed. The UN's institutions for managing peace-support operations (PSOs) have been forced to operate, particularly in terms of the effectiveness of their command and control, to an unprecedented degree. Furthermore, the command and control arrangements have faced a variety of challenges: they are required to set and reconcile the objectives and the operations of an increasing variety of bodies and agencies both horizontally (that is, in terms of arrangements between bodies with different, non-hierarchically arranged functions) and vertically (that is, between differing bodies arranged in a hierarchical structure). Multifunctionality and institutional diversity have been compounded by a lack of clear and unambiguous definitions of the nature of the projects that UN military forces have been engaged upon. These have ranged from consent- to enforcement-based mandates and combinations thereof.

UN PSOs have also increasingly, albeit tentatively, been drawn into the reconstruction and rehabilitation of war-torn societies and the removal of the diverse social and economic forces which perpetuate violence within states.[1] Phenomena such as the collapse of state and administrative infrastructures, and the combination of natural disasters with conflict provide a rich but tragic tapestry of experience. This also provides a range of dramatic new challenges to command, control and coordination structures within PSOs' multifunctional components. It forces political, humanitarian and military executive and policy-formulating structures to deal with, in command and control terms, issues arising from the vertical and horizontal integration of their policies and operational responses to crises where there is little articulation of the desired end-states. This chapter explores the generic command problems for a military component within a PSO, as well as the recent institutional evolution of the UN Department of Peacekeeping Operations (DPKO).

GENERIC COMMAND AND CONTROL DIFFICULTIES

Institutional confusion, a lack of unity of direction, inappropriate mandates and insufficient resources have impinged heavily on the adequacy of command and control arrangements in UN operations such as those found within Bosnia, Rwanda and Somalia in the early 1990s. However, any exploration of specific UN command and control failings would be incomplete without some examination of the generic difficulties in command and control arising in multinational headquarters.

The principles to be followed in the division of labour between the various levels of command structures are relatively easy to define. Palin, for example, suggests that:

> At the highest level, the political authorities determine the political objectives, set the politico-military guidelines for the operation and superintend its strategic direction. Within the theatre, the appointed force commander and his staff plan, direct and conduct the operation within those guidelines. In between, a superior military headquarters commands the overall operation, sets the operational concept, deals with the strategic issues, acts as the interface between the political authorities and the theatre commander, and coordinates the supply of reinforcements and logistic support.[2]

In order for this to work effectively there are a number of what Palin describes as governing principles that should be applied. The political objectives and mandate should be clearly defined and the linkage between the political and military objectives should be such that the military task is achievable. The chain of command should be integrated both vertically and horizontally in order to provide unity of command and purpose and rapid decision-making, where appropriate. Such a system requires a clear delineation of responsibilities and a span of command which is sufficiently

20

limited so that control can be maintained. In essence, this can be reduced to two clear prerequisites for effective command and control: first, clearly defined and achievable political and military objectives; second, both vertical and horizontal integration throughout the intervening organisation.

However, there are likely to be a range of generic difficulties which plague any operational level, multinational, command and control structure. At the operational level these often relate to the way in which troop-contributing countries regard a headquarters. Governments frequently regard multinational headquarters as places where they can continue politicking for national advantage and the division of labour within any multinational headquarters provides opportunities for national advancement. Within long-established headquarters, the division of such political spoils has long since been established. However, new and adapting headquarters provide significant opportunities for inter-governmental competition. Efforts to divide such advantages are therefore likely to coincide with the point when cohesion and unity of command are most required: the start up phase of an operation.

National interference also impinges upon the unity of purpose of a multinational headquarters in additional ways. It allows the importation of a number of 'discrete national links with specific national responsibilities'.[3] Governments therefore distort both the command structure and the decision agenda within it. Within established structures this happens far less, as the mechanisms for the formulation of politico-military advice are formalised over a period of years. The lines of national communication into and throughout the organisation are well understood and agreed upon. Within new structures the norms underpinning such arrangements are in a process of flux. Often, as was the case with the United Nations Protection Force (UNPROFOR) in Bosnia-Herzegovina and the United Nations Operation in Somalia (UNOSOM I and II), missions are so comparatively ephemeral that the lines of political command and control cannot be formalised and regularised before the mission's ending.

For many, particularly smaller nations, involvement in multinational formations becomes an instrument of domestic and foreign policy. For example, it might be argued that the British involvement in NATO's Allied Rapid Reaction Corps (ARRC) was a means of insulating those formations committed to the ARRC from further defence cuts in the aftermath of the British defence-policy paper *Options for Change*. Similarly, recent French negotiations to secure high-level appointments in the NATO military structure clearly reflected the long-standing goal of developing a high-profile European defence identity with French leadership. For the United Kingdom, Belgium and Holland, NATO's increased emphasis upon multinationality enables their armed forces to retain command appointments at the corps level, even if only in rotation, in situations where the nation can no longer field corps-level structures. Appointments to command positions within such structures become a means of maintaining under-resourced national capabilities and also of preventing other nations from dominating such structures and gaining influence. Multinational forces therefore become instruments of foreign policy and appointments are reduced to being the currency of state power rather than a means of improving operational efficiency.

The effectiveness of new multinational structures and *ad hoc* coalitions is further undermined by the inability of commanders to rely upon the certainties that underpin the cohesion of national command and control structures; namely, full and sole command over assigned troops, and a common ethos, military culture and language.

THE BONFIRE OF CERTAINTIES

Commanders within all multinational formations often find that they have not been given sufficient control over the troops assigned to them and that troop-donating governments frequently limit the employment options available to a UN commander. Where trust exists in the nature of the political objectives established and the command structures, and the risk of casualties is limited, operational command of assigned troops will often be granted. However, where trust in the command and control structure is limited and/or the risk of casualties is high, the norm has been to transfer a much lower level of command authority: tactical control. In such a case the troop-contributing nation retains an effective veto over which missions can be assigned to their forces. In military terms success frequently depends upon unity of command and the striving for a common purpose, but limited command and control authority, disparate ethos, cultures, and varying qualities of troops and equipment serve to undermine achievement.

Furthermore, command structures frequently involve several layers of organisations, and the relationship and the division of labour between these organisations are often critical to operational success. However, the creation of an effective architecture often takes several decades to achieve even in ideal conditions; that is, where finance is relatively secure, where there is bureaucratic and political support for such change and the institution is not constantly bombarded with new operations. Within the UN system such procedures are still being developed and in comparatively more demanding circumstances.

It is also interesting to view the failings of the UN command and control capacities within the setting of the failure of national structures. It is worth noting, for example, that during the Falklands War both Britain and Argentina encountered numerous difficulties as a result of inappropriate command and control structures. Neither side had adequately defined the nature of the relationship between military and political authorities nor had each determined the extent to which political involvement in the establishment of military priorities was considered appropriate or just meddlesome.[4] Similarly, neither Britain nor Argentina effectively resolved the nature of the mechanisms for ensuring 'horizontal' integration of forces within the theatre so that the objectives of the single-service or component commanders reinforced the process of achieving, rather than of hindering, the mission. British command structures have addressed this range of problems only relatively recently with the creation of a Permanent Joint Headquarters (PJHQ) and the idea of a deployable, theatre-level Joint Commander. This delay in implementation should be seen in the context of a relatively unitary state with comparatively secure funding; arguably, therefore, such a reform would be much more difficult in the context of a poorly funded international organisation.

PSOs are also complicated by the fact that missions are increasingly multifunctional. The overarching operation is not, in principle at least, necessarily dominated by a military agenda. Ensuring an appropriate and synergistic balance between the military, the political and the humanitarian agendas at the operational level can be enormously problematical. Furthermore, the sources of accountability for the institutions involved are clearly very different, ranging through the Security Council, the General Assembly, national capitals, institutional mandates, international law and donors. Reconciling such diversity in order to maintain unity of purpose is certainly not always possible and probably not even desirable.

This creates a peculiar set of operational difficulties. Each agenda is likely to develop a momentum of its own and this will tend to pull the components of a mission in differing directions. Consequently, developing an appropriate balance between the elements of the mission and maintaining such a balance throughout the mission life may be difficult. Experience in Somalia and the Former Yugoslavia suggests that in multifunctional missions where consent is not uniform throughout the theatre and, where it exists, is limited, a military and political agenda will dominate the humanitarian.[5] Command, in the sense of horizontal integration between the multiple components of a PSO, therefore becomes hugely complicated.

Such multifunctionality has an additional dimension. Organisations themselves may be multifunctional in two senses. First, they may develop an agenda which contains two or more elements drawn from the broad range of humanitarian, political and military issues. For example, military involvement may not be limited to the provision of security but may encompass involvement in small-scale community-based relief and reconstruction projects. Similarly, humanitarian non-governmental organisations (NGOs) may also provide both humanitarian assistance and small-scale security through the hiring of guards and the negotiating of agreements with local power brokers. The problem in this case is partly that of ensuring an appropriate division of labour between organisations and also of ensuring coordination between activities which impinge upon other organisations' agendas. An additional difficulty is that the same activity conducted by different organisations, from what are in effect different functional sectors of the international response and conducted for different purposes, may impact upon the way in which other institutions' activities are perceived. The different elements of the international response (humanitarian, political and military) can therefore become intermingled in the minds of belligerents. Perceived neutrality, for humanitarian organisations, may suffer as a consequence of increased association with multifunctional political and military organisations.

The second element of multifunctionality arises when an organisation possesses what could be described as internal multifunctionality. In this case an organisation may focus on issues drawn from essentially one agenda, whether it be political, humanitarian or military. However, even within what might be described as a single agenda there may be a significant absence of internal consistency between such activities. For example, an NGO mandated to conduct consent-based, emergency relief may have difficulty in overtly involving itself in human rights advocacy work without prejudicing its relief activities.[6] Similarly, military involvement in the provision of security, where the mandate extends so that it effectively becomes a belligerent party to the conflict, may prejudice other aspects of its mandate such as the development of consent for the presence of a humanitarian mission. Consequently multifunctionality has what could be described as inter- and intra-sectoral dimensions. Horizontal coordination to ensure even basic operational consistency within and between such sectors is therefore likely to be exceptionally difficult.

Furthermore, the UN is plagued with structural difficulties in terms of its priority setting and implementing structures. At the most obvious level the combination of high politics in the Security Council and the delegation of authority through the UN Secretariat have had adverse effects upon the unity of purpose and effectiveness of strategies adopted by the UN. The enormous division within the policy-formulating elements of the UN system, principally the Security Council, has placed burdens upon the Secretariat to rationalise the Council's direction in terms of its operational advice to commanders.[7] However, the Secretariat is cognisant of the fact that it does not possess the authority or legitimacy to make, in effect, strategic political decisions which facilitate the conversion of political agreement in the Council into a realistic operational mandate. This ensures that the Secretariat is ill placed to provide effective strategic-level guidance and direction and is poorly structured to act as an operational-level headquarters for peace-support missions. Consequently, the onus falls upon the UN theatre headquarters, which is itself ill equipped to deal with the strategic priority-setting function.

The massive growth in the scale and complexity of tasks forced upon the UN in the aftermath of the Cold War has highlighted these structural weaknesses within the command and control structures. These structural problems can be examined in two ways: first, the problems of defining objectives, mandates and resources within the Security Council (which is beyond the scope of this chapter); and secondly the institutional weakness of the UN itself.

UN INSTITUTIONAL WEAKNESSES

The capacity for UN command and control is further weakened by UN institutional weakness at the level below that of the Security Council. Berdal produces a particularly convincing critique of what he terms the difficulties with both horizontal and vertical integration between individuals and departments in the UN system.[8] This has been complicated by the existence of multiple layers of management between the Security Council and the field and the continuing decentralisation of responsibility through an increasingly disaggregated system.

Berdal defines vertical integration as the attempt to enhance resources and streamline decision-making within an institution. He differentiates this from horizontal integration which he describes as 'those measures aimed at improving overall coordination among the various departments, offices and divisions involved in UN field operations'.[9] These would include departments such as Peacekeeping Operations (DPKO), Political Affairs (DPA), Humanitarian Affairs (DHA), Administration and Management (DAM), the Office of Legal Affairs, the UN Development Programme (UNDP) and the UN High Commissioner for Refugees (UNHCR).

The UN Secretariat is not structured to fulfil the role of what could be described as a strategic- or operational-level headquarters. It was established essentially to support the legislative bodies of the UN. Operational functions and responsibilities were essentially divested to the specialised agencies. The clear exception to this generalisation was, and is, peace-keeping. However, the simplicity and scale of many Cold War peace-keeping missions limited the requirements for radical institutional changes both within the DPKO and the wider secretariat.

Furthermore, Cold War competition ensured that the provision of formalised military advice from either superpower or their supporters was limited to one military adviser to the Secretary-General. This advice and planning vacuum limited the nature of the UN's ability to plan, control and sustain operations. The Cold War also limited the nature of the UN's security role in other ways, ending the idea of collective security through the effective internationalisation of force and changing the concept of the Security Council from a form of international Leviathan into an organisation providing discrete but limited security 'maintenance' services; it became something of a security 'cleaner-fish' to the superpower sharks.

As a consequence of limitations on role and institutional structure, the function of the Cold War UN headquarters was limited to what could be described as management and facilitation, negotiating the deployments of troops with contributing states and securing logistic support in an environment that was often far less volatile than many situations encountered since the end of the Cold War. This legacy, to a degree, still permeates the way in which the DPKO operates.

ICARUS'S RISE

The DPKO was overwhelmed by the massive increase in scale and complexity of UN operations in the early 1990s. Consequently, partly as a result of institutional weakness and partly as a consequence of organisational overstretch, it had difficulty in planning, mounting, sustaining and controlling operations. The result of these pressures was to increase reliance upon *ad hoc* solutions and the development of what could be described as 'personal', rather than 'institutional' solutions to problems in the field. However, the DPKO has not remained institutionally static. It has nearly doubled staffing levels since April 1994 and now comprises two major sub-departments: the Office of Planning and Support and a department of 'Operations' organised into several functional units including a Situation Centre, a Policy and Analysis Unit and a Mission Planning Service.

The Office of Planning and Support was created to improve planning on staffing, procurement, logistics and finance and also to oversee the work of the Field Operations Division (formally known as the Field

Administration and Logistics Division and located within the Department of Management). This has now been incorporated into DPKO (after much bureaucratic resistance) in order to simplify the dual reporting lines from the field to the headquarters in New York; a much more integrated form of mission support structure is the result. The Mission Planning Service has also been developed significantly both in terms of competence and experience and has subsequently been involved in the planning for a number of missions: the deployments of the UN Angola Verification Mission III (UNAVEM III), UN Assistance Mission for Rwanda (UNAMIR), the withdrawals of UNOSOM II (Somalia) and UNPROFOR as well as contingency planning for operations in Sierra Leone and Liberia.[10]

Mission sustainability is being further enhanced by the creation of a 'contingent owned equipment system'.[11] This provides a means for identifying the range of assets that are required from a troop-donating country in order to support a given level of force and may contribute to reducing the frequency of troop contingents being deployed to an operational theatre without sufficient resources from their own country to sustain them. Such changes are vital given the reluctance of states to contribute troops to missions in potentially volatile regions in the absence of effective mission planning and support.

However, despite an enormous improvement in the capacity of the UN to plan operations, mission planning is likely to remain essentially reactive and prompted to a large degree by Security Council deliberations and resolutions. Statements of missions are drawn from specific Security Council resolutions and, as a consequence, the shapes of actual missions are difficult to predict. This problem was highlighted with the plans to deploy a multinational force to the Great Lakes region in 1996 and 1997 and again with the contingency plans for the creation of humanitarian corridors for the return of Rwandan refuges dispersed throughout eastern Zaire. The consequence of this is largely to preclude the type of long-range planning routinely conducted by national ministries of defence.

The DPKO has recognised this difficulty and efforts have been made to address these issues both in terms of specific contingencies and the creation of generic capabilities for a range of mission types. The latter is a clear and necessary response to the changed nature of the international security environment and the unpredictability of threats. It also parallels the type of national defence planning which generates generic capabilities rather than responses to specific country based or regional crises.[12] The other difficulty with the reactive nature of mission planning results from the late appointment of the Special Representative of the Secretary-

General (SRSG) and the force commanders. Whilst there has been increased pressure to appoint SRSGs and force commanders as early as possible they still, generally, have only a limited involvement in mission planning and are often not appointed before the DPKO is tasked with writing the report which precedes Security Council debate and mandate formulation. This situation, while not entirely unknown even within Western militaries, is not satisfactory, although it may be unavoidable so early mission planning therefore may continue to exclude the very individuals who might be expected to have a critical input.

A further institutional weakness in the DPKO has been the paucity of military officers, particularly those from the more sophisticated militaries, which has had a number of results. It has ensured that, in the absence of a sizeable military presence within the headquarters, the management culture of the UN as a whole has permeated the DPKO. At the most basic level this led to a lack of 'operationality' or task focus. Certainly the nature of the decision-making and the support from the DPKO, in addition to difficulties arising out of the nature of Security Council decision-making, have contributed to the frustration of many former UN commanders.

The frustrations felt by the increasing number of, particularly Western, military contingents has led to attempts to inject the DPKO with an increased sense of 'operationality'. This has been effected through the direct provision of 'gratis military officers' (GMOs) to the DPKO. GMOs are staff officers provided on loan and without charge by, predominantly, former Warsaw Pact and current North Atlantic Treaty Organisation (NATO) members. By the end of 1996 there were over a hundred GMOs and they introduced a considerable sense of urgency and realism into the work of the DPKO. They provided benefit by not only changing the culture of the DPKO but also by the systematisation of military planing and the creation of what the more powerful armies would recognise as the sinews of military professionalism: common doctrine, standard operating procedures and attempts at preparing for contingencies. In effect, they represented a core decision-making and 'working' structure within an otherwise amorphous and somewhat disembodied UN department. In this they resembled a development that was occurring at the level of UN theatre and operational headquarters. Within these, force commanders increasingly attempted to transpose either national preformed command structures (as, for example, in UNPROFOR's Sector Sarajevo and South West from 1994 to 1995) or, where this was not possible, to generate headquarters staff structures which employed a kernel of officers of similar ability, language and often even nationality through which the real decision-making authority passed. This was often termed 'hard wiring' a headquarters by those who performed it and 'hijacking' by those who could not. However, both the provision of GMOs and 'hard wiring' head-quarters was resented by states who, unable to provide GMOs or the kernel of a theatre- or operational-level headquarters, were consigned to providing troops and risking casualties without gaining the kudos or influence of effective representation within a multinational headquarters.

In New York the provision of GMOs became a matter of dispute between those states that were unwilling or unable to provide such forces and those that did. For states such as Pakistan, GMOs were a means by which the principal debtor nations in the UN system gained influence through two mechanisms: securing influential appointments within the DPKO and exerting leverage by withholding funds. For such states the appropriate means through which the DPKO should have been reformed was to formalise the GMOs, making their funding part of the regular budget and making DPKO appointments subject to the same requirement for universal and equitable representation that governs the recruitment of all other UN permanent staff. The result of this dispute was the suspension of the GMO system through General Assembly Resolution 51/243; the last of the GMOs finally left UN headquarters in early 1999.

ICARUS'S FALL

While the removal of the GMOs was viewed by many states as a victory (even by some within the UN Secretariat, which originally feared the cultural change that the GMOs had brought with them), it was somewhat pyrrhic. States would support UN involvement in the management of military operations only if the organisation had a demonstrable capacity to do so: the GMOs effectively provided that capacity and their removal weakened the organisation's credibility immeasurably. In the aftermath of the often perceived failures in Angola, Rwanda, Somalia and Bosnia, this was yet another way that the UN could be lambasted. Ironically, at just the point at which the DPKO was becoming most institutionally capable of managing operations, the removal of the GMOs clipped its wings.

The parlous state of UN finances also creates difficulties in creating new UN missions. Unable to finance the start-up costs of every mission, some states are able to step into the breach, provide logistic support and expect a greater degree of political influence than would otherwise be the case. To some extent this was the case with the high degree of British control of military logistics and infrastructure during the UNPROFOR[13] mission.

For many years the UN was also criticised for failing to provide some form of situation centre. Such a centre, however, was established in 1993 in order to monitor events in Somalia and this has continued to be developed. The US has supplemented its limited intelligence collection capacity through the provision of the Joint Deployable Intelligence Support System (JDISS), a useful, albeit limited, enhancement to the UN's capacity to use intelligence, including satellite imagery. However, there has been little real improvement or willingness to countenance the improvement of the capacity of the UN to collect and disseminate its own intelligence and dependence upon US intelligence continues to limit the ability of a global institution to act without active US support. For example, in UNOSOM in 1993 the US withdrawal led to significant reduction in the intelligence gathering and analysis capacities of the remaining UN forces, effectively blinding the Turkish commanding General Civek Bir.[14] The clear limitations upon the generation and use of intelligence remain evident in many continuing missions.

Several UN operations – UN Transitional Authority in Cambodia (UNTAC) and UN Transition Assistance Group (Namibia) (UNTAG), for example – have also suffered from the absence of a dedicated, pre-constituted UN headquarters which can be deployed to start new missions. The use of a preformed NATO headquarters in order to establish the UNPROFOR operation in Bosnia demonstrated the positive aspects of using a pre-existing structure[15] and led to the announcement in 1995 of a standby headquarters component in the Mission Planning Service of the DPKO.[16] Consequently, the Rapid Deployable Mission Headquarters (RDMHQ)[17] is in the process of being established. Comprising some 80 personnel it will act as the core command and control structure during the first few weeks of a mission and will facilitate a more rapid, and possibly coherent, initial military response.

Perhaps the greatest institutional weakness faced by the DPKO is the absence of readily and rapidly available troops. The lack of both political will and a dedicated pool of soldiers meant that the UN system was unable to react rapidly to the impending genocide in Rwanda in April 1994. Consequently, the UN Standby Initiative System (UNSAS) has, since 1994, improved the potential of the UN to provide reinforcements and act quickly. However, member-state willingness to deploy forces has not matched the willingness to join the system. The system therefore provides administrative help in the problem of troop deployment, but the fact that it is essentially a system for registering non-binding pledges of troops does not provide any remedy for the absence of political will to prevent or remedy crises. It also does little to provide for reinforcements held at the operational level.[18] These are still generally not available, and, when requested, require the agreement of the Secretary-General and are subject to veto by member states on the Council[19] and often the troop-donating governments as well. Consequently, UN commanders are limited in their capacity to exploit and reinforce success or respond to crises by redeploying troops. Furthermore, commitments of less visible but perhaps even more critical resources such as communications, logistics and engineering troops are lacking in depth and a sizeable proportion of them are not available within the critical first 30 days of the mission start. The result is that while there is no 'lack of willingness to make troops and equipment available for peacekeeping operations, the United Nations is currently far from having a rapid reaction capability'.[20]

However, some nations have sought to remedy this through the enhancing of regional capacities for UN operations. Several Latin American, African and European countries have developed arrangements for augmenting the UNSAS with multinational forces of up to brigade size.[21] These will provide augmentations to the UN capacity but also represent a move towards the practice of operating outside UN structures rather than the developing of its institutional capacity. Similarly, arrangements designed to improve regional organisations' capacities to manage PSOs, such as the US-sponsored African Crisis Response Initiatives (ACRIs), represent an obfuscation rather than a solution to the problems of the UN's lack of capacity. They also do little to provide a theatre- or operational-level reserve of troops for the force commander.[22] Such measures, in effect, highlight the absence of UN operational military capacity and undermine governmental confidence in its ability.

The DPKO has also made considerable efforts to improve what could be described as the lexicon of peacekeeping. Work on the establishment of command and control definitions, of agreed doctrine and of rules pertaining to the transfer of command authority have certainly facilitated a smoother start to UN missions than has hitherto been the case. Similarly, the creation of a Lessons Learned Unit designed to identify the main issues arising out of specific missions has begun the process of developing institutional memory. However, these developments have been slowed by a lack of funding. Throughout 1995, for example, the Policy and Analysis Unit was staffed with only one UN military officer tasked with the production of peacekeeping doctrine.

The increased strengthening of the DPKO and the reforms initiated by Boutros Boutros-Ghali and Kofi Annan are not likely to solve the central command difficulties of the UN. In many ways they are likely to reinforce some of them. Berdal, for example, points to the fact that 'the growing decentralisation of peacekeeping functions in the secretariat and the consequent diffusion of authority' in the management of the operations'[23] is likely to fragment further the decision-making processes. This will increase reliance upon *ad hoc* solutions to problems of command integration. However, in multicomponent, large-scale missions, *ad hoc* responses to command problems are unlikely to prove sufficient. New York is not suitable to act as an operational headquarters. The multiplicity of different operations reduces its capacity to invest sufficient effort in most of these and the result is the actual and prescribed devolution of responsibility to the field through the SRSG.[24] UN HQ remains, in essence, a headquarters which can mount and support rather than fully command operations.[25]

THE OPERATIONAL COMMANDERS – THE CIVIL AND MILITARY DIMENSIONS

As a consequence of such institutional failings the SRSG becomes, in effect, the executive director of the mission. However, his role is complicated in a number of ways. First, he represents the Secretary-General, who is clearly subordinate to, where so defined, the wishes of the Security Council. As a result, and in the absence of a peace agreement, his actions may simply reflect the lack of political will or divisions within the Council. The last SRSG for UNPROFOR, Yasushi Akashi, was, in many ways, a perfect example of this problem. He resisted calls for the use of air-power in Bosnia, particularly in 1994, when many international journalists and prominent US politicians were calling for the increased use of air-strikes against the Bosnian Serbs. Unsure that the Security Council would support large-scale enforcement action against the Bosnian Serbs and with a peacekeeping rather than war-fighting force deployed in both Bosnia and Croatia, he resisted robust military action. Consequently, to expect an individual who is tasked with the coordination of a multicomponent mission to resolve the problems generated by an inappropriate and under-resourced mandate is naive.

The effectiveness of an SRSG will also be eroded by other factors. For example, the confused lines of accountability from the military to the political levels within a PSO can lead to national interference which erodes a degree of control over troop contingents. Furthermore, the SRSG has little real influence over policy formulation in the Security Council. The SRSG, therefore, suffers to a large extent from accountability without influence.

Force commanders in UN missions face a range of difficulties as a result of the multiple personalities and differing quality of the units under their command as well as the diverse lines of accountability. As a consequence, force commanders often lack effective command authority over all their troop contingents.

National interference may be felt in a wide variety of ways. For example, US commanders effectively bypassed UN institutions in their pursuit of General Aideed in Somalia in 1993. However, such actions are not limited to the US: neither the Zimbabwean nor the Indian contingents to UNOSOM accepted deployments to Mogadishu; similarly, the French troops refused to take over positions vacated by the Australians when they withdrew. Such limitations were not confined to UNOSOM, as could be seen during UNPROFOR's existence: the then French President Jacques Chirac bypassed UN commanders on several occasions and gave direct orders to French units deployed in Sarajevo. In May 1995 this interference led to French UN troops taking the first ground-based offensive action against Bosnian Serb units on the Vrbanja bridge in Sarajevo. Similarly, Turkish UNPROFOR troops provided limited logistic and medical support to Bosnian Muslim Armija units during their offensives against Serb positions on Mount Vlasic during early 1995.

General Sir Michael Rose, a former Commander of UNPROFOR's Bosnia-Herzegovina Command, suggested that such national interference was commonplace: 'Every troop-contributing nation had its own national command structure within the main UN staff, and each nation had its own political agenda as well as a chief of contingent who held the national red card.'[26] Such actions potentially hinder the formation of the perception that UN forces are impartial and they can only undermine the unity of effort.

National interference is often more formalised but less visible. For example, the British maintained a separate national command structure in theatre during the first 18 months of their involvement in UNPROFOR that was eventually incorporated into the UNPROFOR chain of command in early 1994. However, during its existence it countermanded UN orders[27] and occasionally developed an agenda which reflected national rather than UNPROFOR interpretation and priorities. The likelihood of such national interference with the operations of national troops deployed in UN missions increases with the volatility of the environment in which they are used. In part this explains the enormous degree of national interference with the operations of UNPROFOR troops.

However, in many ways the UN's command and control structures become victims of their own failures. The perceived failings of UN command and control capacities combine with the organisation's difficulties in sustaining troops in the field to increase the reluctance of national authorities to assign the command of their troops to UN structures. The result is to increase the use of what could be described as coalitions of the willing, or of unilateral responses within a multilateral framework. For example, the deployment of French, British and American troops after the Rwandan genocide was, in effect, a set of parallel national responses within a multilateral setting. The UN's perceived weakness therefore undermines trust and, consequently, the willingness even to remedy the failings.

FINANCE AND EFFECTIVE COMMAND AND CONTROL

The UN's financial crisis also creates additional command and control difficulties. It ensures that the UN may sometimes be unable to fund the start-up costs of all missions and, even once begun, the procurement of the vital assets of a mission is often slow. This is reinforced by an administrative rather than operational culture that is, along with many national civil services, rule dependent, which leads to what has already been described as a lack of 'operationality' in the UN system. Furthermore, many states, envious of their hard-currency resources, are sometimes unwilling to provide troops for UN duties if they are unable to reclaim the hard-currency costs of that support.

The failure of states to pay their contributions to both the peacekeeping and the regular budget of the UN has also led to understaffing at a time when the UN's activities have generally been growing. This has been keenly felt in the DPKO where nearly half the short-term contracts have been threatened with non-renewal.

The funding crisis has had another effect: it effectively prevents the UN from reimbursing states who contribute troops and equipment to missions. As such, the US, as the primary debtor state, often spreads the burden of debt to Third World countries. Furthermore, it also ensures that the UN uses peacekeeping money to bankroll the regular budget, in effect reducing the money available for missions. Even if the US were to repay the outstanding debt, this money would be used to reimburse those states who are owed money, thereby ensuring that little new money would appear immediately in mission budgets. Peacekeeping is, therefore, not only out of political favour but also in economic recession.

HORIZONTAL INTEGRATION

The massive increase in the scale of multicomponent missions and the diversity of actors operating within them has led to enormous difficulties in the horizontal coordination of activities performed by different agencies, departments and institutions within the mission. This has two aspects. First, the DPKO is not the only UN institution with responsibility for operations associated with peacekeeping; consequently, these intra-

UN departmental activities require coordination. Second, peace-support tasks involve a multitude of political, humanitarian and military organisations. The failure to coordinate effectively with the addition of the increasing numbers of actors has, in effect, reinforced the fragmentation of authority within a PSO.

The UN system possesses, or has possessed, a variety of coordination mechanisms for internal, horizontal coordination. The Inter-Agency Standing Committee (IASC) and the relatively newly appointed Emergency Relief Coordinator's office, for example, provide means for coordinating the activities of the humanitarian agencies at what could be described as the strategic level. Similarly, the creation of a 'cabinet'-type office has contributed to strategic-level, horizontal coordination. The Planning Division in the DPKO and the Secretary-General's Task Forces on UN operations (established in 1994) provide a somewhat more limited framework for coordination with the other departments and specialised agencies. Other efforts have attempted to clarify the delineation of responsibilities in order to provide a clearer division of labour. For example, the March 1994 report of the Secretary-General entitled 'Improving the Capacity of the United Nations for Peacekeeping' seeks to delineate the responsibilities of the DPA, DPKO, DHA and DAM. Consequently, the DPA is described as the 'political arm' of the Secretary-General while the DPKO is his 'operational arm for the day-to-day management of peacekeeping operations'. The responsibilities of the DHA are described as 'coordination and humanitarian operations'. However, this distinction has proved to be difficult to sustain within a field operation and has resulted in duplication.

Both Boutros Boutros-Ghali and Kofi Annan have strengthened the Executive Office of the Secretary-General, in order to use it as an institutional coordination mechanism. Such responses clearly make sense, yet they introduce another layer between the Secretary-General and the relevant departments and could potentially result in obfuscating rather than coordinating the mechanisms.

While Kofi Annan's reforms have aimed at a greater degree of sophistication than those in the past they have not addressed the root causes of coordination difficulties, namely: institutional overlap, duplication, institutional turf wars and increasing layers of management.

COORDINATION WITH OTHER AGENCIES

The paucity of mechanisms for horizontal integration in the field is also complicated by the resistance, by both UN humanitarian agencies and departments, and NGOs, to positive coordination. In the past, host-government Memoranda of Understanding[28] and the activities of the UNDP have provided mechanisms for coordinating humanitarian responses; but in failing states or in the context of UN-authorised enforcement action such mechanisms may be absent or insufficient. The result is a significant reduction in unity of purpose.

The problems of coordination between agencies begin with their differing sources of accountability. In multicomponent missions, therefore, there is no real sense in which the institutions involved are accountable to a common, central source. Even the new Office for the Coordination of Humanitarian Affairs (OCHA), headed by Sergio de Mello (a contributor to this volume), has failed to make a significant impact on the problem of coordinating the UN agencies. His department is split between New York and Geneva and its schizophrenic nature does little to improve its chances of controlling the five main agencies, themselves split between Rome, Geneva and New York. Separate mandates provide these agencies with a means for resisting any centralising authority. This is replicated in exaggerated form by humanitarian NGOs, which not only have differing mandates but also have markedly different operating principles to add a richness to the tapestry of operational coordination which is, arguably, unsurpassed in any other walk of public life.

However, such problems are not new. The operational-level coordination of the UN specialised agencies, particularly the humanitarian agencies (such as the World Food Programme, the Food and Agriculture Organisation, the High Commissioner for Refugees and the Children's Fund), has historically proved to be difficult.[29] Clearly the simplest solution to the problems of duplication and institutional overlap is to reform the mandates of these agencies; however, such draconian steps have been resisted by donor countries and agencies alike, fearful of the idea of creating a large UN 'super' humanitarian agency which would replace the institutional 'alphabet soup' which currently prevails. For donor states this move would have the effect of improving the capacity of UN institutions to compel states to react to problems, thereby eroding their freedom of action – and inaction.

Mackinlay and Kent have indicated that the problem of turf wars between potentially rival UN agencies is not simply one of mandate duplication. In many ways this problem has been accentuated by the difficulties arising out of different forms of accountability. The UN specialised agencies have their work rooted in a humanitarian mandate reflecting humanitarian rather than political imperatives, whereas the work of the DPKO and DPA reflects the political realities of the Security Council and the General Assembly to a much greater degree. Consequently, turf battles between the DPKO and the DPA on one side and the DHA on the other have represented something deeper than simply a battle for bureaucratic influence.

The problem of coordination at the operational level is also compounded by expectations as to what coordination should involve. Broadly speaking, governments and military commanders often expect active or positive coordination: the authoritative allocation of priorities and the maintenance of a common effort and unity of command. However, in the broadly defined civil and humanitarian sectors, coordination is defined in much more vague terms. It becomes what could be described as passive coordination, 'consensus building' in order to reconcile differing agendas and operating principles; the sharing of information in order to avoid duplication. Coordination among humanitarian NGOs is also complicated by competitive pressures which exist to a far-reduced degree within military hierarchies. Such differing conceptions of what is coordination have proved stubbornly persistent. They also ensure that within the broad range of institutions encompassed by a PSO, effective and positive command and control become relegated, in reduced form, to the national military hierarchies.

UN involvement in PSOs has been complicated quite significantly by deployment alongside a range of diverse institutions whose activities impact upon UN military forces and the specialised agencies. The linkage of institutions as diverse as those for war-fighting (such as NATO) through to those for peacebuilding[30] has compounded the problems of vertical and horizontal integration of command. Defining institutional relationships at all levels, in terms of both political and bureaucratic precedence, is compounded by the difficulty of identifying the nature of an organisation. Many organisations involved in a PSO possess what could be described as an evolving 'nature': the inability to predict the shape that the operation will eventually take and the consequent inability to make decisions that reflect this shape complicate relationships with the PSO enormously.

For example, the association of humanitarian organisations with military formations is made more difficult if it is difficult to predict how a military formation itself will shape a crisis. A case in point is the French General Philippe Morillon's unscripted promise of UN protection to the population of Srebrenica in 1993 that helped to generate a climate in the Security Council that allowed the passage of the ill-considered safe-areas resolutions. Furthermore, differing military doctrines may lead to very different rules of engagement and approaches to the use of lethal force. For example, close air support (CAS) may be an apparently limited use of military force, except where casualty intolerance by the providing nation requires the large-scale suppression of regional and local air-defence systems in order to minimise the threat to air crews. In such a case (as occurred in Croatia in 1994 with the air attack on the Udbina airbase), an apparently limited retaliatory raid may generate a considerable target list which serves to reduce the proportionality of the response. This is clearly likely to generate an escalation of the conflict.[31] Arguably, therefore, military involvement has elements of unpredictability which go beyond the problems generated by institutional weakness in the UN system.

Horizontal coordination between institutions has been compounded by the range of issues generated by contemporary complex emergencies. Increasingly 'solution-based' approaches to conflict effectively undercut the factors which cause and perpetuate violence. This demands an enormous range of operational responses from third parties. Hence environmental pressures are increasingly likely to generate an increasing diversity of function – multifunctionality – within missions. The road to multifunctionality and the blurring of humanitarian, political and military mandates within UN operations was, to a large extent, signposted by the former UN Secretary-General Boutros Boutros-Ghali. *An Agenda for Peace, the Supplement to An Agenda for Peace* (UN: New York, 1992) and *An Agenda for Development* (UN: New York, 1994) clearly pointed to the idea that UN military involvement in peacebuilding within complex emergencies needed to progress beyond the separation of formerly warring factions and the organisation of elections. UN military involvement in complex emergencies should be increasingly directed towards undermining the forces which created intra-societal violence. *An Agenda for Development* made it clear that where the appropriate UN agencies were not present the UN PSO forces should be involved in peacebuilding tasks until the conditions were right for the return of the UN's civil agencies. This represents a two-fold change. First, it extends the range of tasks that are expected of the UN military into a potentially open-ended commitment to the implementation of the rather poorly defined concept of peacebuilding. Second, it implies that building peace may begin at a much earlier stage in the conflict than concepts such as post-conflict reconstruction have traditionally allowed for. In short, it promises a far more complicated division of labour between institutions and a significant complication in terms of the horizontal integration of efforts.

CONCLUSION

The UN faces a diverse range of potentially intractable command, control, cohesion and priority-setting problems. These stem partly from the nature of decision-making in the Security Council and the varied institutions which populate the contemporary battlefield, but they also arise from the confused and sometimes incompatible sources of political control over deployed troops and the institutions with which they endeavour to cooperate. The peculiar mixture of national and international responsibilities for the support and maintenance of troops precludes effective and efficient management and direction.

The UN remains institutionally ill equipped to deal with the wider problems of policy and operational coordination, as well as the specifically military concepts of command and control. As a consequence it becomes difficult in complex crises to turn political objectives into achievable, precise and effectively resourced military mandates. Palin makes the critical point that within a multinational organisation such as NATO the 'lines of communication into and within the organisation are well understood and accepted'.[32] Within UN structures these lines are much more diverse and become a source of competition between states. The *ad hoc* nature of UN institutional responses to complex emergencies and PSOs ensures that the opportunities for such competition are great. *Ad hoc* responses bring with them additional problems; organisations that have different cultures, languages, communications equipment, standard operating procedures, troop quality, equipment and levels of training, and degrees of national interference on the part of troop-donating governments are only some of the factors that serve to undermine cohesion and unity of purpose.

Nevertheless, the UN has many strengths which serve to offset some of these weaknesses. It has a degree of legitimacy as a result of its status as the instrument through which the international community can, at times, formulate responses to events. Its role is quite well defined in terms of legal statute and it possesses a unique capacity for a range of humanitarian, political, developmental and military actions which no other multinational body currently has. While its fortunes in terms of institutional capacity to coordinate such activities, like Icarus, have risen and fallen, it still retains enormous value.

NOTES

The opinions expressed here are those of the author and do not necessarily reflect those of either the Ministry of Defence or RMA Sandhurst.

1. M. Pugh, 'Peacekeeping as Developmentalism: Concepts from Disaster Research', *Contemporary Security Policy*, 16, 3, December 1995, pp. 320–46.
2. R. H. Palin, 'Multinational Military Forces: Problems and Prospects', *Adelphi*

Paper No. 294 (Oxford: Oxford University Press/IISS, 1995), p. 15.
3. Ibid., p. 16.
4. See L. Freedman and V. Gamba-Stonehouse, *Signals of War: The Falklands Conflict of 1982* (London: Faber, 1990), pp. 142, 147 and 247–72.
5. S. Ogata, 'UNHCR in the Balkans', in W. Bierman and M. Vedset (eds), *UN Peacekeeping in Trouble: Lessons Learned from the Former Yugoslavia* (Aldershot: Ashgate Publishing, 1998).
6. K. Van Brabant, 'Cool Ground for Aid Providers: Towards Better Security Management in Aid Agencies', *Disasters*, 22, 2, June 1998, pp. 109–26.
7. See R. Caplan, *Post Mortem on UNPROFOR* (London: Brasseys, 1996). Caplan describes the difficulties faced by DPKO in implementing the ambiguously constructed Security Council Resolution 836 (which created the safe areas regime in Bosnia in April 1993) which contained the potential for contradictory enforcement and consent-based provisions.
8. M. Berdal, 'Reforming the UN's Organisational Capacity for Peacekeeping', in *A Crisis of Expectations: UN Peacekeeping in the 1990s*, pp. 181–93, and M. Berdal, 'Whither UN Peacekeeping?', *Adelphi Paper* No. 281 (London: Brasseys, 1993).
9. M. Berdal, 'Reforming the UN's Organisational Capacity for Peacekeeping'.
10. Private interview with senior officials from the Mission Planning Service.
11. C. Van Egmond, 'The Situation in UN HQ', in Bieman and Vedset, *UN Peacekeeping in Trouble*.
12. UK defence planning after the Cold War, for example, is predicated on the creation of capabilities rather than the existence of specific threats.
13. Private interview with senior UNPROFOR staff officers, Gorni Vakuf, UNPROFOR Sector Headquarters, Bosnia-Herzegovina, 1995.
14. *UN Command and Control Review*, New York, 9 November 1993.
15. W. Durch and J. A. Schear, 'Faultlines: UN Operations in the Former Yugoslavia', in W. Durch (ed.), *The UN and the Uncivil Wars of the 1990s* (London: 1996).
16. UN press release SC/95/67, Geneva, 19 December 1995.
17. This was proposed by the Canadian government in September 1995. It was described as the Vanguard Concept and envisaged a small, deployable, multinational headquarters capable of preliminary contingency planning and, subsequently, of deployment as a cadre for an operational-level headquarters. See Government of Canada, *Towards a Rapid Reaction Capability for the United Nations* (Ottawa: September 1995).
18. There are three levels of warfare: strategic, operational and tactical. 'Tactical' usually refers to the level below that of the brigade and often means the immediate battle; 'strategic' relates to the level of the theatre; while 'operational' is, in essence, the level between the two.
19. As at 3 December 1997, 67 countries had expressed a willingness to participate but only 12 had signed memoranda confirming their participation. See *SIPRI Yearbook 1998* (London: Macmillan, 1997), p. 9.
20. UN Doc. S/1995/943, 10 November, p. 5.
21. For a full explanation of these arrangements see the *SIPRI Yearbook 1998*, p. 9.
22. These are often rejected by troop-contributing nations as providing force commanders with an excessive and dangerous capacity for robust independent action. For example, UNPROFOR was prevented throughout 1994

from reorganising its troops so as to provide for a theatre-level reserve.
23. M. Berdal, 'Reforming the UN's Organisational Capacity for Peacekeeping'.
24. However, this is, to some extent offset by the decline in the numbers of new missions authorised after 1994.
25. Private interview with senior DPKO staff.
26. See General Sir M. Rose, *Fighting For Peace* (London: Harvill Press, 1998), p. 106.
27. Private interviews with senior British and UNPROFOR staff officers 1994–95.
28. Even the operations of UN humanitarian agencies in the Kurdish safe havens in northern Iraq (1991) were guided by a memorandum of understanding with the Iraqi authorities.
29. See J. Mackinlay and R. Kent, 'UN Humanitarian Reform', in *The World Today*, July 1997. See also S. Vieira de Mello, Ch. 7 in this volume.
30. See M. Pugh, 'Peacebuilding as Developmentalism'.
31. For a further discussion of this point see S. Gordon, Ch. 13 in this volume.
32. See Palin, 'Multinational Military Forces', p. 17.

3

European Approaches to Peacekeeping: The Muddled Legacy of the Yugoslav Wars

ROSEMARY DURWARD

In December 1995 NATO deployed a multinational peace Implementation Force (IFOR) to Bosnia-Herzegovina to implement the terms of the Dayton Accord. The smaller Stabilisation Force (SFOR) replaced IFOR in December 1996 with the primary task of contributing to the secure environment necessary for the resumption of peace. SFOR was initially expected to be deployed for 18 months. Because of the continuing fragile state of Bosnia-Herzegovina, Europe and the United States concluded in June 1997 that the criteria on which it would base a decision for withdrawal should be the 'end state', rather than a previously agreed time limit. Despite the continuing requirement for a NATO presence in Bosnia, the operation is often viewed as a success because it has stopped the pattern of violence and provided conditions in which peacebuilding can take place.

The IFOR and the SFOR operations are radically different in mandate, structure and politics from their predecessor, the UN Protection Force in Bosnia-Herzegovina (UNPROFOR). The UN peacekeeping operation was confused by mixed mandates combining peacekeeping with peace enforcement, thus putting the lives of peacekeepers at risk and damaging the organisation's reputation for impartiality. The protracted UNPROFOR operation, undertaken in the midst of a civil war, underlined a useful lesson for peacekeeping, which is that 'success' in any form of unarmed or lightly armed intervention can be achieved only in conjunction with a satisfactory and lasting political solution. The UN was not able to impose a political solution by deploying lightly armed peacekeepers in Bosnia, with or without NATO, where there was no peace to keep.

Against that background, in late 1998 the governments of Europe tried to develop a coordinated approach to the crisis in Kosovo, where the Albanian population demanded independence from Serbia and threatened to precipitate a war between the Serbian army and the insurgent Kosovo Liberation Army (KLA). In an attempt to defeat the Kosovar Albanians, President Milosevic of Serbia had engaged in widespread massacres, displacing Kosovars from their towns and villages. In October 1998 thousands of Kosovars took refuge in the hills, facing the prospect of death from exposure but unable to return to their homes for fear of further reprisals. The USA and Russia initiated separate talks with Milosevic to try to halt the excesses of the Serbian army. American Ambassador Richard Holbrooke brokered a ceasefire in October 1998 and Milosevic agreed that an unarmed Kosovo Verification Mission (KVM), under the authority of the Organisation for Security and Cooperation in Europe (OSCE) and numbering 2,000, would verify compliance on the ground. In time, it would help to implement the expected political settlement by the parties, supervise elections, provide support in building democratic institutions and assist with police force development in Kosovo.[1] Under the terms of the agreement, the government of the Federal Republic of Yugoslavia guaranteed the safety and security of the KVM and its members and agreed to 'permit and cooperate in the evacuation of Verification Mission members should it become necessary'. The agreement allowed the OSCE to establish coordination with other organisations it deemed 'appropriate' to allow the KVM to accomplish all its objectives.[2] President Milosevic also agreed to NATO establishing an air-verification mission over Kosovo.[3]

Russia endorsed the OSCE role but it refused to back NATO's threat of air-strikes, which was first made in early October 1998. NATO is convinced that these threats, combined with diplomacy, played some part in persuading the Serbs to accept a ceasefire and OSCE and NATO verification measures. In Ambassador Holbrooke's words, it was the 'credible threat' of imminent NATO air strikes that induced Milosevic to comply.[4]

NATO maintained the implicit threat of force by establishing a reaction force with forward elements deployed to the Former Yugoslav Republic of Macedonia and numbering some 2,300 French-led troops, with the agreement of the government of Skopje.[5] NATO threatened to use force again in January 1999 when Serbian forces massacred civilians in the village of Racak. By the end of January some 2,000 people were reported dead in Kosovo and 300,000 had lost their homes. After successive breaches of the ceasefire, NATO began preparations to send troops to impose peace in Kosovo or to police a political settlement.

These preparations were made coincidentally with a political initiative from the Contact Group of the United States, France, the United Kingdom, Germany, Italy and Russia. At the end of January they summoned President Milosevic and the leaders of the KLA for talks at Rambouillet, near Paris, to begin on 6 February 1999, with an expectation of their conclusion by 20 February. NATO reinforced the political process by threatening to bomb the Serbs and cut the KLA off from its foreign arms supplies if the violence in the Federal Republic of Yugoslavia continued and if the two sides failed to reach agreement on substantial autonomy for Kosovo and accept a NATO peacekeeping force. Deadlines had to be adjusted and conditional political agreement was reached, although the issue of NATO policing of the agreement remained an obstacle.

A new round of talks was arranged at Rambouillet for three weeks later. Whatever the outcome, many difficulties remained in the way of a permanent peaceful settlement to the Kosovo crisis. According to one observer:

> In essence, the big powers are trying to do another Dayton, the accord that ended the Bosnian War. It will be harder. The Bosnian War produced a weariness and an eventual balance of force. In Kosovo, the Serbs have the big guns, and believe that without foreigners restraining them they could roll up the KLA as an organised force. The Kosovar Albanians feel destiny and demography are with them in their push for independence.[6]

Neither side seemed likely to achieve its objectives but both refused to accept this. By their refusal they threatened a conflagration which could sweep across the entire Balkan region. The events in former Yugoslavia highlight the dilemmas of peacekeeping in Europe and, indeed, whether there should be a regional response to such crises from Europe's security institutions.

THE EUROPEAN VISION AND EUROPE'S SECURITY INSTITUTIONS

To be European should, in principle, bind its inhabitants to a club. To the outside world this 'club' seems to have exerted a disproportionate influence on world affairs, given the fact that, geographically, Europe is relatively small. Today, three of the five permanent members of the UN Security Council are European. This gives them significant influence over matters relating to the maintenance of international peace and security, be they humanitarian, political, military or economic.

Europe stretches from the Arctic Ocean in the north, the Atlantic Ocean in the west, the Mediterranean Sea in the south, and the Ural Mountains, the Ural river and the Caspian Sea in the east. The dominance of Christianity combined with the imprint of two ancient civilisations, Greek and Roman, has exerted a profound influence on European culture. Nevertheless, Europe's modern history is one of diverse nations, of shifting national boundaries brought about by wars and the clash of empires. World Wars I and II are testament to the awful capacity of Europeans to slaughter each other. The division of Europe between the democracies of the West and communist states of the East after World War II offered only an uneasy peace. Stability was found at a price, in a nuclear stand off.

Since the end of the Cold War there have been a number of institutional initiatives to try to bind Europeans together. The European Union (EU)'s moves towards monetary union and a Common Foreign and Security Policy (CFSP) represent a unique form of 'clubbing', the objective of which is to be able to compete economically with outside powers, especially the United States, and to present a common foreign policy on economic, political and security matters. This vision of an 'ever closer union' has the underlying agenda of minimising nationalist forces which have been the cause of the world wars. However, the absence of real social and economic homogeneity between the peoples of Europe continues to hamper the process. The ideal has a great deal of support but the practical steps to achieving it are far from clear. A tension exists between the preservation of sovereignty and the so-called 'federal goal'. Most obviously, the fruits of union are currently available only to a select number of West European states. Poland, Hungary, the Czech Republic, Estonia, Slovenia and Cyprus have been named as potential candidates, but the process is still awaiting the successful integration of existing members. So long as the EU remains exclusive, economic inequalities within Europe are likely to persist.

NATO's focus since the end of the Cold War has been to adapt its structures and strategy to new security challenges in Europe and 'extend a hand of friendship' to Central and Eastern Europe in order to enhance stability on its borders. NATO's North Atlantic Cooperation Council (NACC) and Partnership for Peace (PfP) programmes have paved the way for enlargement, taking in Poland, the Czech Republic and Hungary in 1999, with the possibility of further enlargement in the future. NACC's successor, the European-Atlantic Partnership Council (EAPC), with 44 members, and the NATO–Ukraine Charter draw Central and Eastern Europe (CEE) states closer to NATO, developing a common understanding on security matters, including peacekeeping. The countries of Central Europe have welcomed NATO's initiatives. Their main security concern is the latent threat from Russia and many have signed up to PfP to enhance their chances of joining the Alliance.

NATO has singled out Russia for special attention in an effort to transcend old animosities and, to some extent, as a form of appeasement to allow enlargement to go forward. The NATO–Russia Permanent Council, created in May 1997, has given Russia the opportunity to participate in NATO discussions, without giving it a veto over NATO action, thus significantly elevating its status and influence. Whether NATO will enlarge further is a moot print. The impact of enlargement from 16 to 19 on consensus decision-making will have to be assessed before a firm decision can be made. The strengthening of PfP and the EAPC may confer sufficient political and security advantages beyond NATO's borders as to make institutional enlargement unnecessary. While Russia remains vehemently opposed to a further extension of NATO's boundaries, a move which would almost inevitably mean NATO touching Russia's borders, deeper levels of cooperation will be hard to achieve.

The Western European Union (WEU) has a unique role to play in giving expression to the EU's CFSP and a European voice in NATO. Unlike the EU, it has an operational role with the potential for low-level peacekeeping.[7] Its membership overlaps with European members of NATO (except Norway, Denmark, Turkey and Iceland) and non-neutral states in the EU. Norway, Turkey and Iceland have become associate members of the WEU. Many NATO partners have adopted WEU associate partner status, although the suspicion remains that in view of the WEU's limited responsibilities at present, they see this as a route into NATO. Denmark, along with neutral EU member states, has adopted WEU observer status. The total number of states making up the so-called WEU 'family of nations' is 28. In July 1997 at the NATO Madrid Summit Alliance members gave their support to the notion of a European Security and Defence Identity (ESDI) and pledged to enhance cooperation with the WEU, taking advantage of NATO's Combined Joint Task Force (CJTF) concept. Plans for CJTF Operational Headquarters have progressed within NATO but, despite more communication and the sharing of intelligence between the two organisations, nothing material has yet emerged.

The Commonwealth of Independent States (CIS) binds together in a political, economic and security arrangement most of the states of Eastern Europe that were part of the former Soviet Union. There is evidence that at least some members of the CIS have been coerced into it. The case of Georgia is worth recording: Russia allegedly encouraged instability in Georgia and, as a result, Georgia was forced to invite in Russian peace-keepers to restore order.[8] Russia has tried, unsuccessfully so far, to be given a UN mandate to legitimise this force.[9] The CIS has not reciprocated NATO's steps towards transparency by embracing the countries of Western Europe and an uneasy relationship exists between the two.

The OSCE, with its 55 participating states, represents the only European institution which is pan-European. Since its inception as the Conference on Security and Cooperation in Europe (CSCE) in 1973, it has provided a unique forum for diplomacy in Europe. At the 1992 Helsinki Summit the CSCE extended its interests to include early warning, conflict prevention, crisis management and peacekeeping. It changed its name to the OSCE in 1994 following a decision at the Budapest Summit to reflect the transition from a 'process' to an organisation. A recent initiative, flowing from the 1996 Lisbon Summit, has been the European Charter which, among other things, aims to make sense of the relationship between the OSCE and Europe's other security organisations.[10] Because the CIS does not currently conform to many of the OSCE's principles, such as transparency and genuinely voluntary and equal membership, it may not be able to sign up to the OSCE Charter.

PEACEKEEPING COOPERATION AT THE OPERATIONAL LEVEL

The idea that there can be a common European response to crises, now that the Cold War is over, is extremely attractive. In Western Europe the act of 'clubbing together' in NATO and the EU has reinforced a pattern of consultation and cooperation which has considerably reduced the likelihood of war. Where long-standing hostilities exist, such as between Greece and Turkey, membership of NATO has defused tensions. Links between Europe's security institutions, and between institutions and individual countries have grown since the end of the Cold War with positive results.

Today, there is scope for a great deal more flexibility in peacekeeping arrangements in Europe than was the case at the end of the Cold War. In institutional terms, the idea of a 'new European security architecture' involving 'interlocking institutions' within the OSCE area was popular in the immediate post-Cold War period.[11] But the slow and relatively disunited European response to the developing crisis in the Balkans meant that it represented little more than an image for institutional enlargement and overlapping membership. By 1996 the concept of the 'new European security architecture' had been substituted by the notion of 'mutually reinforcing institutions', describing the cooperative effort undertaken by NATO, the WEU, the EU and the OSCE, following the Dayton Accord.

At a practical level, NATO's CJTF concept offers possibilities for willing Europeans to respond to regional crises. Potentially, the WEU and NATO's partners could deploy peacekeepers under the command of deputy Supreme Allied Commander Europe (SACEUR), using NATO assets. The Eurocorps could also make a contribution, as might the emerging peacekeeping battalions in Central and Eastern Europe. Importantly, CJTF allows for the deployment of European forces even if the USA prefers to remain aloof. The IFOR/SFOR operation is often described as a generic CJTF. Driven primarily by military requirements, it was operating long before NATO could reach agreement on the CJTF concept, where politically sensitive command issues challenged national interests. Following on from the experience in Bosnia-Herzegovina, the US Secretary of State Madeleine Albright has proposed that NATO and Russia form a joint brigade for peacekeeping and crisis-management missions.[12]

The idea of 'coalitions of the willing' has also gained currency in Europe because of the political and operational flexibility that it offers. It was first put into practice in the crisis in Albania in 1997. Neither NATO, the WEU nor the OSCE offered forces for a peacekeeping operation. Instead, neighbouring Mediterranean states responded under Italian leadership by creating a Multinational Protection Force (MPF).[13] The EU provided aid and the OSCE undertook election monitoring and coordinated the several aspects of the operation.

The formation of 'coalitions of the willing' does, of course, rest upon a series of assumptions. First, that a coalition can be found which is willing; second, that a coalition is suited to dealing with the scale of the crisis; third, that the states that volunteer for this coalition are acceptable to the host state; and fourth, that the coalition is acceptable to the international community. In the case of the Albanian crisis, all these criteria were satisfied. The crisis itself was relatively self-contained; it attracted peacekeeping contributions from southern Mediterranean states with an interest in local stability and which were no doubt seeking recognition by NATO of their own security needs. Finally, the force they organised was acceptable to Albania. Hence, there was a relatively swift response.

The deployment of unarmed OSCE verifiers to Kosovo under the protection of NATO constitutes a previously untried experiment in conflict management on the ground. The OSCE had never fielded such a large number of personnel to a conflict zone. In line with Russia's ambitions, the operation has arguably elevated the OSCE in relation to other European security institutions and underscored the possibilities for pan-European cooperation in the interests of crisis management, peacekeeping and stability. As NATO's Secretary-General Dr Javier Solana pointed out in a speech to the North Atlantic Assembly in November 1998, 'This is the new European security structure – not on paper, but at work'.[14]

UNDERLYING TENSIONS: THE LEGAL FRAMEWORK FOR PEACEKEEPING IN EUROPE

Such optimism should not obscure the fact that NATO, the EU, the WEU, the OSCE and the CIS have quite separate identities and institutional and national rivalries impact on cooperation. Tensions remain not only between the old adversaries of Russia and the USA but also in relations between these two states and Europe. Russia, because of its nuclear weapons status and its dominant geographical position in Europe, and the USA, because of its political, economic and military influence, continue to exert a disproportionate influence on European affairs. West Europeans share a schizophrenic attitude towards the USA. They welcome its capacity to give vital leadership and direction, as well as provide a balance to Russian power. But its equal capacity to stifle the European vision causes rifts among West European states. The formation of a Contact Group to deal with the crisis in Kosovo in early 1999 may be heralded as an important indicator of cooperation, at least to the extent that all its members enjoyed the same goal of peace in Kosovo, but the Group has been divided over critical matters such as how, where and when to use force in the event that coercion became necessary.

The principles of consent, impartiality, respect for sovereignty and minimum force associated with traditional peacekeeping have developed as a consequence of the legal framework for the peaceful settlement of disputes. The UN Charter distinguishes between the pacific settlement of disputes under Chapter VI and enforcement action under Chapter VII. The Charter requires a Security Council mandate in the case of enforcement under Chapter VII, except in cases of self-defence or breaches of territorial integrity. This distinction between peacekeeping and peace enforcement has applied as much to regional as to international crises until now. Regional *peacekeeping* by a group of states or a regional organisation would be entirely legal without specific endorsement by the UN, according to Chapter VIII. Indeed, it actively encourages regional arrangements in the pacific settlement of disputes. But Article 53 makes it clear that no *enforcement* action may be taken without authorisation from the Security Council.

The challenges of UN peacekeeping in Europe as Yugoslavia disintegrated after the end of the Cold War led to the UN passing successive mandates under both Chapter VI and Chapter VII. So-called 'mixed mandates' were passed which, in Bosnia, allowed for a combination of UN peacekeeping and peace enforcement. Western academics talked enthusiastically about Chapter 'Six and·a Half' operations, a halfway house between peacekeeping and peace enforcement.

These developments provoked a radical revision of peacekeeping doctrine among Alliance countries. In Britain *Wider Peacekeeping* replaced the British Army manual designed for traditional peacekeeping operations. It tried to provide rules for peacekeeping operations carried out with the general consent of the parties but in an environment that might be highly volatile.[15] However, the combination of UN peacekeeping and peace enforcement in Bosnia proved counter-productive. Attempts at coercion challenged the impartiality of the peacekeepers, bolstered opposition and left a legacy of hostility and violence.

In the British Army's latest statement on doctrine, *Peace Support Operations*, there is a recognition that *Wider Peacekeeping*'s definition of peacekeeping:

> stretched traditional peacekeeping doctrine too far. It is agreed that PK doctrine should not be applied to, and PK forces relying on consent should not be deployed into, a civil war involving widespread human rights abuses ... the restriction of human rights abuses, and the creation of safe areas and other tasks requiring enforcement, can only be accomplished, and should only be attempted, by a force capable of overmatching whatever level of opposition it may be offered.[16]

The sense of this was borne out in Bosnia with the deployment of IFOR under robust rules of engagement (ROE) backed up by a heavy armour capability for possible enforcement.

Peace Support Operations states that enforcement should be 'undertaken under Chapter VII of the UN Charter'. It explains that enforcement is coercive and concerned with victory. It defines peacekeeping as 'generally undertaken under Chapter VI of the UN Charter, with the consent of the major parties to a conflict, to monitor and facilitate the implementation of a peace agreement'. It proposes that peace-support operations, which may incorporate a range of responses including peacekeeping, peace enforcement, conflict prevention, peacemaking, peacebuilding and humanitarian operations, are concerned with the desired end state which includes the creation of conditions for a lasting settlement which is self-sustaining. It further states that peace-support operations are conducted impartially in support of a UN or an OSCE mandate.[17] This has been widely accepted within the Alliance and among PfP states. Now British, American, French, Swedish and NATO doctrines all distinguish peace support from warlike operations which aim for the defeat of the designated enemy.[18]

Until recently, where peacekeepers have been deployed or where force or the threat of force has been applied, NATO has insisted that this should be sanctioned by the UN or the OSCE. In NATO's 1993 *Athens Report*, for example, it stated that

> the basis for any mission is a clear and precise mandate of the UN or the CSCE, developed through consultations with contributing States and organisations and/or interested parties, covering all of the essential elements of the operation to be performed.

It went on:

> In all types of operations, the extent to which force can be used needs to be clearly defined either in the mandate or in the terms of reference ... Forces involved in any operation retain the inherent right of self-defence at all times.[19]

In the light of widespread atrocities against civilians in Kosovo, the USA became particularly keen to argue that NATO does not need a UN mandate for using force in Kosovo. It can draw upon Article 52, which states that nothing in the Charter prevents regional arrangements from dealing with matters relating to the maintenance of international peace and security, 'provided their activities are consistent with the Purposes and Principles of the UN'. Whereas Article 53 insists that 'no enforcement action shall be taken under regional arrangements or by regional agencies without the authorisation of the Security Council', effectively the USA wants to separate traditional enforcement involving victory and a Chapter VII mandate from the use of force for humanitarian goals. This would widen the scope of Chapter VIII of the Charter to allow not just peace-keeping but peace support operations and would avoid the requirement for a Chapter VII mandate.

While NATO threatened the use of force in Kosovo to coerce President Milosevic and the KLA towards political agreement, a consensus on the use of force, except as mandated to protect the verifiers, was fragile. Some European NATO allies, such as Germany and France, stressed the traditional legal interpretation of Chapters VII and VIII of the Charter and insisted on a Chapter VII mandate for NATO military action in Kosovo. Their concern was the consequences of violating Serb sovereignty, not simply for the Balkans but for international order.[20] There were also practical difficulties to surmount, notably the safety of the verifiers. Lessons could be drawn from the UNPROFOR operation where NATO's bombing in support of UNPROFOR exposed the peacekeepers to hostage-taking. Those verifiers could become hostages of President Milosevic or, indeed, of the KLA.[21]

At the moment of writing (January 1999), Russia, which has historical sympathies with Serbia, is opposed to the use of force in Kosovo and would veto any attempts by the Security Council to sanction a Chapter VII mandate. While the Russian military see good sense in the principle of deploying appropriately armed troops with suitable ROE in a non-consenting environment,[22] there is little support at the political level for endorsing it. Russian political leaders argue that air-strikes would solve nothing and only make a dangerous situation worse. Russia's legal position, explained on successive occasions in NATO forums, is that force should be used only in self-defence and NATO has no right to undertake even traditional peacekeeping in Europe without a Security Council mandate, based on Chapter VIII of the Charter.[23] This is consistent with Russia's demand for a legitimising mandate from the Security Council for its peacekeeping role in the near abroad and its determination to prevent NATO from becoming a European policeman within Russia's 'sphere of influence'.[24] NATO nations have always viewed a mandate for traditional peacekeeping in Europe as unnecessary because Chapter VIII actively encourages the peaceful settlement of disputes at regional level. Establishing the precedent that all operations require a UN mandate, even when minimum force is used only in self-defence, would give Russia an unacceptable veto over NATO's freedom of action.

During the Cold War the Security Council was notorious for not mandating action in the face of territorial aggression because of Cold War rivalries. This undermined the credibility of the UN. Post-Cold War obstruction of the effective functioning of the UN by any state, for narrow political advantage, is hard to tolerate after the UN's more active role in maintaining international peace and security since the Gulf conflict.[25]

There is a moral imperative to the notion of peace-support operations which, in emphasising the end state, is consistent with and reinforces the purposes of the Charter. Article 1.2 defines one of the purposes of the UN as: 'To develop friendly relations among nations based on respect for the principle of equal rights and self-determination of peoples, and to take other appropriate measures to strengthen universal peace'. Article 55 commits all members to universal respect for, and observance of, human rights and Article 56 provides that 'all members pledge themselves to take joint and separate action in cooperation with the Organisation for the achievement of the purposes set forth in Article 55'. Article 2.2 also places responsibilities on members to 'fulfil in good faith the obligations assumed by them in accordance with the present Charter ... in order to ensure to all of them the rights and benefits resulting from membership'.

Subsequent UN resolutions endorsed these principles, notably the Universal Declaration on Human Rights which stressed the inseparability of human rights and peace.[26]

To some extent, the development of doctrine born out of the demands made on troops on the ground since the end of the Cold War has out-stripped the traditional legal framework for peacekeeping provided by the UN Charter. Whilst custom and practice has been for a Chapter VII mandate to make the use of force legal, the Charter is just one source of international law. The Geneva Convention of 12 August 1949 and its protocols, for example, extend to protect any person affected by armed conflict. Whether in the case of armed conflict or severe non-international armed conflict, the Convention prohibits murder, torture, corporal punishment, mutilation, outrages upon personal dignity, the taking of hostages, collective punishments, execution without regular trial and cruel and degrading treatment,[27] all of which have been perpetrated in Kosovo. Article 1.1 of the UN Charter states that 'adjustment or settlement of international disputes or situations which might lead to a breach of the peace' must be in 'conformity with the principles of justice and international law'. The OSCE appears to be moving in that direction in its Charter on European Security, established in 1996 at the Budapest Summit, and confirmed at Istanbul in 1999. Provisional guidelines suggest that in exploring actions that may have to be taken in accordance with the Charter of the UN in the event of a threat to the sovereignty, territorial integrity or political independence of any state, and in case of an internal breakdown of law and order, member states

> shall ensure that the presence of foreign troops on the territory of a participating State is in conformity with international law, the freely expressed consent of the host State, or a relevant decision of the United Nations Security Council.[28]

There may now be a case for legitimising the use of force to impose peace without necessarily having the authority of a Chapter VII UN mandate. Such regional operations, consistent with international law and with the principles of the UN Charter, could fall under the rubric of a notional Chapter VIII and a Half operation.

THE POLITICS OF PEACEKEEPING IN EUROPE

The legitimacy of peacekeeping and peace-support operations in Europe rests not only upon strict legal definitions but also upon the consensus of opinion in Europe and, to some extent, the consistency of response.

Ideally, humanitarian intervention in Europe's crises should be guided by Grotius's doctrine contained in *De jure belli et pacis*. Published in 1625, the Dutch jurist, diplomat and founder of international law argued that natural law may override the law of nations as manifested in state practice. According to Grotius, a number of a *priori* rights exist, including human rights, and it is perfectly legitimate and praiseworthy for states to defend these rights on behalf of other states or their citizens. The doctrine allows the full-scale use of force, as required, to end human suffering.[29]

At present, the legal framework appears confused to the extent that post-World War II norms about the central role of the Security Council and the importance of the great powers in it are being challenged. The UN Charter was written by states and designed to preserve their interests, the principal ones being sovereignty and territorial integrity, through the power of veto. There are clear dangers that humanitarian intervention which has the support of the majority of the citizens of Europe may undermine international order between states, particularly if it becomes an excuse for imperialism. That is why, although humanitarian intervention has become more legitimate since the end of the Cold War, it has, up until now, been activated only by the Security Council.

The OSCE has the potential to confer legitimacy on a peacekeeping operation because it is pan-European, although it has no treaty basis on which to mandate action. It can confer legitimacy by virtue of its size and its decision-making, based upon consensus among the 55, and because it is a designated regional organisation of the UN. However, in the case of Europe's crisis in Kosovo the legitimacy of NATO intervention was weakened by the absence of a European-wide consensus and particularly by Russian opposition.

With a note of desperation, NATO's Secretary-General urged Russia to behave as a responsible member of the international community over the Kosovo crisis:

> Russia's weight and importance must rest on its ability to contribute to common solutions, not on its ability to deny them. And such is the responsibility of a UN Security Council member. And such should be the logic that guides modern Russia into the 21st century.[30]

Russia's promised veto on a Chapter VII mandate to use force in Kosovo was ironic, given the record of Russian peacekeeping in the 'near abroad' in the early post-Cold War years. A certain hypocrisy was evident in Russia's position since Russia has used excessive force or threatened it in Georgia and Tajikistan. In Georgia's South Ossetia Russia's threat of force was sufficient to establish a ceasefire. In Tajikistan the Russians used force before the ceasefire was in place and continued to do so after the peace-keeping force and the ceasefire were established.[31] Indeed, its peace-keeping doctrine stresses the early use of force.[32] Clearly, Russian policy and practice differ widely.

It was concern about Russia's *modus operandi* which prompted the OSCE to become engaged in the crisis in Nagorno-Karabakh. In 1994 the OSCE promised to deploy peacekeeping troops to the Armenian enclave in Azerbaijan, but only in the event of a lasting peace settlement. The settlement has proved elusive and progress in planning for the peace-keeping operation has been slow. Not all states who have offered troops for peacekeeping are acceptable to the neighbouring states. Turkey and Azerbaijan have both opposed a large contingent of Russian troops in any peacekeeping force, fearing the long-term consequences for Azerbaijani independence and Turkish security. Yet Russia is the only country which was prepared to deploy troops in sufficient numbers to carry out the planned tasks. The US, because of its interest in oil from the Caspian Sea, has tried to motivate West Europeans to play their part through the OSCE, but it recognises that to lead such a contingent or to encourage NATO to do so would be unacceptable to Russia. Spheres of influence still exist, particularly in the 'near abroad', to the extent that 'coalitions of the willing' might, cynically, be substituted by 'coalitions of the possible'.

The West has recognised that Russia has an important role to play in this area but concludes that, if Russia is to attain the international recognition and even the financial support it seeks for such operations, the West in turn needs guarantees that Russia would not regard recognition of its involvement as giving it *carte blanche* in the former Soviet Union (FSU).

In December 1993 the then British Secretary of State for Foreign Affairs Douglas Hurd and the Russian Foreign Minister Andrei Kozyrev agreed, provisionally, to a set of peacekeeping principles[33] designed to deal with so-called 'third-party peacekeeping' involving Russian peace-keeping in the near abroad. This laid out the conditions upon which the OSCE and Europe would approve of Russian peacekeeping. Hurd and Kozyrev reiterated their assent to traditional peacekeeping principles: peacekeeping must be agreed on a case-by-case basis; peacekeeping in the former Soviet Union must comply with internationally recognised principles; respect for the sovereignty of the newly independent countries must remain paramount; there must be an invitation from the government concerned and the consent of the parties to the conflict. However, as a safeguard, Hurd also insisted on a commitment to a parallel political peace process: a clear mandate setting out the role of the peacekeeping forces which would, wherever possible, be multinational in character, and an exit strategy for the peacekeeping forces deployed. Kozyrev at first agreed and then subsequently rejected these principles, resenting the degree of interference proposed, particularly in the negotiation of a settlement.

Efforts to negotiate third-party peacekeeping principles have not been resurrected since 1993. However, it may now be the right time to consider a set of principles, perhaps incorporated into the OSCE's Charter, which would apply to peacekeeping and peace-support operations involving intervention on humanitarian grounds. In both cases the requirement for a parallel political process which engages all interested parties, even if only as observers, and the principle of multinationality would seem to be essential for intervention to have legitimacy.

During the Cold War it was accepted that in most peacekeeping operations neighbouring states and the superpowers did not take part. This principle has lapsed and, indeed, for regional initiatives to work they largely depend upon the intervention of neighbouring states. Hence, as well as agreement on the legal aspects of peacekeeping, a set of peace-keeping principles needs to be agreed which is relevant not only to peace-keeping today but also to peace-support operations. Europeans need to settle their differences and arrive at a set of mutually acceptable principles which are, quite possibly, peculiarly European.

The experience in the Balkans of searching for political solutions while at the same time trying to establish the 'appropriate' level of intervention in a timely fashion has been challenging. It has encouraged greater flexibility at the operational level but much remains to be done at the political one. In the peacekeeping operation in Bosnia tactical-level practitioners took the view that UNPROFOR's perceived failures were not due to a lack of military or civilian competence in the field but resulted from insufficient political will and commitment from the international community.[34] Although there has been a great deal of progress since the end of the Cold War in creating links between the institutions in Europe, as yet there has been no truly coherent institutional or political framework to give legitimacy to a European peacekeeping operation. It is probable that a far higher level of cooperation will have to be sought at the political level than has hitherto been the case if the chances of a regional response to European crises are to be improved. With such differing approaches within Europe, any regional response to crises is likely to continue to be a process of 'muddling through'.

NOTES

The opinions expressed here are those of the author and do not necessarily reflect those of either the Ministry of Defence or RMA Sandhurst.

1. Agreement signed in Belgrade on 16 October 1998 by the Minister of Foreign Affairs of the Federal Republic of Yugoslavia, H. E. Zivadin Jovanovic and the Chairman-in-Office of the Organisation for Security and Cooperation in Europe (OSCE) H. E. Bronislaw Geremek providing for the OSCE to establish a verification mission in Kosovo (S/1998/978), including the undertaking of the Federal Republic of Yugoslavia to comply with UN Resolutions 1160 (1998) and 1199 (1998). The mission never exceeded 800 personnel because of repeated violations of the peace agreement.
2. Agreement on the OSCE Kosovo Verification Mission, Belgrade, 16 October 1998.
3. Agreement signed in Belgrade, 15 October 1998 by the Chief of the General Staff of the Federal Republic of Yugoslavia and the Supreme Allied Commander Europe of NATO providing for the establishment of an air-verification mission over Kosovo (S/1998/991, annex), complementing the OSCE verification mission.
4. Special State Department press briefing on Kosovo, 28 October 1998.
5. State Department briefing by Secretary of State Madeleine Albright, Office of the Spokesman, 27 October 1998.
6. 'Peace Push', *Financial Times*, 1 February 1999.
7. On 19 June 1992 WEU Foreign and Defence Ministers issued the Petersburg Declaration which outlined three missions for the WEU: humanitarian and rescue tasks; peacekeeping tasks; and tasks of combat forces in crisis management including peacemaking. In addition, they pledged their support for conflict prevention and peacekeeping efforts in cooperation with the CSCE and the UN Security Council.
8. Mark Galeotti, 'Russia and its neighbours: partner, threat or problem?', in *Jane's Defence '96: The World in Conflict*, p. 96. An alternative view is that if Russian assistance was given to local Ossetian militias in Georgia, 'it may have been the result of local initiative or venality rather than a component of an official policy of Russian aggrandisement'. See N. A. Kellett, *Russian Peacekeeping, Part III: Peacekeeping Operations since 1991* (Revised Version), Directorate of Strategic Analysis Policy Group, Research Note 98/03, Department of National Defence, Canada, March 1998, p. 36.
9. H. E. Andrei V. Kozyrev, '"Neoimperialism" or Defence of Interests of the Democratic Community? – Russian Peacekeeping in the CIS', *NATO's Sixteen Nations*, No. 2 (1994), p. 52.
10. See 'Guidelines on an OSCE Document-Charter on European Security', Decision No. 5, OSCE Ministerial Council, Copenhagen 1997, MC(6). DEC/5, 19 December 1997.
11. See Rome Declaration on Peace and Cooperation, NATO Summit Meeting, Rome, November 1991.
12. 'Albright proposes joint NATO–Russia peacekeeping unit', *The Times*, 19 February 1997. For further discussion on the emerging peacekeeping battalions in Central and Eastern Europe see P. Latawski, Ch. 4 in this volume.
13. The force, consisting of 6,000 troops from Italy, France, Turkey, Greece, Spain, Romania, Austria and Denmark, deployed under UN Resolution 1101 to 'facilitate the safe and prompt delivery of humanitarian assistance, and to help create a secure environment for the missions of international organisations'.

14. Secretary-General Javier Solana's Speech at the North Atlantic Assembly Annual Session, Edinburgh, 13 November 1998.
15. See Army Field Manual Vol. 5, *Operations Other than War,* Part 2, *Wider Peacekeeping* (London: HMSO, 1994).
16. *Peace Support Operations*: Joint Warfare Publication 3-50, Appendix 1-4 (Llangennech: MOD CSE).
17. *Peace Support Operations*: JWP3-50, p. 1-1 (Llangennech: MOD CSE).
18. *Peace Support Operations*: JWP3-50, p. 1-6 (Llangennech: MOD CSE).
19. See 'Follow-on to the 1993 Athens Report on Cooperation in Peacekeeping', NACC Meeting, 6 December 1995, press release M-NACC-2(95)123, pp. 3–5. See also Chairman's Summary, Seminar on Peacekeeping and its Relationship to Crisis Management, p. 1, Annex 11 to Progress Report to Ministers by the Political–Military Steering Committee/*Ad Hoc* Group on Cooperation in Peacekeeping, NACC Meeting, 2 December 1994, press release M-NACC-2(94)119.
20. See Richard Caplan, 'International Diplomacy and the Crisis in Kosovo', *International Affairs*, 74, 4 (1998), pp. 754–5.
21. See James Gow, 'Coercive Cadences: The Yugoslav War of Dissolution' in Lawrence Freedman (ed.), *Strategic Coercion: Concepts and Cases* (Oxford: Oxford University Press, 1998), p. 285.
22. Lt-Gen. Lebed, former commander of the Russian 14th Army in Moldova, has argued that a readiness for decisive action and absolute superiority in force will deter and break the will of opponents of the 'peacekeeping forces'. See Roy Allison, 'Russian Peacekeeping – Capabilities and Doctrine', *Jane's Intelligence Review – Europe*, December 1994, p. 546.
23. Russian delegate Professor Federov spoke from a paper on these matters at the NACC Peacekeeping Seminar on the Legal Aspects of Peacekeeping, 10–12 July 1995, Bucharest. His position was reiterated at the NATO Seminar on the Modalities for Cooperation with the UN and OSCE, Including the International Legal Basis and Legitimacy of Peacekeeping Operations, Oslo, 22–24 June 1998.
24. See Michael Orr, 'Peacekeeping – A New Task for Russian Military Doctrine', *Jane's Intelligence Review – Europe*, July 1994, p. 307.
25. On 25 February 1999 China exercised its veto in the Security Council to prevent an extension of the UN's conflict-prevention force in Macedonia because of Macedonia's diplomatic recognition of Taiwan. John M. Goshko, 'To Punish Macedonia, China Vetoes UN Mission', *Washington Post*, 26 February 1999.
26. 'The Universal Declaration on Human Rights', UN General Assembly Resolution 2174 (111), 10 December 1948.
27. Summary of the Geneva Conventions of 12 August 1949 and Their Additional Protocols, in *Joint Warfare Publication 3-5*, Appendix 3-1, para. 4 (Llangennech: MOD CSE).
28. See Guidelines on an OSCE Document-Charter, para. 5c and 5d, pp. 2–3.
29. See Tonny Brems Knudsen, 'Humanitarian Intervention Revisited: Post-Cold War Responses to Classical Problems', *International Peacekeeping*, 3, 4, Winter 1993, pp. 147–8.
30. Javier Solana, Secretary-General of NATO, Speech at the North Atlantic Assembly Annual Session, Edinburgh, 13 November 1998.
31. See Kellett, *Russian Peacekeeping*, p. 99.

32. See Orr, 'Peacekeeping', p. 307.
33. 'Challenge of Peacekeeping: Douglas Hurd and Andrei Kozyrev on a possible framework for cooperation', *Financial Times,* 14 December 1993, p. 16.
34. *Peace Support Operations*: Joint Warfare Publication 3-50, Appendix 1-4 (Llangennech: MOD CSE).

4

Bilateral and Multilateral Peacekeeping Units in Central and Eastern Europe

PAUL LATAWSKI

During the Cold War Soviet political constraints limited the participation and interest in peacekeeping by the communist states of Central Europe. Although a few of these states, such as Poland, contributed to a number of United Nations operations – beginning with the Supervisory Commission of Neutral States in Korea (SCNS) in 1953 – the Polish presence in these peacekeeping missions could not be described as stemming from a position of political neutrality nor a desire to serve only the interests of international peace and security. Indeed, Soviet political and ideological limitations precluded the pursuit of independent policies by any of the countries of the Warsaw Pact. The end of the Cold War, however, opened up the possibility of participation in peacekeeping by the former communist states of the region on a scale unimaginable during the period of Soviet hegemony.

Since 1989 there has been a marked increase in interest and participation in peacekeeping by the former communist states. Free to make their own security policies, many of these states began to develop their capability and to contribute to peacekeeping operations of several kinds. Undoubtedly, this enhanced interest in peacekeeping took root in the favourable climate of the early 1990s. With the dramatic growth in post-Cold War regional conflict, demand for UN peacekeepers was never higher. Indeed, the revivification of the UN's role in peacekeeping was accompanied by a lively conceptual discussion on peacekeeping, stimulated by the publication of papers such as *An Agenda for Peace* by the then Secretary-General of the UN Boutros Boutros-Ghali in 1992. Although the need for UN peacekeepers and conceptual discussion has waned in the late 1990s, the Central European enthusiasm to continue to develop a capability in peacekeeping has not lessened.

Throughout the 1990s Central Europe has been at the forefront of efforts to create bilateral and multilateral peacekeeping units, ostensibly to provide a standby capacity for the UN and the European collective security efforts of the Organisation for Security and Cooperation in Europe (OSCE). The scale of the effort devoted to the development of joint peacekeeping units in the region suggests the existence of a political–military agenda that goes beyond simply contributing to traditional UN peacekeeping.

REGIONAL POLITICAL AGENDA: SECURITY SUBSIDIARITY AND INTEGRATION

The motives driving this proliferation of peacekeeping units in the region are complex. They include a *prima facie* desire of former communist states to contribute in a constructive manner to the maintenance of international peace and security through contributions to traditional peacekeeping. Within the region, however, they serve a very different function. As the Lithuanian Foreign Minister emphasised in his address to the UN General Assembly in September 1997, the peacekeeping units are an important statement of cooperation in the Central European region:

> Together with Estonia, Latvia, and with Poland, Lithuania is developing joint peacekeeping units. Apart from its genuine objective – to contribute to the UN goals – this exercise is, in itself, a testimony of full understanding and cooperation among the neighbouring countries of our region.[1]

Other reasons for the creation of joint peacekeeping units are linked to the security aspirations of the states. Apart from potentially contributing to traditional peacekeeping operations, these bilateral and multilateral peacekeeping units are seen as building blocks of wider European security. Many examples of such thinking may be found in the statements of policymakers. The Polish Foreign Minister, Bronislaw Geremek, in addressing an international conference on sub-regional cooperation in Stockholm in October 1998, typified Central European views on the importance of security cooperation at the sub-regional level to the general security of Europe:

> Sub-regional co-operation makes a tangible contribution to security in the OSCE area. It is the embodiment of the principle of

subsidiarity in security terms. It is designed to solve problems at the lowest possible platform of interaction. Sub-regional cooperation underlines the importance of the 'neighbourhood' as a security factor. Good neighbourliness constitutes the fabric of European security. Without a solid bilateral basis of relations between neighbours, all references to a new security era on the continent will ring hollow.[2]

The Slovenian Foreign Minister emphasised the same theme in an address given in March 1997 pointing towards an eventual Hungarian–Italian–Slovenian joint peacekeeping project:

> The security integration must not be limited to the Euro-Atlantic area alone; it also has to consist of regional cooperation, which is an important component of the overall Euro-Atlantic security cooperation. Slovenia therefore together with Hungary and Italy established trilateral cooperation in autumn 1996. A significant part of this co-operation is the security dimension which is aimed not only at these three countries, but also towards the broader region. The experience gained in the initial security cooperation confirms us in the belief that regional cooperation represents the territorial nucleus of the new European architecture.[3]

The joint peacekeeping units therefore serve as instruments in building a layered model of European security. In Central European thinking they contribute to good 'neighbourliness' at a bilateral level, extend the web of cooperation within the sub-region and are necessary components for building a pan-European security architecture.

The eagerness to form joint peacekeeping units also serves national interests in Central Europe. Most, if not all, of the states that plan to or already participate in joint peacekeeping units aspire to membership of Western security institutions such as NATO. Peacekeeping units are therefore seen as a means to eventual membership of these security organisations. The cooperation they foster at a bilateral and sub-regional level is meant to be a concrete signal of suitability to join the NATO 'club'. They are visible examples of military cooperation between countries that may have had significant conflicts in the past and demonstrate the ability to overcome them. This impulse to replace previous conflict with cooperation has fitted well into NATO's Partnership for Peace (PfP) programme. One of PfP's key objectives has been to promote cooperation in such areas as peacekeeping.[4] As NATO places great stock on close military-to-military contacts as the lifeblood of cooperation necessary to make a multinational alliance function, the joint peacekeeping battalions are a means of generating these military links.

As a practical matter, these joint peacekeeping units are meant to serve as military transmission belts 'for improving national defence capabilities and promoting interoperability with NATO'.[5] The actual utility of the joint peacekeeping units as a means of enhancing national defence capabilities is open to question: apart from these former communist states lacking any military infrastructure or capability on acquiring sovereignty, the joint peacekeeping units bring few revelations in the military art. Similarly, these joint units offer only the most rudimentary, if useful, opportunities for promoting interoperability with NATO. Despite these limitations, the joint peacekeeping units are viewed by their participants as fostering a process of acculturation into the practices of Western security organisations. Most of these projects to form joint peacekeeping units have certainly succeeded in attracting the support and, in some cases, the direct participation of NATO and non-NATO European states.

REGIONAL MILITARY DEVELOPMENTS: JOINT PEACEKEEPING PROJECTS

The first joint peacekeeping unit was the trilateral Joint Baltic Peacekeeping Battalion (BALTBAT) with troop contributions from Estonia, Latvia and Lithuania. Since BALTBAT's creation in 1994 five other bilateral, battalion-sized projects and four multilateral initiatives on the scale of a brigade have followed. The status of these ten projects is summarised in Table 1. Most of these joint battalions and brigades are in the process of formation and how many of these joint peacekeeping units will achieve operational readiness is by no means certain. Although some of them, such as the BALTBAT, will achieve a high level of multinational military integration *à la* Eurocorps, at the other end of the spectrum they are likely to consist of a joint headquarters with a multinational menu of sub-units assigned to the larger joint peacekeeping unit. It is also possible that political, military or financial constraints could see some of these joint peacekeeping projects, such as the Bulgarian–Romanian joint battalion, stillborn. Nevertheless, the majority of these projects can measure tangible progress toward their realisation.

Militarily these joint units are structured to participate in peace-support operations (PSOs). Within the broad array of operations contained under the PSO rubric they are clearly not configured for more muscular peace enforcement operations. What all of these formations have in common are roles, unit structures and equipment more appropriate to participation in humanitarian or traditional peacekeeping operations. Indeed, almost all of these joint units from Central Europe

Aspects of Peacekeeping

TABLE 4.1. Joint Peacekeeping Units in Central and Eastern Europe

Units	Acronym	Date Proposed	Date Operational	Overall Strength
Bilateral				
Bulgarian–Romanian Peacekeeping Battalion	?	January 1998	?	?
Czech–Polish Peacekeeping Battalion	?	February 1997	?	?
Hungarian–Romanian Peacekeeping Battalion	?	May 1997	2000	1,000
Lithuanian–Polish Peacekeeping Battalion	LITPOLBAT	February 1995	1999	800
Polish–Ukrainian Peacekeeping Battalion	POLUKRBAT	November 1995	1999	500
Trilateral				
Joint Baltic Peacekeeping Battalion	BALTBAT	September 1994	1999–2000	721
Joint Hungarian–Romanian–Ukrainian Peacekeeping Battalion	?	January 1999	?	?
Joint Hungarian–Italian–Slovenian Peacekeeping Brigade	?	April 1997	?	?
Multilateral				
Central European Nations Cooperation in Peace Support. Participating states: Austria, Hungary, Slovakia, Slovenia and Romania. Observer states: Czech Republic and Switzerland	CENCOOP	March 1998	2000	5,000
Multinational Peace Force Southeastern Europe (MPFSEE). Participating states: Albania, Bulgaria, Greece, FYROM (Macedonia), Romania and Turkey. Observer states: Slovenia and the United States. Unit title: South Eastern European Brigade	SEEBRIG	October 1997	1999	3,000–4,000

contain the word 'Peacekeeping' in their title, giving them a narrowly defined military role. The contributions of the collaborating states in these projects consist of either a company or a battalion-sized contingent.

Joint Peacekeeping Battalions

With troop contributions from Estonia, Latvia and Lithuania, the idea of forming a joint peacekeeping unit was first proposed by Lt-Gen. Aleksander Einseln, the commander of the Estonian Defence Forces, in autumn 1993. Subsequent military and political meetings in January and March 1994 developed the idea further and on 13 September the three Baltic states reached agreement in Riga on the formation of BALTBAT. BALTBAT consists of a trinational headquarters and logistics company and three national infantry companies: Estonian Company (ESTCOY), Latvian Company (LATCOY) and Lithnanian Company (LITCOY). Each of the three contributing countries provides roughly one-third of the 721 assigned personnel and command of the battalion is rotated between the three states with English as the language of command.[6]

From its inception the BALTBAT project has enjoyed considerable external support. The Memorandum of Understanding Concerning Cooperation on the Formation of a Baltic Peacekeeping Battalion was signed on 11 September 1994, creating a framework to coordinate international support for the development of BALTBAT. Apart from the three Baltic states, Denmark, Finland, France, Germany, the Netherlands Norway, Sweden, the United Kingdom and the United States are all signatories of the memorandum of understanding (MOU). The motivation behind the assistance to the Baltic states varies among this eclectic group of states: for countries as distant as the United Kingdom it is to promote wider stability in Europe; for states such as Sweden there is a more direct security interest in the Baltic region.[7] Denmark leads and coordinates the efforts of this group through a Steering Committee that is assisted by an Ad Hoc Military Working Group. The material and financial aid to equip and train BALTBAT has been considerable, with virtually all of its equipment needs having been met by donations from Denmark, Norway, Sweden and the United States.[8] The value of the initial material supplied by donors to BALTBAT amounted to about US$10 million.[9] The training of the battalion has been undertaken by the MOU signatory states. Britain, for example, has been responsible for providing English-language training and infantry training undertaken by Royal Marines.[10]

The original Western aid timetable envisaged only three years of coordinated support for BALTBAT. It seems highly unlikely that aid will dry up just as the battalion is approaching a state of operational readiness.

At the same time, Western governments are going to be unwilling to maintain an open-ended commitment to the project and there is an expectation that the Baltic states will eventually be able to sustain BALTBAT from their own resources.[11]

Despite the considerable external aid lavished on BALTBAT the project has had to overcome some significant difficulties. The two most significant problems have been the recruitment and retention of BALTBAT personnel and the need to improve or establish the infrastructure necessary to support the battalion.[12] Many key personnel joined the battalion in 1994–95 on two- or three-year contracts and when these expired, BALTBAT lost well-trained key personnel who had acquired experience from abroad.[13] All of the problems besetting the BALTBAT project served only to delay the preparations necessary for the battalion's operational employment. Exercises in October 1997 highlighted these problems, including the poor command of English among BALTBAT officers, that made its operational deployment to Bosnia inadvisable.[14] As a consequence, operational experience has been limited to the companies that have been deployed to Lebanon attached to a Norwegian battalion or to Bosnia as part of Danish and Swedish battalions.[15]

When BALTBAT's problems are measured against the fact that the three Baltic states are having to build their armed forces from nothing, the progress made in establishing the joint battalion looks far more promising. Indeed, from the very beginning, the three Baltic states saw BALTBAT as a vehicle to help in building their armed forces. The Minister of Foreign Affairs of Lithuania Saudargas, reflecting the Baltic viewpoint, stated that 'these projects are improving national defence capabilities and promoting interoperability with NATO'.[16] Future plans for developing BALTBAT include adding a mortar and an anti-tank platoon and such an upgrading will allow it to participate in a wider spectrum of PSO operations. Sweden has agreed to loan, without cost, the Bofors BILL RBS 56 medium-range anti-tank missile system to BALTBAT.[17] The decision to move forward with the upgrading of the capability of BALTBAT clearly enjoys continuing international support and will act as a further conduit of military expertise into the Baltic armies.

The best indication of BALTBAT's role in fostering the development of the armed forces of the Baltic states can be seen in the series of trilateral projects that build on the BALTBAT initiative. In the course of 1997 the political leaders of the three states agreed to form a Joint Baltic Naval Squadron (BALTRON) equipped for mine-hunting and a Baltic Airspace Surveillance Network (BALTNET) to provide comprehensive radar coverage over the three states. During early 1998 the decision was also taken to establish a Baltic Defence College (BALTDEFCOL) for training the relatively small number of senior officers required by the Baltic states. With the support of foreign staff and instruction in English, BALTDEF-COL was scheduled to open in August 1999. The new military infra-structure thus generated will be equitably shared out between the three states: BALTBAT headquarters remain in Latvia; BALTDEFCOL will be based in Tartu in Estonia and the regional air-surveillance centre for BALTNET will be in Lithuania. These outgrowths of BALTBAT indicate the key role that the peacekeeping battalion has played in the develop-ment of the armed forces of the states.[18]

The only other trilateral peacekeeping battalion is a joint Hungarian–Romanian–Ukrainian project, which also has the distinction of being the most recent initiative to form a joint unit. With the plan for its creation announced in Kiev in January 1999, the trilateral unit is named the Tisza (Tysa) battalion and its 'deployment area' will be near Vinogradovo where the borders of the three participating states meet. The battalion is unique in so far as it will be a joint engineering unit. Its organisational structure has yet to emerge but the roles of the battalion include cross-border relief operations in the event of a natural disaster and the peacebuilding element of PSO operations.[19]

The efforts to create Czech–Polish, Lithuanian–Polish and Polish–Ukrainian joint battalions represent an important cluster of peacekeeping projects. Two of these bilateral battalions (Lithuanian–Polish and Polish–Ukrainian) started a year after BALTBAT. The first was the Lithuanian–Polish Peacekeeping Battalion (LITPOLBAT). This battalion emerged against the backdrop of efforts to create a more favourable post-communist Lithuanian–Polish political relationship. Of all the bilateral relationships between Poland and its neighbours the one with Lithuania has proved the most difficult. Eventually differences were satisfactorily resolved with the signature of a Treaty of Friendly Relations and Good Neighbourly Co-operation on 24 April 1994.[20] This aided the beginning of one of the most far-reaching reconciliations in post-communist Central Europe. Even before the signature of the treaty, military relations between the two countries were rapidly developing. Substantial donations of military equipment, which have since continued at regular intervals,[21] came from the Polish side in February 1993; indeed, the scale of Polish aid suggested something akin to a Polish PfP programme. However, improvement in bilateral relations has not been one-sided and has led to a blossoming strategic partnership.

The Lithuanian President Algirdas Brazauskas first proposed the creation of a joint peacekeeping battalion in February 1995. After a pro-tracted gestation, a formal inter-governmental agreement to establish the joint battalion was signed in June 1997.[22] Since then, steady progress has been made toward the goal of making the peacekeeping battalion operational. LITPOLBAT has a strength of 800 men with a joint command company, a logistics company and two mechanised companies from the Lithuanian 'Iron Wolf' Brigade and two from the Polish 4th Mechanised Brigade. The joint headquarters of the battalion is in the Polish town of Orzysz in north-eastern Poland. Details of the battalion's equipment are scarce but its table of organisation includes 170 vehicles. Only the Poles are able to contribute armoured vehicles to the unit and it is likely that they provide the Lithuanians with the equipment they are lacking.[23] In autumn 1998 LITPOLBAT completed the last exercise – 'Grunwald Wind 98' – before it was to be declared operationally ready in early 1999.[24]

The launch of the Polish–Ukrainian Peacekeeping Battalion (POLUKR-BAT) followed a few months after LITPOLBAT and by autumn 1995 an agreement to form a joint Polish–Ukrainian peacekeeping unit was initialled. The Polish–Ukrainian project symbolised the dawn of a new period in Polish–Ukrainian bilateral relations and it represented a highly visible effort to put former mutual antagonisms behind them. From 1993 onwards Polish–Ukrainian relations showed many signs of growing military cooperation. These included a presidential consultative committee established to consult regularly on security matters.[25] The creation of a joint peacekeeping battalion was the logical outgrowth of this cooperation and was given a further impetus by the Polish–Ukrainian experience gained in working together in the United Nations Protection Force (UNPROFOR) in Bosnia-Herzegovina.[26] The early momentum of cooperation soon translated into a solid political commitment to the formation of the joint unit. In mid-1996 a joint communiqué issued after a meeting between Polish President Aleksander Kwasniewski and his Ukrainian counterpart, Leonid Kuchma, in Warsaw stressed that the 'work on the creation of a joint Polish–Ukrainian unit for participation in UN peace operations and other security structures is particularly important'.[27]

The initial target date for the formation of the joint Polish–Ukrainian battalion was to be one year after the signature of the agreement.[28] With English as the language of command, the total strength of POLUKRBAT was set at about 500. The battalion's organisation consists of a mixed HQ company, three mechanised companies (two Polish, one Ukrainian), a mixed combat-support company and a logistics company. The battalion will reportedly possess 40–50 armoured fighting vehicles (mostly BMP infantry-fighting vehicles), six 120mm mortars, three or four wire-guided, anti-tank missile launchers, and ten 23mm anti-aircraft guns. The Polish troops assigned to POLUKRBAT at present come from the 14th Armoured Brigade at Przemysl and the Ukrainian component from the 310th Mechanised Infantry Regiment at Rawa Ruska.[29] The battalion staff and headquarters are at Przemysl. POLUKRBAT will require 30 days' notice to deploy on a UN or OSCE operation with the agreement of both governments.

Although the battalion was not ready by autumn 1996, it had nevertheless made good progress in its effort to become operational. However, one of the problems identified early in the training cycle was the need to have adequate numbers of officers who speak English; as a consequence, special courses of instruction were organised for both Polish and Ukrainian officers assigned to the battalion.[30] Another potential problem for the battalion stems from the looming disbandment of the 14th Armoured Brigade as part of a major reorganisation of the Polish armed forces. The battalion HQ is likely to remain in Przemysl, but the Polish element will be drawn from the nearby 21st Highland Infantry Brigade at Rzeszów and this change may lead to the disruption of personnel assigned to the battalion. By September 1998 though, the joint battalion participated in a PfP exercise in western Ukraine and in the same month POLUKRBAT received its battalion standard symbolising the unit's role in promoting a more cooperative phase in Polish–Ukrainian relations.[31]

The Czech–Polish peacekeeping battalion is the most ill-defined of the three projects between Poland and its neighbours. Agreement to launch a 'joint Polish–Czech unit' was reached in a meeting of the two countries' defence ministers in February 1997 in Prague.[32] The initial enthusiasm for the project by the then defence ministers – Stanislaw Dobrzanski of Poland and Miloslav Vyborny of the Czech Republic – was not followed up with much action. Indeed, subsequent discussions between the two governments did not reach agreement on the size of the unit. The debate centred on whether the unit should be of battalion or company strength![33] It is difficult to see what added value both countries could gain in pursuing this project in a financial climate of tight resources and with the reality of their membership in NATO.

The remaining bilateral peacekeeping battalions have been the Hungarian–Romanian and the Bulgarian–Romanian projects. Of these two, the Hungarian–Romanian battalion is the more advanced in its formation. First proposed in May 1997 by the Romanian government, a series of ministerial meetings between the two countries fleshed out a proposal,[34] with a formal agreement to form the joint battalion signed in March 1998. The details of the agreement followed the pattern seen elsewhere in the region: each country will contribute 500 men to the joint unit; the Hungarian contingent will come from the Berzsenyi Brigade in Hodmezovasarhely and the Romanian element from Arad; command of the battalion will be rotated in the joint battalion command structure; and

English will be the language of command. The role envisaged for the joint battalion is peacekeeping and humanitarian operations mainly in the region but also to areas outside Europe. It is planned to have the joint battalion ready by 2000.[35]

According to the agreement, the plan to set up the joint Hungarian–Romanian peacekeeping battalion could be established only after the agreement was ratified by the parliaments of both countries. This process, however, has proceeded at a desultory pace with the political process acting as a brake on military preparations.[36] Although talks between the two defence ministries concentrated on technical issues, the actual preparations remained stalled by the ratification process. Difficulties in financing the project also appear to have hindered progress toward the launching of the joint battalion.[37] On 22 September the Hungarian Parliament ratified the agreement and the Romanian government submitted a bill to its Parliament to ratify the agreement at the beginning of October. A month later the Romanian ratification was still pending. Nevertheless, despite the deliberate manner in which the ratification process has advanced no major political obstacles remain to block the creation of the joint battalion.[38] Like some of the comparable projects between Poland and its neighbours, the battalion's significance lies in its role as a confidence-building measure between two countries whose relations in the past have been dogged by frontier disputes and conflict. Moreover the joint battalion builds on the growing web of Hungarian–Romanian military contacts and cooperation.

The Bulgarian–Romanian peacekeeping project has registered far less progress than its counterpart to the north. Apart from agreeing to form a joint peacekeeping battalion in January 1998, there has been little movement by the two countries toward the realisation of this project. Indeed, there are indications that it could be subsumed into a wider Balkan initiative to form a joint peacekeeping brigade. The Bulgarian–Romanian peacekeeping battalion points to the need for some rationalisation of the peacekeeping projects in the region. There is, in the case of this one, a degree of overlap that does not justify expenditure of limited resources on efforts that only duplicate each other and achieve the same military and political goals.[39]

Joint Peacekeeping Brigades

The most ambitious, if least developed, joint peacekeeping units in Central and Eastern Europe (CEE) are the brigade-sized projects. Most of them also differ from the joint battalions by the participation of NATO members or non-NATO Western European states in the projects. The first joint brigade to be proposed was the Hungarian–Italian–Slovenian brigade in April 1997. Consistent with virtually all such projects, the joint brigade was to be structured for peacekeeping operations and could be deployed only with the approval of all three countries.[40] A formal agreement to form the joint brigade followed in November 1997.[41] The trinational brigade will use the Italian Julia Brigade as its framework; the joint command structure will be based on the Julia Brigade with each country supplying an infantry battalion and Italy providing artillery, logistics and medical service battalions. Within the trilateral brigade will be the equivalent of six national battalion commands.[42] Given the prominence of the Italian contribution, it is clear that Italy is playing a leading role in the development of this project. The largest beneficiary is likely, however, to be Slovenia as this initiative links it militarily to two NATO member states and will undoubtedly add to Slovenia's credibility as a candidate for Alliance membership.

The boldest joint peacekeeping project emerged out of a meeting of eight defence ministers from south-eastern Europe held in Sofia in October 1997. Consisting of NATO or PfP members, the meeting included representatives from Albania, Bulgaria, Greece, the Former Yugoslav Republic of Macedonia (FYROM), Romania, Slovenia, Turkey and the United States. The purpose was to encourage confidence and security-building measures in the Balkans.[43] One of the proposals to emerge was the Multinational Peace Force South-Eastern Europe (MPFSEE). The project was welcomed by all the participants although the participation of Slovenia and the USA would be as observers. During the course of 1998 a series of meetings at the 'expert level' was held to flesh out the MPFSEE project: Ankara (16–18 March), Bucharest (15–16 April), Sofia (11–17 May) and Athens (26–28 June). An extra meeting was included in Tirana on 22 May where a letter of intent for the initiative was signed.[44] By autumn 1998 a draft final agreement to create a joint peacekeeping brigade was ready for signing at a ministerial level meeting of the eight states held in Skopje in September.[45]

From the Skopje meeting came the South-Eastern European Brigade (SEEBRIG) which has the role of participating in a 'possible NATO or WEU-led conflict prevention or other peace-support missions that would be conducted through the UN or OSCE mandate'.[46] Participation in any operation is up to each of the SEEBRIG member states. The total strength of SEEBRIG is eventually to be 3,000–4,000 soldiers.[47] The national contributions to SEEBRIG include mechanised or motorised battalions from Bulgaria, Greece, Romania and Turkey; infantry companies from Albania and Macedonia; and an Italian framework regiment. In addition, Turkey will provide additional support elements: a reconnaissance company, an artillery battery and a logistic framework battalion. HQ and signal companies will be rotated among SEEBRIG members. The sharp end of SEEBRIG comprises 11 mechanised companies and three light infantry companies.[48] However, determining the location of SEEBRIG's HQ proved to be a more politically vexing problem. Eventually a deal was struck in Athens in January 1999 whereby the SEEBRIG HQ and command positions would be rotated. Bulgaria will initially host the HQ at Plovdiv.[49]

Of all the joint peacekeeping initiatives in CEE, SEEBRIG faces the most difficult political problems. The legacy of mistrust and conflict is perhaps most acute in the Balkan region and the process of creating SEEBRIG has already seen Greece and Turkey in rivalry over aspects of the project.[50] However, against this, SEEBRIG enjoys strong American support and no doubt American observers will seek to resolve the differences among its members. Although SEEBRIG offers a number of political and military challenges, the Macedonian Minister of Defence Dr Lazar Kitanoski expressed the benefits to be derived from the joint brigade:

> Formation of a unit for peacekeeping and humanitarian operations composed of troops from ... South-eastern European countries ... would be a significant step forward in confidence building and a new way for cooperation of the countries in this region. Regardless of the fact of whether this idea seems realistic or not at this point, I believe that it should be considered seriously because the joint functioning within such a unit will make a huge contribution to the overcoming of the differences.[51]

In March 1998 another CEE country, Austria, initiated an ambitious, collaborative, peacekeeping brigade. CENCOOP, the Central European Nations Cooperation in Peace Support, includes among its participants Austria, Hungary, Slovakia, Slovenia and Romania. with the Czech Republic and Switzerland having observer status. In the letter of intent signed on 19 March 1998 the aim of CENCOOP was 'to improve the capabilities of the Central European Nations in order to respond more effectively to peace-support operations' challenges and achieve a higher profile through regional cooperation'.[52] The CENCOOP brigade is intended to be in line with the PfP framework and contribute to UN standby-force arrangements. It is intended that the joint brigade should be able to contribute to a full spectrum of PSO operations. Participation in an operation will be entirely a national decision for CENCOOP members. The joint brigade, with a maximum strength of 5,000, will be deployable within 60 days and be fully operational by 2000.[53] The CENCOOP project overtly emulates the UN Stand-by Forces High Readiness Brigade (SHIRBRIG) launched in 1995 as a Danish initiative.[54] Following the signature of a letter of intent in Vienna, during the course of 1998 there ensued a series of discussions between the CENCOOP states on the structure of the brigade and aspects of participation. Although few details have emerged regarding the military structure and contributions to CENCOOP, the second ministerial meeting held in Vienna on 9–10 November 1998 agreed that the HQ for the brigade would be in the Martinek Barracks in Baden just south of Vienna and that the senior positions in the CENCOOP unit would be rotated among its members.[55]

The CENCOOP project brings together a group of states that, with the exception of Switzerland, were all at one time part of the Habsburg patrimony. The project's political and military significance, however, rests on contemporary goals rather than nostalgic sentiment and the fact that Switzerland has joined the CENCOOP marks a cautious and modest step away from the confines of its traditional neutrality toward a greater engagement in European security cooperation. For the former communist states not yet in NATO, CENCOOP is another stage that can advertise their suitability for membership of the Alliance. In particular, the timing of the emergence of the CENCOOP project could not have been more fortuitous for Slovakia: it allows Slovakia to improve its standing as a candidate for NATO membership after the recent improvements in its domestic political climate. Slovak government policy strongly endorses the CENCOOP project and has made it a visible element in external policy.[56] Finally, the leading role taken by Austria also demonstrates its willingness to cultivate connections with NATO (in this case with PfP) and perhaps is a harbinger of its eventual membership of NATO.

The proliferation of peacekeeping units certainly seems to be creating a bandwagon effect. During a recent visit of Lt-Gen. David Tevazde, the Georgian Minister of Defence, to meet his counterpart in Bucharest, he suggested the creation of another peacekeeping brigade based on a group of countries in the Black Sea and Caspian Sea area. The core of this project might initially consist of Georgia, Ukraine, Azerbaijan and Moldova (the GUAM group). The GUAM brigade is seen as a vehicle for these states to establish closer relations with NATO.[57] Although the proposal embraces countries beyond Central and Eastern Europe, it does highlight the degree to which joint peacekeeping projects have become a ubiquitous feature of the security landscape of the former communist east.

CONCLUSION

The security phenomenon of joint peacekeeping units is a distinctly Central and East European contribution to post-Cold War security developments in Europe. Although some might view them as security fashion accessories of limited political and military utility, such a judgement is premature given the fact that only a handful of these units will reach operational readiness by the arrival of the new millennium. From the perspective of peacekeeping, the question remains as to how they can be employed in the future. On this point, Western security organisations such as NATO and the Western European Union (WEU) need to consider what kinds of link could best take advantage of this pool of peacekeeping assets. For NATO this might mean developing the Combined Joint Task Force (CJTF) concept in new directions. Hitherto NATO's work on CJTF has been focused on headquarters arrangements for command and control.[58] Assigning some or all of these joint peacekeeping units to the CJTF headquarters could add to the menu of assets available for a NATO-led PSO operation.

For the WEU, the reason for adding these joint peacekeeping units to its list of assets is even more compelling. Most of these units are configured for the sort of 'Petersburg tasks' assigned to the WEU in 1992.[59] Contributing to UN standby arrangements for peacekeeping is perhaps potentially the least difficult way to make use of these units.

The importance of these joint projects, however, goes beyond peacekeeping. The former communist states of Central Europe are pioneering new ground in the political and military functions of these collaborative ventures in peacekeeping. They have transformed their interest in creating joint peacekeeping units into a regional confidence and security-building measure and a mechanism for promoting their integration into Western security organisations. Although the wider international community derives benefit from the larger supply of peacekeepers that NATO, the UN or the WEU can draw on, the national and regional security benefits in Central Europe may in fact eclipse those associated with traditional peacekeeping functions.

NOTES

The opinions expressed here are those of the author and do not necessarily reflect those of either the Ministry of Defence or RMA Sandhurst.

1. Speech by Algirdas Saudargas, Minister of Foreign Affairs of Lithuania, 52nd Session of the General Assembly of the UN, 5 September 1997, *Newsfile*

Lithuania Weekly, Issue 319 (500), 5–12 September 1997.
2. Speech by Bronislaw Geremek, Minister of Foreign Affairs of Poland, International Conference on Sub-regional Cooperation, Stockholm, 13 October 1998.
3. Address by Zoran Thaler, Minister of Foreign Affairs of the Republic of Slovenia, 24 March 1997.
4. 'Partnership for Peace: Framework Document', 10 January 1994, NATO website http://hq.nato.int.
5. Presentation by Algirdas Saudargas, Minister of Foreign Affairs of Lithuania, *The Baltic Sea Region in the Emerging European Security Architecture*, Warsaw, 6 August 1998.
6. 'The Baltic Peacekeeping Battalion: Regional and International Cooperation in Action', 14 April 1998, Estonian Ministry of Foreign Affairs website http://www.vm.ee; Paul Beaver, 'BALTBAT bonds the Baltics', *Jane's Defence Weekly*, 4 March 1995; and Capt. Kristian P. Lorentzen and L/Cpl Steffan Skov, 'Baltic Peacekeeping Battalion', *The ARRC Journal*, December 1997.
7. For an overview of Baltic security issues see Clive Archer, 'The Baltic–Nordic Region', in W. Park and G. Wyn Rees (eds), *Rethinking Security in Post-Cold War Europe* (London: Longman, 1998), pp. 117–34.
8. 'The Baltic Peacekeeping Battalion'.
9. Paul Beaver, 'West Shows Way for Baltic Peacekeepers', *Jane's Defence Weekly*, 4 March 1995.
10. 'The Baltic Peacekeeping Battalion'.
11. Lorentzen and Skov, 'Baltic Peacekeeping Battalion'.
12. Ibid.
13. Henning A. Frantzen, 'The Baltic Response to NATO's Enlargement', *Jane's Intelligence Review*, October 1997.
14. Vera Rich, 'Baltic States – Delays as BALTBAT Proves Ineffective', *Jane's Intelligence Review*, 1 March 1998.
15. Lorentzen and Skov, 'Baltic Peacekeeping Battalion'.
16. Saudargas, Minister of Foreign Affairs of Lithuania, *The Baltic Sea Region in the Emerging European Security Architecture*, Warsaw, 6 August 1998.
17. Hans Andersson, 'Swedish Accord Grants Guns, Training Aid to Baltic States', *Jane's Defence Weekly*, 25 November 1998 and Lorentzen and Skov, 'Baltic Peacekeeping Battalion'.
18. 'The Baltic Peacekeeping Battalion'. See also *Newsfile Lithuania Weekly*, Issue 301 (482) 1–9 May 1997; Issue 332 (513) 9–15 December 1997; Issue 339 (520) 27 January–2 February 1998; and Issue 350 (531) 15–22 April 1998.
19. Hungarian News Agency MTI, 5 January 1999 and 'Trinational Battalion Formed', *Jane's Defence Weekly*, 13 January 1999.
20. Leon Brodowski, 'Stosunki z Litwa', in *Rocznik Polskiej Polityki Zagranicznej 1995* (Warszawa: PISM, 1995), pp. 115–17 and Gunnar Artéus and Atis Lejiņš (eds), *Baltic Security: Looking Towards the 21st Century* (Latvian Institute of International Affairs, 1997), p. 61.
21. 'Po wiekach, znów pod Grunwaldem', *Rzeczpospolita*, 16 July 1993, report by Lithuanian Radio, 25 June 1997, BBC Monitoring, FS1-Lithuania-Poland and Polish News Agency PAP, 25 March 1998.
22. Hubert M. Krolikowski, 'Poland Strengthens Ties with Lithuania and Ukraine', *Jane's International Defence Review*, 1 January 1997 and

'Lithuania and Poland to Establish Joint Peacekeeping Battalion', *Newsfile Lithuania Weekly*, Issue 307 (489), 20–27 June 1997.

23. Krolikowski, 'Poland Strengthens Ties with Lithuania and Ukraine', 'Miecze w pokojowej sluzbie', *Rzeczpospolita*, 19–20 September 1998 and 'Wspólny batalion w drodze', ibid., 26 March 1998.

24. 'Orzysz: przygotowania do cwiczen LIPOLBAT', Polish News Agency PAP, 8 September 1998.

25. Malgorzata Leczycka, 'Nie ma wolnej Polski bez wolnej Ukrainy', *Polska Zbrojna*, 26–28 November 1993, Piotr Koscinski, 'Bliscy sasiedzi, bliska wspólpraca', *Rzeczpospolita*, 5 February 1993 and 'Wspólpraca, nie sojusz', ibid., 2 February 1993.

26. Krolikowski, 'Poland Strengthens Ties'.

27. Text of Polish-Ukrainian Joint Declaration, 25 June 1996, Polish News Agency PAP, 26 June 1996.

28. *Zycie Warszawy*, 26 November 1995.

29. Artur Golawski, 'Batalion przez granice', *Polska Zbrojna*, 27 March 1998 and Krolikowski, 'Poland Strengthens Ties'.

30. Golawski, 'Batalion przez granice'.

31. Maj. Janusz Grochowski, 'Batalion nowej Europy', *Polska Zbrojna*, 5 December 1997 and 'Polsko-ukrainski batalion otrzyma w piatek sztandar', Polish News Agency PAP, 17 September 1998.

32. *Mlada Front Dnes*, 28 February 1997.

33. 'Polacy plus Czesi', *Polska Zbrojna*, 6 June 1997.

34. Duncan Shiels, 'Hungary and Romania Sign Pact', *Independent*, 18 February 1997; Romanian News Agency, Rompres, 7 April 1997; Hungarian News Agency MTI, 24 June 1997 and 9 July 1997.

35. Budapest Kossuth Radio, 20 March 1998 in *Daily Report*, FBIS-EEU-98-079 and Hungarian News Agency MTI, 20 March 1998.

36. Budapest Duna TV, 24 March 1998 in *Daily Report*, FBIS-EEU-98-084, Hungarian News Agency MTI, 24 March 1998 and 13 July 1998.

37. Hungarian News Agency MTI, 10 August 1998.

38. Ibid., 16 October 1998 and 6 November 1998. Romanian Euro-Atlantic Club Chronicle, 28 September–4 October 1998, website http://www.domino. kappa.ro

39. Report Romanian Radio, Bucharest, 21 January 1998, BBC Monitoring, 138 EU-1 Romania–Bulgaria.

40. Hungarian News Agency MTI, 4 April 1997.

41. Hungarian Radio, 13 November 1997, BBC Monitoring Service, EE/3077.

42. Hungarian News Agency MTI, 11 March 1998, 'The Italian Army: Restructuring Aims to Meet Changing Roles', *Jane's Defence Weekly*, 11 February 1998 and *Slovenska Vojska*, 10 April 1998 in *Daily Report*, FBIS-EEU-98-134.

43. Bulgarian News Agency BTA, 27 August 1997 and 3 October 1997.

44. Albanian News Agency ATA, 22 May 1998.

45. 'Joint Statement at the Defence Ministerial in Skopje on 26 September 1998, Macedonian Ministry of Defence website http://www.morm.gov.mk

46. 'Briefing on Multinational Peace Force South Eastern Europe' by Ismet Sezgin, Minister of Defence of the Republic of Turkey, 26 September 1998, Macedonian Ministry of Defence website http://www.morm.gov.mk

47. Correspondent Report, Skopje, Macedonia, Voice of America, Radio

Transcripts, 1 October 1998.
48. 'Briefing on Multinational Peace Force South Eastern Europe' and Zoran Kusovac, 'Balkan States to Set Up Rapid Reaction Force', *Jane's Defence Weekly*, 20 January 1999.
49. Macedonian Press Agency (Greece), 12 January 1999.
50. 'Turkey and Greece Compete for Balkan Peacekeeping', *Jane's Defence Weekly*, 25 March 1998.
51. 'Security in Southeastern Europe', speech by the Macedonian Minister of Defence, Dr Lazar Kitanoski, Brussels, 3 December 1997, Macedonian Ministry of Defence website http://www.morm.gov.mk
52. 'CENCOOP Fact Sheet', in Österreiches Bundesheer im Internet (Austrian Defence Ministry website http://www.bmlv.gv.at).
53. Hungarian News Agency MTI, 19 March 1998 and 'Statement by the Austrian Defence Minister, Dr Werner Fasslabend', 19 March 1998, in Österreiches Bundesheer im Internet (Austrian Defence Ministry website, see n.52 above).
54. 'Zentraleuropäische Kooperation für Operationen zur Friedenssicherung', 10 March 1998, in Österreiches Bundesheer im Internet (Austrian Defence Ministry website, see n.52 above).
55. 'Verteidigungsministertreffen der CENCOOP', 9–10 November 1998, in Österreiches Bundesheer im Internet (Austrian Defence Ministry website, see n.52 above).
56. Information Bulletin, SIA, No. 4/1998, Slovak Information Agency website.
57. 'Romania and Georgia – Strengthening the Bilateral Military Relations', *Romanian Military Newsletter*, 3, 17 December 1998.
58. Lt-Gen. Mario da Silva, 'Implementing the Combined Joint Task Force Concept', *NATO Review*, No. 4, Winter 1998.
59. *WEU Today*, WEU Secretariat-General, Brussels, March 1998, p. 12.

5

Regional Initiatives and Non-UN Forms of Intervention in Sub-Saharan Africa

EDMUND YORKE

INTRODUCTION

On 8 May 1998, during a visit to Muwire village in Rwanda, the United Nations Secretary-General Kofi Annan addressed a crowd of villagers. He said, 'Your tragedy is our tragedy; your pain is our pain'. In Muwire in 1994 over 3,000 Tutsis and moderate Hutus had been brutally killed. Annan's emotionally charged comments were greeted by a stony silence, punctuated by occasional angry heckling. The villagers' reaction was symptomatic of the locally perceived gross failure of the UN in resolving perhaps the most tragic of recent African conflicts. This mini drama was preceded by stinging criticism of Annan in the Rwandan Parliament where Anastase Gasana, the Foreign Minister, had furiously lambasted the UN's failure to prevent the massacres. That evening the Rwandan Vice-President and Prime Minister[1] boycotted a 'welcoming dinner' for the Secretary-General. Indeed, the series of snubs was eerily reminiscent of the furious local protests launched by Somali demonstrators against his predecessor Boutros Boutros-Ghali during his December 1992 visit to war-torn Mogadishu.[2]

These incidents have been indicative of the perceived escalating crisis of UN peacekeeping on the African continent.[3] The huge scale of the problem has become abundantly clear: between 1989 and 1996 30,000 out of 80,000 troops involved in UN peacekeeping were undertaking missions in Africa. During the past quarter of a century over 30 wars have been fought in Africa alone, the vast majority of them intra-state in origin. In 1996 14 of the 53 countries of Africa were afflicted by armed conflicts, accounting for more than half of all war-related deaths worldwide and resulting in more than eight million refugees, returnees and displaced persons. Three million of these are Angolan, the product of virtually continuous war over the past 30 years.[4] Africa has therefore presented a unique challenge to both the UN and those other institutions and agencies seeking conflict resolution on the continent. This chapter will examine the future prospects for UN peacekeeping in Africa, focusing primarily on the Sub-Saharan African region and also critically evaluating the record and role of selected non-UN Western and African initiatives.

RETREAT FROM AFRICA

The immediate aftermath of the Gulf War represented the highwater mark of post-Cold War UN global activism. The political willingness of the Western powers to intervene had been clearly demonstrated through Operations Safe Haven and Provide Comfort when, following the poor performance of the UN agencies and 'non-governmental organisations (NGOs) during the post-Gulf War humanitarian crisis, the principle of 'military humanitarianism', of using military personnel both to alleviate suffering caused by man-made and natural disasters and protect a UN-mandated relief operation was established. The optimism was short-lived. It was an African state, Somalia, which provided a mortal blow to both large-scale peacekeeping operations in Africa and Western willingness to intervene direct in African conflicts. The massacre of 24 UN Pakistani peacekeepers in Mogadishu in June 1993, followed by the fiasco of a misconceived punitive military operation in which 18 US servicemen were killed, proved to be a watershed not only in the minds of a horrified American public and its government but also in the minds of the UN mandarins.[5] As Christopher Smith has succinctly observed:

> Just as the period of détente in the 1970s was said to have been buried in the sands of Ogaden so the concept of a cohesive UN peacekeeping force was, to some extent, buried in the streets of Mogadishu in October 1993, as dead US soldiers were dragged through the streets by the supporters of General Aideed.[6]

The UN Secretary-General himself recently confirmed that memories of that operation continue to haunt the UN capacity to respond sufficiently and decisively to crisis – the United Nations' operation in Somalia was also the first UN operation to be withdrawn by the Security Council before completing its mission'.[7] For the USA – the key player in any concept of international peacekeeping – it had an even more devastating impact with a radical review of America's role in global peacekeeping and African peacekeeping in particular.[8] Presidential Decision Directive 25, issued in May 1994, led to a virtual cessation of the use of US ground forces in peacekeeping operations and severe budgetary cutbacks. Such lessons were not confined to the USA. Critical reports regarding the poor behaviour of Canadian, Belgian and Italian UN peacekeeping troops in Somalia, with allegations of torture and murder, also contributed to this marked phase of Western disengagement. The immediate consequences are well known as reluctant, chastened Western governments and the UN lay largely paralysed during the horrific 1994 genocidal massacres in Rwanda, in which up to a million, mainly Tutsi, Africans were systematically and brutally murdered by Hutu militias.[9]

PEACEKEEPING VACUUM

The Somali débâcle served to underline the extreme complexity of African conflicts and the relative futility of conventional military solutions. The absence of sovereign authority structures in Somalia and the problem of achieving consent, of crossing the 'Mogadishu line', were illustrated at terrible human and moral cost. Paralleling other parts of Africa, humanitarian aid has become a political weapon in the indigenous power struggle for control of resources. As a result, in the words of Mark Duffield, 'military humanitarianism has … begun to wane … rather than a blueprint for a New World Order it is probable that military protection for humanitarian programmes will remain exceptional'.[10] Instead, the trend of the mid to late 1990s has been towards a more sophisticated if more risky 'operational evolution of UN negotiated access', where humanitarian assistance has become much more closely integrated with the dynamics of violence, UN/NGO plans are cleared in advance with the warring parties and aid is delivered according to set times and corridors. Angola presents one example of this trend which has had a possibly detrimental impact on local power relations and facilitated the emergence of a private and corporate NGO sector which, in some cases, can act as a law unto itself and involve even higher risks to lives of relief workers.[11]

A further, perhaps more sinister development, which partly reflects the growing security vacuum and the retreat of both the UN and the West in general from direct military involvement, has been the proliferation of private, mainly European and American security agencies and consultancies, assisting ailing African governments in restoring stability. The South African-based Executive Outcomes has become the most notorious of these. As Anthony Clayton has pointed out:

80

Until the 1980s large commercial interests may have funded one faction or another in a conflict. In the 1980s and 1990s commercial involvement became more direct with companies, often of former soldiers, notably ex-SAS men, assuming specific security commitments and thereby acquiring a corporate identity.[12]

The lack of accountability of some of these companies and their nefarious role in conflicts have become a major cause for concern, as illustrated by the recent political row in Britain over the role of Sandline, the Chelsea-based private company and offshoot of Executive Outcomes, which played a leading role in restoring to power the deposed president Ahmad Tejan Kabbah of Sierra Leone. Particularly alarming has been the alleged involvement of local diplomats and Foreign Office officials in Sandline operations, which suggests that some Western governments may now be surreptitiously using such agencies as surrogates, perhaps to compensate for their own lack of political willingness to intervene militarily at ground level.

'AFRICA MUST LOOK AT ITSELF'[13]

As the politics of development aid and security underwent a radical change, so, in the aftermath of the Somalian and Rwandan crises, has the UN's perception of, and approach to, conflict resolution in Sub-Saharan Africa. In April 1998 Kofi Annan, significantly the first black African to head the UN, delivered a key manifesto speech – indeed blueprint – for democratisation and economic reform on this troubled continent. Associating himself with the new 'liberal' generation of African leaders such as Jerry Rawlings of Ghana, Yowery Museveni of Uganda, and Major-General Paul Kagame of Rwanda, and carrying out what Thabo Mbeki of South Africa has termed an 'African Renaissance', the Secretary-General has argued that Africa must now stop blaming its colonial past and look towards solving its own problems.

'Today more than ever,' he boldly asserted, 'Africa must look at itself.' Targeting in particular the misgovernment of many ruling African élites he asserted: 'the nature of African political power in many African states, together with the real and perceived consequences of capturing and maintaining power, is a key source of conflict across the continent'. Pinpointing the ruthless aggrandisement of many African dictatorial regimes he observed how 'frequently' it was 'the case that political victory assumes a winner-takes-all-form with respect to wealth and resources patronage and the prestige and the prerogatives of office'. Directly promoting key concepts of liberal democracy, he concluded:

Where there is insufficient control of leaders, lack of transparency in regimes, inadequate checks and balances, non-adherence to the rule of law, absence of a peaceful means to change or replace leadership or lack of respect for human rights, political control becomes excessively important and the stakes become dangerously high.[14]

His full official report, undoubtedly partially aimed at the increasingly dictatorial regimes in Kenya and Nigeria, recognised the extent of social breakdown in Africa and included a particular plea for the protection of civilians who had become 'chief indirect victims of fighting between hostile armies'. 'Women', the Secretary-General continued, were 'suffering in disproportionate numbers while often also being subjected to atrocities that included organised rape and sexual exploitation.' Endorsing the notion of children as 'zones of peace', the Secretary-General particularly lambasted 'the targeting of children for attack and recruiting or abducting them into military forces', a problem which 'must be specifically addressed in any future war crimes, statements or prosecutions'.[15] In a sense this major initiative was a reflection of key developments over the past five years in the rapidly changing nature and pattern of peacekeeping and reform in Sub-Saharan Africa, namely, the drive towards 'surrogate peacekeeping' and the Africanisation of conflict resolution.

SURROGATE PEACEKEEPING

As part of its radical review of its African peacekeeping policies, and what might be construed as a distinct desire to divorce itself from any UN-led missions after Somalia, the American government has launched a series of initiatives to support indigenous African conflict resolution. In September 1994, for instance, Congress passed the African Conflict Resolution Act providing for $25 million of assistance for sub-regional organisations engaged in peacekeeping activities. The role of the USA since the disastrous Somalia episode has, however, been limited and reactive. The two recent American operations in the Central African Republic and Liberia were both strictly limited to the protection of US lives and property. The emphasis has been much more on politico-diplomatic initiatives spearheaded by leading American government officials and, more recently, by President Clinton himself. The first major diplomatic mission since Somalia was led by Secretary of the State Warren Christopher in October 1996 and was designed to promote African support for, and participation in, an African Crisis Response Force (ACRF). The key components of the programme, estimated to cost between $25 and 40 million, included a proposal for a force of 5,000–10,000 troops (eight to ten battalions), training support by US Special Forces in joint exercises, and compatible communications and training equipment (for instance, uniforms, computers and mine-detection equipment). Ethiopia, Malawi, Mali, Senegal, Tunisia and Uganda began receiving training in 1997 and Ghana followed in 1998.[16] At the G7 summit in Colorado in June 1997, this initiative received some international credibility when all seven members as well as Russia agreed to support it. However, the response on the African continent was generally lukewarm. A follow-up mission by Madeleine Albright in 1997 fared little better. Even President Clinton's major African 'safari' in March 1998, aimed at promoting trade and peacekeeping cooperation and carefully arranged to visit only those six 'renaissance' countries (Ghana, Uganda, Rwanda, Ethiopia, Eritrea and South Africa) considered to be most further advanced in adopting Western concepts of plural democracy, was widely seen to be one more example of noble rhetoric rather than evidence of major American engagement. Clinton's bold statement to the South African Parliament that 'Africa still needs the world but more than ever the world needs Africa' largely rang hollow, being widely interpreted as a sop or appeasement gesture to the black caucus in Congress.[17]

The generally negative local reaction towards these initiatives is perhaps understandable. Many African critics feared it was simply designed to avoid Western involvement in future African crises. The financial aid to set up the ACRF was seen as paltry. African leaders were particularly incensed by the lack of prior consultation over ACRF, the American failure to recognise the growing role in conflict resolution of sub-regional organisations such as the Economic Community of West African States (ECOWAS) and the Southern African Development Community (SADC), by the lack of definition of the proposals and by its obvious appearance as an eleventh-hour response to an ongoing regional crisis. Indeed, the recent decision to rename the ACRF as the African Crisis Response *Initiative* (ACRI) underlined the sensitivity felt by many Africans about external meddling and their frequently expressed fears of neo-colonialism. On his mission Clinton was 'also confronting for the first time the Third-World realities of most of Africa which lie behind the continent's suspicion of his new "trade not aid policy"'.[18] Moreover, it remains clear that the American policy towards Africa itself remains deeply divided. In the traumatic aftermath of Somalia, while a statement from the 1997 National Security Strategy (NSS) stressed the attenuation of regional conflict, the growth of democratic institutions, regard for human rights, sustained economic development and security from weapons of mass destruction and trans-national threats as key American interests in the region, an earlier, 1995, Department of Defense document bluntly contradicted it by declaring that, in the post-Cold War period, the USA had 'very little traditional strategic interest in Africa'.[19]

Moreover, America's two main European allies in Africa, Britain and France, key players by virtue of their major colonial legacies and post-colonial cultural and trade links have, to some extent, duplicated and pre-empted these American initiatives. From 19 to 21 March 1997, for instance, France conducted its first large humanitarian training exercise (Operation Nangbeto) under which nearly 4,500 troops from Benin, Burkina Faso, France and Togo rehearsed the establishment of a security zone and provisional humanitarian aid in a country torn by external strife. France also organised a seminar in Dakar, Senegal, in October 1997 to 'reinforce' African peacekeeping capabilities.[20]

Britain has also not been slow to act. In April 1997, for instance, Britain similarly sponsored a joint peacekeeping exercise (Blue Hungwe) involving troops and observers from Angola, Botswana, Swaziland, South Africa, Lesotho, Malawi, Mozambique, Namibia, Tanzania, Zimbabwe and the United Kingdom. The aim was to develop operational logistics and communication doctrines for joint operations. However, British plans to train two battalions in Sierra Leone had to be suspended because of the ongoing emergency there.[21]

Even at this minimal level Britain and France, like the USA, still suffer from accusations of neo-colonialism, with the financial resources allocated for African peacekeeping also being regarded as less than adequate. France, in particular, attracted major international criticism for her military role in Rwanda in 1994 (Operation Turquoise) where she was widely seen to be acting more on behalf of her own self interest in trade and prestige terms rather than as a humanitarian protector. France (like Belgium) focused mainly on protecting expatriate and diplomatic facilities while French troops were even alleged to have turned a blind eye to nearby massacres. France's presence, in Clayton's view, probably 'had more to do with French suspicions that Anglophone Africa, backed by the United States and in the person of Museveni (of Uganda), was trying to take over a Francophone land'.[22] Mel McNulty, a fierce critic of French policies in Rwanda, even predicts that the

> Legacy of France's Rwandan intervention not only will be the abandonment of French ambitions across the African continent, but also the discrediting of all foreign military intervention and the consolidation of a new assertive political climate within which regional solutions become not only desirable but the most practicable.[23]

The recent decision by the French government to cut back garrisons and diplomatic missions significantly in West and Central Africa suggests that this prophecy may yet be fulfilled.

REGIONAL AFRICAN SOLUTIONS

Increasing Western reticence and difficulties in the context of African peacekeeping notwithstanding, the UN Secretary-General's own direct clarion call for Africa to 'help itself' leads us to a critical assessment of recent indigenous African initiatives. In the words of May and Cleaver, in the specific case of Rwanda,

> The precipitate withdrawal of the Belgian contingent of UNAMIR [UN Assistance Mission for Rwanda], after securing the safety of Westerners, the apparent disinterest of the United States, the questionable role of France and the failure of the UN to reinforce its ongoing mission and alter its mandate to deal with genocide, all combined to support a growing belief within Africa that Africa's problems could only be effectively addressed by themselves.[24]

As the only continent-wide organisation of African states, the Organisation of African Unity (OAU), founded in 1963, has naturally assumed primary responsibility for matters of security and conflict resolution.[25] In this context an early major advance was the 1993 establishment of a division entitled Mechanism for Conflict Resolution, Management and Prevention (MCRMP) and a Peace Fund to help to finance this work. The New York-based International Peace Academy (IPA) assisted in this process with a 1997 meeting of the OAU/IPA Joint Task Force on peacemaking and peacekeeping in Africa, including the preparing of a report to improve the mechanism and publicise it throughout Africa.[26] The OAU's greater sense of urgency and responsibility in seeking 'African solutions to African problems' after the Somalian and Rwandan crises was also indicated by two major conferences held on peacekeeping in Cairo and Harare in January and February 1995. The Harare conference, in particular, revealed the huge problems still confronting the deployment of African forces in a peacekeeping context. Predictably, most speakers pinpointed finance as a key obstacle. One paper concluded that,

> In spite of Africa's viewpoint that the continent must solve its own problems and the West's support of this viewpoint, the OAU does not at this stage have the ability to accomplish it without the complete backing of the international community.[27]

Another paper observed how the OAU was 'perennially in financial difficulties often with accounts arrears amounting to about twice the annual budget of the organisation', while there were 'still sensitivities about accepting outside funding'.[28] Considerable doubt was expressed about Western motivation and initiatives, which, while amounting to 'almost a process of disengagement', could also be interpreted as 'an attempt to explore new ways in which they can expand their political influence in Africa, either directly in the case of the French or through the UN as with the British and the USA'.[29] Much stress was also laid upon the OAU's biggest problem in terms of ground-level peacekeeping, that of logistics, especially the chronic lack of radio communications, vehicles, and air transport resulting in an undignified 'begging syndrome' and a 'humiliating reliance upon donor countries'.[30] The OAU's first sponsored peacekeeping operation in Chad merely resulted in almost total reliance upon French logistic support. Similarly, the OAU's first sponsored observer group, the Neutral Military Observer Group (NMOG), deployed to Rwanda in 1993, was paralysed by an almost complete lack of vehicle support. The OAU Mission in Burundi (OMIB) was also emasculated by an almost total failure of communications, with a lack of contact with Bujumbura lasting 'sometimes almost for a month'.[31] Outside South Africa and Egypt there is still no fully operational, brigade-level communications system in Africa. Internal political divisions also continue to hamper concerted OAU action with, for instance, Zaire and Kenya refusing to ratify the resolution on the MCRMP because they believed that it would 'act as a licence to powerful countries to interfere in the internal affairs of other countries which is prohibited under the OAU Charter'.[32]

Even with adequate financial and logistic support African military capacities are, as May and Cleaver observe, 'small' both in absolute terms and as a percentage of the population, with a total manpower pool of 'little in excess of a million'. They continue:

The vast majority ... have armies numbering less than 50,000 men. Nineteen states have armies less than 10,000 strong, a further five have between 10,000 and 20,000 men and ten have forces between 20,000 and 50,000. Only five states have armies in excess of 50,000 strong and of these three – Angola, Sudan and Ethiopia – either are or have recently been engaged in civil wars.[33]

They are effectively, in Orth's words, 'mere skeletons of Western militaries',[34] generally lacking manpower, equipment stocks and complex logistic capabilities. However, as peacekeepers African states do have one or two major advantages. Several have considerable experience in peace-keeping techniques, especially UN peacekeeping, with 22 African states participating in a total of 21 UN operations since 1960. Several profes-sional African militaries have ably 'demonstrated this capability', inclu-ding the Botswana Defence Force (BDF) in Somalia and Mozambique and the Zimbabwe National Army (ZNA) when deployed in Somalia and Ethiopia.[35] Indeed, in this specific context it may be argued that the West has little to teach many African countries and there is a danger of dupli-cation of effort. When the USA sent 60 members of its Special Forces to teach peacekeeping methods to 800 UN-experienced Senegalese soldiers, 'Senegal was happy to get one million dollars worth of supplies ranging from baseball caps to food rations, but its Army spokesman said its troops had learnt nothing the French had not already taught them!'.[36]

Some observers have also argued that the greater cultural affinity of many African states has enabled them to enjoy enhanced legitimacy over non-African peacekeeping contingents. In both Somalia and Rwanda, for instance, militarily less capable African countries have 'displayed a significant degree of "cultural sensitivity"'.[37] Botswana, in particular, by developing a philosophy of 'give them smiles', promoted excellent relations with local Somalis as it 'respected the local population, tried to learn the local language and built upon the importance of pride in Somali culture by treating the Somalis as equals'.[38] This is not to say that non-African peacekeeping nations cannot achieve the same aim. The Australian contingent's excellent hearts-and-minds record in Somalia in 1993 remains a testament to this alternative viewpoint.

Two current case examples, both involving the regional heavyweights of Sub-Saharan Africa, South Africa and Nigeria, will serve to illustrate that, while possessing relatively sophisticated Western-style military establishments even they, particularly as regards the key issue of legiti-macy, can face enormous difficulties in carrying out their peacekeeping tasks.

Liberia and Sierra Leone 1989–99

The twin conflicts in Liberia and Sierra Leone have revealed many of the worst features of the current mode of primeval savage warfare, aptly described by one observer as 'a retreat from modernity'.[39] In these con-flicts, where the mortality rate has only been dwarfed in scale by the 1994 Rwanda genocide, thousands of children as young as ten have, as in Uganda and elsewhere, been recruited, abused, exploited and even encouraged to indulge in ritual killings of their own village elders and relatives, sometimes as a debased form of tribal puberty rites. As elsewhere in Africa the ready availability of thousands of cheap conventional armaments in the post-Cold War era has facilitated a ferocious struggle between warring factions, accompanied by widespread looting and burning of villages and towns. Significantly, both countries have also suffered from a distorted post-colonial infrastructure and the current implosion of their social structures has unleashed huge regional and ethnic tensions particularly between the coast and hinterland peoples.

The Liberian civil war began in 1989[40] when the rebel ex-minister Charles Taylor launched a guerrilla invasion from the Ivory Coast in an attempt to overthrow the government of President Samuel Doe. In July 1990, when a force sent by the ECOWAS abjectly failed as intermediaries in the conflict, a West African peacekeeping force, the ECOWAS Monitoring Group (ECOMOG), initially comprising troops from Gambia, Ghana, Mali, Nigeria and Togo, was sent to intervene. As Doe's Armed Forces of Liberia (AFL) suffered defeat both at the hands of Taylor's National Patriotic Front of Liberia (NPFL) and a breakaway faction, the Independent National Patriotic Front of Liberia (INPFL), and internecine massacres by all sides continued, the ECOMOG forces' mandate was changed to one of enforcement. The early potential for depravity in this particular conflict was soon graphically illustrated by the televised torture and killing of President Doe on 10 September 1990. Although the first ECOMOG commander was a Ghanaian, Nigerian dominance was inevitable from the start (Nigeria supplies 80 per cent of ECOMOG's 12,000 soldiers) and Nigeria's role was seen as a test case for its fitness and capability as a key future regional peacekeeper for Africa. As Clayton has pointed out, 'ECOMOG is significant as the world's first regional peacekeeping force not sponsored by the United Nations'.[41] Indeed, the limited UN presence in the form of UN Observer Mission in Liberia (UNOMIL)[42] is, perhaps, further evidence of the tacit surrender of peacekeeping roles to African regional organisations.

The Sierra Leone war[43] was effectively a spill-over from the Liberian conflict when, in July 1991, Charles Taylor retaliated against the Freetown government for supplying ECOMOG with bases and logistics support and, in particular, allowing the Nigerian Air Force to conduct bombing missions on his positions from Sierra Leone. The insurgent movement, the Taylor-backed Revolutionary United Front (RUF) led by Corporal Feday Sankoh, attacked towns in the south and the east, exploiting the ethnic tension between the élite coastal Creole and the northern Temne and the southern Mende hinterland peoples; the latter were the main basis of his support. As Dowden has observed, resource competition has been a special feature of the Sierra Leone conflict. The Sierra Leone war

> is an even clearer example of people, especially young people in the hinterland rejecting the domination of a coastal capital. They also reject, sometimes violently, their parents' acceptance of that domination. Their propaganda is filled with references to the wealth of the fields and rivers, the gold and diamonds under the ground, the wealth of the city dwellers and the poverty of the people. This appears a much stronger motivation in this war than ethnic or regional loyalties.[44]

In both these 'seesaw conflicts' the focus has been on securing the control of local economic resources rather than any wider ambitions of national political control. For ECOMOG and Nigeria in particular it has been a peacekeeping performance of mixed success. In Liberia the key problem from the outset has been the distinct lack of impartiality with francophone and anglophone countries demonstrating overt partisanship. The ECOMOG forces, led by Nigeria, have blatantly taken sides against Taylor while francophone countries have continued to support him and, on at least two occasions, ECOMOG prevented the NPFL from capturing the capital.[45] Furthermore, Nigeria's own patent lack of democratic accountability at home under the Abacha regime had already seriously compromised its role in the eyes of many neutral observers. There have even been suggestions that UNOMIL was in place more to monitor Nigeria's behaviour as much as the indigenous peace process. More ominous has been growing evidence of the widespread involvement of Nigerian troops in incidents of organised looting and general ill discipline in both Liberia and Sierra Leone. Similarly, Nigerian officers serving with ECOMOG have been accused of indulging in corrupt commercial deals designed either to sell off ECOMOG equipment for profit or even acquiring stakes in, for instance, the country's rich gold and diamond mining industry.[46] Such incidents have further undermined the legitimacy and credibility of ECOMOG as an acceptable peacekeeping force. Equally worrying has been the recent evidence of the impact of these two long attritional wars upon Nigeria's logistic and financial capability.[47] Partly as a result of this the Sierra Leone government has been forced to rely increasingly upon private military companies for the protection of its key assets. In January 1999 even Britain felt compelled to provide an extra one million pounds to support ECOMOG forces in Sierra Leone, mainly to purchase lorries, communications and other logistic backup, although, perhaps surprisingly, she still continued her arms embargo on Nigeria for its alleged violation of human rights at home.[48]

Lesotho 1998

The other key regional heavyweight in Sub-Saharan Africa, the new South Africa, has also faced considerable difficulty in its first reluctant and tentative steps towards a peacekeeping role. Until September 1998 both President Mandela and his designated successor Thabo Mbeki had ruled out a specifically military peacekeeping role outside the country's borders. Priority was to be given to internal reconstruction, meeting pressing social priorities such as health and employment reform, and completing the complex task of integrating the old South African Defence Force and the military wings of the 'liberation movements' into the South African National Defence Force (SANDF). The new South African government was also unfortunately aware of the embarrassing political legacy of South Africa's incursions into neighbouring countries during the apartheid era.[49] In a speech delivered in 1995 the Deputy Foreign Minister Aziz Prahad summed up the government's position on external peace-keeping, one based largely upon a diplomatic role:

> In the light of the so-called Africa fatigue prevalent among many of the principal industrialised and military powers and the understand-ing that South Africa cannot prosper in splendid isolation in a continent not at peace with itself, it is in the national interest to play an important role in conflict prevention and resolution in Africa, especially Sub-Saharan Africa.

However, he confirmed,

> South Africa should not act – or be perceived to act – as the superpower on the continent ... the most important contribution that South Africa can make in preventive diplomacy at present is the moral authority it has derived from its own process of national reconciliation and democratisation.[50]

On 24 September 1998, however, South Africa was suddenly and unexpectedly plunged into an armed intervention across the borders of the neighbouring state of Lesotho. Pretoria's African National Congress (ANC)-dominated government rapidly lost its 'diplomatic virginity' when, under the auspices of the SADC,[51] 600 South African soldiers were deployed to put down an armed mutiny against Pretoria's ally King Letsie III. Designed to prevent, in Mandela's words, 'chaos and anarchy', it was significantly 'the first foreign deployment of South African military muscle since the demise of the last National Party government in May

1994'.[52] The bungled operation, which cost the lives of nine SANDF and 58 Lesotho Defence Force soldiers, degenerated into a politico-military fiasco. It took outnumbered South African and later BDF troops 48 hours just to seize key bases in Maseru and take control of the Katse Dam in the midst of widespread confusion. The most damning criticism came from SANDF commanders themselves, with the Deputy Chief of the Army, Major-General Roland De Vries, bluntly stating that 'the wrong forces have been sent in without adequate intelligence, planning or prepa-ration'.[53] Other sources spoke of the command and control problems emanating from the incomplete reorganisation of the SANDF. In an observation which can be paralleled with Nigeria's relatively poor military performance in both Liberia and Sierra Leone, the prominent political commentator Tom Lodge noted, 'South Africa's stature as the region's professional and competent military power has taken a fair knock'.[54] The damage to South Africa's political credibility, her perceived legitimacy as a vehicle for regional peacekeeping, has been even more catastrophic. Some South African Foreign Office officials described the intervention as 'unnecessary, unwise and unconstitutional'.[55] Another commentator noted that 'no defence treaty exists between the two countries. No United Nations Security Council resolution had been taken. No constitutionally valid request had been made by Maseru and the SADC had not formally agreed to empower Pretoria to intervene.'[56] In Lesotho itself the intervention incited a wave of popular hatred. Angry at the perceived violation of Lesotho's sovereignty, one local protester defiantly declared 'we don't want to be another province of South Africa'.[57] Even Chief Seeso, brother of the Oxford-educated King Letsie III, deprecated not only the lack of warning but 'the violation of the sanctity of Lesotho's people ... We are all perturbed by this open aggression by a neighbour who, for a long time, has seen the sense in exploring diplomatic rather than military solutions.'[58] The justification for intervention was also widely doubted in view of the Lesotho government's poor political track record, with widespread dismay over the recent (May 1998) election results in which the ruling Lesotho Congress for Democracy Party took 79 out of 80 seats. The election was perceived by many observers as blatantly fraudulent.

Above all, the crisis engenders (as for ECOMOG's role in Liberia and Sierra Leone) serious implications for the unity and credibility of the SADC as a future regional peacekeeper. The intervention was questioned by several SADC members on purely constitutional grounds and only 200 BDF troops belatedly joined the hurried operation. The general lack of legitimacy was not welcomed within an SADC already hamstrung by earlier disputes between members over the recent military intervention

91

by Angola, Namibia and Zimbabwe in the Democratic Republic of Congo, an operation designed to prop up President Kabila's politically and morally compromised regime.[59] The Lesotho crisis had thus come as a major embarrassment to the new South Africa which, like Nigeria, is now widely seen as yet another heavy-footed regional giant. It will take some time before the moral authority of these regional powers can be restored and both be seen as legitimate and credible vehicles for future peace-keeping operations. As R. W. Johnson has succinctly observed:

> The Lesotho Crisis has come as a rude awakening: unless South Africa can deal more competently with the minor troubles of this neighbouring micro-state its ambition on the broader world stage – to lead Africa, to champion the Third World and to preach with moral authority to the West – could come to seem almost risible.[60]

CONCLUSION

It is clear from this analysis that Sub-Saharan Africa has a considerable distance to travel before, in the words of Kofi Annan, it can effectively both 'look at itself' and its governments can carry out peacekeeping operations with any form of independence or confidence. The financial and logistic gaps are still far too great – even Nigeria, a comparatively wealthy regional giant, is experiencing logistic difficulties in Sierra Leone and Liberia, while both South Africa (after Lesotho) and Nigeria have the additional problems of political credibility as regards peacekeeping outside their borders, which will take some time to resolve. UN and individual or collective Western support, both financial and logistical, is still critical, but all these external actors, in the wake of the Somalian and Rwandan crises, are still suffering from an evident lack of political will. The impact of this loss of will, a reluctance to intervene at ground level, can only be detrimental with often less accountable security agencies increasingly filling the vacuum and creating further chaos in these already traumatised conflict areas. The African Crisis Response Initiative can be seen as one stopgap but even this cannot be sufficient to deal with the complexity and sustained barbarity characterising many of Africa's small wars. For the USA, the key outside power, there must be some solution to the current paradox in her foreign policy, both towards Africa as else-where for, 'to be an imperial power, even today, demands a sacrifice in blood' which as 'the only power capable of acting imperially', she 'is simply not prepared to pay'.[61] In recent months only Britain, a lesser power, has, albeit on a small scale, been prepared to bite the bullet and undertake some intervention in the Sierra Leone crisis in the form of a frigate and a possible ground-level troop intervention. For South Africa, still the pre-eminent and most politically credible regional Sub-Saharan power, both by virtue of her military capacity and internal democratic credentials, there must be a greater awareness (despite her Lesotho mistakes) that Africa is, indeed, part of a 'global village', that she shares an intrinsic common destiny with the rest of Africa and that domestic peace and stability cannot be achieved while there is regional instability. The physical evidence of this stark reality is already there in the form of several million illegal immigrants, many fleeing war zones and themselves causing significant social disruption within her own borders.

Despite all these difficulties there remains some ground for optimism. The OAU is demonstrating great political will despite its financial and logistic shortcomings and individual African countries, notably Ghana and Togo, have recently put forward feasible schemes for more efficient peacekeeping. Of these, arguably the most comprehensive have been the Togo proposals, which 'have all the legal and administrative ingredients needed to bolster action on the formation of the much vaunted pan-African Peacekeeping Force'.[62] Moreover, they have great legitimacy, the product of wide consultation with other African states, notably Senegal, and, more importantly, the benefit of a mandate conferred on Togolese President Eyadema in 1994 by France at the Francophone Summit in Biarritz. The Togolese proposals envisage a force nucleus of 3,000 troops accompanied and monitored by a flexible, military-dominated, military-controlled but non-permanent body with the declared aims of preventing conflicts, keeping and restoring peace, consolidating peace and carrying out humanitarian missions for refugees and displaced persons, and, if necessary, enforcing or imposing peace. The plan has benefited from South African support and observers hope that the initiative in the wake of the American-sponsored ACRI will provide 'a bridge between France and the USA, and both countries' individual determination to help Africa tackle its quagmire of internecine war and destructive political/ethnic conflict'.[63] In the meantime, the UN has strongly supported the expansion of preventive diplomacy as a response to the threat of continuing and future conflict. The Secretary-General has, in particular, pointed to the 'major difference' made by this strategy in the Central African Republic, where 'an explosive situation has been contained by African mediation efforts, local perseverance and an African security force, the Inter-African Mission to Monitor the Implementation of the Bangui Agreement (MISAB) supported by France and the United Nations Development Programme'.[64] This has sent a 'positive and important signal to the region and to Africa as a whole'.[65] Where preventive diplomacy is irrelevant and conflicts are ongoing, another observer has pointed out some interim ways of achieving at least partial security for civilian victims. As Quentin Outram has observed, in Liberia, where in October 1995 alone it was estimated that 700,000 people were displaced and another 727,000 were refugees with up to 200,000 deaths recorded to date, ECOMOG's 'safe zone' established around the capital Monrovia, although 'lacking factional consent and under constant military pressure', played a 'major role in the relatively successful provision of aid to a large population that has remained inside and fled to it'.[66] Such policies do not solve wars but they do provide partial protection for civilians in such imploded states where all semblance of authority has perished.

Military intervention and enforcement is, of course, only a short-term remedy for many of these conflicts. What is needed in the continuing absence of significant Western aid is a major initiative from the global economic mandarins, principally the International Monetary Fund and the World Bank which, by rescheduling or restructuring debt (as in the recent case of Nigeria) or even cancelling the debt of the hardest hit countries of Somalia, Sierra Leone, Liberia, Rwanda, the Democratic Republic of Congo and Burundi, enable African societies to begin to rebuild socio-economic structures, the partial or total collapse of which has been at the core of virtually all Sub-Saharan conflicts. Alongside this, as so many UN reports have highlighted, must be some comprehensive plan for widespread disarmament in the region if only to remove the tools of conflict.[67] Notwithstanding these two key remedial measures there is, it must be reiterated, an enormous fund of political will in Africa. As one OAU speaker at the 1995 Harare Conference confirmed, Africa and specifically the OAU is

> still in the process of learning. We have just started. And like a child trying to learn how to walk we are bound to fall down from time to time. Yet we believe we are not bad students either ... It is the OAU's belief that the UNO, Britain, the Americans, the French, the Germans, the Scandinavian countries, Belgium and all other friends of Africa will continue so that one day we will be talking of wars just as history and not as a reality.[68]

In a continent of preponderantly weak or weakening states the alternative is for large areas to descend into a nightmare scenario of virtually 'organised chaos' for, in the words of Christopher Clapham

> As the relative stability conferred by the agreement to maintain the post-colonial order continues to erode, the new Africa is likely to

94

owe as much to its pre-colonial origins, with zones of reasonably effective government interspersed with ones in which anything readily identifiable as a 'state' is hard to discern ...[69]

NOTES

The opinions expressed here are those solely of the author and do not necessarily reflect those of either the Ministry of Defence or RMA Sandhurst.

1. L. Tunbridge, 'UN Chief Heckled by Survivors of Rwanda Genocide', *Daily Telegraph*, 9 May 1998.
2. See, for instance, 'Somalia; beyond the Pax Americana', *Africa Confidential*, 33, 25, 18 December 1992.
3. For an erudite analysis of the escalating UN peacekeeping crisis in the mid-1990s see A. Roberts, 'The Crisis in UN Peacekeeping', *Survival*, 36, 3, Autumn 1994, pp. 93–120.
4. Report of the UN Secretary-General to the Security Council, 'The Causes of Conflict and the Promotion of Durable Peace and Sustainable Development in Africa', UN (New York), 13 April 1998. For a precise summary of the underlying causes of the current destabilisation of Sub-Saharan Africa, emphasising the role of colonial and Cold War legacies, arms proliferation, debt crises and natural disasters see ibid., paras 8–15.
5. For a detailed discussion of this 'disaster' see, for instance, J. Clark, 'Debacle in Somalia', *Foreign Affairs*, 72, 1, pp. 109–24.
6. C. Smith, 'Peacekeeping in Africa: a state of crisis', *Jane's Defence '96: The World in Conflict*, p. 97.
7. Report of the UN Secretary-General (UN: New York, 1998).
8. See M. Michaels, 'Retreat from Africa', who detected signs of America's withdrawal from Africa even before the Somalia débâcle, *Foreign Affairs*, 72, 1, 1993, pp. 93–109.
9. For a deeper discussion of the West's and the UN's role in this tragic conflict and, in particular, the abject failure of the UN Standby Arrangement System when, in April 1994, the armed forces of 19 UN states refused to intervene militarily, see R. M. Connaughton, 'Military Support and Protection for Humanitarian Assistance in Rwanda April–Dec. 1994', *Strategic and Combat Studies Institute*, 18, 1996 and J. M. Vaccaro, 'The Politics of Genocide: Peacekeeping and Disaster Relief in Rwanda', in W. J. Durch, *Peacekeeping, American Policy and the Uncivil Wars of the 1990s* (London: Macmillan, 1997), pp. 367–407.
10. M. Duffield, 'Complex Emergencies and the Crisis of Developmentalism', *Institute of Development Studies*, 25, 4, 1994, p. 42. For further discussion of the 'politics of aid' see A. De Waal, 'Democratising the aid encounter in Africa', *International Affairs*, 73, 4, 1997, pp. 623–9, and T. G. Weiss and K. M. Campbell, 'Military Humanitarianism', *Survival*, 33, 5, September/October 1991, pp. 451–65.
11. As J. Prendergast has observed: 'The complex crises which exist ... in Africa require more meaningful political engagement ... the substitution of humanitarian action for deeper political engagement allows symptoms of emergencies

to be treated leaving root and proximate causes relatively intact and allowing egregious violations of fundamental human rights to go unaddressed', in W. S. Clarke, 'Waiting for the "Big One": Confronting Complex, Humanitarian Emergencies and State Collapse in Central Africa', *Small Wars and Insurgencies*, Spring 1998, p. 287.

12. A. Clayton, *Frontiersmen, Warfare in Africa since 1950* (London: UCL Press, 1998), pp. 155–6. See also, 'Militias and Market Forces', *Africa Confidential*, 23 October 1998.
13. J. Bone, 'UN Chief Tells Africa to Reform', *The Times*, 12 April 1998.
14. Ibid.
15. Report of the UN Secretary-General (UN: New York, 1998).
16. 'Conflict Prevention, Management and Resolution', *SIPRI Year Book 1998* (Oxford: SIPRI, 1998), p. 51.
17. See S. Kiley, 'Uneasy Ghosts of Genocide Haunt Clinton's Safari', *The Times*, 23 March 1998 and A. Russell, 'Clinton Tributes Fail to Win over S. African MPs', *Daily Telegraph*, 27 March 1998.
18. Russell, 'Clinton Tributes'.
19. D. Henk, 'US National Interests in Sub-Saharan Africa', *Parameters*, Winter 1997–98, p. 95.
20. 'Conflict Prevention, Management and Resolution', pp. 51–2.
21. Ibid. Britain is also providing military assistance and training to military colleges in South Africa, Zimbabwe and Ghana and an Anglo-French joint commission on peacekeeping was established following President Chirac's visit in May 1996. R. May and G. Cleaver, 'African Peacekeeping: Still Dependent', *International Peacekeeping*, 4, 3, Summer 1997, p. 4. See also, 'Vox Militaris: Southern African Peacekeeping Exercise – a Great Success', *Army Quarterly and Defence Journal*, 3, 1997, pp. 299–302.
22. Clayton, *Frontiersmen, Warfare in Africa since 1950*, p. 185.
23. M. McNulty, 'France's Rwanda Débâcle', *Kings' Department of War Studies Journal*, 2, 2, Spring 1997, p. 20. See also McNulty, 'France's Role in Rwanda and External Military Intervention: a Double Discrediting', *International Peacekeeping*, 4, 3, Autumn 1997, pp. 24–44.
24. May and Cleaver, 'African Peacekeeping', p. 2.
25. See Salim Ahmed Aslim, 'Africa in Crisis: Response of the OAU and future challenges', *Ethioscope*, June 1995, pp. 3–15.
26. 'Conflict Prevention, Management and Resolution', p. 59.
27. 'International efforts to establish collective security mechanisms for Africa', Collected Papers, Zimbabwe Peacekeeping Workshop, Harare, 23–27 January 1995, p. 8.
28. Ibid., p. 3.
29. Ibid., p. 12.
30. Ibid., p. 2.
31. Ibid., p. 3.
32. Ibid.
33. May and Cleaver, 'African Peacekeeping', p. 8.
34. R. Orth, 'African Operational Experiences in Peacekeeping', *Small Wars and Insurgencies*, 7, 3, Winter 1996, p. 314.
35. G. Cleaver and R. May, 'Peacekeeping: The African Dimension', *Review of African Political Economy*, 22, December 1995, p. 495.
36. 'An African answer to African Wars', *Economist*, 18 October 1997, p. 85.

37. R. Orth, 'African Operational Experiences', p. 313.
38. Ibid.
39. R. Dowden, 'Africa's Wars: a Continent in Turmoil', *Jane's Defence '96: The World in Conflict*, p. 92.
40. For a summary of the origins of and recent developments in the Liberian civil war see W. Reno, 'The Business of War in Liberia', Current History, 95, 607, May 1996, p. 211, who contends that the war can be 'traced to the cutoff of aid after the Cold War's end and the collapse of patron–client politics that had bound Liberia's politicians to one man'.
41. Clayton, *Frontiersmen, Warfare in Africa since 1950*, p. 194. For a detailed examination of ECOWAS/ECOMOG's role in Liberia see W. Ofuatey-Kodjoe, 'Regional Organisations and the Resolution of Internal Conflict: The ECOWAS Intervention in Liberia', *International Peacekeeping*, 1, 3 (Autumn 1994), pp. 261–302 and J. Adisa, 'Nigeria in ECOMOG: Political Undercurrents and the Burden of Community Spirit', *Small Wars and Insurgencies*, 5, 1, Spring 1994, pp. 83–110.
42. For UNOMIL's role in Liberia see F. Olonisakin, 'UN Cooperation with Regional Organisations in Peacekeeping: The Experience of ECOMOG and UNOMIL in Liberia', *International Peacekeeping*, 3, 3 (Autumn, 1996), pp. 33–51.
43. See W. Reno, 'Privatising War in Sierra Leone', *Current History*, 96, 610, pp. 227–30 for the background to the conflict in this former British colony.
44. Dowden, 'Africa's Wars', p. 94.
45. See Reno, 'The Business of War', pp. 212–14, especially regarding Taylor's diplomatic and commercial links with France and the Ivory Coast.
46. See, for instance, Dowden, 'Africa's Wars', p. 94, for examples of looting and commercial malpractice.
47. See J. Adisa, 'Nigeria in ECOMOG', p. 107, suggesting that Nigeria has spent up to 5 billion naira on Liberian operations since 1990 with a significant impact on the economy.
48. M. Binyon, 'Cook Cash for War on Rebels in Sierra Leone', *The Times*, 6 January 1999.
49. For an extended discussion of South Africa's peacekeeping dilemma before the Lesotho crisis see J. Cilliers and M. Malan, 'A Regional Peacekeeping Role for South Africa: Pressures, Problems and Prognosis', *African Security Review*, 5, 3, 1996, pp. 21–31. See also F. H. Toase and E. J. Yorke, *The New South Africa: Prospects for Domestic and International Security* (Basingstoke: Macmillan, 1998), especially Ch. 7.
50. A. Prahad, 'South Africa and Preventive Diplomacy', in G. Mills and J. Cilliers (eds), *Peacekeeping in Africa* (Braamfontein: Institute for Defence Policy/South African Institute of International Affairs, 1995).
51. For brief details of the SADC and its regional role see, for instance, 'Southern Africa Dreams of Unity', *Economist*, 2 September 1995.
52. 'Militants and Monarchs', *Africa Confidential*, 39, 10, 25 September 1998.
53. 'To a Little Kingdom', *Africa Confidential*, 39, 2, 9 October 1998.
54. E. O'Loughlin, 'South Africa Blows Its Image', *Independent on Sunday*, 27 September 1998.
55. 'To a Little Kingdom'.
56. Ibid.
57. A. La Guardia, 'Lesotho Fury at S. African Invasion', *Daily Telegraph*, 23

September 1998.
58. Ibid.
59. See A. La Guardia, 'Mutiny Rumours as Harare Sends Police to Congo', *Daily Telegraph*, 21 November 1998.
60. R. W. Johnson, 'Lesotho Crisis Exposes Inept Foreign Policy', *The Times*, 24 September 1998.
61. R. Harris, 'Decline and Fall of the American Empire', *Sunday Times*, 10 January 1999.
62. E. Godwin, 'Blueprint for Enforcement', *West Africa*, 6–12 October 1997.
63. Ibid. For a further military perspective see J. P. J. Brookes, 'A Military Model for Conflict Resolution in Sub-Saharan Africa', *Parameters*, Winter 1997/8, pp. 108–20.
64. Report of the UN Secretary-General, 13 April 1998. See also Report of the Secretary-General to the General Assembly, 'Improving Preparedness for Conflict Prevention and Peacekeeping in Africa', UN (New York), 1 November 1995.
65. Report of the UN Secretary-General, 13 April 1998. See also F. MacFarlane and M. Malan, 'Crisis and Response in the Central African Republic: A New Trend in African Peacekeeping?', *African Security Review*, 7, 2, 1998.
66. Q. Outram, 'Cruel Wars and Safe Havens: Humanitarian Aid in Liberia 1989–1996', *Disasters*, 21, 3, 1997, p. 202.
67. For an extended discussion of this key priority for future stability see G. Mills, G. Oosthuysen and J. Katzenellenbogen, 'Disarmament and Arms Control in Africa: A South African Perspective', *Defence Analysis*, 12, 1, 1996, pp. 113–31.
68. Collected Papers, Zimbabwe Peacekeeping Workshop, Harare, 23–27 January, 1995.
69. C. Clapham, 'Discerning the New Africa', *International Affairs*, 74, 2, 1998, p. 264.

SECTION II
Humanitarian Action and Peacekeeping

6

'Those who have the power to hurt but would do none': The Military and the Humanitarian

JIM WHITMAN

In the first months of 1996 the British Army initiated a recruitment campaign with a series of billboards. The first featured a photograph of a pitifully distraught refugee, with the caption 'Fifteen thousand care-takers required'. The second depicted a war-shattered urban centre and the words, 'Fifteen thousand repairmen needed'. Finally, above a photo-graph of the planet itself, there appeared the words, 'Wanted: Fifteen thousand security guards'.

Can or should the military be humanitarian? It certainly seems that someone thinks so. But who comprises this constituency? How large and how important is it? Is this passing fashion or the visible surface of a more profound change? To ask the question at all is to invoke wider questions about the business of professional soldiering; about doctrine, training, equipment and financing, and, at a deeper level, about public expectations, civil–military relations and about conceptions of the national interest and the place of the military in obtaining foreign-policy goals.

Can the military be humanitarian? Should it? The 'can' part of the question may be divided between competence and capacity, but it is difficult to muster a great deal of interest in the question of military competence to undertake or support humanitarian tasks. For all the differ-ences between non-governmental organisations (NGOs) and armies, professionals at work on saving and protecting human life have little trouble recognising one another. This is not to trivialise the differences between professional militaries and civilian organisations in emergency operations; important as these are, competence is not usually on the agenda. But the question of the military's capacity in view of the rapid contraction of developed nations' armed forces is quite another matter.

The 'should' question, although obviously linked to capacity, is essentially political. To ask whether the military should be humanitarian is not to wonder over the possibilities for altruism in the field. In democratic states militaries serve political purposes determined by elected governments. So the much more interesting question is 'How and why have humanitarian issues assumed such political importance?'. Indeed, to what extent does military involvement in humanitarian crises show that they have?

We are accustomed to a neat fit between a determination to dispatch soldiers to battle and the politics which inform such decisions. For all that war may fairly be characterised as a failure of policy, there is at least a visible logic, if not a compelling need, driving the commitment of troops in such instances, sufficient to ensure public support before the fact – and its willingness to brace itself for the possibility of casualties, as was clear in both the Falklands War and the Gulf War. Perhaps more importantly, we expect that behind such emergencies is a well-considered and carefully articulated national interest – those things which we employ our military to secure or defend *in extremis*. But how is it that a considerable degree of both public expectation and professional military energy is now devoted to the military acting in a humanitarian capacity? If, as is proper, the dispatch of soldiers abroad is understood as a political commitment of the utmost seriousness, what is its counterpart in the ordinary conduct of the nation's affairs? The question 'Can or should the military be humanitarian?' is not free-standing then, but follows from the much larger and more compelling question, 'Can or should our nation be humanitarian?'.

To understand how we have come to this juncture and to try to decide whether it is a turning point or just a whistle-stop, it is worthwhile to consider some of the larger currents of history. The rich material of history supports an abundance of hardy perennials and, if the 'lessons' seem ambiguous, there is the consolation that even those issues which seem wholly contemporary often have surprising precedents. Consider, for example, the debate concerning the possible formation of a United Nations (UN) Army or a UN Rapid Reaction Force. Regarded as a theme, this might appear to extend back only as far as the legal provisions in the UN Charter; however,

> As early as the year 1000, French princes of the Church declared their willingness to wage 'war against war' by the intervention of collective military forces under religious leadership. A little later,

Archbishop Aimon of Bourges ... led a number of punitive expeditions with an international army of priests against groups of recalcitrant knights.[1]

Likewise, although the phrase 'humanitarianism and the military' has quite specific contemporary meanings and raises a great many relatively novel practical issues, it comes to us lodged between long and by no means consistent historical trends.

One trend is the 5,000-year history of efforts to bring force within the orbit of law. Today, we can see in our social and governmental structures and in our laws and norms the fruits of countless, often untold, struggles of peoples to wrest absolute power from tyrants and to harness coercive power for collective purposes, collectively determined. Our willingness to distinguish lawful killing from unjustified slaughter is rooted in the ancient struggle to make power the instrument of law and is of a piece with our willingness to employ military force to halt or prevent genocide. In our time the natural counterpart of legal limits on the extent and conduct of war-fighting is the military acting in humanitarian capacities. Much of this is rooted in the codification of human rights. Against the knowledge that human rights are frequently and sometimes grossly violated, the force of human rights as an idea and ideal is nevertheless undiminished – and universal. If once the struggle was largely to assert these rights against the militaries of unsavoury regimes – as it is currently in Burma – now, at least occasionally, we see fit to charge our soldiers with the defence of the helpless or the threatened.

The UN is more than simply an institutional convenience for this purpose: the Charter of the UN is international law. It hardly requires a cynical disposition to regard the Gulf War as a happy conjunction of international law, global responsibility and national interest, yet the imposition of sanctions and the use of force were acts of law enforcement. Beyond the letter of the Charter the UN embodies and furthers a good deal of the normative architecture of international relations, while peacekeeping – now more commonly known as 'traditional' or 'classic' peacekeeping – has grown out of and in turn contributed to the UN's non-legal authority – what some mean when they speak of the organisation's 'legitimacy'.

None of us would argue that UN peace-support operations are the culmination of a stately progress of virtue in human affairs, yet they serve as an embarrassment to the 'one-damned-thing-after-another' school of history. But in condensing and simplifying for the purpose of describing a trend there is a danger of appearing to falsify the past or to deny the present. Any decent newspaper will make plain that many millions have more to fear from the domestic security apparatus of their own state than from any external force. And an historical trend sketched over centuries invites a sense of inevitability or irreversible progress. Against this notion it is worth recalling that in 1933 the German polity turned its back on a deeply rooted and well-articulated legal tradition for the persecution and eventual genocide of the Jews and other minorities.[2]

We are not on the history train bound for the New Jerusalem, yet, contrary to what was briefly a fashionable conviction, there is no end in sight to this history. After all, asking ourselves today whether or not the military should be humanitarian is hardly a pause on the banks of the Rubicon. And in pondering its possible extension, consolidation or institutionalisation, or by trying to get to grips with its practical implications, we are furthering and extending the long history of efforts to assert liberty and justice over tyranny and brute force; and law over chaos and barbarous competition. If our unwillingness or inability to act in so many instances seems more consequential than our efforts, the fact of them is nevertheless considerable in human as well as historical terms. And here, the military is on the front line.

For a second, conflicting trend, we need go back less than 250 years to the Enlightenment. George Steiner's single, poignant example will suffice:

> Asked why he was seeking to arouse the whole of Europe over the judicial torture of one man, Voltaire answered, in March 1762, '*C'est que je suis homme*'. By that token, he would, today, be in vain and constant cry.[3]

This was written more than 20 years before 'Sarajevo' became shorthand for the return of slaughter and terror wreaked on civilian populations in Europe and for the stain it has left on public and political life well beyond the borders of the former Yugoslavia.

The looming millennium will no doubt give us a good many gloomy reflections on the blood-soaked history of the twentieth century. Behind the awful statistics, however, is something still more disturbing: our apparent ability as peoples, particularly within the political cultures we create, for a progressive accommodation of the worst products of human endeavour. Perhaps what is truly horrifying in twentieth-century history is not the mechanisation of mass slaughter, but its rationalisation.[4] Possible courses of action once thought unconscionable now seem unremarkable – 'news' only for as long as such things now last. This was certainly the case with the aerial bombardment of cities, for example, up to the eve of World War II.

It is not only the weight of historical events which presses down on us, but the brutalising, numbing effect on our sensibilities and expectations of the collective insanity of the nuclear arms race; and the re-emergence of genocide in our lifetimes – most recently, even as a lively debate ensued over whether there is a legal right of humanitarian intervention.

If the first trend described depicts the gradual articulation, enactment and formalisation of shared values, these find expression in a nation willing to dispatch its soldiers for the protection of a people against the genocidal intent of a tyrant. Yet the same British government which deployed its soldiers in defence of the Kurds had earlier sold weapons-making capacity to Saddam Hussain after Halabja – that is, in the full knowledge that he was a genocidal killer. Our ability to accommodate both the inhumane and the humanitarian has many such expressions, by no means confined to a single state. We have all heard assertions as to the difficulty of 'threading principle through the intricacies of the world', but it will not wash: such actions are an affront to our heritage and to what we profess to believe. These are not the 'tough decisions that have to be made' – they are an obscene scribble across the accomplishments of principle and law. And they have practical import: in the Gulf War, for example, British soldiers faced weapons purchased from British companies with money loaned by British banks and underwritten by export credit guarantees. British taxpayers are left with unpaid Iraqi debts of £652 million.

We know in detail that nations which have demonstrated as well as asserted their commitment to humanitarianism have, at the same time, pursued other goals which, because they cannot be publicly justified, are more commonly given a reassuring gloss or hidden from view altogether. But if the human rights records of Iraq and Indonesia did not debar them from purchasing weapons from this country, what values are evinced in the sending of soldiers to a humanitarian emergency? Should the *military* be humanitarian?

There is nothing in history or the news which obviates the need for defence of the realm, much though the particulars continue to change over time. Any number of new tasks might befall the military in the coming years and, though most would probably be variations on familiar themes, these too would require a range of thinking and planning – and a juggling of resources – much as the demands of humanitarian remits do now. For example, the only novelty in the idea of the military playing a role in 'protecting biodiversity' is the phrase: in 1886 the management of Yellowstone Park was turned over to the American Army. So successful was it that

> Professor Charles S. Sargent, an eminent dendrologist of Harvard, suggested that, because of the excellent example established in

protecting the Yellowstone, the guardianship of all the nation's forests should be confined to the Army and 'that forestry should be taught at West Point'.[5]

There is considerable interest in the degree to which the British and the American governments in particular have stressed the 'green' aspects of their militaries – most tellingly, if a little comically, in the United States Marine Corps recycling its familiar 'The Marines are looking for a few good men' to 'The Marines: we're saving a few good species'.[6] But a good deal of this is 'passive' – firing ranges and training grounds as conservation areas – or more at the level of environmental degradation having been perceived as a security threat and absorbed into broader 'national security' remits. This is not without beneficent initiatives – using military assets to help developing countries to curb the poaching of endangered species or to patrol fisheries, for example – but all too easily shades into 'strategic materials', access to resources – and more familiar military roles.[7]

But for all that there is a large and probably expanding range of tasks for the military, it is not difficult to understand why it is that humanitarian roles command such strength of feeling, within publics at large as well as within militaries themselves. I believe that only a part of this is the essentially moral character of the work. For the rest, in this and several other countries, I think it is connected to the common perception that our militaries embody a good deal of what we regard as the best in ourselves as peoples.

This too has a long history. Behind the supposition of some that 'military' and 'humanitarian' are an oddly assorted pair lies the difficulty that it is not a simple matter to filter out qualities we revere from situations we abhor – to praise heroism in battle even as we feel revulsion over war, for example. And beside a history of war replete with barbarity, cruelty, rapacity and wanton destructiveness, there emerged across centuries and cultures notions of honour, laws regulating conduct, codes of humane decency and an acute sense of the shared humanity between antagonists in battle.[8]

As developed nations have abandoned conquest and colonialism, the extent to which professionalism in the military has come increasingly to embrace values, both formally and informally, has also increased. Little wonder then that professional militaries require men and women of character and humane instincts as well as competence and intelligence. Some years ago the British Army ran an officer-recruitment campaign in national magazines. In the manner beloved of copywriters, desirable traits of character were phrased as rhetorical questions and framed in a simple, multiple-choice style: 'A brave and passionate man will kill or be killed.

A brave and calm man will always preserve life. Of the two, which is preferable?' Such was the style, but these lines come from the *Tao Te Ching*, written in China 2,500 years ago.[9]

The changing disposition of professional militaries has its counterpart in civilian attitudes toward the military. While these are largely unexamined and even unremarked in Britain, they are nevertheless deep and enduring – and have considerably strengthened in this century. With World War I still on the periphery of living memory, the wholescale destruction of a generation of young manhood in a war of attrition is no longer conceivable – and most certainly not 70,000 men in a single, pointless battle. Although we are accustomed to thinking about World War I as a war of the modern era – with the forces of industrialism on both sides being brought to bear – socially, it is of a wholly different milieu. It is obvious that this has more to do with changing public norms than changing standards of generalship or political direction, that is, with the advance of human rights.

There are those who doubt the substance as well as the efficacy of human rights and who might argue that human rights have made no difference to the business of professional soldiering, except to expand the range of its possible tasks. But how is it then that it is not only no longer done but no longer *possible* to regard soldiers as cannon fodder? There is a good deal more to the Geneva Conventions than the letter and the extent of the law – a splendid subject for reflection on the manner in which changing norms find expression in law and laws in their turn widen and strengthen norms.

It is in part because as societies we have come to individualise and cherish the lives of soldiers that missions which expose them to danger are strongly felt. This is much more acute in the USA, where sensitivity to casualties is such as to make the political risks of troop deployments ever more considerable, and problematic; but it is no less real in Britain for all that public expectations are perhaps a bit more realistic.

In both countries and beyond, because we do not ask servicemen and women to risk their lives except for our core values, the recourse to military means often brings these to the surface of public awareness and makes them a subject of reflection and debate as at almost no other time. Although war and its prospect are obviously more strongly felt, this is true of mercy missions as well as battles. Consider the following quotation of a high-minded prescription of political values for Great Britain. Who is addressing whom – and when?

> If we speak of democracy we do not mean a democracy which maintains the right to vote but forgets the right to work and the right

to live. If we speak of freedom we do not mean a rugged indivi-
dualism which excludes social organisation and economic planning.
If we speak of equality we do not mean a political equality nullified
by social and economic privilege. If we speak of economic reconstruction we think less of maximum production (though this too will
be required) than of 'equitable distribution'.

This is not the 1997 election manifesto of the Labour Party but a leader
in *The Times,* written a few weeks after the evacuation from Dunkirk.[10]
It is one of the hallmarks of a democratic nation that core societal
values should find expression in the tasks given to the military; and it is
genuinely heartening that values which extend beyond war and defence
of the realm should also be accorded a place in our felt obligations. But
how far do our humanitarian obligations extend? The significance of the
phrase 'War is a failure of policy' is that soldiers must risk their lives
picking up the pieces. If those same soldiers are to risk their lives in
extending humanitarian assistance to the starving, threatened or dispossessed, what kind of failure engenders it? Are peace-support operations
a failure of policy and if so, whose? Or are Britain and its affairs so
removed from, say, Zaire and Rwanda that the commitment of troops
there is essentially an act of charity?
Of course, the phrase 'in the national interest' is a wonderful
ministerial fall-back – but in every instance, we are entitled to expect that
it contains some substance, particularly if soldiers are to be put in harm's
way. As it happens, it is perhaps more difficult for governments to justify
their inconsistency than their choices: since there seems to be a considerable if not inexhaustible public willingness to act in some of the worst
humanitarian tragedies, '*not* in the national interest' will be the more
telling pronouncement. Sometimes this is shorthand for a calculation of
political ends and military means which are not deemed acceptable. In
fairness to our politicians, they bear the shouts of the chorus, 'We must
do something', while shouldering their responsibility not to throw 'blood
and treasure' at a problem. Sometimes, the answer has to be no.
We might also reasonably expect one or a number of other considerations – political, diplomatic, economic – to figure in such calculations.
This is neither surprising nor necessarily malign. Overseas development
assistance and disaster relief have political intent as well as humanitarian
meaning and effect; nor is it a disjuncture that a government should have
an agenda which accommodates but extends beyond the simpler and more
straightforward humanitarian impulses of many citizens.
But while there is much to be said for enhancing a nation's diplomatic
standing through assistance to the distressed, there are limits to the span

of purposes which the full range of government initiatives can seek to achieve before its actions become dysfunctional. If we send in troops to pick up the pieces, we also look to our governments to take such non-emergency and non-military action as they are able to ensure that things do not fall apart again. The more astute and professional emergency and development charities work on this principle, as they seek to address the causes of poverty as well as alleviating the worst of its effects. In other words, we might expect that the dispatch of soldiers to humanitarian emergencies is only one expression, albeit the most serious, of a consistent, well-considered commitment to humanitarianism. In fact, there is much to suggest that the sending of troops to emergencies is, increasingly, a substitute for political engagement with the underdeveloped world.

It is not my intention to slight the contribution made by armed forces for the relief of human suffering. In the worst instances it is the presence of military forces which makes the initiation or continuance of work by NGOs and UN agencies possible. In Rwanda in 1994 I spent a day travelling with members of the British contingent, from the Parachute Regiment, who were particularly well-regarded for their untrumpeted, quiet competence. Many NGO workers who have long been ambivalent at best about working closely with the military were deeply impressed with the troops' willing cooperation and range of skills. They accomplished more than one kind of bridge-building – to say nothing of the great credit which accrues to this country by their professionalism.

But there is a limit to what the military can accomplish in such situations. We train, equip and sometimes require our armed forces to deal with the sharp end, but the blunt substance of humanitarian emergencies is considerable, daunting and long-term. Military logisticians can work wonders in feeding the starving and troops can protect food convoys, but it is not the Army's job to address the causes of hunger; and they can build bridges and keep roads open during the rainy season, but what happens when they go home? Had British troops been sent to Zaire in December 1996 the deployment would have been limited to a period of about four months. But the surge in refugee flows that prompted the pledge is only a symptom of deeply impacted conflicts and widespread chaos which grip the entire African Great Lakes region.

If we are to address a certain class of humanitarian disasters at all the military is essential, but never will it be sufficient. That might seem obvious enough, but there is a trend in greatly reducing humanitarian provision, both before and after the fact, even as we continue occasionally to offer a military contribution. Britain's and other nations' humanitarianism is fast acquiring an emergency/charity ethos. The effect of raising the frequency and profile of peace-support operations while reducing long-term assistance and development is to dilute humanitarian obligation into humanitarian commitments – belated, discrete, limited, palliative, while at the same time, high-profile, benign, low-cost and, as far as possible, low-risk. Put another way, we are taking from the human and material resources devoted to policy provision and placing a fraction of them in emergency provision.

The evidence is abundant:

> ... the European Union [drew] on funds from its development budget to finance the Belgian peacekeeping contingent in Somalia. As the UN budget for peacekeeping has increased from $230 million in 1987 to $3.6 billion in 1994, the aggregate development assistance expenditure of OECD countries (albeit a larger absolute amount) has witnessed a stagnation ... In general, there has been a notable decline in funding for development activities within the UN system in contrast to funding for emergency relief operations. In recent years, for example, there has been a fifteen per cent reduction in the core resources of the UN Development Programme as compared to an almost doubling of resources for the World Food Programme, the bulk of which has been devoted to relief food assistance.[11]

Those for whom the words 'peacekeeping' and 'United Nations' are synonymous will not be surprised that in 1995 the UN's peacekeeping expenditure was more than twice as much as the organisation's regular budget. But the heart of the UN Charter is not law enforcement, emergency relief or even peacekeeping but development. All of us applaud the strenuous efforts that have been made to make operations more efficient, better coordinated and more cost-effective. But the state of the world is now such that, in addition to asking how we can make ourselves better fire-fighters, is it not time to ask why it is there are so many fires to fight?

Such a question should not occasion the United Kingdom any embarrassment. After all, it pays its UN assessed contributions in full, has a well-respected Minister for Overseas Development and its military has a history of participation in peacekeeping and humanitarian assistance operations which is a justifiable source of pride to its citizenry. Yet beneath this shining surface is a peculiar, disturbing reality. Britain and the other four Permanent Members of the UN Security Council account for 86 per cent of all weapons sales to developing countries. Even Britain's Overseas Development Administration (ODA) has suffered manipulation: it is one thing to argue that a relatively prosperous country such as Malaysia should have a call on Britain's meagre and declining ODA budget against claims from genuinely impoverished regions; it is quite another that this should have been done for a *quid pro quo* in arms purchases from the UK. The action was found to have been illegal and the ODA budget duly compensated, but the following year the ODA's budget was cut, as it was again at the end of 1996.

The then British Secretary of State for Defence Michael Portillo, announcing Britain's willingness to send a contingent of troops to Zaire to ease the crisis there, pre-empted the question as to why Britain should become involved in a place far from home where there was no vital national interest. His answer was 'because Britain is a civilised nation. We can see that people are about to die in their thousands and we are one of the few nations on earth who have the military capability to help at least some of them.' But why Zaire? And why a militarised emergency? Every day we can see that poverty, malnutrition and curable diseases are also about to kill people in their thousands – more an ambient roar than head-line news, but audible to anyone who cares to listen. We have the spectacle of a nation which can send its soldiers into volatile and dangerous environments when there is no apparent national interest at stake – that is, for humanitarian reasons – but, faced with no end of worthwhile projects for the elimination of absolute poverty, instead gives millions in aid for the construction of a dam which the Malaysians themselves can afford, apparently because it is too embarrassed to subsidise Britain's arms manufacturers direct. The nation shows a willingness to send its troops to a humanitarian emergency in Zaire, while at home it is left to the Red Cross to feed asylum seekers.

Can the military be humanitarian? Should it be? The military marches off under the banner of humanitarianism, but are what soldiers term 'our political masters' marching in step? The USA deployed its Marines in Somalia for the purpose of feeding the starving Somali people and suffered some gruesome casualties while there. Yet the US government is now preparing to cut by two-thirds – and within three years eliminate – its funding for the International Fund for Agricultural Development (IFAD). This Fund represents one of the most comprehensive efforts to reduce poverty as well as malnutrition and is 'one of the few international agencies to attract virtual unanimous approval from the world's govern-ments, and even among the anti-UN Republican majority in the US Congress'.[12] What are the prospects for what the UN Charter terms 'international peace and security' with 800 million malnourished human beings? Where are our humanitarian obligations in all of this? The effect of our inconsistent, even dysfunctional humanitarianism at the level of government policy, here and elsewhere, is rather like the prayer of St Augustine, 'Make me a good man, Lord, but not yet'. We appear humanitarian – intermittently, briefly, televisually – but the larger facts and mechanisms of our ways of life remain unchanged.

This is not advocacy for national self-denial; quite the opposite, since moral considerations and a sharp sense of self-interest need not be antagonistic. For example, the motives behind America's Marshall Plan from 1948 are instructive. In declining order of importance, these were: first, enabling Europeans to purchase American goods; second, ensuring that Western Europe was sufficiently strong and coherent to withstand external pressures; third, obviating the need for further direct US involvement, and finally, addressing humanitarian need. The greatest beneficiary of the Marshall Plan was the USA. The markets to be found in a stable and prosperous Sub-Saharan Africa, Central America and elsewhere dwarf the sums now being earned by the morally odious sale of weapons to repressive regimes. Yet at the end of 1996 – the end of the International Year for the Eradication of Poverty – Britain's ODA budget was cut by £180 million. Dolly Parton once remarked, 'You'd be surprised how much it costs to look this cheap'.

One is commonly met with the argument that it is fine to stand on the moral high ground so long as there are people prepared to deal with life's hard realities. But to ask whether the military can or should be humanitarian is to engage both at once. Can the military be humanitarian? Should it be? A large proportion of the populations of this and similar countries think it should be and the strength of feeling behind it is linked to conceptions of morality and justice as much as to order and self-interest: to an understanding that the strong have a responsibility to protect the weak; and that the best test of fitness for the possession of power is a certain reluctance to wield it – 'those that have the power to hurt but would do none', in Shakespeare's wonderfully apposite phrase.

But note: if we hope and expect citizens to support military humanitarianism, we are asking them to engage public policy with humane values and broadly shared standards of moral worth. We should hardly be surprised, then, by the breadth and depth this engagement sometimes assumes. Recently, four women using household hammers disabled a Hawk military aircraft bound for export to Indonesia. Naturally, a prosecution was brought for criminal conspiracy and criminal damage. The women involved did not deny their action but defended it under national and international law. They detailed the history of Indonesia's genocidal campaign against East Timor, had eye-witness accounts that Hawk aircraft from a previous sale had been used to bomb villages, and explained the many appeals they and others had made to the British government and

British Aerospace to halt the sale, to no avail. Citing law and precedent from the Criminal Law Act 1967 to the Tokyo and Nuremberg War Crimes Trials, the Genocide Convention and the Geneva Conventions, they argued that they had taken reasonable action to prevent the crime of genocide. A jury of their peers found them innocent.

Any number of fascinating discussions can spring from this tale – on behaviour aberrant or courageous as one judges it, on the applicability of international law in domestic courts, the perversity of juries, or what the verdict means in terms of public standards and expectations. But what about humanitarian principles, which were so readily brought to the fore to justify a deployment of troops to Zaire?

In 1995 the British *Statement on the Defence Estimates* assured us that 'Our success in winning export orders has been achieved against a background of very strict export controls. All exports are considered on a case-by-case basis in the light of established criteria.'[13] In view of what we have subsequently learned, it is fair to wonder which is worse – the criteria themselves or the fact that they are 'established'?

Can or should the military be humanitarian? Yes, of course. But it is not enough. Nor, in my view, is it decent that the military should be on the frontline in a double sense. If we are willing to risk the lives of soldiers in the name of humanitarianism then it is right that they should be addressing the worst of our failed humanitarian initiatives, not our failure to enact humanitarian principles. We have work to do on the humanitarian disposition of our public bodies – the work of citizenship, of soldiers and civilians alike, as we go marching on.

NOTES

1. Gabriella Rosner, *The United Nations Emergency Force* (New York: Columbia University Press, 1963), p. 207.
2. Ian Kershaw, 'The Extinction of Human Rights in Nazi Germany', in Olwen Hufton (ed.), *Historical Change and Human Rights: The Oxford Amnesty Lectures, 1994* (New York: Basic Books, 1995), pp. 217–46.
3. George Steiner, *In Bluebeard's Castle: Some Notes Towards the Re-Definition of Culture* (London: Faber, 1971), p. 43.
4. Daniel Pick, *War Machine: The Rationalisation of Slaughter in the Machine Age* (New Haven: Yale University Press, 1993); Michael S. Sherry, *The Rise of American Air Power: The Creation of Armageddon* (New Haven: Yale University Press, 1987).
5. Quoted in Bruce A. Byers, 'Armed Forces and the Conservation of Biological Diversity', in Jyrki Kakonen (ed.), *Green Security or Militarised Environment* (Aldershot: Dartmouth Publishing Co., 1994), p. 116.
6. Andrew Ross, 'The Future is a Risky Business', in George Robertson *et al.* (eds), *FutureNatural* (London: Routledge, 1996), p. 9.

7. For a survey of United States DoD initiatives, see Kent Hughes Butts, 'Why the Military is Good for the Environment', in Jyrki Kakonen, pp. 83–109. For a contrary perspective, see D. Deudney, 'The Case Against Linking Environmental Degradation and National Security', *Millennium*, 19, 3 (1990).

8. A summary of useful sources is contained in Adam Roberts and Richard Guelff, *Documents on the Laws of War* (Oxford: Clarendon Press, 1989), p. 2, fn. 3–6.

9. Lao Tsu, *Tao Te Ching*, trans. Gia-Fu Feng and Jane English (New York: Random House, 1972).

10. Quoted in William De Maria, 'Combat and Concern: The Warfare-Welfare Nexus', *War and Society*, 7, 1 (May 1989), p. 75.

11. Olara Otunnu, *The Peace and Security Agenda of the United Nations: From a Crossroads into the Next Century*.

12. Geoffrey Lean, 'Clinton cut means that millions could starve', *Independent on Sunday*, 17 November 1996, p. 4.

13. *Statement on the Defence Estimates 1995*. Cm. 2800 (London: HMSO), p. 78.

7

The Evolution of UN Humanitarian Operations

SERGIO VIEIRA DE MELLO

At present, the United Nations is called upon to address an increasingly diverse and complicated set of humanitarian emergencies. The nature of the challenges and conflicts is different from those which confronted the UN in the past. In order to understand the direction in which the UN is proceeding it is useful to analyse a number of significant changes which have occurred with regard to how member states have chosen to utilise the UN in the field of peacekeeping and humanitarian affairs.

Historically, peacekeeping has been perceived as an *ad hoc* response undertaken by the UN as an interim arrangement pursuant to Chapter VI of the Charter to contain fighting, prevent the resumption of hostilities and restore international peace and security. In order to be effective, peacekeeping forces need to be seen as legitimate, neutral and impartial in the eyes of all the relevant parties. Legitimacy is derived from the consent of the warring parties. Neutrality and impartiality, on the other hand, are ensured by the multinational composition of the force, in addition to the limited nature of its armaments and its ability to use those armaments only in self-defence. Peacekeeping forces are not authorised to use force, and although equipped with light defensive weapons, they may use them only as a last resort. Traditionally, the focus of peacekeeping efforts has been on the advanced stages of a conflict, usually after a cease-fire agreement has been reached and the parties in dispute have agreed to cooperate with UN forces monitoring the agreement. There are several examples of such operations, including the UN Transition Assistance Group (UNTAG) in Namibia, the UN Observer Mission in El Salvador (ONUSAL), the UN Transitional Authority in Cambodia (UNTAC), the UN Operation in Mozambique (ONUMOZ) and most recently the UN Angola Verification Mission (UNAVEM).

Peace-enforcement operations, on the other hand, are the antithesis of the traditional peacekeeping operation. They are established pursuant to Chapter VII of the Charter and authorised to use force in carrying out their mandate. Peace-enforcement actions precede a ceasefire and may even assist in bringing one about. Thus they are usually launched in the midst of conflict rather than after a peace agreement has been brokered. In this context the maintenance of a neutral position is more difficult to sustain, as the pursuit of a political objective will generally be perceived as detrimental to the interests of one faction while being beneficial to another. UN or multinational operations which received the blessing of the Security Council and were conducted in conflict environments without any pre-existing peace agreement before deployment include the coalition intervention in northern Iraq, the UN Operation in Somalia (UNOSOM), the UN Protection Force (UNPROFOR) in Bosnia-Herzegovina and the UN Assistance Mission for Rwanda (UNAMIR).

Integration between peacekeeping and humanitarian operations is more easily achieved in countries where a comprehensive peace settlement has been attained before the deployment of a UN mission. In the case of Cambodia, for example, the humanitarian objectives had been clearly defined and agreed upon within the parameters of a peace settlement well before the arrival of UNTAC. UNTAC was a truly integrated operation with civil affairs, human rights, humanitarian and military components organised under a strong, political leadership. The arrival of the first UNTAC self-contained battalion in March 1992, the Indonesian Rangers, was brought forward in order to enable the UN High Commissioner for Refugees (UNHCR) to launch its repatriation operation in Cambodia. For more than a year, UNTAC's Military Component assisted the Repatriation Component in organising and protecting nearly 500 convoys. Thanks to this cooperation, the UNHCR succeeded in repatriating some 370,000 refugees by road, rail, river transport and air with few incidents, despite numerous difficulties including the Khmer Rouge's policy of non-cooperation with UNTAC. The success of the repatriation operation was linked to the larger, integrated UN effort to address humanitarian and human rights issues in conjunction with the underlying political and military issues.[1]

The situation in Cambodia, like those in Angola, Mozambique and El Salvador, was rooted in and sustained by superpower rivalries. Peace was brought about only through the cooperation of the superpowers. UN operations in these countries represent the final chapters to stories that were vestiges of the Cold War. In the second category of operations, where operations are launched with no pre-existing peace agreement as in Bosnia or Somalia, the UN has become involved in operations that are, arguably, unique to the post-Cold War era. UN peacekeeping has evolved from inter-state to intra-state operations in countries characterised by the breakdown of state authority and the eruption of ethnic violence. The simple will of the superpowers is no longer sufficient to bring about peace. By reviewing recent UN efforts at humanitarian relief and peacekeeping in these situations, one can better foresee the nature of conflict in the post-Cold War era and what challenges the UN will face in the coming years.

FROM IRAQ TO RWANDA (1991–96)

Northern Iraq

The first major humanitarian operation in the post-Cold War period occurred in Iraq. Saddam Hussain's repression of the Kurdish population in northern Iraq in 1991, following the Gulf War, created a humanitarian crisis that resulted in hundreds of thousands of Kurds fleeing towards the Turkish border. This was the first time that a humanitarian crisis was recognised by the UN Security Council as constituting a threat to inter-national peace and security. In April 1991 the Security Council passed Resolution 688, which condemned the Iraqi violation of human rights and recognised the consequent mass displacement of civilian populations in Iraq as a threat to international peace and security. The resolution made it clear that international military intervention was necessary to stop the flow of Kurdish refugees into neighbouring states. The resolution effectively enabled a coalition of UN member states to create a safe haven for internally displaced persons within Iraq, allowing for the provision of both humanitarian aid and military protection pursuant to Chapter VII of the UN Charter.[2] This in turn made it possible for the displaced Kurds to remain safely in Iraq rather than flee to neighbouring states as refugees. The combination of the coalition security umbrella and international humanitarian assistance worked well in containing a large-scale humani-tarian tragedy.

Somalia

The success in northern Iraq signalled a turning point in humanitarian intervention. Cold War norms of non-intervention seemed to be giving way to a new international consensus in which minimum humanitarian standards within states were to be enforced by the international com-munity with the use of force if necessary. Subsequently, in April 1992 the

Security Council authorised the deployment of UNOSOM I to provide military protection for the delivery of humanitarian assistance in Somalia. It determined that it was 'the magnitude of the human suffering' in Somalia which constituted a threat to international peace and security.

The security situation in Somalia deteriorated and humanitarian efforts in the field broke down. Another international military force was authorised, this time under Chapter VII of the Charter and armed with greater powers of enforcement and action. In December 1992, under the pressure and scrutiny of intensive media coverage and criticism, President George Bush announced his intention to send 30,000 American soldiers to Somalia to assist with the humanitarian emergency. The Security Council passed Resolution 794 under Chapter VII, which authorised 'all necessary means' to create a 'secure environment' for the delivery of humanitarian relief in Somalia. This resolution led to the formation of the Unified Task Force (UNITAF) with some 37,000 troops, mostly from the USA. UNITAF was deployed in Somalia and ordered to protect humanitarian operations at key points around the country. The US-led operation was successful in accomplishing the objective of delivering humanitarian assistance to the most devastated parts of the country.

With the initial success of UNITAF, responsibility for the Somalia operation was handed over to the UN under Resolution 814 of March 1993. The resolution created UNOSOM II and launched an enforcement action of an unprecedented nature. Its mandate was to restore law and order, monitor the arms embargo and assist in relief and economic rehabilitation. This was the first Chapter VII military operation ever launched under the actual command and control of the UN.

However, following a number of armed attacks on UNOSOM II troops, a strengthened US task force, operating under a Security Council mandate, attempted to detain and forcibly disarm those responsible. In the subsequent fighting several US Rangers and a large number of Somali citizens were killed. The UN had become embroiled in Somalia's internal conflict. Having suffered casualties and with no readily identifiable interests to defend in the region, the USA decided to withdraw its forces and other states soon followed.

The UN experience in Somalia reflects how humanitarian assistance and intervention in the post-Cold War era can become more complicated and difficult than in traditional peacekeeping operations which have occurred in the past. For instance, the intervention in northern Iraq occurred without the consent of the government concerned but was the result of a unique situation in that it was preceded by an unambiguous military victory over Iraqi forces in the Gulf War. Security Council Resolution 688 was largely made possible by what Adam Roberts of

Oxford University calls the logic of the rights of victors over a defeated country. It may be correct to say, as a result, that this was a *sui generis* episode. In Somalia, by contrast, an effort was made to undertake a humanitarian initiative under Chapter VII, in an ongoing war without consent and without a clear military advantage. The consequences of the UN's action in Somalia are still evident. The fear of repeating the same mistakes has influenced, or rather inhibited, every subsequent UN deployment.

Bosnia-Herzegovina

The provision of humanitarian assistance was the foundation upon which the UN's multilateral response in Bosnia was constructed. For the first time a UN military peacekeeping force was given the primary objective of assisting a humanitarian operation in the context of a full-scale civil war. Humanitarian objectives were again pushed to the fore with mixed results. The fear of being drawn into the conflict, on the one hand, combined with overwhelming pressure to contain the atrocities being perpetrated before the international media, on the other, led to a blurring of the division between Chapter VI and Chapter VII operations.

Tactics that were successful in northern Iraq worked less well in Bosnia-Herzegovina. As in Iraq, the UN attempted to create safe havens for civilians in need of protection and humanitarian assistance without threatening the integrity of the state in question. In early 1993 the Security Council established safe havens in Bosnia under Resolution 836. The safe areas were to have a strategic significance, yet, on the other hand, they were established to serve 'humanitarian purposes'.[3] The Security Council did not delineate the geographical boundaries of the areas nor did the Council clarify their exact status. Furthermore, no formal requirement for their demilitarisation existed and the language of the resolution was contradictory regarding the level of force the UN could use. Although the mandate sounded more like a Chapter VII enforcement operation, the force deployed in Bosnia was too small and vulnerable to be effective. This was a typical case in which capabilities did not match commitments.[4]

The UN mandate for peacekeeping forces in Bosnia reflected the disagreement which existed between proponents of a traditional peacekeeping force on the one hand and an enforcement action on the other. The UN peacekeepers had a tenuous mandate to provide security for humanitarian operations and to protect civilian populations in safe areas. Fear of crossing what has become known as the 'Mogadishu line', the transition from neutral peacekeeper to participant in a conflict, kept the UN almost paralysed.

Rwanda

By the spring of 1994, after having suffered setbacks in both Bosnia and Somalia, the optimism of the early 1990s had largely evaporated. The initial enthusiasm experienced in 1991 with the possibilities of multi-lateral action had soured into scepticism and fear. When on 6 April 1994 the Presidents of Rwanda and Burundi were killed, General Dallaire, the UNAMIR Force Commander in Kigali, called for a modest increase in troop numbers in order to try and contain the outbreak of genocide. The international community reacted with extraordinary speed by hurriedly withdrawing a large proportion of their troops from the region.

The consequences of this act represent one of the saddest chapters in the history of the UN. The world stood by as hundreds of thousands were massacred and one million people fled to what was then called Zaire, among them many of those responsible for the genocide. The presence of the refugees posed a serious threat to the integrity and stability of the country. To bring about any solution, while the refugees were still under the leadership of the 'genocidaires', was, however, impossible. The international community responded to the conflict by settling for the provision of humanitarian relief isolated from any parallel political or military action. In a travesty of the humanitarian ideal, aid was provided totally divorced from any concern for the political and military require-ments necessary to re-establish human security. The result proved inade-quate and drew fierce criticism.

The presence of former Rwandan army and militia troops in the refugee camps made it difficult to maintain their desired civilian character and contributed to a deterioration of the security conditions within them. In order to separate former soldiers and militia from civilian refugees, UNHCR requested international assistance. The Secretary-General Boutros Boutros-Ghali made a number of efforts to solicit peacekeeping forces for deployment in the camps to carry out the separation of ex-militia and other so-called intimidators – 90,000 or so – from the rest of the refugee population. No state apart from Bangladesh, however, offered its troops for such a mission.

As the consequences of the 1994 inaction took on dramatic pro-portions in October–November 1996, an attempt was made at providing the humanitarian agencies with the necessary military support. The Security Council recognised 'that the present situation in Eastern Zaire constitutes a threat to international peace and security in the region'. Security Council Resolution 1080 was adopted on 15 November 1996. What was originally intended to be an exclusively humanitarian oper-ation, the Multinational Force (which was not, as such, a UN force but rather a so-called 'coalition of the willing') was still, however, not

authorised to separate military elements from the civilian refugee populations. It was mandated only to assist in providing access and humanitarian aid to the more than one million refugees dispersed by the conflict
and to assist with their repatriation to Rwanda. Despite its limited terms
of reference, it failed to materialise.

After the sudden return of more than 500,000 refugees in a matter of
days, international commitment and interest evaporated. Questions, however, remain as to whether or not tens of thousands of refugees could have
been saved had a lightly armed UN force been deployed in a rapid and more
forceful manner. To this day, the exact number of Rwandans who perished
in the forest of the Eastern Democratic Republic of Congo is unclear.

The evolution of the UN's engagement in humanitarian operations
from Iraq to Rwanda is indicative of the difficulties and challenges
confronted by the UN. In the case of Iraq, coalition forces established a
secure environment and UN humanitarian agencies subsequently deployed
and provided humanitarian assistance. In the cases of Bosnia and Somalia,
on the other hand, humanitarian agencies were present and active before
the deployment of an international military force. In both operations,
however, the subsequent deployment of UN forces allowed for the
provision of humanitarian aid, where it would not have otherwise been
possible. Then came Rwanda, where humanitarian agencies were left
largely on their own.

Even where states have been unwilling to send highly trained and well-
armed troops, the humanitarian agencies have continued to act and,
ironically at times, have been criticised for not doing more. Humanitarian
agencies are now confronted with a painful paradox: the more insecure
the environment for humanitarian operations, the less likely governments
are to provide military protection and support, in particular high-risk
support such as that which was required in Rwanda. Increasingly, however, in post-Cold War conflicts, humanitarian organisations are, by their
very mandate, entrusted with the task of protecting and assisting civilian
populations in addition to exposing their own staff to the same risks as
the victims. Should humanitarian agencies refuse to intervene in the
absence of adequate security conditions? What would the consequences
of such a stance be?

LESSONS FOR THE FUTURE

In 1991 President Bush spoke of a New World Order. In 1992, in the
context of Bosnia, he spoke of humanitarian aid having to get through
'no matter what it takes'. Today, a few years on, this assertiveness and

faith in the power of multilateral action have faded. States have become more inward-looking, hesitant to take risks unless there are clear strategic interests to be defended. While the link between humanitarian problems and peace is recognised, humanitarian agencies are often left to act alone.

In terms of what is to come, it is clear that multinational arrangements are not the panacea for the future. The Security Council has grown more reluctant to engage in missions that run the risk of turning into long-term commitments with an uncertain outcome and an unclear exit strategy. Instead, there is a move by the Council to have *ad hoc* regional coalitions armed with an international mandate. Regional arrangements, such as the Monitoring Group (ECOMOG), established under the auspices of the Economic Community of West African States (ECOWAS) for Liberia, may prove more successful, especially where strong international political, logistic and financial backing is provided.[5]

The future of regional initiatives is tied to a larger debate over the future of American support for peacekeeping and UN peacekeeping operations in general. Recent UN reform legislation enacted by the US Senate addresses American policy in this context by endorsing a strategy to encourage the UN to subcontract peacekeeping to regional organisations.[6]

There are other lessons that may be drawn from the mixed experiences of recent years. The most obvious is the need for greater efforts to focus on prevention. From Burundi, to the republics of the former Soviet Union, efforts to contain crises before they reach unmanageable proportions are essential.

Another lesson is the importance of an integrated approach in dealing with conflict and the humanitarian suffering that inevitably accompanies it. The three facets – political, military and humanitarian which invariably constitute the pillars of international response to an emergency situation – must be integrated both structurally and temporally in a ratio proportional to the complexity and intensity of any given conflict.

It has often proved very hard to mobilise a comprehensive response. In complex emergencies of the post-Cold War era political leadership is perhaps the most important – yet often the most elusive – element in the successful interface of the different ingredients. In Bosnia, the UN operation was left abandoned in an open, high-intensity conflict situation, divorced from the protracted and timid search for political solutions and deprived of a resolute and cohesive political plan which should have provided it with clearer rules of engagement including, in particular, the credible threat of the use of force. No military or humanitarian operation can succeed without political resolve and direction.

The Canadian study on a rapid reaction capability force for the UN, which was presented to the General Assembly in September 1995, could help to meet some of the concerns outlined above. The study recommended a wide range of measures; but its key proposition was the establishment of a standing, rapidly deployable, operational-level head-quarters-planning cell which could form the nucleus of new peacekeeping operations. The objective of this cell would be to prepare several contingency plans so that once a mandate was obtained from the Security Council for a given operation, military and civilian resources could be deployed in the theatre, quickly and efficiently. The Canadian study was intended precisely to respond to appeals such as General Dallaire's in Rwanda.

What is significant for humanitarian agencies is that this cell is envisioned to be multifunctional. There would be civilian staff in the headquarters to plan for civil affairs contingencies, humanitarian affairs, human-rights-related issues and administrative matters as well as military concerns. Underlying this is a recognition of the insistence that a joint or integrated approach to an operation is critical at the planning stage, well before such challenges are faced on the ground. Peacekeeping operations are not an exclusively or predominantly military affair and one cannot ignore the civilian components described above in planning or training for a peacekeeping operation for the future.

Whatever the UN may be called upon to deploy tomorrow, all the relevant components and departments, whether from a military, political or humanitarian background, should have a comprehensive strategy in mind. With increased planning, coordination and an organised programme for prevention and early-warning, the UN can better meet the challenges of the future and reignite the vigour and enthusiasm of the early 1990s but in a manner better suited for the post-Cold War era.

NOTES

The views expressed in this article are those of the author and do not reflect the position of the United Nations.

1. Eric Morris, 'The Role of Peacekeeping Forces in Humanitarian Operations', Tokyo Seminar on *Legal Aspects of Peacekeeping Operations,* 19–23 February 1996.
2. Many states felt, however, that Security Council Resolution 688 would set a dangerous precedent that could open the way to diverting the Council away from its basic functions and responsibilities to safeguard international peace and security. China abstained, declaring at the time: 'this is a question of great complexity, because the internal affairs of a country are also involved. According to Paragraph 7 to Article 2 of the Charter, the Security Council should not consider or take action on questions concerning the internal affairs

of any State. As for the international aspects involved in the question, we are of view that they should be settled through the appropriate channels. We support the Secretary General in rendering humanitarian assistance to the refugees through the relevant organizations.' (UN Doc. S/PV.2982), pp. 55–6.

3. For further discussion of the 'safe areas' issue see Gordon, Ch. 13 in this volume.

4. Without UNPROFOR escorts and security provision in and around Saravejo airport UNHCR could not have established the airlift that nurtured the city, nor could it have kept up the convoys that penetrated through to other populations under siege in Central and Eastern Bosnia. But the senselessness of providing relief where there was no security, where shelling and sniper fire took their daily toll on those recently 'assisted', was all too apparent. At the height of the war a prominent French academic compared the provision of assistance to Saravejo to the handing out of sandwiches through the gates of Auschwitz.

5. It should be noted that recently Security Council member states have placed particular emphasis on the importance of Africa's capacity to respond quickly to crises, where the need and political will are the greatest.

6. USFY 98 State Department Authorization Bill.

8

Positioning Humanitarianism in War: Principles of Neutrality, Impartiality and Solidarity

HUGO SLIM

INTRODUCTION

In Dante's *Inferno* there is a special place of torment reserved for those who have been neutral in this life. Their sin is so particular that they do not even merit a space in Hell. Instead, they are confined to the outer part, or vestibule, of Hell and separated from the rest of the damned by the river Acheron. The precise sin of this group of people is that of indecision and vacillation. They have never made a stand for one thing or another in their life. True to form, Dante inflicts upon them a torment which neatly fits their crime. They are destined to rush forever behind a banner which 'whirls with aimless speed as though it would never take a stand', while at the same time being chased and stung by swarms of hornets.[1]

There may be many United Nations peacekeepers and relief workers who feel that they have already experienced the particular anguish of Dante's punishment. On many occasions the international humanitarian system might be accurately described by Dante's image: a great crowd of international agencies rushing frantically behind the whirling banner of international concern which seldom actually takes a definite stand by planting itself firmly in the ground. Indeed, the urgent and relentless flapping of UN and non-governmental organisation (NGO) flags from thousands of fast-moving white vehicles around the world today seems uncannily reminiscent of Dante's vision. And even if relief workers and peacekeepers have not yet experienced such hell, there are those today who might be tempted to think that such a fate should certainly await them when the day of reckoning arrives. African Rights, in particular, has made a severe critique of the 'neutralism' of humanitarianism and of what it considers to be the absurdity of current relief agency claims to humanitarian neutrality in political emergencies and war.[2] Yet in classical humanitarianism neutrality is prized as one of its essential operational principles.

So why has neutrality become a dirty word? Is it really a sin? Or do Dante and African Rights have a different understanding of the word from that of conventional humanitarian practitioners? Is neutrality inevitably unprincipled or is it, in fact, the operational means to highly principled ends? Is real humanitarian neutrality really impossible when any humanitarian action inevitably plays to the advantage of one side or another? A passionate debate now rages along these lines about the positioning of humanitarian agencies and peacekeeping forces. And as most relief agencies and UN forces alike abandon the idea of neutrality, they are clinging with renewed vigour to other traditional humanitarian principles such as humanity and impartiality, or going beyond traditional humanitarian principles by justifying their position in terms of solidarity or more nuanced interpretations of impartiality.

The debate surrounding humanitarian neutrality and its associated humanitarian principles is one about the position of third parties in other people's wars. Where should an international agency or a UN force stand in a violent dispute between several groups? As an aspect of peacekeeping, such humanitarian positioning is important for two reasons. First, because every peacekeeping force needs to establish its own position in any given conflict.[3] And, second, because it is essential that peacekeeping forces are able to interpret the positioning of the many civilian relief agencies operating in their area. Positions taken by such agencies may often have important repercussions on a peacekeeping force seeking to cooperate with a diverse group of civilian agencies. The issue of positioning not only concerns relief organisations and peacekeeping forces at a corporate level, but also at an individual level. In order to operate in the midst of war a UN force or a relief agency needs to make its organisational position in that conflict known to the combatants. But at a personal level it is also essential for morale that each individual has a strong sense of an individual position in relation to the violence around him or her. Playing a third-party role in the midst of violence and injustice is personally taxing, and is one of the greatest challenges facing soldiers and relief workers in today's emergencies. The ability to do so with a sense of moral conviction and international legality is crucial to the morale of relief worker and UN soldier alike.

The purpose of this chapter is to explore the difficulties of organisational positioning for international aid workers and UN peacekeepers operating as third parties in the midst of war. Both groups, UN soldiers and international aid workers, share a common third-party status in today's emergencies and both groups have worked hard to conceptualise and communicate this status for the benefit of their operational effectiveness. The chapter begins by identifying the essential problem of organisational positioning as that of locating humanitarian values within a context of organised inhumanity. The main part of the text then explores organisational positioning by examining the current usage of the terms humanity, neutrality, impartiality, solidarity and consent. The chapter then looks briefly at the morale implications for UN soldiers and relief workers of operating as non-combatant third parties in war. In particular, it examines their experience in terms of what I describe as 'bystander anxiety' with its simultaneous feelings of compassion, powerlessness, frustration, anger, fear and outright hostility. A final section recognises that a range of different positions is both inevitable and desirable in a given conflict. Behind the various reconfigurations of traditional humanitarian language lies a common desire by all civilian and military organisations to finesse humanitarian action with the ability to speak out or shoot out, while also maintaining immunity within the conflict. To combine all three objectives in a single position may often be extremely difficult. To do so without obscuring the language which traditionally conveys important humanitarian principles may be impossible. The chapter thus concludes by emphasising the responsibility on any third-party organisation (military or civilian) to be transparent in its position and to preserve rather than distort traditional humanitarian principles.

THIRD PARTIES AND HUMANITARIAN VALUES IN WAR

UN peacekeeping forces and relief agencies have problems with their identity and position within today's wars because they are trying to do something which is intrinsically difficult: they invariably find themselves trying to represent the values of humanity and peace within societies which are currently dominated by the values of inhumanity and violence. More often than not, therefore, they are swimming against the current of that society, or certainly of its leadership. They are representatives of values which are often seen as a threat by leaders and people committed to violence and war. If humanitarian values are given too much room in situations of war or political violence, political and military leaders fear that they might undermine the violent spirit of their followers or provide succour to their enemies. Nevertheless, it is part of the paradox of human nature that humanitarian values may be present in war and since time

127

immemorial have usually coexisted with violence to some degree.[4] Where there is organised violence there is often mercy too. But the intricacies of the Geneva Conventions which were put together after World War II show how even the most united and victorious military and political leaders prefer humanitarian values to be tightly circumscribed to prevent their becoming an excessive threat to the war effort.

The task of representing humane values to combatant parties will, therefore, always place a humanitarian third party in a difficult position. In most cases the values represented by the humanitarian or peacekeeper will be greeted with distinct ambivalence. They may be recognised and even strangely cherished in some quarters of the warring parties (many humanitarians have a story about a gentle warrior whose cooperation was critical to saving many lives), but they will also be treated with the utmost suspicion by crucial sections of any warring party and perceived as a threat to the violence they are embarked upon. In turn, the organisation and the individual who dares to represent the values of humanity in war will also be perceived as a threat. And, as we have seen in Somalia, Bosnia, Burundi, Chechnya and most recently in Rwanda, violent factions are not afraid to shoot the messenger who comes to represent such values in the midst of war.

While it has always been difficult to represent and position humanitarian values in war, the proliferation of relief and development agencies working in today's wars now seems to make that positioning even more difficult. One of the main reasons why humanitarian principles have been so difficult to clarify and affirm in the last five years must be because there are now so many different organisations trying to assert themselves as 'humanitarian'. The proliferation of NGOs in particular (which has been an inevitable consequence of Western donor policy in recent years) has led to wide differences in the ethical maturity and political sophistication of organisations all competing to work in the same emergency. Anyone surveying the swarm of NGOs delivering primarily governmental humanitarian assistance in many of today's emergencies would be unwise to accept them all as equally principled and professional. With so many organisations trying to establish a humanitarian position within today's wars, and with all of them using the same, tired, humanitarian language to do so, it is hardly surprising that the humanitarian position has become overcrowded, garbled and somewhat undignified.

So what concepts are relief agencies and UN forces now using to distinguish their third-party and humanitarian position in war? Many of the more mature relief agencies and experienced national military forces have done some hard thinking about the principles of their position and the nature of their stance in today's conflicts. But despite their commitment to such thinking, attempts at a real breakthrough in the development of an overarching principle for their position have remained in the doldrums. To a large degree this is because different agencies have different views on where they stand. As a result, the new NGO codes and principles still lack the kind of resounding clarity, brevity and irresistible persuasion which might impress militiamen at checkpoints or convince a beleaguered government enduring the attacks of a rebel army.[5] The established humanitarian principles and conventional language with which relief agencies and peacekeepers have traditionally been accustomed to formulate their humanitarian stance are sounding distinctly hollow. It is perhaps small wonder that the precise meaning of words such as impartiality has evaporated in a world where, in the same emergency, a Red Cross nurse can use the term to describe her medical programme and a UN commander can use the same word to describe air-strikes.

HUMANITY, NEUTRALITY AND IMPARTIALITY

Humanitarianism traditionally describes its position with the three key terms of 'humanity', 'neutrality' and 'impartiality'. These three guiding principles (which also herald the opening of UN General Assembly Resolution 46/182 (1991) which attempted to define humanitarian assistance in the 'New World Order' after the Cold War) are, of course, lifted straight from the top three of the Red Cross/Crescent movement's seven guiding principles as formalised in 1965.[6] Indeed, most humanitarian language which emerges from the mouths of NGOs and UN forces is, in fact, little more than the rebounding and frequently distorted echo of the language and principles of the Red Cross and the Red Crescent. These three ideals are currently being actively reaffirmed in various forms in an effort to make them work again for today's civil wars and for the new range of international third-party organisations which seek to find a role within these wars. The confusion seems to arise because different agencies are using the same language to describe different positions.

Minimal Humanity

The first principle, that of humanity, remains the least controversial, or at least the principle most easily retained by agencies and UN forces alike. The core of its Red Cross/Crescent definition is the desire *'to prevent and alleviate human suffering wherever it may be found ... to protect life and health and to ensure respect for the human being'*. A crucial point to note in this definition is that while humanitarianism is often caricatured as a purely physical pursuit, aimed only at saving life, the actual meaning of humanity transcends mere physical existence to embrace 'respect for the human being'. This phrase is essential as it extends to rights beyond the simple right to life (such as religious freedom or fair trial) which are clearly spelled out in the Geneva Conventions. As Pictet points out, the humanitarian ideal of the Red Cross/Crescent actually extends to a person's 'life, liberty and happiness – in other words everything which constitutes his existence'.[7]

One of the major complaints by NGOs and human-rights groups about the classical humanitarian position is that it does not embrace broader human-rights concerns. But such a view seems to be based on a misunderstanding of the principle of humanity and its development in the Geneva Conventions. To interpret humanitarianism as an essentially minimalist endeavour relating to simple human survival is a misreading of its first principle. The Geneva Conventions and their Additional Protocols are full of civil, social and economic rights as well as of rights relating to simple physical survival. Recognition of this fact has serious implications because, as we shall see, NGOs in particular seem to have convinced themselves that a humanitarian position and a human-rights position are somehow at odds with each other. This is obviously not the case – a truly humanitarian position on the plight of civilian populations in war as articulated in the IV Geneva Convention is firmly grounded in the full spectrum of human rights.

In humanitarian discourse today the principle of humanity thus remains central, but is being slightly but significantly distorted along minimalist lines. This is exemplified in some new language. Instead of the simple principle of humanity, most relief agencies have now adopted the more cumbersome (and perhaps sinister) term 'the humanitarian imperative'.[8] This is presumably in the hope that, by giving the principle of humanity an imperative gloss and making it unreservedly a moral absolute, the phrase will present humanitarianism as a non-negotiable, almost genetic and biological force, so always overriding the position of the warring factions. In addition, the humanitarian imperative usually seems to relate solely to 'humanitarian assistance' – a term which has come to describe that minimum package of relief *commodities* which donor governments are prepared to allow as emergency aid. As such, the new nuances of the term 'humanitarian imperative' contain two serious distortions of the principle of humanity.

First, very much in the Gallic humanitarian tradition, it gives humanitarianism a non-negotiable aspect.[9] This is at odds with the spirit of classical humanitarianism which has always recognised that it must negotiate its place in violence, assuming the right of human beings to wage

130

war but seeking to limit the effects of that war with the consent of the warring parties. The Geneva Conventions recognise that warring parties have rights as well as obligations in agreeing how humanitarianism should be realised in war.[10] By implying that the rights are all on the side of the relief agencies and the victims of war, current interpretations of 'the humanitarian imperative' may optimistically (and even illegally) imply the automatic presence of relief agencies in war and undermine the serious negotiation which needs to take place between warring leaders and humanitarians to ensure that humanitarian action is fair. In reality, unless it is delivered by force (as it increasingly is), humanitarianism will always be negotiable. Those who have experience of representing humanitarian values in war realise that they are usually pleading for a minority position and one which has to be nurtured rather than imposed.

Secondly, as it is currently framed, the notion of the humanitarian imperative over-identifies the concept of humanity with a minimal and essentially materialistic package of 'humanitarian assistance'. For example, in affirming that 'the humanitarian imperative comes first', the Code of Conduct states 'the right to receive humanitarian assistance, and to offer it, is a fundamental humanitarian principle which should be enjoyed by all citizens of all countries'. By speaking only of humanitarian assistance and not of humanitarian protection, this tends to restrict humanitarian concerns to relief commodities, so precluding many other vital aspects of the Geneva Conventions which relate to Pictet's notions of liberty and happiness. Without this idea of a full humanitarianism, humanitarian minimalism may actually limit the rights of those it seeks to help.

Finally, it is also worth noting that relief agencies and peacekeeping operations tend to be extremely selective about the many humanitarian 'imperatives' around the world. In an Orwellian fashion, it seems that all humanitarian crises are imperative but some are more imperative than others. The more imperative emergencies are, of course, usually determined by the *realpolitik* imperatives of relief agencies' donor governments, and by the financial, publicity or market imperatives of competing relief agencies. Thus behind the rhetoric there is an element of bluster and even hypocrisy when relief agencies talk about 'the humanitarian imperative'. Dropping the new term and reverting to the more extensive and more dignified original principle of humanity might be wise.

Abandoning Neutrality

Of the three classical principles which seek to underpin a humanitarian position, neutrality is the one from which most agencies and all military peacekeeping doctrine are in retreat. As suggested above, there is now a majority view that neutrality is either undesirable because it is equated with being unprincipled, or is simply unachievable in practice because relief aid is so frequently manipulated. However, the recent pariah status of neutrality in the humanitarian's lexicon seems to stem from a widespread misunderstanding of the term. As Denise Plattner has pointed out, although it is much talked about, there is no definition of neutral humanitarian assistance, and her 11 criteria go far in determining the parameters of what such a definition might encompass.[11]

In its strict sense, humanitarian neutrality is not the neutralism of Dante and African Rights. Truly neutral relief workers and peacemakers are not indifferent, unprincipled and vacillating creatures destined for the vestibule of Hell. On the contrary, they have a determined commitment to particular ideals. They have already taken a stand and for them neutrality is ultimately the operational means to achieve their humanitarian ideals within an environment which is essentially hostile to those ideals. For the International Committee of the Red Cross (ICRC) and for other relief agencies which choose such a position, neutrality is thus a pragmatic operational posture. Far from being unprincipled or amoral, it allows them to implement their ideals within the limits prescribed by international humanitarian law.

The Red Cross/Crescent definition of neutrality is enshrined in its third fundamental principle: '*In order to continue to enjoy the confidence of all, the Movement may not take sides in hostilities or engage at any time in controversies of a political, racial, religious or ideological nature.*' Within this principle, Pictet has emphasised the important distinction between military neutrality and ideological neutrality.[12] Being neutral means taking no part in military operations and no part in ideological battles either. Plattner deduces that the three key ingredients to a neutral position are abstention, prevention and impartiality. For an organisation, as for a state, abstention means no involvement in military or ideological activity. Prevention obliges that organisation to ensure that neither party is able to use the organisation to its advantage. Impartiality requires the organisation to apply equal terms to the warring parties in its dealings with them.[13] As such, Plattner concludes that 'neutrality may therefore be understood as a duty to abstain from any act which, in a conflict situation, might be interpreted as furthering the interests of one party to the conflict or jeopardising those of the other'.[14]

While perhaps approving of this definition in theory, seasoned peacekeepers and relief workers will, of course, seize quickly on the word 'interpreted'. As they know only too well, in the extremely contested atmosphere of war and political emergencies, the devil is in the interpretation of actions and events. Perception is everything and varies from

132

faction to faction in conditions where one group's legitimate relief is seen by another group as an obvious contribution to the war effort of the enemy. African Rights is thus correct in condemning the 'tendency to believe that neutrality need only be asserted to be proved'.[15] In reality, it has to be proved by rigorous adherence to abstention, prevention and impartiality, and by constant negotiation, thorough appraisal of the conditions of the respective parties and continual recourse to the precepts of the Geneva Conventions.

Apart from the Red Cross/Crescent movement which still rigorously upholds the concept, few other agencies still draw on the concept of neutrality to stake out their position in war. One determined exception is the UN Children's Emergency Fund (UNICEF) and its Operation Lifeline in South Sudan which has worked hard to draw up and disseminate a set of 'humanitarian principles'. In doing so it has firmly embraced the principle of neutrality: 'The guiding principle of Operation Lifeline is that of humanitarian neutrality – an independent status for humanitarian work beyond political or military considerations.'[16]

The many NGOs which have rejected the notion of neutrality have done so for two main reasons. First, as Plattner points out, they feel that it often imposes an unacceptable silence upon them in the face of grievous violations of human rights.[17] What Pictet has described as the inevitable 'reserve' required of the neutral[18] is considered to be too high a price to pay for NGOs which mandate themselves as advocates of human rights and social justice. Second, abiding by neutrality's commitment to prevention and abstention seems increasingly impracticable in the light of what we now know about the manipulation of relief supplies and the fact that combatants and civilians are intrinsically mixed in today's civil wars. For example, in the same article in which UNICEF argues for neutrality, the apparent paradox of its position is made clear. Within a matter of a few column inches it also eloquently makes the case as to why such neutrality is not so simple and is perceived by many as impossible to achieve in today's wars:

> The military are not a distinct group, separated from the civilian population, but are fathers, brothers, sons frequently returning to their homes. Clearly, in such circumstances, women and children who have received aid from OLS [Operation Lifeline Sudan] agencies are not going to refuse to feed their own family members.[19]

Despite these problems, UNICEF is one of the few agencies which is trying to keep and apply the principle of neutrality in its work. But while neutrality may be right for some organisations, it is certainly not right for all of them. Some are bound to find it offensive to the mandates they give themselves. Also, as African Rights points out, the majority of organisations will find that they simply do not have the means in terms of diplomatic and political contacts, finances or professional competence to negotiate and secure a rigorous position of neutrality in their relief work.[20] Nevertheless, these factors do not mean that neutrality in itself is not possible nor that it is an unprincipled means of operating. In the right hands and in pursuit of the right ideals recognised in international humanitarian law, neutrality is an extremely valuable principle. Relief agencies need to decide whether they are going to abide by it or not. If they are, they should skill-up accordingly. If they are not, they should not discredit the principle simply on the grounds that it is at odds with their own mandate and capabilities.

Few UN military forces use the concept of neutrality to describe their position as third parties in war and it would be inappropriate for them to do so. Plattner argues[21] that by bringing force into a situation – even an interpositioning or minimum peacekeeping force – they can no longer claim abstention from the conflict. Their appearance with force forfeits their military neutrality because by their presence and deployment they are automatically participating in and influencing the pattern of hostilities. This is particularly true when their force levels are such as to be genuinely coercive and means that any humanitarian assistance which is provided under such conditions cannot be described as truly neutral.

Embracing Impartiality

Because of their difficulties with neutrality most UN forces and NGOs alike have abandoned the concept and embraced its close relation 'impartiality'. The classical definition of impartiality from the Red Cross/ Crescent principles is that an organisation '*makes no discrimination as to nationality, race, religious beliefs, class or political opinions. It endeavours to relieve the suffering of individuals, being guided solely by their needs, and to give priority to the most urgent cases of distress.*' As Pictet[22] and others have pointed out, the principle of impartiality is therefore built on the twin pillars of non-discrimination of person and proportionality of need. In other words, the similarity of all people but the differences in their needs should at all times determine the judgements of the impartial humanitarian in the light of the objective precepts of humanitarian law.

The attraction of impartiality over neutrality for most UN forces and NGOs is that the concept permits the impartial person to be judgemental, albeit not gratuitously so but in line with agreed values. Pictet caricatures the difference between neutrality and impartiality thus: 'the neutral man refuses to make a judgement whereas the one who is impartial judges a situation in accordance with pre-established rules'.[23] Thus military peace-keeping doctrine and NGOs have pounced on the objectivity of imparti-ality and its potential for being judgemental. For advocacy-driven NGOs and robust peacekeepers alike, impartiality seems to offer the most scope for justifying a strategy of speaking out or shooting out while also main-taining humanitarian values. And consequently a more nuanced notion of impartiality is emerging which involves a hardening of the principle of impartiality into a more robust principle determining punishment and sanction as well as relief. This new form of impartiality in military doctrine inevitably allows for more forceful peacekeeping action while prizing even-handedness in any response.[24] It is, therefore, determinedly not neutral and abstentionist. Military action will be taken against people or groups on the basis of what they do but not on the basis of who they are. Impartiality in this harder form rejects the idea of abstention in the face of human-rights abuses and might therefore be summed up as impartiality to persons but partiality to their actions.

LEANING TOWARDS SOLIDARITY

There is a fourth concept gaining increasing currency within debates about humanitarian positioning, that of 'solidarity'. This represents the stance of those who wish to abandon both neutrality and impartiality, arguing that in many political emergencies and wars the notion of solidarity might be the most appropriate guiding principle around which UN forces and relief agencies could align their operational position. In its paper *Humanitarianism Unbound*, African Rights states that: 'It is arguable that solidarity is the most important principle of all', adding that 'what solidarity operations have in common is a political goal shared with the people'.[25] It defines 'genuine solidarity in relief work' as including four main components:

> 1. Human rights objectivity and the pursuit of justice. This means a commitment to pursuing an agenda based on a set of rights.
> 2. Consultation with and accountability to the people with whom solidarity is expressed. 3. Shared risk and suffering with the people.
> 4. Concrete action in support of the people and their cause. This may include providing relief and/or political or human rights lobby and advocacy.[26]

The idea of solidarity obviously involves taking sides. Such a concept may be anathema to many people who give to and work for NGOs and it is certainly in opposition to classical humanitarian and peacekeeping principles. But there is an important tradition of taking sides in both Christian moral theology and development work based on social justice. Albert Nolan, a Dominican veteran of the South African liberation struggle, is a leading advocate of this position:

> In some conflicts one side is right and the other side is wrong ... In such cases a policy of seeking consensus and not taking sides would be quite wrong. Christians are not supposed to try and reconcile good and evil, justice and injustice; we are supposed to do away with evil, injustice and sin.[27]

Such a solidarity-based approach is obviously easier when the sides are clearly drawn, when right and wrong are as distinct as night and day, and when the wronged can be easily identified from the wrong. But such clarity is not always the case in today's internal wars and the principle of solidarity can seldom be applied with confidence in many conflicts. Solidarity is a principle which was right for those who backed long (and often non-violent) resistance movements such as the civil-rights movement in the USA or the liberation movements in South Africa and Eastern Europe. It is also one which should always be actively applied in genocide, as in Rwanda. But in wars such as those in Somalia, Liberia, Sierra Leone and even Former Yugoslavia, the good sides are not so clear. At a practical level, the application of solidarity faces problems too. The tenuous nature of the chain of command in today's wars may compromise the principle of taking sides. Leaders often have little control over those who carry out atrocities in their name (whether intentionally or unintentionally), meaning that solidarity may all too easily become solidarity with excessive and uncoordinated violence.

In an attempt to avoid these pitfalls, a certain part of humanitarian discourse has adapted the notion of solidarity and claimed solidarity, not with those who are 'right', but with those who are somehow regarded as 'innocent'. In this analysis (which might be called innocence-based solidarity) the lowest common denominator of innocence is usually drawn along lines of sex and age. So women, children and the elderly are stereotyped as the innocent and as 'vulnerable groups' who merit the solidarity of relief agencies. But as the quotation above from UNICEF makes clear, such a position is often over-simple and ill-informed. This kind of innocence-based solidarity is thus equally precarious as a general principle of humanitarian action. And Levine's lament about current humanitarian action is apt when one considers the conflict between classical humanitarianism and its detractors: 'we have not worked out what it means to be neutral in a conflict yet in solidarity with all its victims'.[28] On the one hand, ICRC would claim that this is something it has worked out years ago, while Duffield and African Rights would probably claim that such a position is both undesirable and impossible.

ORGANISATIONAL POSITIONING AND PERSONAL MORALE

Beyond the desire to clarify humanitarian principles, there is another reason why a clear sense of the positioning of third-party organisations in war is so important: its effect on staff morale. Being a third party to the wanton cruelty and violence in so many of today's civil wars is personally testing for individual UN soldiers and relief workers. Even with the clearest sense of purpose, an individual may feel all the recriminations of being a bystander in the face of appalling atrocities. Experiencing the violence and destruction around them in places such as Rwanda, Bosnia and Liberia, it is usual for most relief workers and UN soldiers to go through a gamut of emotions which range from pity and compassion through powerlessness, frustration and fear, to anger and outright hostility to all concerned.[29] It is common for several of these emotions to be experienced simultaneously in an individual. It seems equally common for individuals to swing from one end of the spectrum to another at different intervals. At the hostile end of the spectrum it becomes common to stereotype a whole people as somehow deranged and subhuman.

Humanitarians seldom do anything obvious to stop the causes of the violence around them. They are usually palliative in their impact, at best becoming some small beacon of alternative humane values in the midst of inhumanity. Because of their frequent inability to stop the violence around them, many humanitarians and peacekeepers have to deal with what might be termed 'bystander anxiety'. In the mass of literature which has sought to analyse the Jewish holocaust of World War II, the word bystander has emerged as one of the most damning.[30] It is this bystander anxiety which perhaps underlies the concerns of NGOs in particular to be dissatisfied with classical humanitarianism and move towards notions of active impartiality and solidarity. Although not necessarily the case, public silence is feared as the hallmark of the bystander and so advocacy becomes all important to NGOs.[31]

In such a context it becomes extremely important for soldiers and relief workers to know where their particular organisation stands and what position it is taking as a third party. Their own personal contribution must make sense as an active one within the violence around them, and such activity must be clearly explained in terms of whichever principle – neutrality, impartiality or solidarity – their organisation has chosen to pursue. In this way, the individual can interpret his or her role within the violence beyond that of a bystander, consciously countering the invidious feelings of bystander anxiety with a definite vision and understanding of his or her position.

BEHIND THE WORDS

To sum up, the semantic manoeuvring around humanitarian principles which currently preoccupies humanitarian and military policymakers alike is symptomatic of the confusion arising from so many different types of third-party organisation seeking to clarify their position in political emergencies and war today. Not surprisingly, however, the disparate nuancing of classical humanitarian language creates something of a cacophony and has not yet given the humanitarian community a decisive moral banner under which to go about its business. Indeed, with so many different organisations now involved in and around humanitarianism it is doubtful whether any single banner can now be found. The result is that the notions of humanity, neutrality and impartiality, which traditionally underpinned classical humanitarianism, are being stretched or abandoned and so risk being undermined in a process in which they come to mean different things to different people.

With so many agencies (civilian and military) now operating in and around humanitarian programmes, a range of positions from classical neutrality to solidarity is to be expected and even desired in any given emergency. But there is a responsibility on every agency to make its own position clear. For the sake of the credibility of the important principles involved, a UN force or relief agency must seek to clarify the humanitarian terms it uses and the principles to which they refer, so preserving their legitimacy and the effectiveness of humanitarian principles in war. Failing to be transparent by draping one position in the language of another would indeed merit a place in Dante's Hell, for deception if not for neutralism.

NOTES

1. Dante, *The Divine Comedy: The Inferno* (Harmondsworth: Penguin, 1984), Canto 3, lines 53–4. Translated by Mark Musa.
2. African Rights, *Humanitarianism Unbound* (London: African Rights, November 1994), pp. 24–8.

3. It seems appropriate to talk of the humanitarian positioning of peacekeeping forces when the objectives and mandates of such forces are frequently drawn up in humanitarian terms by the Security Council.
4. See Jean Guillermand, 'The Historical Foundations of Humanitarian Action, Part I. The Religious Influence', *International Review of the Red Cross*, No. 298, 1994.
5. See, for example, the Code of Conduct for the Red Cross Movement and NGOs in Disaster Relief (Geneva 1994); the Providence Principles from Brown University (1991); and the Mohonk Criteria for Humanitarian Assistance in Complex Emergencies, World Conference on Religion and Peace (1994).
6. The seven fundamental principles of the Red Cross/Crescent movement were proclaimed by the 20th International Conference of the Red Cross in Vienna 1965. They are humanity, impartiality, neutrality, independence, voluntary service, unity and universality.
7. J. Pictet, *The Fundamental Principles of the Red Cross: A Commentary* (Geneva, Henri Dunant Institute, 1979), p. 26.
8. See, for example, the Code of Conduct for the Red Cross Movement and NGOs in Disaster Relief.
9. Gallic thinking on humanitarianism has tended to be particularly strident in recent decades, evolving around the notion of '*sans frontièreism*' and its conviction in the '*droit d'ingérence*'. While such robust relief ideology has its place alongside military intervention, it lacks a certain subtlety in situations where forceful intervention is not available or not necessary and where negotiation is inevitable and desirable.
10. See, for example, Article 23, IV Geneva Convention.
11. Denise Plattner, 'ICRC Neutrality and Neutrality in Humanitarian Assistance', *International Review of the Red Cross*, No. 311, 1996.
12. Pictet, *The Fundamental Principles*, pp. 54–9.
13. Plattner, 'ICRC Neutrality', p. 164.
14. Ibid., p. 165.
15. African Rights, *Humanitarianism Unbound*, p. 24.
16. Iain Levine, 'Sudan: In Pursuit of Humanitarian Neutrality, Aid Under Fire', *Issues in Focus Series*, No. 1 (Geneva: UNDHA, 1995).
17. Plattner, 'ICRC Neutrality', pp. 169–70.
18. Pictet, *The Fundamental Principles*, p. 53.
19. Levine, 'Sudan: In pursuit of Humanitarian Neutrality'.
20. African Rights, *Humanitarianism Unbound*, p. 24.
21. Plattner, 'ICRC Neutrality', pp. 177–8.
22. Pictet, *The Fundamental Principles*, pp. 37–43.
23. Ibid., p. 53.
24. See, for example, British Army (1998), *Peace Support Operations*, Joint Warfare Publication 3-01, Ratification Draft.
25. African Rights, *Humanitarianism Unbound*, pp. 26–7.
26. Ibid., p. 27.
27. Albert Nolan, *Taking Sides* (London: Catholic Institute for International Relations, 1984), p. 5.
28. Iain Levine, 'Humanitarianism and Humanity', *DHA News*, 19 (Geneva, August 1996).
29. My recent interviews with returned British peacekeepers and civilian-aid

agency staff illustrate this range of emotions in aid workers and peacekeepers alike.

30. See, for example, Raul Hilberg, *Perpetrators, Victims and Bystanders: The Jewish Catastrophe 1933–45* (London: Lime Tree, 1993).
31. Effective action is not always to be equated with speaking out. Much can be achieved in silence. Indeed, discretion and secrecy may be the optimal strategy in many situations.

9

Understanding, Promoting and Evaluating Coordination: An Outline Framework

KOENRAAD VAN BRABANT

INTRODUCTION

The coordination of international intervention in conflicts is an old sore. Although nobody is in principle against coordination, in practice efforts to achieve coordinated action lead to irritation and frustration. Coordination efforts can quickly provoke institutional 'turf' wars. The discussion about coordination then degenerates into one of power and authority. If successful coordination then still occurs, this is mainly because of 'personal chemistry' and 'leadership', the ingredients that analysts consistently identify as the key factors.[1] However, another reason why discussions about coordination remain frustrating is that it is often not clear what is understood by the term; in effect, there is no common frame of reference. This also makes it difficult to evaluate coordination.[2]

The so-called 'international humanitarian system' is not a 'system'. It is an arena with a complex array of institutional actors which come together in varying and dynamic configurations in different settings. Much has been written about coordination between different 'sub-groupings' of the humanitarian world. There is a rich, but poorly analysed and disseminated experience of non-governmental organisation (NGO) coordination. However, there is a developing experience and doctrine of civil–military collaboration or coordination. Similarly, there is a rapidly growing body of documented experience and ongoing debate about coordination in the United Nations.[3] Despite this, there is only a little documented experience of donor coordination, and even less of the coordination of humanitarian action by national governments. However, rather than take the institutional entry-point into an analysis of co-ordination, this chapter starts from the premises that the conflicts that are the object of international intervention are dynamic, and that coordination is not an end in itself but an attempt to enhance the quality and impact of the international intervention in and on these conflicts. The concept of coordination also encompasses many things: such as integrated planning, common standards and common positioning. It also includes several aspects which are less sharply delineated, working in ways that are less exclusive, more 'orchestrated' and 'convergent', 'coherent' and 'informed of and by each other'. Conflicts, the responses to them and the impacts of these responses, are fluid; they evolve and change. 'Coordination', therefore, is an ongoing activity, a process, rather than, as has often been the case, a 'blueprint'.

This chapter establishes an analytical framework. It is a means of focusing debate as well as serving as a tactical guide for those wanting to strengthen the coordination efforts. Similarly it provides a frame of reference in order to evaluate the effectiveness of coordination practices. The chapter has six major sections. The first identifies three interlocking levels of the coordination of conflict interventions; the second provides a critical review of common objections and of institutional obstacles to coordination. The third discusses a range of functions that a coordinating process at field level may perform. It explores which functions are taken up and which not, in an effort to determine whether the coordination effort remains fairly 'hollow' (agency-oriented) or becomes more 'substantive' (task- and target-oriented).[4] The fourth section addresses the issue of coordinating action which is designed to facilitate the creation of humanitarian space, while the fifth section deals with coordination that is designed to facilitate conflict management. The final section identifies the, still elusive, 'strategic coordination' as one of the major challenges facing the humanitarian community.

THE LEVELS OF COORDINATION OF HUMANITARIAN INTERVENTIONS IN CONFLICT

This section examines the coordination of conflict interventions from a humanitarian perspective; yet it is clear that 'humanitarian objectives cannot be separated from the issue of conflict resolution'.[5] Humanitarian action in conflict must be related to action *on* conflict. Nevertheless, conflict interventions take place at different levels and for different purposes, and it seems useful to distinguish these and the coordination that is required at each.

At field level, the level where 'operations' take place, there are the humanitarian assistance programmes provided by a wide range of actors. These require programmatic coordination. At the other end of the scale there are the political attempts to bring the violence and the conflict to an end. Conventional wisdom holds that international efforts to effect this stand an improved chance of being 'successful' if they are 'coordinated'. The humanitarian agencies on the ground, in order to realise their programmes of assistance and protection, require what could be described as 'humanitarian space'. The nature and the scope of that space, however, is not determined by them but by the effective power brokers on the ground. It is from them that a 'framework of consent'[6] needs to be obtained. However, these power brokers first and foremost have their own political and military agendas. The assumption, therefore, is that humanitarian agencies will improve their chances of obtaining more consent, or enlarge the available humanitarian space, if their negotiation efforts are orchestrated.

'Humanitarian space' is not an abstract notion. It is related to concrete assistance and protection efforts. Assistance and protection cannot be provided without a certain amount of humanitarian space, but that space needs to be sustained through the responsible provision of assistance and protection. Programmes and consent are therefore interlocked. Ultimately, however, the only power of aid agencies is that of moral authority and argument. They, therefore, may require support from the international political actors, through pressure or through incentives, to convince the power brokers in the conflict to provide more humanitarian space. It is on the issue of humanitarian space then that the political and assistance strategies (should) 'meet', a meeting that needs to be 'coordinated'.[7]

TABLE 9.1. Humanitarian Space 'Meeting' Political and Assistance Strategies

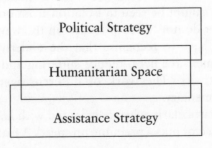

143

OBJECTIONS AND OBSTACLES TO OPERATIONAL
COORDINATION

More effective operations and more humanitarian space for aid providers and civilians alike seem eminently pursuable aims. Why does this unity of purpose then not lead to greater support for collaboration and coordinated approaches? Those trying to promote and facilitate coordination will have to face a range of objections to it, and part of their task will be to provide convincing arguments that can overcome these. This is something that is largely within their control. At the same time, the humanitarian world operates in ways that offer strong disincentives to those considering more effective coordination. These make field-level coordination difficult and need to be addressed at higher organisational levels but, above all else, also by donors.

There are a variety of systemic, or structural, obstacles to effective coordination. The humanitarian sector is a rather saturated market where implementing agencies are competing for limited funds. The visibility of the individual agency is seen as a key element in ensuring its long-term financial survival. This competition unfortunately also extends, to a degree, to official aid donors. Yet it seems not totally outlandish to believe that the excesses of what has become unhealthy competition can be tempered by a greater emphasis on 'profile' rather than 'visibility'; that is, an agency's 'reputation' for professionalism rather than a surplus of publicity. Donors can create incentives for collaborative work and co-ordinated action by providing what amount to financial rewards. Donors and agencies alike in their communications to 'audiences at home' can offer positive messages about collaboration.

Similarly, 'mandate' issues are often overemphasised by humanitarian actors. This usually smacks of overt organisational self-interest, with little regard for the interests of the intended beneficiaries. Fundamentally, humanitarian agencies do not have different mandates. They may specialise in certain sectors or focus on different target groups, such as children, refugees or mine victims, but it is obvious that population categories and sectoral assistance cannot be seen in isolation from one another. People afflicted by disaster do not 'slice up reality' in the way that aid agencies tend to. Agencies have to recognise that the underlying humanitarian mandate is the same: save lives, reduce suffering and try to protect or restore local capacities. The work of different agencies is therefore inherently complementary.

Furthermore, particularly when confronted with an acute emergency, the humanitarian sector puts a premium on speed. A fear arises, therefore, that the coordination efforts will generate delays.[8] The point is not that this argument is without substance, but that it applies only in a minority of circumstances. Many crises become protracted, so that the most effective response is not necessarily the speediest one.

There is also institutional resistance to the creating of yet another layer of bureaucracy. If coordination attempts are indeed so unprofessional and ineffective as to be nothing more than 'bureaucracy', then they are indeed wasteful. Yet at the same time few would fail to recognise that unco-ordinated work also creates much wastage and unfilled 'gaps' in terms of assistance. The reservation therefore does not seem to be against coordination *per se*, but against ineffective coordination. The challenge then becomes one to render coordination mechanisms and processes effective.

Coordination has a cost. It is time- and therefore staff-intensive. It also needs to be properly resourced and this imposes a financial burden. The difficulty is that while such 'overheads' are obvious and quantifiable, 'wastage and duplication avoided' through coordination do not show up in the books. Consequently, it is difficult to demonstrate that the co-ordination effort, even from a financial perspective, has provided value and 'cost-saving'. However, given that the same senior managers who object to inter-agency coordination probably see it as an important aspect of their internal management responsibilities, the stumbling block may in reality be more a desire to retain 'authority' rather than a concern over 'cost'.

Furthermore, there is a rather strange, although quite common, belief that coordination complicates accountability. While it may be true that where resources are pooled in a coordinated effort it may become more difficult to trace the end-use of specific funds and donations, this leads to a rather distorted concept of 'accountability'. Ultimately aid funds are provided to bring assistance. There cannot therefore only be accounta-bility upwards to the financial auditor; there has to be accountability in terms of the effectiveness of the work and its impact upon the recipients. Financial accountability cannot be limited to the figures that appear in the accounts. Consequently 'wastage', as a result of unnecessary dupli-cation of efforts, even if it does not appear in an agency's formal accounts, is no less a management failure.

However, few organisations have clear policy declarations which place an importance on the active pursuit of collaboration and coordination efforts. Few, if any, agencies even describe such objectives in the job descriptions of agency field representatives. As a consequence, the attitude of an agency towards coordination efforts is left entirely to the whim of individuals and, perhaps more importantly, may change as the individuals change. This is both irresponsible and unprofessional and needs to be corrected at the level of agency policy.

Familiarity with the purposes and mechanisms of coordination is generally lacking in the professional knowledge of many aid workers. The result is that an individual from a particular agency located in one country may be acting as a major opponent of coordination, while the same agency in another country is taking the lead. Even where agencies have formally signed up to a coordination protocol, field representatives tend to be totally unaware of this.[9] Basic knowledge about inter-agency coordination should become as much a part of the 'general knowledge' of managers as the basics of personnel management. However, there is an obvious risk in the humanitarian world that organisational self-interest predominates over the interests of the beneficiaries and private donors. This conflicts with agencies' proclaimed humanitarian ethos and principles and should therefore be exposed and confronted.

THE COORDINATOR: OPERATIONAL COORDINATION

If the effectiveness of coordination efforts is so reliant upon the persuasiveness of an individual, what then are the desirable qualities of a good coordinator? If intellectual leadership is a hallmark, then the person will adopt a 'coordination by argument' rather than 'coordination by authority' approach. This will require a thorough understanding of the situation, of different perceptions of it, and of the organisational incentives that work against more coordinated action. The challenge will be to show leadership in identifying the topical agenda issues, to offer the most convincing analysis, to raise the key questions and to take a lead in exploring what might be the best possible way of responding to them.[10]

A crucial characteristic of an effective coordinator is the ability to run effective meetings. Few things in the humanitarian sector are quite as prevalent, yet motivation-killing, as ineffective meetings. Consequently, to prepare a meeting properly, ensuring that the right people attend, and managing it effectively in order to produce results, is a key skill. To a degree this requires a certain type of personality and, to a degree, this skill can be learned or developed. Beyond that, coordination facilitators need to possess relevant knowledge about and experience of coordination if they are, themselves, to demonstrate effective coordination skills. They need to have an understanding of the mandates, cultures and operational practices of the variety of actors whose work needs to be coordinated. They will definitely benefit from having knowledge about other aid coordination experiences. Where decision-makers arrive in theatre without experience or knowledge of the benefits of coordination it may be necessary for others to provide information to this effect.

The aims and rationale for operational coordination are straightforward: similar standards of quality, the cost-effective use of resources, the rational allocation of tasks, a working towards agreed priorities, all of which will improve the impact of humanitarian assistance. As such, operational collaboration, or coordination, covers the various moments of the project cycle: assessment of needs; programme planning (including the prioritisation of target groups, areas and sectors and the allocation of tasks); resource mobilisation and allocation (and implementation to avoid duplication but also to avoid gaps); optimising the use of the available logistics and communications; and monitoring and evaluating the impact of the programmes on the existing needs and capacities of the target populations. It should also include the concentration of efforts to strengthen local capacities.

An examination of who holds authority to conduct the coordinating function is largely beyond the scope of this chapter, although in practice it is extremely relevant. Disputes over this issue also seriously distract attention from the question of what can be done to make the coordination function most effective. Table 2 provides an overview of the possible functions that a coordinating forum of aid agencies can fulfil. The horizontal axis presents a continuum from service to members-oriented functions, through information-focused functions, to task- and target-group oriented functions. The vertical axis represents the degree of controversy of the function for the participants in the coordination forum. The assumption is that the more task- and target-oriented the function becomes, the more substantive, but probably also the more controversial, it will be. However, the very act of strengthening coordination is to render it more substantive.

A key function is the provision of a contact point to facilitate information flows and situation updates. These are often the classical core of coordinating entities. However, such structures may also provide support services (relating to training and legal and administrative requirements) to members/participants in the coordination forum. Other potential functions are more task-oriented and concern programming, political analysis, representation and strategic decision-making.

The diagram is both a tool and a guide. For example, those wanting to promote better coordination may conduct a participatory mapping exercise in order to determine how controversial certain functions are perceived to be. If there is a high level of unease among aid agencies it may be tactically wise first to build trust and cooperation by starting with some less controversial functions before moving into the more controversial domains.

147

TABLE 9.2. Field-level Coordination

MEMBER-ORIENTED FUNCTIONS	INFORMATION-FOCUSED FUNCTIONS	TASK AND TARGET-ORIENTED FUNCTIONS
SERVICES	CONTACT POINT OF AID COMMUNITY	POLITICAL ANALYSIS
Registration		Agendas
Tax & labour laws		Scenarios
Documentation centre		
	SITUATIONAL UPDATES	PROGRAMMING
	Needs assessments	Project database
	Political developments	Sectoral standards
	Agency plans	Collective planning
	Resource flows	
	SECURITY	COLLECTIVE REPRESENTATION
	Security updates	Common appeals for funds
	Technical support	Collective positioning &
	Coordination contingency management	negotiations for consent
	Incident analysis	
TRAINING	LEARNING	STRATEGIC MANAGEMENT
Training inventory	Report collection	Common programming
Standardise curricula	Thematic networking	Strategic monitoring
Training provision	Review discussions	Vetting of agencies
	Evaluations	Discipline renegade
		Fund control

Degree of controversy over function

Possible functions fulfilled by coordinating forum of aid agencies

It is important to note that each function may encompass several activities that themselves have different degrees of controversy. The agencies may, for example, welcome an inventory of training on offer, but be more hesitant when the coordinating entity tries to facilitate the standardisation of training programmes. For the coordinating entity itself to become a training provider may be highly controversial, certainly if there are training providers among the participating agencies. As regards security, technical support particularly on communications and security updates are likely to be welcomed. However, for a coordinating entity to get involved in the investigation of a security incident, let alone to assume a stronger role in the coordination of the security strategies of several agencies, would be much more controversial. An underexplored area of activity is the potential for coordinating forums to foster learning through inter-agency information exchanges on programmes. Sectoral task forces could be developed into 'thematic' learning groups. In order for this to be accomplished a climate would have to be created whereby critical review is no longer perceived as threatening. The coordinating forum could become, ideally, the central repository of reviews and evaluations, a locus of inter-agency learning and a forum for critical but constructive discussion of programme approaches. The developing of a perception of review and evaluation as non-threatening would need to come first. However, the direct commissioning of reviews and evaluations by the coordinating authority would, again, be highly controversial.

Very task- and target-oriented, but highly controversial, is strategic or integrated common programming. This would involve, in its most developed form, the identification of priority work, the screening and vetting of aid agencies for work in a particular area and the allocation of tasks and resources among several agencies. Ideally, but not inevitably, this would require a pooling of financial resources even if the coordinating entity itself does not need to be in a position of authority over the control of funds. The closest approximation to this ideal of common programming is the assistance strategy to Afghanistan. Efforts have been made for a coordinating body, the Afghanistan Programming Body, to oversee the entire assistance strategy. This body comprises representation from donors, UN agencies, NGOs and the Red Cross. Interestingly, the official donors themselves have objected to the pooling of resources in a trust fund. As already mentioned, however, operational coordination of assistance and protection efforts in conflict situations cannot be totally separated from the search for humanitarian space. The effectiveness of humanitarian operations is strongly influenced by the humanitarian space that belligerents allow and the degree of political support that can be mobilised to secure and broaden this space. At the same time, the credibility of those demanding humanitarian space also depends on the capacity then to deliver the promised assistance.[11]

There seems to be a role therefore for a coordination forum to bring the aid and protection agencies together in order to develop common political and economic analyses and to orchestrate 'humanitarian diplomacy' and negotiations with power brokers. Such a forum would address issues such as what do the agencies request and from whom, what negotiation strategy and tactics should they pursue, and is collective representation possible? Such a role is indeed recognised in the terms of reference of the Office for the Coordination of Humanitarian Affairs, but rarely in the field-based coordination forums, although it is primarily at field level that humanitarian space is negotiated.[12]

COORDINATING FOR HUMANITARIAN SPACE

Humanitarian space is ultimately determined by the warring parties. The assumption is that the chances to obtain or to enlarge the space will be increased if the humanitarian agencies negotiate collectively rather than individually.

Before a concerted approach to the power brokers of the conflict can be considered, there has to be some clarity as to what 'humanitarian space' means in practical terms. Furthermore, the extent to which individual agencies feel comfortable with strategies and tactics being proposed within a given coordination structure needs to be identified. These discussions often tend to become confused. Consequently, this section endeavours to indicate some considerations that might help to foster greater clarity.

First, we need to discuss what we mean by humanitarian space. What is it that we want to negotiate or exercise pressure for? The most common understanding of it among aid agencies is unrestricted access.[13] This implies that they have full freedom of movement and operation and can make their own independent needs assessment. Another possible understanding of it is that the belligerents fight in line with the regulations of international humanitarian law, under which the integrity of civilians, non-combatants and aid workers needs to be protected and non-military targets avoided. That is clearly the line of the International Committee of the Red Cross (ICRC). Note needs to be taken, however, that international humanitarian law recognises the concerns of the belligerents and that these may lead to a restriction of access. A third possible understanding is that of a real, geographical space which is protected from fighting. Softer expressions of this are the notions of 'zones of tranquillity', 'humanitarian corridors' and 'safe areas', while a 'safe haven' has a more assertive tone to it.[14] Presumably civilians, aid workers and peacekeepers are protected in such spaces. The risk is, of course, that the warring parties assume that they no longer have the obligation to respect and protect civilians outside the now delineated 'humanitarian space'.

A second area for discussion and clarification is that of the meaning of humanitarian space for civilians. Aid agencies normally agree about access and security for their resources and personnel, but tend to react differently over the issue of the protection of civilian populations. This is because it is seen as leading to human-rights work with a potentially confrontational style and dangerous consequences in terms of the relationships with the power brokers. There is general agreement that the physical integrity of civilians needs to be respected. But does one take a stance, and with what arguments, when civilian populations are forcibly displaced? Can their livelihoods be destroyed, houses shelled and crops burned? Can civilians be used as forced labour or forced into sexual services? Coordinating the negotiations among the humanitarian community appears to require that, first, consensus is achieved on the nature of the 'humanitarian space' which will be pressed for.

Furthermore, what does an agency consider within its realm of responsibility? What guidance do headquarters offer to the field representatives? Table 3 is a possible tool to try and structure the discussion at the level of principle and mandate. One possible interpretation of the 'humanitarian' mandate is that it responds to unmet needs. This is a widespread inter-

TABLE 9.3. Humanitarian Space

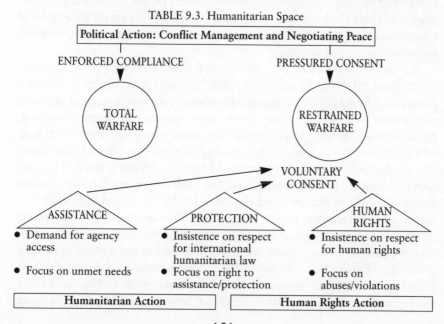

151

pretation which has led to a strong emphasis on humanitarian 'assistance' through the supply of goods and services and based on 'needs assessments'. A somewhat stronger, more political, argument asserts that people afflicted by conflict have a right to assistance. Therefore the national government, for example, even in a civil war, has an obligation to recognise and honour basic entitlements. If it cannot itself do so, or does not want to, then it or other warring factions should allow aid agencies to provide assistance. The right-to-assistance argument therefore supports a demand for access.

Such arguments may also be used against donor governments in order to encourage a greater allocation of aid funds. Such a right of assistance focuses upon broad social and economic rights. From there, then, it appears a logical step to move towards an even broader 'protection agenda'. While this may be logical, it is often resisted by 'relief' agencies as it brings them into the realm of civil and political rights (the classical 'human rights' agenda) which warring parties tend to perceive as 'political advocacy' and therefore no longer 'neutral'.

Such hesitations are also noticeable among the political actors. For example, although Kosovo is recognised as a political problem for which a political solution needs to be found, the international political actors have always been careful to describe the destruction of Kosovar villages and livelihoods as a 'humanitarian' rather than as a 'human rights' crisis. However, there is a framework of humanitarian law that provides guidance for such difficulties: international humanitarian law. This is supported by other legal instruments: refugee law, the Convention on the Rights of the Child, the Convention for the Elimination of all Forms of Discrimination against Women and more recently the 'guidelines for internally displaced people'.

Despite their existence, beyond the ICRC, the UN High Commissioner for Refugees (UNHCR) and the United Nations International Children's Emergency Fund (UNICEF), many members of humanitarian aid agencies are rather unfamiliar with these instruments. As a consequence, humanitarian agencies in particular have been investing efforts in articulating 'codes of conduct'.[15] The primary aim of these is to bring about some coherence in the behaviour of aid agencies on the ground. They are also instruments for self-regulation. Two codes in particular, the Ground Rules in southern Sudan[16] and the code for Sierra Leone, aspire also to influence the behaviour of warring parties. What seems missing, however, is a broader knowledge of the more formalised legal codes and instruments and their more regular use in the formulation of agency operating principles. This lack of familiarity, for example, hampered the articulation of a clear inter-agency position towards the government of Sri Lanka and the leadership of the Liberation Tigers of Tamil Eelam (LTTE), following the displacement of the population of Jaffna town (autumn 1995) and increased restrictions on humanitarian access.[17] By contrast, a common humanitarian policy grounded in humanitarian law was developed with regard to the *camps de regroupement* in Burundi.[18]

An additional policy question is whether an agency sees it as within its mandate to address the political and military strategies of the warring parties. This is not simply a theoretical question. It has profound implications for one's analytical perspective, for the position adopted by an agency and for the nature of its advocacy. It is one thing, for example, to denounce the death of civilians in an air-raid by the Sri Lankan airforce (an 'incident'), but another to inquire whether indiscriminate bombing is part of the military strategy of the government. Similarly, it is one thing to consider the rapid displacement of the Jaffna population in autumn 1995 as a 'potential humanitarian crisis', but another to inquire whether it was not part and parcel of the military and political strategy of the LTTE. Finally, there is the question of the so-called 'root causes' of conflict and whether an agency considers it within its mandate to address these. The ICRC, for example, does not. With 'root causes' we understand the historical politics of inclusion and exclusion, of patronage, humiliation, repression and impoverishment that have finally spilled over into organised violence. Including this in one's mandate implies engaging with the questions of justice, good governance and 'democratisation'. As we progress in this reflection, we move from 'needs' to 'rights', from the 'immediate' to the 'longer-term', from the 'micro-' to the 'macro-' level and from working *in* conflict to working *on* conflict.

At each step, an agency may wish to decide the nature of its engagement. It can consider certain of the steps described above as outside its mandate or it can choose to recognise them and include the full picture in its analysis, but to limit its actions and advocacy to certain components or levels. Or it can choose to 'act', practically or through advocacy, on all aspects of the conflict. One problem is that few agencies seem to have clear policies on this and, even among those that do, individual representatives often appear to turn their own personal judgement or preference into 'agency policy'. Trying to get some clarity about where agencies position themselves here may be a useful first step towards a more coordinated approach.

The discussion then has to move on to the level of practice. How *practically* can the protection of civilians and the access and security of aid providers be advanced with the warring parties? This is a difficult discussion about tactics and 'bottom-lines'. What guidance does the field have to offer to headquarters? Discussions on such issues tend to get bogged down in assertions that humanitarian and human-rights work are not compatible, or that it is not the role of the humanitarian actors to get involved in politics. The dilemmas are real and the complexities great, but the obligation remains to develop the argument, to be informed about the nature and rationale of each other's tactics, and to keep their validity and effectiveness under review. In recent years there has been a recognition that humanitarian action may have been too 'pragmatic' and that a new, more principled approach may be required. This is healthy, as excessive 'pragmatism' and 'fieldcraft' eventually may turn into complicity. It is possible, however, also to err on the other side and to forget that modern day conflicts are reflections of an 'unprincipled world' and that to work under tremendous constraints and threat of violence will inevitably require adaptations. There are no easy solutions, but the understanding of this can be deepened by more rational analysis of the constraints and of the possibilities and opportunities available to broaden the humanitarian space. Such approaches may help us to explore middle ways between remaining silent and public denunciation.

An understanding of the nature of 'humanitarian space' also requires the humanitarian actors to develop an understanding of the political economy of the warring parties. What is their power base, their structure of command and control; what are their goals and aspirations; where lie their sensitivities; what are their strategies and tactics; do they recognise any social contract towards the civilians? Furthermore, what are the perceptions, relating to all of these issues, of the people that one wishes to protect? Do the displaced, for example, wish to return and under what conditions? What do the target populations expect from a humanitarian intervention and what do they recommend as the best strategy? What are the implications for the military strategies of the belligerents of what the aid agencies say and do? What form does the bargaining power of the aid agencies take? In whom can they find an ally in their negotiations with the warring parties? What will the negotiating strategy be, which arguments will be put forward and who speaks on behalf of the humanitarian actors? In short, where may they find leverage and opportunities for influence?

Finally, if humanitarian space is denied or increasingly restricted, what can the aid and protection providers do? How effective is discreet dialogue and private protest? Under what conditions does one speak out publicly and what are the potential benefits for those one tries to protect and the risks for those who speak out? How will the message be phrased and what 'protocol' adopted to minimise the risks? Is there a possibility for a combination of tactics, with an 'orchestrated' division of labour? Self-evident as these considerations may seem, in practice one sees few examples of agencies sitting together and developing a detailed, common analysis or even structuring their approaches to these topics. Interestingly,

154

the discussions of the 'Emergency Group' of international humanitarian agencies confronted with war and a humanitarian crisis in Sri Lanka in 1995–96 did not lead to greatly increased access. However, it stimulated a much greater awareness of the politics of war and of the political implications of their presence, actions and statements. From this arose a more consistent approach to the belligerents.

Discussion between humanitarian organisations can facilitate the identification of the bottom line in terms of approaches to security. Security tends to be something that agencies on the ground usually agree upon as a minimum requirement, although even on this issue there is often a divergence of opinion between NGOs and the UN.[19] Discussion may also help to determine common approaches to restrictions. For example, if one is unable to work independently on humanitarian programmes, or agencies do not have access to all those in need without discrimination, what common approaches can be developed? Under what level of restrictions, either bureaucratic or as a result of the nature of the fighting, should one declare a threshold beyond which one should question the continuation of one's work? Currently agencies tend to make these assessments in isolation, and it is clearly their right to make the decision individually. However, it appears that all may benefit from a collective, critical and detailed assessment before making decisions on an agency basis; critical, because questions must be asked why agencies sometimes have different experiences. For example, why are some NGOs routinely interfered with by the Taliban in Afghanistan and the ICRC far less so? Is it the nature of their programme – is food aid, for example, politically much more sensitive than a vaccination programme? Or does it say something about the style of the agency and its representatives? Often the suspension of programmes or the withdrawal of aid is contemplated as a form of protest or pressure on a warring party. However, has one reflected on whether that warring party cares at all? Rarely do agencies attempt to establish common terms of either engagement or disengagement.[20]

Humanitarian and human rights operators on the ground, however, typically have only limited bargaining power with belligerents. Where belligerents, such as in Sri Lanka, are essentially prepared to accept a degree of regulation of the conduct of war (as embodied in international humanitarian law), these operators can exert a degree of influence through their arguments and negotiations. However, where the belligerents engage in 'total war' they are fairly powerless and need political backing. As the events in the Great Lakes have shown, humanitarian agencies cannot obtain much humanitarian space if they have to operate in a 'political vacuum'.[21] This underlines the need for aid agencies to lobby the external political actors for concrete support; something that can best be done collectively.

155

Discussions to ensure that the political and assistance strategies are 'better informed' about each other have been taking place, for example, in Afghanistan in the context of the 'strategic framework'.[22] Similar approaches are being developed in the Caucasus[23] and were developed during the period 1993–94 in Angola, where the Special Representative of the UN Secretary-General (SRSG) provided effective support when the humanitarian actors needed it.

A not uncommon experience, however, is for the political agenda to dominate the humanitarian one. In 1993, in Liberia, for example, the SRSG chose not to support the humanitarian agencies in their protests against the restrictions of the Economic Community of West African States Monitoring Group (ECOMOG) on their access and even attacks on humanitarian convoys, so as not to jeopardise the negotiations for the Cotonou peace accords.[24] Similarly, during the Bosnian war humanitarian exemptions to the internationally imposed sanctions tended to be subjected to political manipulation. In North Korea the political agenda dominates and there is little political will to provide help for the agencies to gain better access and the right to independent monitoring of the food assistance.[25]

An additional difficulty in ensuring greater coherence between the political and the assistance strategies is the increasingly popular demand (among certain donors) that aid should 'build peace'. Whereas the Rwanda evaluation concluded that aid cannot substitute for political action,[26] this expectation or demand could imply that aid *has* substituted for political action. A detailed discussion of this is beyond the scope of this chapter, but it is an issue that may increasingly have to be addressed by aid agencies. The broad issue is not so much that aid can be manipulated by the warring parties into becoming a political and economic resource for the war, this is largely accepted, but that there is an issue of proportion. If victims of conflict were really totally dependent on aid they would be dead. Similarly, if aid were the mainstay of the war economy the war effort would probably soon come to a halt if the aid were removed. Consequently, such observations may provide scope for addressing peace at a local level. However, in the absence of effective political engagement and progress it seems well beyond the control and the power of aid providers to address the macro-dimensions of war and peace. Again, assistance providers may benefit from joining efforts to develop that analysis and argument.

Developing the strategies and tactics to facilitate a widening of humanitarian space thus involves the analysis of the relationships between the political, military and humanitarian agendas and the articulation of credible, and shared, arguments. A coordination forum and its facilitators have a clear role to play in this process.

THE COORDINATION OF POLITICAL ACTIONS

Only in recent years have humanitarian actors been paying more attention to the political efforts to prevent or end conflict. Traditionally this has been the domain of political scientists and international lawyers. There are probably several reasons for this. However, there is a clear perception among the humanitarian community that they (the agencies themselves) frequently operate in the context of a 'policy vacuum', unsupported by a vibrant political process. Critically, the humanitarian community wants support from the political actors in order to obtain a framework of consent for their actions from the local power brokers. Ideally, they want the political actors to help to bring about an end to the conflict, without which the humanitarian assistance requirement will not end. The implication is that the humanitarian actors need to include the actions and motives of the political players, not only of the conflict entrepreneurs but also of those attempting to 'resolve' the conflict, in their strategic analysis, lobbying and advocacy.[27]

An approach might be to recommend evaluating the political efforts aimed towards conflict resolution as well as those other political considerations that shape the attitudes and actions of the political actors. With regard to direct political attempts towards conflict resolution, the effectiveness of international efforts may be undermined by a lack of clarity or differences among international actors in their analyses of the conflict, in their perception of the objectives of the international efforts and in the strategies they use to realise these objectives. Some examples may help to illustrate this. The international response to the outbreak of war in Bosnia was complicated by the confusion over whether this represented a 'civil war' or an 'act of international aggression'.[28] Similarly, when the Belgian government, in April 1994, withdrew its troops from the UN Assistance Mission for Rwanda (UNAMIR) the dominant 'analysis' was that 'tribal fighting' had broken out again, not that it was a preprepared genocide created as part of a political power struggle and using 'ethnicity' as a mobilising factor. In Sierra Leone the analysis of the conflict began to change when the Revolutionary United Front (RUF) came to be seen as an armed opposition that represented some genuine grievances, rather than simply as a predatory and ragtag militia.

There is usually a degree of agreement among the political actors as to the broad goals of their efforts to resolve conflict: an end to the fighting and a durable peace. Where the difficulties arise is over the ways of achieving this. There may be different views over the specific political objectives that need to be pursued. When the Yugoslav war of dissolution started in 1991 there were divided opinions in the international 'community' about whether to try and maintain the Yugoslav Federation or to accept the break-up into new states.

Political objectives may also evolve. The coalition that allied itself under UN auspices after the Iraqi invasion of Kuwait in August 1990 did not seek the overthrow of Saddam Hussain. That, however, has become a policy objective of the USA, even though other members of the coalition feel uncomfortable with such a goal. Differences may also arise between political actors over what should be the guiding principles: respect for the integrity of the national territory or respect for the right of self deter-mination? Similarly, should peace be pursued vigorously in order to end violence rapidly or, alternatively, may delays in achieving peace be accept-able if those delays secure peace with justice? In such an event what, in practice, would 'justice' mean? Differences may also arise within the so-called international 'community' over the compromises between moral principles and basic pragmatism. Does one accept the *de facto* 'peace and stability' that come from a victorious war leader, such as Hun Sen in Cambodia, or a movement such as the Taliban in Afghanistan, or only the, perhaps, more fragile peace and stability that come from elections and a broadly based government? Does one accept that non-Serb refugees cannot return to their homes in what is the Respublika Srpska in order to save the 'broader' objective of maintaining the Dayton Accords?

There may also be differences among the conflict resolvers about what methods may best be used to try and achieve the political objectives. In terms of political strategies, two major approaches are possible, one that uses incentives and another one that uses disincentives. In terms of instruments, essentially there are three: the political, the economic and the military instrument. One approach may be to pursue constructive engagement with a warring party, another may be diplomatic condem-nation or exclusion. Different actors may adopt different strategies. Between the two world wars Britain sought to contain Germany through 'appeasement', while France adopted a strategy of 'encirclement' through political alliances against Germany. Today, the USA and Britain adopt an aggressive stance towards Saddam Hussain, while France and Russia are more inclined to attempt constructive engagement. Canada advocated stronger political action against Abacha's government in Nigeria, particu-larly after the execution of the Ogoni activists, while Britain preferred a less antagonistic stance.

The military instrument can also be used as an incentive: former colonial powers engage in 'military cooperation' with African countries; former Eastern Bloc countries are incorporated into the NATO alliance via the Partnership for Peace (PfP). Or it can be used as pressure. In Bosnia, for example, the USA advocated a 'lift [the arms embargo against the

Bosnian government] and strike [with air-power]' policy to apply pressure to the Serbs, a strategy that the countries with peacekeeping troops on the ground were far from content to adopt. One can offer trade and funds for reconstruction and development as incentives, or one can advocate the imposition of trade sanctions or restrictions on access to international capital and the suspension of aid. Clearly, where the actors seeking to resolve the conflict are using different approaches, the warring parties can play them off against each other and undermine the effectiveness of the approach.

It would be naïve, however, to assume that the attitudes and policies of international political actors are shaped only by the desire to bring about an end to conflict. There are other political factors which tend to determine the degree of 'political will'. Individual countries clearly have their own 'national' interests that influence their stance towards a particular conflict. These may be geopolitical or economic or simply relate to the wish to limit the movement of populations across borders. Such factors tend to be fairly 'stable' or predictable, at least in the medium term. In addition, there are factors relating to the creation and maintenance of coalitions: the search for appropriate forums and means for decision-making. For example, the international efforts to manage the wars of dissolution of Yugoslavia led to a veritable odyssey from the European Union to the UN Security Council and the International Conference on the Former Yugoslavia to the five nation 'Contact Group', with the North Atlantic Treaty Organisation (NATO) and the Western European Union (WEU) as additional sideshows.

Even when coalitions are established, 'coalition-politics' continue. Some states may deliberately adopt a position divergent from that of their allies, to underline their importance as interlocutor or leader within the coalition. This can generate rivalries as states compete for influence and credit. At the same time, there is often a concern to minimise the differences among 'allies'. Avoiding the collapse or degradation of a coalition, such as NATO, for example, can become an important policy objective in itself. The result may be political approaches to a specific conflict that have little relevance to the realities of the conflict, but are highly appropriate for maintaining the coalition.

Furthermore, volatility in terms of domestic political considerations may have a dramatic impact upon coalitions. For example, what is the level of domestic public support in a country for its government's involvement in conflict resolution elsewhere? The media, lobby and advocacy groups play a large role in defining the range of possible actions and in shaping public support. The concern for public support can also act to make governments wary about casualties, especially among their own

159

peacekeeping troops. This can discourage participation or, after intervening, encourage excessive limitations on mission types or even precipitate withdrawal.

Several conclusions may be drawn from this overview. First, an analysis of the political dynamic and the political economy of the so-called 'international community' that tries to resolve a particular conflict is essential. This is well understood by the Western military, who have always been deployed under a political mandate and under political direction. However, it is a fairly new exercise for the humanitarian actors, whose desire to be politically and operationally independent has led them to neglect, to a degree, the importance of being 'politically informed'. Second, such an analysis should indicate where advocacy and lobby efforts may have to be directed: towards the analysis, objectives and strategies for conflict resolution; towards mobilising political will; or towards indicating points of leverage on the warring parties? Third, when uncoordinated the actions and approaches of the political actors trying to bring about a resolution of the conflict are likely to undermine each other and can be manipulated by the warring parties. Finally, it should be borne in mind that coordination itself does not lead to more effective action. The key to the ending of violence in many cases is, ultimately, a question of either a preponderance of military force leading to a decisive outcome or a balance of military power leading to protracted stalemate, which itself generates war weariness and eventually a desire to settle. Even where the political will is high, external actors may not be able to exercise a decisive influence on the warring parties.

STRATEGIC COORDINATION

Recently there has been renewed interest in coordination efforts. This has led to a growing number of studies of coordination experiences and the lessons learned. In the UN system there have been attempts at *rapprochement* between the Office for the Coordination of Humanitarian Affairs and the major operational agencies. Reflection is under way about major coordination 'frameworks' such as the Consolidated Appeal Process, the Development Assistance Framework and the Strategic Framework. Reflection and discussion are taking place about how a Resident Co-ordinator/Humanitarian Coordinator and an SRSG can best focus their efforts and relate to each other. The biggest challenge and current stumbling block, however, is how to integrate the many coordination forums that exist. There may already be several coordination forums at the field level.[29] To these should be added coordination mechanisms at the level of the headquarters of humanitarian actors. The assistance strategy, however, should be coordinated with the political strategy in order to ensure an overall 'strategic approach'. This is a widely recognised need;[30] however, to achieve it in practice has proved elusive and continues to represent a challenge.

NOTES

1. A. Donini, *Afghanistan: Co-ordination in a Fragmented State* (New York: DHA, 1996), p. 45.
2. J. Borton, *An Account of Coordination Mechanisms for Humanitarian Assistance during the International Response to the 1994 Crisis in Rwanda* (Tokyo: Sophia University, Institute of Comparative Culture, 1996), p. 17.
3. J. Bennett, *Meeting Needs: NGO Coordination in Practice* (London: Earthscan, 1995).
4. Borton, *An Account of Coordination Mechanisms*, p. 6; and Donini, *Afghanistan*, p. 24.
5. J. Sanderson, 'The Humanitarian Response in Cambodia: The Imperative for a Strategic Alliance', in J. Whitman and D. Pocock (eds), *After Rwanda: The Coordination of United Nations Humanitarian Assistance* (London: Macmillan, 1996), p. 181.
6. S. Lautze, B. Jones and M. Duffield, *Strategic Humanitarian Coordination in the Great Lakes Region 1996–1997* (New York: OCHA, 1998), p. 13.
7. Ibid., pp. 13–16.
8. L. Minear, U. Chelliah, J. Crisp, J. Mackinlay and T. Weiss, *United Nations Coordination of the International Response to the Gulf Crisis 1991–1992* (Providence, RI: Brown University, T. J. Watson Institute for International Studies, 1993); B. Doppler, 'The ICRC in Complex Emergencies: An Outsider or Part of a Team?', in Whitman and Pocock (eds), *After Rwanda*, p. 134.
9. J. Kunder, *Evaluation of NGO Field Cooperation Protocol* (Washington, DC: InterAction, 1988).
10. M. Walsh, 'The Role of the Humanitarian Coordinator', in Whitman and Pocock (eds), *After Rwanda*; also K. Van Brabant, *The Coordination of Humanitarian Action: The Case of Sri Lanka* (London: Overseas Development Institute, 1997), p. 20.
11. Van Brabant, *The Coordination of Humanitarian Action*, p. 17.
12. S. Lautze et al., *Strategic Humanitarian Co-ordination*, pp. 16–17.
13. T. Lanzer, *The UN Department of Humanitarian Affairs in Angola: A Model for the Coordination of Humanitarian Assistance?* (Oxford: Refugee Studies Programme, 1996), p. 16. Also K. Van Brabant, 'Security and Humanitarian Space: Perspective of an Aid Agency', *Humanitares Volkerrecht*, 11, 1, 1998, pp. 14–24.
14. J. Honig and N. Both, *Srebrenica: Record of a War Crime* (London: Penguin, 1996), p. 104.
15. N. Leader, 'Codes of Conduct: Who Needs Them?', *Relief and Rehabilitation Network Newsletter*, 14, 1999, pp. 1–4.
16. I. Levine, *Promoting Humanitarian Principles: the Southern Sudan Experience*

(London: Overseas Development Institute, 1997).
17. Van Brabant, *The Coordination of Humanitarian Action*, p. 20.
18. Lautze *et al.*, *Strategic Humanitarian Coordination*, p. 48.
19. The discussion over NGO support for the withdrawal of all international UN staff from Afghanistan (August 1998–March 1999) illustrates this.
20. One recent exception that it is hoped may become a precedent comes from the Caucasus. See G. Hansen and L. Minear, *Waiting for Peace: Humanitarian Impasse in the Caucasus* (Providence, RI: Brown University, T. J. Watson Institute for International Studies, 1998), author's manuscript, p. 5.
21. Lautze *et al.*, *Strategic Humanitarian Coordination*, p. 2.
22. M. Keating, 'Dilemmas of Humanitarian Assistance in Afghanistan', in W. Maley (ed.), *Fundamentalism Reborn? Afghanistan and the Taliban* (London: Hurst, 1998), pp. 135–44.
23. G. Hansen, *Humanitarian Action in the Caucasus: A Guide for Practitioners* (Providence, RI: Brown University, T. J. Watson Institute for International Studies, 1998), pp. 62–7, and G. Hansen and L. Minear, *Waiting for Peace*, manuscript.
24. C. Scott, *Humanitarian Action and Security in Liberia 1989–1994* (Providence, RI: Brown University, T. J. Watson Institute for International Studies, 1995).
25. J. Bennett, *North Korea: The Politics of Food Aid* (London: Overseas Development Institute, 1999).
26. J. Erikson, *The International Response to Conflict and Genocide: Lessons from the Rwanda Experience. Synthesis Report* (London: Overseas Development Institute, 1996).
27. Lautze *et al.*, *Strategic Humanitarian Coordination*, p. 16.
28. J. Gow, *Triumph of the Lack of Will: International Diplomacy and the Yugoslav War* (London: Hurst, 1997), p. 8.
29. Van Brabant, *The Coordination of Humanitarian Action*, pp. 13–18.
30. Borton, *An Account of Coordination Mechanisms*, p. 20; Lautze *et al.*, *Strategic Humanitarian Coordination*, p. 47; Donini, *Afghanistan: Coordination in a Fragmented State*, p. 45.

10

Armed Protection for Humanitarian Action: What Are the Questions?

KOENRAAD VAN BRABANT

INTRODUCTION

Armed protection and humanitarian action remain uneasy bedfellows. Humanitarian aid agencies have been struggling with the issue and particularly since the negative experiences with the protection racket of some Somali militia guards and the mixed feelings about the use of military peacekeepers in Bosnia. Although in reality many agencies at one time or another have used some form of armed protection, few so far have tried to think through the issues in a systematic way, and the debate quickly turns emotive. This chapter is an attempt to provide a more systematic framework for considering the question of armed protection and to stimulate thinking in coming to an informed and well-argued decision.

The essay is not intended to be an argument for armed protection. It explores a line of reasoning concerning security for humanitarian action, focused on armed protection. The nature of the topic means that the text continues to explore the 'yes' options. At every step, however, it is possible to come to the conclusion that armed protection is not the option. Discussing armed protection should not cover up the fact that armed protection actually may increase the risk by turning the aid agency into a 'legitimate' target. On the other hand, the general effectiveness of non-armed protection against outright crime and banditry by perpetrators not restrained by any formal command or social control remains to be demonstrated.

INCREASED VULNERABILITY

Security in recent years has become a major concern among aid workers. Although road accidents and medical cases continue to do the most harm, there is a perception that aid workers are at increasing risk of violence.[1] In the absence of adequate statistics this perception is hard to confirm or refute. The International Committee of the Red Cross (ICRC) and United Nations data show an increase in the number of incidents that threaten the physical integrity of aid workers. The ICRC data show a serious increase in the number of incidents classified as acts of crime or banditry.[2] Irrespective of their statistical importance, the apparently increasing number of targeted kidnappings and assassinations of aid workers in recent years, notably but not exclusively in the Caucasus, has been instrumental in making security a major concern.

There are a number of contextual factors that contribute to the increased risk of aid workers being harmed through acts of intentional violence. One of these is increased exposure as more aid agencies work more closely to the centre(s) of conflict. However, there are a broad range of additional factors: the breakdown of central authority and its monopoly of violence; the spread of small arms and the use of violence to 'transfer assets' in the absence of many other viable economic opportunities; the conscious manipulation of civilians and their humanitarian needs as part of political and military strategies; the incorporation of aid resources in the political economy of violent groups; the loss of the perception that aid agencies are neutral, impartial and non-political; and the perception that aid agencies are a 'wealthy' and 'soft' target.

There are also a number of factors that aggravate the vulnerability to acts of violence. Among these are the continuing inability of some agencies to grasp fully the realities of working in new types of violent environments and to approach this as a major management challenge. Consequently there remains the belief that the risk is random and cannot be dealt with in a more professional way. This is compounded by the lack of competency in aid agencies regarding risk management and the comparatively weak discipline of aid personnel. An analysis of aid agency practice and recent security incidents reveals some common deficiencies.[3] These include field security guidelines that are not based on a realistic threat assessment and retrospective incident analysis; security guidelines written by untrained managers, which are not underpinned by training or rehearsal and are weakened by poor staff discipline; failures to analyse incidents in order to expose problems with the agency or its operations in a violent context; and an unwillingness to share the analyses that are made.[4]

SECURITY STRATEGIES

The most spontaneous response to the perceived increase in threats and risks is to try and 'harden the target' by reducing the vulnerability of the agency through protective procedures and devices. Protective devices include the erecting of compound walls or barbed-wire barriers, sandbagging windows, creating bomb shelters, wearing helmets or flak jackets, as well as the prominent display of the agency emblem. Access to radios is generally seen as an indirect protective measure. Protective procedures take a variety of forms but can include the observance of no-go zones and no-go times (curfews), identity checks and body searches of visitors to the compound, announcing or seeking clearance for movements in advance from local authorities, avoiding routine movements, ruling that no fire-arms are allowed in agency vehicles and compounds, driving in convoy, and, ultimately, evacuation.

However, hardening the target may be a necessary but not a sufficient strategy. It reflects a reactive and besieged mentality. It does not ask the question why the aid agency has become besieged, and whether the threat could be removed or circumvented. It may lead to isolation from the operating environment. It also may lead to a situation where such a defensive strategy hampers operational activity to a degree that is no longer cost-effective.

Risk Reduction

It is possible to identify three mechanisms for reducing risk. One can reduce or remove the threat by gaining widespread acceptance for one's presence and work. One can reduce the risk but not the threat by making oneself less vulnerable with protective procedures and devices. Finally, one can reduce the risk by containing and deterring those who constitute a threat, with a counter-threat. The latter strategy of deterrence may consist of legal, economic or political sanctions and/or armed action. The three major strategies constitute a range from 'soft' to 'hard' approaches.

Individuals, aid agencies and states tend to have 'preferred styles'; that is, a preference for one security strategy above another. With an element of caricature one could say that the preferred strategy of the ICRC[5] and of many non-governmental organisations (NGOs) is to seek 'acceptance'.[6] The ICRC actively seeks explicit consent from all warring parties. NGOs have been accustomed to feel accepted and tend to take consent as a given, sometimes even almost as a right. In contrast, the tendency, or preference, for the UN and some other NGOs is to reduce their vulnerability through protection. Professional security personnel, but particularly the military, have had a preference for deterrence. Indeed, the major justification for the international trade in weapons is the portrayed need for a credible capacity for 'self-defence' that in itself should constitute a deterrent to potential aggressors.

Security problems arise when preferred security strategies fail to match the threats in the environment. For example, the ICRC may have misread the perceived impact of its acceptance strategy in Burundi and had three staff members assassinated in June 1996. The landing of US troops on the beaches of Mogadishu in late 1992 showed a security strategy based on 'deterrence'. Although the full record is more nuanced, there was no over-riding strategy to cultivate acceptance; over time the Somali population, which had initially welcomed the intervention, turned against it.

Acceptance, protection and deterrence are discussed here as ideal types. In any given context a mix of them may be necessary. A potentially confrontational deterrence strategy is typically combined with protective measures. But it may also be combined with measures to gain acceptance among the population at large, as has been more explicitly recognised in the NATO-led peace Implementation Force (IFOR) and peace Stabili-sation Force (SFOR) missions in post-Dayton Bosnia. Activities to increase general acceptance and consent may still have to be combined with protective measures where crime and banditry persist and cannot be controlled by the authorities and/or local populations.

Such examples also highlight the difficulty of matching a security strategy to the threats in the environment. This requires a fairly sophis-ticated and ongoing analysis of threat and of one's vulnerability. The examples also hint at the difficulty in changing from a 'preferred' security strategy to another one.

Armed protection is associated here with a deterrence strategy. Even when a force is small, lightly armed and under instructions to use weapons only in self-defence, the potential use of firepower in the face of threat introduces a qualitative difference from the use of unarmed guards. No less importantly, it also profoundly affects the perception or image of an aid agency.

THINKING THROUGH THE QUESTION OF ARMED PROTECTION

Three major areas of consideration are relevant to an aid agency when deciding whether to use armed protection. These are: principles, context and management.

Principles

Aid agencies are confronted with an array of questions relating to the principles they should apply. Agencies will answer these in different ways, these varied responses posing problems for coordinating structures and the consistency of the humanitarian effort. Such questions include:

- Should one work at all in an area where the level of threat is such that the question of armed protection arises?
- Are there circumstances that warrant the defensive use of force?
- Is armed protection compatible with humanitarian action?
- Is armed protection compatible with advocacy against the arms race or against arms sales?
- Is armed protection compatible with a policy that aid workers should never carry guns or that no weapons are allowed in aid agency vehicles or compounds?
- Is it acceptable to pay for armed protection?
- Should consent be enforced?

Levels of risk

Many agencies work in environments where the risk of violence, whether targeted or not, is very much present. They thereby expose their own personnel to danger and risk their assets. The decision to continue working in such a setting is often an intuitive rather than a considered decision. Evaluating the impact of insecurity on one's operational effectiveness, the likelihood that certain security incidents may occur and the seriousness of their impact is one way of establishing a threshold beyond which the situation becomes one of 'unacceptable level of risk'. Once passed this would warrant a suspension of operations, a physical withdrawal, perhaps, with an attempt at continuing work through local organisations supported by 'remote control'.[7] At worst it could precipitate a termination of operations.

Conditional use of force

Many aid personnel are declared or undeclared pacifists, opposed to violence and the use of force. That sometimes influences their perception of and attitudes to military units deployed in so-called 'peace-support' roles. There is a need, however, to reflect on the distinction between absolute and conditional pacifism and non-violence. Absolute non-violence is the rejection of force under any circumstance. Conditional non-violence can accept the limited and defensive use of force in the face of clear aggression.

Armed protection and humanitarian action

This leads to the question of whether the use of armed protection is against the basic principles of humanitarian action or if it is a response to the conditions in which humanitarian action takes place. Even if it is the latter, when carefully and proportionally used does it necessarily under-mine the basic principles of humanitarian action?

The agency that is probably most explicitly reticent about using armed protection is the ICRC, even though in Somalia it too used armed guards.[8] A closer examination of the ICRC logic, however, reveals that this reticence is not derived from an ethical opposition but from operational considerations. First, there is the concern that armed protection may increase rather than reduce the risk, by turning the aid agency into a 'legitimate' target. Second, as with 'neutrality', 'impartiality', 'indepen-dence' and other principles that guide ICRC actions, the ICRC reasoning is not simply limited to the specific 'here and now' context. The agency operates with a longer time frame and a more global horizon than most other aid agencies. For the ICRC, unlike the UN Security Council, perceived consistency and predictability of its actions and positions are key concerns. Resorting too quickly and too often to armed protection may undermine efforts to persuade belligerents in future conflicts to respect international humanitarian law and the physical integrity of humanitarian aid workers.[9] The point is not so much that armed protection is not compatible with humanitarian action, as that its adoption, globally and in the long-term, is likely to undermine the effectiveness of humanitarian action and protection efforts. A long-term strategy of no armed protection, however, does not necessarily solve the immediate security problem and may not protect against armed criminality and banditry.

Armed protection and proliferation
An argument against armed protection is that, internationally or locally, it contributes to the arms race and the proliferation of arms. This argument needs to be elaborated. Does it stem from an absolute pacifism? If not, then the question perhaps is not about the use of arms *per se* but about their proliferation, that is, the loss of the monopoly of violence by the authorities responsible for security and law and order. An important related point is that arms here may be used only for 'private' protection, notably the aid agency staff and assets, rather than for 'public security'. A principled stance can be taken by an agency not to contribute to the trend of the privatisation of violence which in the medium term seems to create a climate that is detrimental to everybody's security.

Conditional armed protection
The question of whether armed protection is compatible with a policy forbidding arms in aid agency vehicles and compounds can be addressed from two perspectives. Armed protection again can be rejected as a matter

of principled non-violence that is extended beyond the agency 'space'. Or it can be seen in the light of international humanitarian law. The latter does not condemn the use of arms but tries to regulate it, especially in terms of proportionality and the distinction between combatants and non-combatants. International humanitarian law attempts to be a code of conduct for war, not an anti-war declaration. As such, it tries to create 'spaces' in the middle of war, where humanity prevails and no fighting should take place. In the latter approach, armed protection, when kept outside the vehicles and compounds, may be acceptable.

Paying for armed protection
A controversial issue is whether it may be acceptable to pay for armed protection. There are certainly ethical and practical issues to consider, and many humanitarian staff are ill-disposed to pay for hired guns.

On the moral level, one can argue that the 'value' of a life lost in an armed confrontation, be it the life of a guard, an assailant or a bystander, is greater than the value of resources stolen or looted. In contrast, one can argue that the value of such a life is less than the cost, in terms of the suffering and death, caused by the loss of vital and urgently needed relief goods or the suspension of humanitarian assistance (resulting from a lack of security). But the situation may also be one in which people rather than assets are targeted. In such circumstance is investment in armed protection to be considered a cost small in comparison with the loss of life?

A moral and sometimes a legal question is whether paying for armed protection is a legitimate use of donations for charitable purposes. Is it, as a matter of principle, an abuse of such donations, or is it a necessary cost in order to protect the bulk of charitable donations from predation and loss? In justification of the paying for such services it could be argued that the provision of law and order is a necessary part of the functioning of our society. Furthermore, in functioning democracies part of one's tax contributions finances police, 'gendarmerie' and armed forces. Paying directly for armed protection makes only more transparent a reality that is otherwise less visible. Even in countries where there is a nominal police force this may be so under-funded and under-equipped that aid agencies have no choice but to provide the police with material and perhaps financial support for them to be able to perform with some effectiveness. Obviously this should be the responsibility of the state authorities, but then international aid also supports policies and practices that strictly speaking are the responsibility of national authorities, such as basic education or basic health services. Arguably the issue revolves around distinguishing between the payment for armed protection and its use for 'private' rather than public security.

169

In determining the legitimacy of a resort to armed protection one must also weigh the cost of armed protection against the cost of assets looted. A useful equivalent would be to compare the cost of armed protection with that of insurance coverage for assets and people in high-risk areas.

Enforced consent

The reference to the forces of law and order allows us to raise the issue of consent, enforced compliance and acceptance. Some aid workers tend to equate the use of force with the end of consent and freely given acceptance of humanitarian actors.

The notion of consent, for the presence and work of humanitarian agencies, is central to the Geneva Conventions. However, these were drawn up essentially for conditions of organised warfare, between states and, rather by extension, organised non-state armed groups. If not in principle at least in practice, consent is sometimes hard to obtain from 'bandits', 'irregulars' and 'rogue warlords'.

For military units deployed under UN auspices the Bosnian conflict in particular has raised major questions about the relationship between peacekeeping and peace enforcement and concepts of neutrality, impartiality and consent. As peace-support personnel, UN troops are required to be neutral in the sense of avoiding the taking of sides and the use of excessive force. Neutrality, however, does not mean passivity. It should be a principled neutrality. Principled neutrality does require responding to what a violent group is doing, but not because of what faction or side it belongs to, but in the light of a judgement of acts against principles, the mandate or both. It also does not mean abstaining from the use of force under all circumstances, but using the minimum necessary force. There always is a concern for how one will be perceived if one uses force. To avoid any use of force on the grounds that it can be portrayed as taking sides is, however, not the answer. The challenge is to be principled, consistent, transparent and accountable about the use of force. There is no dispute that increased acceptance is the best route to promoting consent but there may be circumstances in which consent may have to be enforced. 'Enforcing consent' as a concept appears problematic. Perhaps it may be better replaced by 'enforcing compliance'. Enforcing compliance has a clearer implicit reference to rules, laws, codes of conduct and agreements that are broadly accepted. All social systems ultimately have recourse to ways of enforcing compliance with social rules. People in some countries may suggest that their police are partial, use excessive force or are corrupt, but few people would question the principle of a competent, controlled and accountable police force capable of enforcing compliance with basic rules to protect basic rights.

The use of force, as the ultimate recourse, may not be met with the consent of those organisations to which it is applied, but there may well exist consent and acceptance within the broader population. The credibility of military peace-support operations has suffered from the failure to establish and maintain broad-based acceptance and consent. But it has equally suffered, in the eyes of local people, from the failure to enforce compliance where it vitally mattered. Many Somalis started wondering about the purpose of Operation Restore Hope if it was not going to disarm the militias. The people in Sarajevo and elsewhere in Bosnia resented the fact that the UN Protection Force (UNPROFOR) at times did little to protect them effectively from shelling, mass expulsion and massacre. The international community has become reticent about forceful intervention in internal conflict. Yet for some analysts of the Bosnian war the crucial factor in creating the conditions for the Dayton Agreements was the decision, after years of procrastination, to use force with greater determination.[10]

The problem with the current thinking about 'consent' is that, derived from a world in which states are the principal actors, it focuses heavily on the authorities, nominal and *de facto*, several of which may be violent power-brokers. It does not pay sufficient attention to the 'consent' and 'acceptance' of those who should be the principal beneficiaries of international intervention, the population at large. Admittedly this may not be easy to establish, and there may exist complex relationships between civilians and armed groups. Yet there is little doubt that most people anywhere favour the basic protection of their lives and property. The neutral, measured and accountable use of force to obtain compliance with basic international standards and norms, which, importantly, should be for the public good, may enhance acceptance among the population at large.

Context
If there is no rejection in principle of the use of force, then thought has to be given to the contextual questions. What threats provoke a potential requirement for armed protection? Are alternative strategies possible? If not, who should provide armed protection, and for what purpose? Finally, who does and should benefit from such protection?

What are the threats and why are there threats?
Threat assessment, currently and retrospectively, through incident and incident-pattern analysis, is not something with which aid personnel are very familiar. While it is not a hard science, it can certainly be rendered more systematic than is currently often the case. Threat assessment

endeavours to identify the nature and seriousness of the major threats in an operating environment: burglary, sexual assault, landmines, hijacking of vehicles, shelling and armed robbery being but a few. It also sets out to define which categories of person are at risk when, where risks may be found and who are the likely perpetrators. It explores too the likely motives of perpetrators. This is a difficult but important task. There is a difference between an agency vehicle being hijacked by bandits or by local strongmen who have complaints about the agency's programme. There is a difference between a female staff member being sexually assaulted because she is vulnerable as a woman or because she is a member of your agency. In the latter case there is a 'message' to the agency that is not present in the first type of assault.

A threat assessment should be complemented by a risk assessment: what is the likelihood that a certain type of incident may happen to you and, secondly, if it did happen, how grave would be the impact on the individual and agency? For example, the risk of burglary may be high, but burglars rarely use arms. Consequently, the impact may be low. Protective strategies can be designed to reduce the likelihood of a threat occurring or to reduce its impact. Blast walls and bomb shelters, for example, do not reduce the risk of an attack but do reduce its impact.

Some aid agencies, for example the ICRC, draw distinctions between war and criminality and consequently will adopt different security strategies. However, in practice it may be difficult to differentiate between both types of threat and they may be present alongside one another. In the Caucasus, for example, kidnapping and hostage-taking may be motivated by a desire for ransom, as a means of discouraging a foreign presence or as 'human shields'.[11] Universally applicable security strategies are difficult to find.

Is armed protection the answer?

If threats occur for 'political' reasons – for example, because the agency is not perceived as neutral in its operations – then increased dissemination and acceptance-building are perhaps a better answer than armed protection. If threats occur because of resentment over the design or implementation of programmes, then broad-based consultation and a review of the programme may be a better answer. If threats occur because your vehicles are seen as a valuable resource then perhaps to change to lower value, less desirable ones may be more appropriate. If threats occur because an agency is viewed as operating outside the local social system then integrating programmes by, for example, placing agency assets under community management may be an appropriate response.

Even where armed protection seems appropriate and necessary the question still needs to be asked whether it will provide a reasonable deterrent or will be more likely to increase the risk. For example, if bandits see an armed convoy they may become more inclined to use lethal violence. Armed protection may turn the agency into a 'legitimate' target.

Who provides the armed protection?

In theory, there are a variety of sources of armed protection, all of which have been used by aid agencies in the past: the national army and police, resistance groups, UN troops and/or civil police, local militia, private security companies and individual armed guards. In practice, an agency considering armed protection should consider a range of questions:

- The 'political' position of a provider of armed protection. For example, national police may be an instrument of government repression. How will your association with such groups impact upon other perceptions of the agency?

- The circumstances under which a protection provider's other objectives override the provision of protection and the consequences of this.

- How professionally resourced and disciplined is the provider? Local police may appear to be the best 'political' choice, but if their morale is low, their discipline weak and they have no vehicles are they effective? Furthermore, can you invest resources, such as vehicles, to improve their capacity and morale?

- How much management control do you need, can you exert and do you want over the provider? Armies have their own chain of command which may be unresponsive to your demands. That of the local militia, however, may be more responsive and you may therefore be able to exert more influence. Having more direct authority over the providers of armed protection brings them more under your control, but also makes you more directly accountable for their behaviour and actions.

A situation may arise where an agency with no objection in principle against the use of armed protection concludes, on the basis of its threat analysis, that such protection is necessary, yet none of the potential providers of protection in the operating environment is acceptable to the agency. In such circumstances the suspending of operations may be unavoidable.

Collective agency strategies?

Aid agency culture overemphasises independence. Different agencies, indeed, need to consider the question of armed protection individually, but this should not absolve them from recognising the implications of their choices for others. There are practical and image implications if aid agencies adopt different strategies. And in most environments local power brokers and populations seldom differentiate between aid agencies. This should be sufficient to encourage security policy coordination.

At the practical level, the fact that some aid agencies use armed protection and others do not may increase the risk to the latter, which become comparatively more attractive targets. The inappropriate use of armed protection, for example where threats arise from resentment over an agency's programming, may escalate a situation in ways that affect all such agencies. At the level of perception the image that the use of armed protection, or of a particular provider of armed protection, creates – not only for the agency concerned but by implication for all aid agencies and for humanitarian operations in general – is another argument that collective discussion is required.

In some circumstances aid agencies may not arrive at a collective position and they might well be correct in doing so; a collective position must not necessarily be the absolute aim of inter-agency dialogue. The purpose of the dialogue is to sharpen the critical arguments around questions of armed protection, to understand the approaches of different agencies and the implications for the agencies collectively, and regularly to monitor and review strategies for security.

For what purpose armed protection?

The threat and risk assessments, and value judgements derived from principles, may help to specify for what purpose armed protection will be used. Will it be to secure physical assets, to protect personnel or to secure an area? An agency may decide to deploy guards at its staff residences, offices and warehouses but not use escorts for aid convoys because this is seen as compromising the humanitarian image and thereby accentuating risk. Alternatively, if there is a strong threat of road banditry, and target populations are in acute need of material assistance, armed escorts may be the only way to ensure passage. The point is, of course, that armed protection should have a specific purpose which reflects a specific threat.

Who benefits from the armed protection?

Determining who benefits and who loses from armed protection is also a critical factor in deciding whether it should be employed.

Would target populations suffer gravely if aid no longer came through because the agency did not want to use armed protection? Does the use of armed protection escalate the level of violence in the area, increasing the threat and risk not only for the aid agency but also for the local population? Do the arms provide only private protection or do they provide more general, public protection?

An issue rather underexplored by aid agencies, although one more familiar to official security forces, including UN peacekeeping troops, is that of securing an *area* rather than an *entity* such as an agency. In north Iraq in the early 1990s, for example, Kurdish Peshmerga fighters were hired and posted on hilltops overseeing main roads to protect traffic against snipers.[12] Clearly this protection was not limited to aid agency traffic. A major issue in the global question of armed protection is not only the privatisation of violence, but also the privatisation of protection. Law and order forces, be they national or international, in principle extend public protection, that is, all people should benefit from the fact that they secure and enforce norms in a particular environment. Dissociating the security of aid operations from the protection of civilians contributes to a trend in which only those with special status and/or monetary resources are safe and protected, while those without remain endangered. Armed protection would gain more widespread acceptance if it were used in ways that provide more public protection. Although more difficult to do, it is preferable for troops to be deployed in ways that secure a road for everyone rather than only to escort an aid convoy. If many agencies have offices and residences in the same neighbourhood, could their armed guards be deployed to patrol the whole neighbourhood, benefiting also the local residents? Can this be raised with the local associations of residents? Would an active neighbourhood-watch scheme or unarmed neighbourhood patrols provide enough protection? Guards themselves will prefer clear and limited responsibilities and may not immediately warm to this type of approach, yet there are potential benefits to be had from it as well.

The relationship between the security of aid agencies and peacekeepers and the protection of local populations is a complex and difficult one. Although in practice local populations tend to understand and accept that foreign aid agencies especially may have to leave for security reasons while they cannot, there is also an inherent tension in humanitarian aid agencies and peacekeepers seeking protection for themselves while, by commission or omission, ignoring the safety of the people they have come to help.[13] The actions, or rather inaction, of UN troops in Rwanda, in Bosnia[14] and, until spring 1999, in Kosovo in the face of ethnic cleansing, massacres and crimes against humanity have exposed the continuing political reservations about international norm-enforcement. Bedevilled by the politics of 'peace', the major international actors have shrunk from protection-enforcement. The peacekeeping equation may include the political, financial and human costs of the peacekeeping operation, but does not seem to include the human cost to the endangered populations. The aim of the Security Council may be to safeguard global peace and stability, but it does not appear to be the safeguarding of (civilian) lives.[15] Again, these are not easy questions to answer, but they should be more actively considered.

Management

Contractual stipulations

A contract may include stipulations related to guard selection criteria, covering aspects such as age, health, literacy, abstention from the use of alcohol or drugs, and refraining from other employment that would preclude adequate sleep. Further specifications may be included regarding the requirements of and for supervisors and minimum standards in supervision. Minimum standards of professional knowledge and training may be identified – for example, log keeping, vehicle- and body-search procedures, package- and mail-search, first aid, office evacuation, local law and the power of arrest. The need for armed protection also raises other issues. The agency may wish to end a contract quite suddenly for particular reasons – for example, because of dissatisfaction with the group providing the armed protection, because the general security situation has improved, or because the agency decides to suspend or end its operations. Are there clear criteria and procedures spelled out for the premature ending of the contract? Shorter term, renewable contracts introduce flexibility here, but may expose the agency to inflating price demands.

Command and control

A crucial question is: to whom are the guards answerable, who has the authority of command, and who is in charge of their discipline? Where external agencies are contracted to provide armed protection, what is the authority of their commander versus that of the agency? Who, for example, determines the rules of engagement? These concern not only the circumstances under which guards can use violence but also its pro-portionality. Different national security forces tend to come with different traditions and cultures, including those about command and control, weaponry, rules of engagement and what is considered 'appropriate' or 'excessive' use of force. Detailed consultation and in-depth discussion may be required to ensure a common understanding between the aid agency and the provider of protection.

As with all things, the devil may be in the detail. Operating procedures may have to include specifications regarding body searches and what to do when someone refuses to be thus searched, whether the personal bodyguards of a visitor may keep their weapons in the agency vehicle or compound, or how far to go in the pursuit of robbers and attackers. Similarly, the defining of disciplinary procedures and agency responsibility will create, at the very least, contractual challenges.

Furthermore, guards often do not own vehicles and the agency will have to decide whether they may use agency vehicles. In some instances agencies have made vehicles, with the logos removed, available to the army to escort aid convoys through bandit-infested areas. Alternatively, vehicles may be rented for the guards' use. Where local security forces provide general protection, for example, in a refugee camp, it will have to be made clear in advance whether or not they may use an agency vehicle for the hot pursuit of robbers.

It is conceivable that an agency may decide that, while armed protection is vital and that a potential provider is suitable, the inability to reach agreement over such issues prevents this. In such a case the agency may also decide to suspend operations.

CONCLUSION

The perception that aid agencies are increasingly at risk of violence has generated a strong increase in security awareness. This chapter has spelled out three ideal type security strategies, a mix of which may be used in any given setting. Armed protection is the most immediate expression of a strategy of deterrence. The chapter then reviewed three major areas of consideration in deciding about armed protection: questions of principle, of context, and of management. In doing so, it does not necessarily advocate armed protection nor does it prescribe answers for the many questions raised. It sets out a framework or a tool for a more systematic and dispassionate consideration of the issues, which one hopes will result in informed decisions that can be objectively reviewed.

ACKNOWLEDGEMENT

Philippe Dind and Stuart Gordon provided valuable comment on an earlier draft. Responsibility for the final version, however, remains entirely with the author.

NOTES

1. J. de Courten, *Towards a More Secure Environment* (Geneva: ICRC, 1997).
2. J. Dworken, 'Where There Is No Data: Patterns, Trends and Unanswered Questions Concerning Wider Security Problems', unpublished discussion paper (1998).
3. For examples, see K. Van Brabant, 'Security and Humanitarian Space: Perspective of an Aid Agency', *Humanitares Volkerrecht*, 1 (1998), pp. 14–24, at pp. 15–16.
4. G. Hansen, *Humanitarian Action in the Caucasus: A Guide for Practitioners* (Providence, RI: Brown University, T. J. Watson Institute for International Studies, 1998), p. 35.
5. P. Dind, 'Security and Humanitarian Space: The ICRC Perspective', *Humanitares Volkerrecht*, 1 (1988), pp. 9–13, at p. 10.
6. See K. Van Brabant, 'Cool Ground for Humanitarian Aid Providers: Towards Better Security Management in Aid Agencies', *Disasters*, 22, 2 (1998), pp. 109–25, for a more expansive treatment of the acceptance strategy.
7. See Hansen, *Humanitarian Action*, p. 41.
8. Council of Delegates, *Armed Protection for Humanitarian Assistance*, ICRC/IFRC working paper (1995).
9. Dind, 'Security and Humanitarian Space', p. 13.
10. J. Gow, *Triumph of the Lack of Will: International Diplomacy and the Yugoslav War* (London: Hurst, 1997).
11. Hansen, *Humanitarian Action*, p. 41.
12. J. Pilkington, 'Beyond Humanitarian Relief: Economic Development Efforts in Northern Iraq', *Refugee Participation Network*, 23 (1997), pp. 21–3.
13. Van Brabant, 'Security and Humanitarian Space', p. 23.
14. J. Honig and N. Both, *Srebrenica: Record of a War Crime* (London: Penguin, 1996).
15. See K. Van Brabant, 'Security and Protection in Peacekeeping: A Critical Reading of the Belgian Inquiry into the 1994 Events in Rwanda', *Journal of International Peacekeeping*, 7, 1 (1999).

SECTION III
Peace-Support Operations and the Military

11

The Legitimation of Strategic Peacekeeping: Military Culture, the Defining Moment

JAMES GOW AND CHRISTOPHER DANDEKER

In the 1990s a new era of cooperation in the United Nations Security Council saw a change in the frequency with which the Council authorised action, as well as in the scope of the action authorised. One of the spheres in which such cooperation was evident was that of peace-support operations (PSOs). This gave rise to the intellectual and practical problem of ensuring the success of complex, multinational, military operations in support of diplomatic efforts to achieve the settlement of armed hostilities, including the use of force in restricted circumstances.

While operations in Cambodia, Somalia, Haiti and Liberia, among others, were important to this evolution, nowhere was more important or more of a focus of interest regarding the evolution of thought, whether among academics or practitioners, than the set of peace-support missions in the former Yugoslav lands. The crucial issues were shaped by the events on the territories of the former Yugoslavia, above all else in Bosnia and Herzegovina – although this focus could never be wholly divorced from the attention given to Croatia and Macedonia, because of the impossibility of separating elements at certain stages. A variety of situations and issues, from assistance in the delivery of humanitarian aid to the deployment of a precedent-setting preventive force, made the former Yugoslav lands a laboratory of new (and rediscovered) developments in the area of PSOs.[1]

There has been a move away from traditional UN military operations of the peacekeeping type – simple, straightforward, one small international force deployed to keep apart two sides that have decided that they want (or need) to call an end to their conflict.[2] Instead, situations have emerged where a number of complex activities are undertaken in the case of a continuing conflict, where effort is designed to assist in bringing the conflict to an end, rather than to give assistance at the end of a conflict. Or there might be a situation in which a concerted and comprehensive initiative to build peace after a conflict requires a major, armed force interacting with a wide range of civilian bodies to assist in the strengthening of peace proactively through presence, activity and action (as opposed to the passive, interpositional role of traditional peacekeeping). These situations pose a number of questions regarding approaches to conflict management, as well as raising questions with regard to the forces actually deployed, both in terms of size and scope.

The multidimensional character of the type of operation under discussion means that it is important to consider the ways in which an appropriate force can be put together and how, in the process of putting it together, it can be made successful. We believe that the key to success is the concept of legitimation, as we argue below. However, understanding the relevance of legitimation to all such operations depends on recognising that they are carried out at the strategic level.[3] For this reason, we term these operations 'strategic peacekeeping'.[4] Operations of this kind involve strategic initiative on the part of those who decide to deploy the forces. That is, the strategic initaitive lies with the international community.[5] Critically, once deployed, however, the force must ensure legitimation. This is a process of diverse elements, many exterior to the force deployed. We maintain, however, that two factors are vital to this process: the military culture of the forces deployed and the degree to which the force (particularly its political and military chiefs) can seize the strategic initiative at what we call 'defining moments'. In order to do this, we shall first review the conceptual background to this case.

THE LIMITS OF THE 'DOBBIE DOCTRINE': FROM TACTICS TO STRATEGY

Having recognised that operations such as those in the former Yugoslav territories are at the strategic level, it is necessary to look at the ways in which the several elements of the mission itself are put together – how the mission is defined, the bases upon which it is framed, the ways in which the different component parts of a force relate to each other. This must be related to a range of questions regarding how to sustain an activity of this kind which is complex and in which it is quite difficult to get people on the same wavelength and, finally, looking at the ways in which it is possible to try to achieve some level of strategic coherence. Again, this is in the context of trying to achieve success. In military terms, the guideline for this is doctrine.

The situation of the multinational armed force in Bosnia and Herzegovina changed greatly from the time troops were first deployed in 1992 to the missions of the late 1990s – and the debate surrounding that force and the type of operation moved on as well. In 1992 and 1993 the British Army began to shape what was called Wider Peacekeeping – what we call the 'Dobbie doctrine'. That debate moved on to embrace work on a new, more appropriate joint-service doctrine. To understand how that debate moved on and its pertinence to our argument it is necessary to go back to the position developed by the Army in the early stages, used for operations and widely embraced by others, academically and pragmatically – the 'Dobbie doctrine'.

The concept of strategic peacekeeping is midway between classic peacekeeping and peace enforcement.[6] We are concerned with the nature and possibilities of those operations which are classic peacekeeping but fall substantially short of peace enforcement. One of the important areas of discourse on this topic has to be that of doctrine development, especially in the British Army. One of the key figures in this debate was an Army officer who was one of the main authors of emerging British doctrine in the earlier phases of interest, Colonel Charles Dobbie.[7] He wrote an interesting, short book, *A Concept for Post-Cold War Peacekeeping*, in which much of the thinking for the doctrine of Wider Peacekeeping was exposed.

What Dobbie was trying to do, in the light of the environment outlined above, was to work out a way through the problem of when and how to deploy peacekeepers on operations in which the strategic initiative lies not only with the contending, conflicting parties but also with one or more elements of the international community. The international initiative is strategic. Dobbie's case, as he was writing in the period 1992–94, during which time the doctrine emerged, was as follows. For some analysts there was a spectrum of operations: peacekeeping to peace enforcement. The type of operation at issue was one in which elements of both might be mixed.

For Dobbie, this was a dangerous mistake. It was dangerous on the ground, it was dangerous for those who had optimistic pictures of the possibilities which might lie ahead for peacekeeping. It was confusing and it was dangerous to think of this line as a spectrum. Rather, there was a clear, conceptual divide between peacekeeping and peace enforcement. Dobbie argued that consent separated peacekeeping, 'including Wider Peacekeeping, defined by the British Army as the wider aspects of peacekeeping operations carried out with the consent of the belligerent parties, but in an environment that may be highly volatile, from peace enforcement'. Consent was the clear, conceptual means of separating the elements of that which some commentators tended to see as a spectrum.

There was, for Dobbie, a conceptual gulf between peacekeeping and peace enforcement. If the external force could not have the consent of the contending parties, then to seek to operate without it would be to mix elements from two discrete operational scenarios. This could only lead to a series of confusions and dangers. Confusion would arise in terms of the countries sending the peacekeepers, in terms of the peacekeepers themselves and danger in terms of uncertainty and misperception in the mission. What Dobbie was trying to do was to evolve a doctrine in which a master term could provide the line of consistency to cut through potential confusion and avert danger. The key term which defined the conceptual gulf between the discrete modes of operation for Dobbie was consent: consent of the parties defined the type of mission.

It should be noted, however, that Dobbie's doctrine was, at the point at which it was written, quite a sensitive and a sophisticated one. Because consent provided the underpinning of the conceptual divide between peacekeeping and peace enforcement, this did not mean that force could not be used as a result of the presence of consent. Its use was a possibility, even a necessity, in operations where consent had been given to the presence of peacekeepers at the strategic level. This was where he drew a distinction between the operational and the tactical levels: consent at higher levels could allow for the use of force at lower levels.

So long as representatives of the contending parties had agreed to the presence of peacekeepers and to some set of arrangements for the settling down of a conflict at the theatre–operational level (probably through a formal agreement), it was legitimate for peacekeepers at the tactical level to use force. For example, this could be against those elements or parties that would not comply with agreements which had been made at the theatre level. So, as long as consent was present at the higher level, this provided a canopy of consent and one of formal authority under which peacekeepers on the ground could and should use force to ensure that the agreements at the operational level were actually policed and enforced at the tactical level.

For Dobbie, however, this arrangement would cease if one of two scenarios were to occur. In the first, if for some reason or other consent were to be withdrawn at the operational level – that is, if one or more of the parties withdrew from the agreement and ripped it up – then the basis for a peacekeeping operation in this volatile environment would have gone and the force would either have to escalate to enforcement or withdraw. In the second scenario, if at the tactical level a series of piecemeal infringements of agreements occurred to such an extent that there was a crumbling effect at the operational level, then the outcome would be the same as in the first scenario: the basis for operating would have gone and, conceptually, the chasm between peacekeeping, based on consent, and peace enforcement would have been proved.

Questions arose over Bosnia and other scenarios as to the fate of what we have called the 'Dobbie doctrine' if a crisis were to emerge in which Dobbie's criteria for the presence of peacekeepers were not to apply. What if a conflict were present in which the contending/conflicting parties did not agree, or did not agree sufficiently to justify the presence of Dobbie's peacekeepers, yet, at the same time, the crisis were creating either a humanitarian disaster or a regional security problem which states felt they had to address? Both out of humanitarian concern, as well as from strategic interest, these states might judge it necessary to do something to address this situation, yet it could be the case that the Dobbie criteria would not allow for it. What should be done? According to Dobbie, the answer would be nothing, because the doctrinal basis for doing so would not be present. This is not a sufficient basis to underpin an intervention in a crisis, however. It is necessary to address this situation at the strategic level.

Strategic peacekeeping provides an analytical basis for addressing this kind of situation. It does so in ways which depart from Dobbie's doctrine. He argued that not only was his concept of wider peacekeeping a basis for intervention, it was also a basis for intervention in which the chances for success, modest though they might be, were high; the chance for no conclusion was high; and the chance, therefore, of the UN or an international force taking responsibility for things that were going to be successful would be higher and, therefore, their credibility would be more likely to be intact than it would be if it became involved in operations where these criteria did not work.

The difficulty with this is that, precisely by applying this kind of doctrine, the UN and other international bodies, as well as their member states, do, in fact, get into a lot of difficulty if they try to operate in this way. Credibility is not maintained by a cautious and restrictive approach of this kind. An approach which says that this doctrine will not be exceeded because, in the prevailing circumstances, we do not believe that it will be successful will not be successful if it meets challenges. To limit the mission to those conditions is, in fact, to bring the very existence of the mission and its credibility into question. This was clear in the debate over the nature and the future of the UN Protection Force (UNPROFOR) in the mid-1990s.

It is, therefore, necessary to understand the way in which a strategic-level force comes to be deployed in this kind of situation and to understand more about the place of the use of force, once the strategic-level decision to deploy it has been taken. Dobbie says that the use of force has a place at the tactical level for dealing with specific incidents, but the use of force has no place at the operational or the strategic level – because that, in itself, would be to bring the mission to an end. There would be no way back. However, the Dobbie position is not enough. To a large extent, once a force has been deployed at the strategic level, to allow the mission to end because of a breakdown in consent is inconceivable, given the original political commitment.

THE EVOLUTION OF STRATEGIC PEACEKEEPING IN BOSNIA AND HERZEGOVINA

With the comfort of hindsight, it is possible, *ex post facto*, to look at the situation in Bosnia and Herzegovina and conclude that the consent argument was wrong.[8] This was a situation in which, first of all, Western European Union (WEU) member states then, branching out (both towards NATO, in terms of infrastructure, and the UN, in terms of authorisation), took a decision in the summer of 1992 to deploy troops to Bosnia and Herzegovina. They took that decision in response to a set of challenges that were emerging from the conflict there.

In particular, there were two concerns.[9] One was the impact of ethnic cleansing, both in terms of a moral imperative and of the pressures of an outflow of refugees, especially into Western Europe. It became a concern for European countries to respond to those challenges in a way which would deal with those aspects. There was a second, perhaps bigger, question which concerned the Serbian project to change the borders of Bosnia and Herzegovina, to break them up through force. This attempt to breach one of the cardinal principles of the international system – that borders should not be changed as a result of the use of force – had to be met with some kind of response. This was therefore a question at the strategic level. It was not simply a matter of recognising that there were some problems on the ground in Bosnia and then deciding that we would like to put troops there to help them.

The difficulty, in this particular case, may have been that there was no strategic definition to accompany a response made at the strategic level.[10] Gradually, the Western European countries, and, through a process of enhancements over a number of years, other countries deployed troops in a complex operation on the ground which was given no clear objective from the outset, but which had the implicit focus of maintaining Bosnia and Herzegovina as a whole and of trying to resist ethnic cleansing as far as possible.

For this reason, given the actual nature of the operation, one possibility might have been to create a refugee haven. This would have meant taking one part of the country – rather like the Kurdish 'safe haven' in northern Iraq – and making a commitment to protect the people within that designated area. To do so, in the eyes of many, including the UN High Commissioner for Refugees (UNHCR) (which had being designated as lead agency regarding this case), would have been to condone ethnic cleansing. To have done so would have been to make a concession to the Serbs by saying, in effect, that they would be able to cleanse outside the designated area. This could, in turn, implicitly be seen to raise questions about the territorial integrity of Bosnia.

The alternative to this was that which, in fact, happened. This was the deployment of a small number of troops on a spider's web of operations to try to help people to stay where they were. On the basis of consent, this was open to people on all sides. The UN operation, as it had become, was going to deliver humanitarian aid to everybody. Humanitarian aid was a useful to tool to explain why a force should be deployed,[11] although, implicitly, it was a force helping communities under siege, as far as possible. It was also open to the Serbs – a way of saying to them that the force was not 'against' them; the idea was not to go to war on the part of the Bosnia government, but to try to bring the conflict to an end at the same time as maintaining Bosnia and Herzegovina as the state framework and resisting ethnic cleansing, as far as possible.

This was a strategic-level question. Yet, the Dobbie doctrine was to be applied at the tactical level. Much of what happened on the ground was defined by tactical-level perceptions, in the absence of any strategic-level vision. This absence was because, at the strategic level, there was a lack of political will and a great deal of uncertainty about the nature of the operation. A large part of this was the problem of bringing together disparate elements from parts of the international community and pitching them against the disparate elements in Bosnia.

There was an essential problem, first, to define what the mission was about and to define it in such a way that it would be acceptable to the contributing member states (on a number of levels – military, official, political and public), those various international organisations involved and to the several communities within Bosnia and its neighbouring countries – at the military, political and population levels. There was a set of different audiences which needed to be kept on board. The key aspect in all of this is legitimation – the concept at the heart of the present analysis regarding the ways in which a degree of success can be achieved in this type of operation.

THE ROLE OF LEGITIMATION IN STRATEGIC PEACEKEEPING

Legitimation has three elements.[12] The first of these concerns the bases for legitimation – which in terms of PSOs means the mandate provided by the relevant Security Council resolutions, as well as why people believe they are there, irrespective of those resolutions – *de facto* what they are actually doing. The second element is performance. This refers to how soldiers do whatever it is they are doing. Crucially, this relates to military culture and whether or not the soldiers are performing well or feel that they are performing well or have the respect of their own national communities, as well as that of other countries and of the host communities. The final layer of legitimation is support. This may mean support either for the performance of the force or for the bases upon which the force is deployed (which may include the mandate or not).

The bases of legitimation at the strategic level may involve UN Security Council mandates, the decisions made by governments (the reasons why they commit the troops), the perceptions and the policies of the host country and population. Each of these has to be kept under review if the mission is to be successful. In terms of the Dobbie doctrine, this generates a number of problems. If there is reliance on consent, but one of the parties sees that it can get what it wants, either by failing to give consent or by relying on the necessity of consent to get away with what it is doing, there is a challenge. Does the force allow the Serbs, for example, in Bosnia to continue with ethnic cleansing? Does it allow attacks on 'safe areas'? Or does it make some kind of a stand? If so, what kind of stand can be made?

Implicitly, this means a possible use of force. Yet the Dobbie doctrine precludes a use of force because that will bring the mission to an end and its purpose will not be served. In fact, the reality is that if ways are not found to operate at that strategic level, to take the strategic initiative, pursuant to the initial strategic-level decision to deploy a force, then the force itself will begin to lose credibility. In addition, the sponsoring international bodies will begin to lose credibility too, and, in the end, the states which contributed to those forces will begin to realise that they themselves are losing credibility – and that the value of the organisations, as well as the values for which they themselves stand, are being brought into question.

This is a serious problem which is not merely one of morality, as it appears on first reading. It is also one of interest. The member states of the UN, NATO and many other bodies are members because they believe that those bodies have value. They are ways of promoting the interests of the states themselves. If, in a situation where it has already been decided that some strategic-level response is required, those bodies are not seen to be able to be successful then the bodies themselves will begin to lose credibility, to fall into disrepute and the member states will have to face the question of how to repair this.

The question is not so much one of simply positing the use of force versus consent, it is, rather, a way of gaining strategic coherence. The importance of strategic coherence cannot be ignored if there is to be an operation which is functioning at the strategic–operational level and which has, to whatever degree, taken the strategic initiative. That may mean using force in certain cases. It may mean the avoidance of force in others. It will probably mean an attempt to maximise the degree of consent so as to oil the wheels of the operation. But it also means that consent cannot be the absolute that it becomes in the Dobbie doctrine at the operational level. But it is not the only factor. It has to be integrated into the framework of whatever it is that the mission is intended to achieve. In this sense the use of force is one particular instance of the salient phenomena which, in terms of legitimation, provide the focus for support: the use of force, or a failure to use force, among other actions, provides the issue around which belief and positive, or negative, discourse revolve.

The point of using force, as with any other salient action, is to maintain equilibrium in the mission. If, however, force is to be used, then it is necessary to have troops of a certain kind. It may not be possible to specify what that type will be on all occasions. But it is certain that they will need to have some degree of common understanding of what they are doing, that they will have to feel confident about what they are doing and that they feel that what they are doing is likely to work and to be respected. These are what we regard as questions of military culture. This applies to individual components of the force and to the international dimension of the force as it is put together.

The other element of strategic coherence is to look at ways in which to frame a strategic programme, either through design or opportunism or, most likely, a blend of the two. This serves to maintain the momentum of the diplomatic, political and strategic processes which the military operation supports. One of the big problems the force in Bosnia faced before 1995, as did others elsewhere, was that, day in, day out, they could do good work and achieve things in positive ways, but that this did not get noticed. Rather, the general outcome and the broad perception of the force's performance were defined by notable, salient moments. These are what we call defining moments. The remaining part of this analysis will examine the importance of these moments and, first, of military culture for the legitimation of strategic peacekeeping missions.

MILITARY CULTURE, RESPECT AND COHERENCE

One of the key ingredients to ensure the legitimation of a strategic peacekeeping operation is the military personnel engaged on it. The military are vital to legitimation in two ways. First, they provide one of the crucial audiences that need to be convinced about the purpose and success of the operation, in addition to their own states, peoples, the wider world and the conflicting parties. Second, the military themselves are a crucial basis of legitimation for the operation. Both in their own perception, with regard, for instance, to morale, and in those of their several other audiences, the performance of the mission by the armed forces is vital. Good performance can overcome deficiencies in the bases of legitimation, as well as add value to bases with broad acceptance, while poor performance can corrode support for the bases of legitimation. In a sense, over time, performance becomes, in itself, a particular basis of legitimation. It is likely to be far more important as a perceived *raison d'être* for the mission, indeed, than many of the technical and formal bases themselves.

It is well known that the military cultures of different countries are more or less compatible with the classical peacekeeping ethos. There is strong evidence to indicate that there may be certain types of soldier that do not make very good traditional peacekeepers. (For example, in the British case, the Parachute Regiment might be argued not be the best suited for such duties.) There are, in contrast, certain societies which find peacekeeping quite amenable to their own military ethos, for example, Sweden. Forces associated with a strong tradition of a warfighting role, particularly the sharper ends of those forces, might find it difficult to adjust to traditional peacekeeping in terms of their own military cultures – as was the case with US forces learning from Scandinavians when operating together in the United Nations' Preventive Deployment to Macedonia (UNPREDEP).[13] Some of the evidence indicates that the morale of peacekeepers drawn from warfighting armies may become low in certain conditions.

Moreover, if this last proposition is considered with regard to non-traditional peacekeeping in general, then, if Dobbie's prescription is

190

followed, the chances of low morale in frustrated strategic peacekeeping might well be acutely high. Soldiers who could take action may become frustrated by the limitations placed upon them and, feeling futile, lose their morale. According to Dobbie, to operate without operational consent is bound to lead to confusion and a corollary of this is the clear risk of low morale. Strategic peacekeeping, as a concept, addresses these issues which are, essentially, questions of military culture. How are military formations going to be attuned to the demands of strategic peacekeeping, whether or not they are drawn from countries which find this type of work more or less amenable? What qualities are important for successful performance? How important is operational acculturation in this process?

There are four areas which have to be addressed in order to resolve these issues of military culture. First, in the context of a strategic peacekeeping operation in which force is a possibility at the strategic level, one of the important points for the military participants to be aware of is that being impartial in the application of a mandate does not mean being a passive, value-neutral observer, simply watching and reporting back to the UN or some other sponsoring agency. On the contrary, in a strategic peacekeeping operation, the crucial thing is the active but impartial application of a mandate even if, four days a week, it looks as though the force may be acting against one belligerent party at the operational level – because that party happens to be the one breaking the mandate the soldiers are impartially applying.

Second, it is crucial to recognise that the mandate must be robustly applied in order for its legitimacy to remain intact. One of the key features of strategic peacekeeping is that the end state cannot be defined in advance by the intervening powers. Rather, it is their role in using force to edge the conflicting parties to a solution that is of their own making. In doing so military commanders have to be able to make the most of a fluid and dynamic situation on the ground – that is, to capitalise on defining moments. This idea poses a sharp challenge to the traditional military mentality that is geared to the supposition that one should use force only if one knows in advance what the end state is, and that one has the necessary means to achieve it, together with knowledge of the time-frame in which the operation will be concluded. The notion of operating without a predefined end state is perceived as particularly unhelpful if forces are having to deploy in a volatile warlike environment. There is a fear of the morale-corroding effects of stasis. This is why our point about momentum is so important.

This discussion of the end state echoes an earlier analysis made by Morris Janowitz in *The Professional Soldier*.[14] Janowitz referred to a constabulary force: one that was continuously prepared to act, focused on the minimal use of force and the pursuit of viable, international relations rather than victory. We would suggest that Janowitz would have been better served by using measured rather than minimum, at least in the context of the kinds of conflict that we are discussing here. Janowitz, however, was acutely aware of how these ideas challenged the values of the traditional warriors or 'heroic leaders'. These tend to thwart the constabulary concept because of their desire to maintain conventional military doctrine and their resistance to assessing the political consequences of limited military actions which do not produce 'victory'. Meanwhile, technologists tend to exaggerate the importance of high-intensity weapons and their importance in international relations.

Third, in applying the mandate, despite the pressures for micro-management in these operations because of the political sensitivity associated with them, it is critical that the military personnel involved have sufficient autonomy to use their initiative in applying the mandate. Without the scope for and presence of initiative, creative opportunities may well be lost, contributing to a deterioration in the standing of the force.

Finally, one of the key elements for the success of the mission and for the maintenance of the military's commitment to these sorts of operation, is the need for a sense of self-respect. If this sense is not there, there will be a loss of commitment to the mission and morale will dwindle.[15] Regarding strategic peacekeeping, a crucial lesson is that impartiality in applying a mandate means respect from the contending parties; but it also means ensuring that there is self-respect. If this is lacking the ability to continue the mission, indeed, to go on and succeed with the mission or to undertake one on another occasion, will be lessened. To ensure self-respect it is necessary to ensure a high degree of strategic coherence, as well as to be seen not to be performing poorly. Central to this is effectiveness in defining moments.

DEFINING MOMENTS: THE SALIENCE OF EFFECTIVE ACTION, OR FAILURE

The foregoing points refer to key elements of coherence – the coherence which goes together to make an operational capability which can be used within the given strategic environment. This coherence is crucial to the legitimation of a strategic peacekeeping operation. However, legitimation is not something easy to gauge. It is not like an arithmetic equation: there is no way of saying, at any stage, that two plus two will equal four. But, in trying to look at the way a force can try to maintain momentum and coherence at the strategic level one of the most important dimensions, we maintain, is that of 'defining moments'. A defining moment is one in which opportunities are either opened up or closed off (depending on the approach and outcome), setting, or contributing to, the tone of the mission for the following period and providing the focal point around which discourse and support for the mission accumulate or dissipate. What this means in practice may be seen with reference to two examples – one a defining moment from the period of conflict in Bosnia and Herzegovina, the other one from the period of peace implementation there.

There were a number of points in the course of the international operations in Bosnia where, irrespective of what was actually happening from day-to-day, there was usually one event which shaped perceptions and either enabled the force to move forward or prevented successful operations for some time. Examples include the Srebrenica crisis of July 1995, the so-called crisis over air-strikes against Pale at the end of May 1995, the Bihac situation at the end of 1994, or Gorazde in April 1994. For present purposes, the example we shall focus on is that of February 1994, the famous Sarajevo market mortar attack. This was a moment which, at the time, was seen to change the course of events and appeared to make life easier for the UN operation for a few months. This example is particularly useful as it makes clear the difference between that which was happening on the ground and the defining moment perception.

Lt-Gen. Sir Michael Rose, the Bosnia force commander at that time, had been involved in Mixed Military Working Group (MMWG) negotiations with all the parties about the artillery around Sarajevo and about the use of the airport. His superior, who at that time was Gen. François Briquemont, had ordered Russian troops deployed in eastern Slavonia (in Croatia) to go to Sarajevo to assist in implementing the agreement for which the MMWG was working. The Russian commander had declined Briquemont's order, saying that he would have to ask Moscow. This was, again, one small but crucial example of the problems in trying to make a force of this type coherent and making it work. These elements were in place, but for the agreement of the Russian commander.

Against this background, there was the market square mortar attack which changed international perception. Suddenly, the French and the Americans were talking in very tough terms, followed by a NATO ultimatum of action – all of which took place at the strategic level, over and above the low-level activity which was happening on the ground and catalysed an agreement. Yet,there was a common perception that it was the NATO threat which got the agreement. In the end, this might have been the case. But much of what happened was in train anyway.

Another common perception was that a Russian diplomatic coup had saved the day. In fact, however, all the Russians had done was to allow their troops to be redeployed in the way that the force commander had already ordered-cum-requested. The point is that this, as a defining moment, gave a sense to the mission for the coming months. It would be two months before that was brought into question at Gorazde by a defining moment of a different kind with a less clear outcome. What the response to the Sarajevo mortar showed was that a force could be carried along, if a defining moment could either be identified in advance or pragmatically seized upon when it arose.

There are two possibilities for the salience of a defining moment. First, defining moments give momentum, in terms of performance, and, by giving momentum, they become foci of identity. In terms of the bases of the operation, the defining moments are a component part of the basis upon which an operation is carried out. The alternative is that the response in a defining moment is inappropriate and the mission is compromised and subject to inertia.

Looking to the second phase of peace implementation in Bosnia – the NATO-led Stabilisation Force (SFOR) – the apprehension of individuals indicted under suspicion of having committed war crimes provides a positive defining moment.[16] SFOR was deployed as the successor to the Implementation Force (IFOR). The first year of implementation was accomplished and elections held successfully, despite some questions surrounding their absolute propriety and outcome. One year of peace, as well as the basic political and constitutional arrangements born of the peace agreement, were consolidated by the holding of elections.

But there was a sense that, with a further 18 months and more of deployment for SFOR and, after that, its reduced, final-phase component DFOR (Dissuasion Force), the key questions concerned how the peace was to be taken forward. On the ground there were local negotiations, local interactions, a bridge built here, a bridge built there, a factory working again somewhere – but none of this created a sense of momentum. It could only be the big, defining moments that enabled the momentum of the force to be carried forward.

Looking at this situation, it was necessary to determine the big issues: the return of refugees; institution building and integration of the two entities under the Dayton peace agreement; solutions to the disputed towns of Brcko and Mostar; and the apprehension of those indicted for war crimes. This was a situation in which, if SFOR were not to get into the same kinds of problem as UNPROFOR had, then it had to be looking for, and take advantage of, defining moments. Such moments were likely to stem from one of those four areas – although one might well have emerged in a way that could not be envisaged. Pragmatically, there had to be a readiness to seize the moment, should it appear, even though the four areas remained the most likely.

Of the four, Brcko was close to insoluble. Whichever way a solution was sought, in the short term at least, this seemed bound to present a serious challenge to the mission overall and to the future of the peace deal. The best therefore in this case was to defer the matter. The same was true of the local elections which were deferred. The return of refugees was far too big a problem to look at in the short term – even though it was given priority by the Office of the High Representative's making 1998 'the year of return'.[17] The apprehension of war criminals was very risky, but, still, the most straightforward and achievable of the relevant objectives.

Following much of the use of force debate surrounding UNPROFOR, it might be consistent to conclude that the objectives were too difficult and too dangerous. Indeed, this was exactly the kind of debate that each of these questions generated in government departments and international bodies. With officials asking themselves, 'What can we do? It's all too risky', there could have been a tendency to conclude that it might be better to concentrate on the security of the force first, rather than seeking to accomplish objectives.

This had to be pitched against the overriding sense that, if the strategic momentum were to be created or sustained, then there would have to be some kind of action, risky though this might be. This would be defining-moment action. The risks of not taking such action would be greater, given the security policy and strategic interests which led the several states and international bodies to be involved in the first place. In this context it is evident that the British lead on apprehending indictees was significant.

The first operation, on 10 July 1997, had a major impact on a number of levels. First, it ensured the momentum and self-respect of the armed force deployed. Second, it conveyed the clear message to the world, to the troop-sponsoring countries and the people and political actors in Bosnia and Herzegovina that the international force would be proactive and could be expected to take firm action. Third, it had the vital strategic effect of sending those implicated in the suspected commission of war crimes and crimes against humanity into hiding, reducing the degree to which they could obstruct the process of peace implementation, while giving opportunities for others, more open to cooperation, to emerge. This is precisely what happened in the Serbian entity, the Republika Srpska, with leaders prepared to cooperate with implementation – such as President Biljana Plavsic and, after subsequent elections, the new Prime Minister Milorad Dodik – moving from strength to strength. Thus, the first incidence of apprehension was a salient moment in defining the course of the Bosnian peace process, supplemented by further operations in November 1997 and in January, April and May 1998.

CONCLUSION

It is necessary to understand that missions such as those in Bosnia and Herzegovina are strategic-level operations. These are strategic peace-keeping operations with peculiar characteristics as a type of operation. In these operations important requirements include the maintaining of coherence and equilibrium. These requirements can be subsumed by the concept of legitimation. Legitimation is vital if the mission is to be successful.

Given that this is the case, then sensitive judgements have to be made about risk calculations and risk itself. These judgements reflect strategic imperatives and the need to seek the strategic initiative. Taking the strategic initiative is vital to the process of legitimation by which the operation can be successful. While this could involve an enormous spread of incidents and events, two issues are of salience: military culture and defining moments, as we have argued.

The military culture of the forces deployed is of vital importance to success. The military are both a constituency of support for the operation, through their self-perception, self-respect and morale and, through their performance, a focal point around which support can form. Moreover, the degree to which force commanders can seize the strategic initiative and turn defining moments to the advantage of the mission is of supreme importance. Defining moments provide the strategic focal points for perception and support and can either close off opportunities or open the way for them, thereby affecting the legitimation of the operation. The defining moments in an operation, cumulatively, define legitimation and, ultimately, success.

NOTES

1. The present analysis stems from a research project conducted jointly by the authors on 'The Legitimation of Multinational Military Peace Support Operations' funded by the Harry Frank Guggenheim Foundation.
2. The conceptual definition of that which we term traditional peacekeeping is clear. Such peacekeeping has three characteristics: a strategically static situation in which third-party assistance is given to people who want it; the second is consent, which flows from the first and the fact that two parties

want the third to be there; and, third, it is based on a non-threatening posture, either unarmed or lightly armed. Essentially, you have a strategically static situation in which a small force is not going to do anything to anybody. There is a not inconsiderable literature on peacekeeping. We have discussed some of the key aspects of this literature and the central conceptual concerns in earlier related work: James Gow and Christopher Dandeker 'Peace-support Operations: The Problem of Legitimation', *The World Today*, 51, 8–9 (August–September 1995) and Dandeker and Gow, 'The Future of Peace Support Operations: Strategic Peacekeeping and Success', *Armed Forces and Society*, 23, 3 (Spring 1997).

3. Thus, in contrast to the strategically static nature of traditional peacekeeping where the initiative lies with parties to the conflict, the type of situation with which we are concerned is strategically dynamic not static. It is one in which, although maximal consent is still the ideal, consent may well be challenged, even where there is some consensual basis for the deployment, as in Bosnia and Herzegovina, where there are still some parts of the mandate which go beyond that and which are subject, for example, to Chapter VII enforcement measures authorised by the Security Council. So there is a complex: the mission is based on the need to maximise consent, as far as possible, while recognising that there is a situation in which consent is not likely to be easily forthcoming – therefore the Security Council has authorised those enforcement measures as part of the mandate (it should be stressed, only as one part of the mandate) to enable certain things to be permissible.

4. Whether or not strategic peacekeeping is the right term is open to discussion. Although it is useful for carrying the discussion forward, it might not be definitive. But it is a problematic term, given that peacekeeping could be seen entirely as a passive activity in which there is no strategic initiative taken by the force or its international sponsors. Similarly, terms such as peace enforcement or the more generic PSOs are used in different ways, depending on the authors involved. The virtue of the label we have adopted for this activity is that it does put the focus at the strategic level.

5. By comparison, in a conventional peacekeeping operation the strategic initiative lies with the parties to the conflict who have made clear that, whatever strategic objectives they had, they have come to the conclusion that they will not be able to get any further and so have said 'Please, help us', and the forces are deployed at the initiation of the parties. In this context there is a difference and that difference is that, at the strategic level, a response is being made to a conflict.

6. This use of terms reflects UN definitions, for convenience. (See Boutros Boutros-Ghali, *An Agenda for Peace*, UN Doc. S/24111, 17 June 1992.) However, as indicated above, terms in this field are subject to debate. Our use of the UN's interpretation of peace enforcement is not consistent with the use of the term in draft British doctrine documents, for example. In seeking to delineate strategic peacekeeping we are acutely aware that, not only are other academic analysts interested in identifying the nature and the possibilities of operating in the middle ground between peacekeeping and peace enforcement, but so are policy planners and military personnel concerned with the preparation and application of military doctrine. In a sense, our work is intended as an intervention in terms of academic research, as well as, we hope, an intervention in policy and doctrine development.

7. The authors interviewed Charles Dobbie, who has since left the Army to train to be a priest, intensively on these matters.

8. However, we have the satisfaction of having published our assessment on this before events took a turn to confirm that analysis. See Gow and Dandeker, 'Peace-support Operations'.

9. See J. Gow, *Triumph of the Lack of Will: International Diplomacy and the Yugoslav War* (New York and London: Columbia University Press and Hurst, 1997); Warren Zimmermann, *Origins of a Catastrophe: Yugoslavia and Its Destroyers* (New York: Times Books, 1996); Laura Silber and Alan Little, *The Death of Yugoslavia* (New York and London: Penguin, 1995); and Susan Woodward, *Balkan Tragedy* (Washington, DC: Brookings, 1995).

10. This insight was offered by a senior British official in discussion with the authors.

11. This point was made by a senior British official in discussion with one of the authors.

12. This approach follows that elaborated in James Gow, *Legitimacy and the Military: The Yugoslav Crisis* (London: Pinter, 1992), pp. 12–14.

13. One US officer, Lt-Col. Carter Ham, for example, noted that the most important aspect of the mission was familiarisation with the Nordic troops and 'the way they work'. Quoted in Richard Calver, 'Blessed are the Peacemakers – Regulars, by God!', *UNPROFOR News* (June 1994).

14. M. Janowitz, *The Professional Soldier* (Glencoe: Free Press, 1973), pp. 424–5.

15. This was strongly put by Gen. Philippe Morillon in our research interviews, as well as in his subsequent public statements.

16. This approach was prefigured in the original presentation of this argument at the doctrine conference which spawned the present volume at the Royal Military Academy Sandhurst in January 1997 and in a presentation to the War Studies Research Seminar two months later.

17. It might be noted that the delineation of an unrealistic aim as the theme for a year was a hostage to fortune, likely to result in a negative definition of the mission's success.

12

British Peacekeeping Doctrine: A Critique

RICHARD CONNAUGHTON

The British government's 1998 Strategic Defence Review implicitly acknowledged the reality that expeditionary conflict as a form of military action required a reappraisal of positions, priorities and policies. This was to be done with the caveat that so-called 'warfighting' capabilities would not be compromised. There is an obvious tension here and a danger of overreaching and attempting to do too much with too little on too small a budget. This factor obviously has to be kept uppermost in our minds but this chapter is concerned with the subject of expeditionary conflict and whether the United Kingdom has the appropriate policies and doctrine for its proper conduct.

The British have had a traditional disdain for doctrine, regarding it as prejudicial to their intuitive and innovative spirit. If we look back to the middle of the nineteenth century to identify the centres of military thinking, we find that in 1859 approximately half of the relevant literature was produced in Germany, a quarter in France and one per cent in Britain. In 1924 J. F. C. Fuller recalled a conversation with the Chief of the Imperial General Staff, who 'considered it to be contrary to military discipline for any officer on the active list to write on military subjects. I hear, on good authority, that he is against the creation of a War College.'[1] War Colleges came, but their effectiveness was brought into question:

> Since the advent of war schools native genius has been crippled by pedantry, not because sound military education is in itself detrimental (such a contention would be absurd), but because the easiest thing to do in a school is to copy the past and the past is something dead and gone, and frequently a thing which was misbegotten.[2]

Today, there is still the thread of anti-intellectualism running through

British military thought processes and too frequently a continuing failure, in Fuller's words, to 'probe into the viscera of living war'. Where there is a poverty of knowledge there remains the tendency to copy the thinking of others, not just in the past but also in the present, without applying the requisite tests and challenges to that plagiarised thinking. The Higher Command and Staff Course was intended to encourage and stimulate original thinking among those officers of the three services assumed to be destined for high command. The problem in a hierarchical organisation headed by a senior reporting officer is that there may be limited scope for subordinates to advise the general that he is not wearing any clothes. There are few military enterprises more personality-dominated than doctrine.

The purpose of doctrine[3] is 'to establish the framework of understanding of the approach to warfare in order to provide the foundation for its practical application'.[4] The formulation of doctrine should follow three evolutionary stages, namely, debate, decision and execution. There is an unbreakable link between doctrine and training since commanders are expected to train their men in accordance with current doctrine.

Although the British Army had the tradition of doing 'what we thought', a great deal of doctrinal guidance was to be found in what were the building blocks of military doctrine, namely the training manuals. 'The Infantry Battalion in Battle' and 'Keeping the Peace Parts 1 and 2' contained much more doctrine than the doctrinal cynic would have cared to admit.

The end of World War II and the emergence of nuclear deterrence did generate a doctrine for general global war, but the implications of such a doomsday scenario also brought into focus the concept of limited war. The year 1948 witnessed the end of the attempt by World War II's victorious allies to draw up a collective security regime centred upon standing forces under the aegis of the United Nations' enforcement Chapter VII. This provides for intensive forms of coercion, not necessarily violent or involving physical conflict. The influence of the Cold War was now apparent and the Permanent Five, unable to work together in the field of collective security, took a back seat in international intervention, confining their efforts in the main to the pursuit of national interests.

What emerged internationally in the conceptual vacuum was an activity not provided for in the UN Charter, but one which found accommodation under the umbrella of Chapter VI of the Charter, the Pacific Settlement of Disputes, namely Peacekeeping. Peacekeeping emerged as a low-risk activity well within the capabilities of lightly trained, often conscript forces. Three basic understandings arose as to the conduct of military operations in these passive inter-state environments. First, the troops were not normally drawn from among the permanent representatives of the Security Council, hence there was no requirement for Britain to contemplate the preparation of a separate doctrine. Second, impartial 'blue berets' used force only for the purpose of self-defence. Third, the monitoring of inter-state borders and ceasefire lines was conducted with the consent of the states involved.

Peacekeeping has invariably been a sponsored activity under the aegis of the UN's Department of Peacekeeping Operations (DPKO). (The notable exception has been the post-Dayton peacekeeping operation in Bosnia which conceptually resembles a traditional UN peacekeeping operation but is a sanctioned, rather than a sponsored, activity.) The DPKO is the operational arm of the UN's Secretary-General, responsible for the day-to-day management of sponsored peacekeeping operations. Command and control of sponsored operations was exercised through a headquarters which reflected the heterogeneous nature, geographical spread, ethnic diversity and mixture of the sexes which the UN is obliged to consider. It did not always provide the most cohesive or efficient of headquarters. On 30 April 1994 *The Economist* observed how the UN 'can try to promote or keep a peace, but it is not equipped physically or mentally to enforce one'. However, traditional peacekeeping is not such a dynamic activity that, in a federal enterprise such as this, the national component commanders could not seek permission from their capitals if required by the UN military commander to do anything out of the ordinary.

It was the Katanga crisis in the Congo which first indicated possible problems with the peacekeeping concept, but there was not to be a revisitation of that looming problem for over a generation. Then, while the actual number of UN operations increased, the number of environments to which traditional peacekeepers were deployed fell as a result of the influence of 'changed circumstances'. For example, the understanding that peacekeepers used lethal force only in self-defence came under increasing pressure when they found themselves engaged in areas where the settlement of disputes with firearms was the norm. Moreover, a contradiction arose in the sending of traditional peacekeepers into hostile, even complicated, environments where the host state and the neighbouring states' armed forces enjoyed a higher level of military competence and capability than the blue berets. The nature of UN military operations had begun to change, but the DPKO did not have the expertise to conduct operations requiring a heightened, proportional, military response by well-trained soldiers. There was little opportunity for manoeuvre or to identify new opportunities for traditional peacekeeping operations. Before 1991, and with the exceptions of South Africa and Rhodesia, the UN steadfastly remained a state-centric organisation in its attitude to inter-national disputes, reflecting the traditional 1945 sense of peace and security.

There are two circumstances under which a state or collection of states may legally engage in armed conflict: first, when backed by a Security Council resolution and, second, in the matter of self-defence under Article 51 of the UN Charter. The 1990–91 Gulf conflict was a Chapter VII inter-state military intervention, the second of its kind after the Korean War. The United States was sanctioned by the UN to lead a coalition to force Iraq out of Kuwait. In a stunning military operation, the immediate objective was achieved and the UN congratulated itself on having author-ised the type of military operation the founding fathers of the UN had envisaged. The problem was that the number of potential inter-state conflicts had become few indeed. Intra-state conflict has always been the most prevalent form of conflict, but until 1991 there was a broad inter-national understanding that states enjoyed domestic sanctity within borders under Article 2(7), which, incidentally, did not exclude the possi-bility of military intervention. At this time there were approximately 28 to 30 ongoing, major, intra-state conflicts – a figure which has been consistently maintained up to today.

The end in principle of this notion of domestic sanctity came in 1991 when 20,000, mostly Western, troops entered northern Iraq in support of the Kurds and without the consent of Iraq's government. The Secretary-General acknowledged:

> While respect for the fundamental sovereignty and integrity of the state remains central, it is undeniable that the centuries-old doctrine of absolute and exclusive sovereignty no longer stands, and was in fact never so absolute as it was conceived to be in theory.[5]

This was a moment of pivotal importance, because it allowed for the intervention of another state or states, when authorised, in another state's domestic affairs when so moved by interest or conscience or both. Choice figured prominently as a factor in putative intervention.

In those heady days after the Gulf conflict there was no shortage of states volunteering their armed forces to serve under the UN – as many as 80,000 servicemen were engaged on military operations on behalf of the UN. There was, however, a paradox. The likelihood of the early repetition of the Chapter VII, Limited War type conflict in the mould of Korea (1950–53) and the Gulf (1990–91) was remote, and examples of traditional Chapter VI peacekeeping were also few and far between. The question therefore is, on what basis and under what understanding was the UN employing so many servicemen? The answer was that a gap, a large one, a grey area, had opened up between the norms and the understanding of Chapters VI and VII. As a consequence, the normal functions of peacekeeping and military intervention were extended and drawn into the vacuum, which colloquially became known as 'Chapter VI½' (although this is not the meaning intended by Dag Hammarskjöld, the man who coined the phrase). The UN therefore found itself in a situation of needing to sponsor or sanction military operations in a broad, new band of military activity for which there were no rules or doctrine. It became apparent to a small number of observers that a review of the UN's 'peacekeeping' *modus operandi* was overdue. There was no overt intention to marginalise the UN, but rather to make it more relevant and better able to respond to contemporary challenges. As Sir Brian Urquhart said, 'The United Nations has many shortcomings and is weak in many respects, but it is still the best, perhaps the only framework in which we can try to develop some kind of effective world order.'[6] However, the UN, 'the palace of the status quo ... insisting on using systems where they cannot be used',[7] was unable and unwilling to reform or to reorder its military operations. There was an urgent need for a positive external stimulus. Unfortunately, the stimulus that did come was extremely negative but welcomed in New York because it enabled the organisation to paper over the wide cracks in its facade.

In 1991 a new Headquarters Doctrine and Training was formed in Britain. The establishment of such a headquarters, with its requisite staff, has to be seen against the defence climate in the country at that time – a period of continuous review and salami-slice reductions in equipment and manpower. The headquarters had to succeed. During 1992–95, the new staff of this organisation produced a doctrine intended for international use which they described as 'Wider Peacekeeping'. At this period of great change, therefore, where it was apparent there were three basic operational situations – Chapter VI traditional peacekeeping, the 'Chapter VI½' 'grey area', and Chapter VII intervention operations – the UK's Doctrine Command announced there to be but two divisions: peacekeeping and peace-enforcement. The formula did not match what was happening in a changing world. It has to be emphasised that the three divisions given here – Chapters VI, VI½ and VII – are not precise entities since they are influenced and distorted by a number of variable factors such as political context, strategic goals and cultural differences. However, to allow for the existence of 'grey areas' is preferable to denying their existence. We have to explore in more detail, with more energy and more enthusiasm, precisely what constitutes a 'grey-area' operation.

There were voices which drew this mismatch to the attention of those in charge of the development of British military doctrine. An emissary from the doctrine staffs advised the Strategic and Combat Studies Institute's (SCSI) academic advisory team, established to be a focus for the study of war – past, present and future – that the new, wider peace-keeping doctrine was not to be challenged. Almost all of the members of the SCSI worked for HQ Doctrine and Training. When alternative options were discussed, those concerned were censured. Thus, one of the vital stages in the formulation of any doctrine, the in-house debate, was not held and the transparent connection of this doctrine with a small number of personalities began to conform with undesirable features of the past. There were voices of encouragement for the dissenting camp, but essentially these came from interested parties unable to speak publicly or from those as far away as Oslo and Rhode Island. Notwithstanding, both the UN Department in the Foreign and Commonwealth Office (FCO) and the Army Doctrine Committee approved the adoption of the 'Wider Peacekeeping' doctrine.

A pamphlet was produced but it was not long before the doctrine was contested. Sir Brian Urquhart expressed the view that the doctrine was an unhelpful diversion because it attempted to take peacekeeping into areas never intended and where it could not exist. 'I believe that the doctrine of wider peacekeeping is very misleading,' he said. 'It is danger-ous nonsense.'[8] The UN Department at the FCO contacted the UK Permanent Representative's office in New York to seek clarification from Urquhart. This request was declined on the grounds that the UK's UN staff in New York believed what had been said to be correct. They told London that they were not prepared to challenge one of the UN's most respected grandees. As a concept, Wider Peacekeeping disappeared from view, but the reality remained of grey-area operations still being under-taken without the benefit of a doctrine.

It was evident to those interested parties supporting the furtherance of peacekeeping that they had also to demonstrate that the two remaining components of peacekeeping, consent and impartiality, its DNA, were transferable into the fields of enhanced military activity. However, while consent and impartiality may be understood in societies which have established the place of the umpire, as in cricket or baseball, they are not concepts universally understood by the parties in the conflicts in which interventionist states will be called upon to intervene. We cannot apply our perceptions and standards universally to every environment with the conviction that they are bound to be appropriate. The inapplicability of consent in operations beyond peacekeeping is receiving wider recog-nition, albeit grudgingly and with little positive application to actual events. In intra-state environments, consent tends not to be a constant but a variable. And as laudable as operating impartially may be, it is a two-sided consideration. It is one thing for interventionists to believe they are acting impartially but quite another to convince the parties to the conflict that that is the case. Political events before military intervention may well damn the soldiers and present them as partial actors. The European Community's (EC) early recognition of Croatia during the Bosnia crisis, for example, meant that forces from EC countries would not be recognised as impartial by the Serbs. Humanitarian aid delivered to one party in the conflict is a less overt form of partiality in comparison to that of arming and equipping the Muslim forces in Bosnia post-Dayton.

Another indicator to look for is the tension and ambivalence that exist between Chapters VI and VII, demonstrating the all too obvious need for the formulation of rules and principles for operations in the grey area. If the reader bears in mind the lessons about to be highlighted, the more surprising is the British Doctrine HQ's assertion that 'the new idea that there is a new middle ground of military operations that lie [sic] somewhere between peacekeeping and peace enforcement is not only specious historically, but dangerously destabilising doctrinally'. Thus the Wider Peacekeeping doctrine encouraged the universal use of the word 'peacekeeping' and its application to environments where there was no peace to be kept. Furthermore, it encouraged the substitution of the term 'peace enforcement' for military intervention when not all military interventions will have as their aim that of enforcing peace.

The description 'peace enforcement' therefore is a sublime statement of virtual unreality. It is a misnomer, for very rarely will it be possible to enforce peace. Organisations or states with such an intention through interest or conscience will require a clear understanding as to how peace is to be enforced, by whom and for how long. The decision-making process will be dominated by three considerations: low risk, low cost and short duration. The portents are not good. The UN Standby Arrangement System (UNSAS), designed to increase UN member states' reactions to crises, was a database containing the details of the military units of member states available in principle to the UN at short notice. In April 1994 there were military units representing 19 member states on the database but, when called upon to assist with intervention operations in Rwanda not one was prepared to do so.

If we take a brief glimpse at operations in Somalia, Rwanda and Bosnia (pre- and post-Dayton) it can be seen that the historic concepts of consent and impartiality are virtually untransferable into the 'grey area' because it is not a benign environment. Analysis of the data indicates the emergence of new grey area criteria, among which, for example, might be the need for intervention forces to be independent of action in the process of securing leverage over hostile parties.

In May 1993 the American UN-sanctioned operation Unified Task Force (UNITAF) handed over operations to the UN-sponsored United Nations Operation in Somalia (UNOSOM II). Although the UNOSOM II mandate was founded upon Chapter VII, Somalia did not need a country-wide mandate, for the problem was largely confined to parts of the capital Mogadishu. The culmination of the crisis which occurred in Mogadishu came about due to the failure of a poorly planned and executed US Ranger capture mission on 3 October 1993. The origin of the crisis lay in Security Council Resolution 837 (1993) of 6 June, when the UN was authorised 'to take all necessary measures against all those responsible for the armed attacks'. Although Gen. Aideed was not specifically mentioned, there is no doubt that that is who Ambassador Albright and Secretary-General Boutros-Ghali had in mind when the Resolution was being prepared. They had both failed to appreciate the political dimension of the crisis. In Mogadishu the UN offered a reward of $25,000 for the capture of Aideed. Consent was demonstrably not a factor. Thus the UN had moved away from any understanding of impartiality and had signed up as a constituent in Somalia's civil war. It became, in effect, a full-blown, counter-insurgency operation. The Americans, not the UN, planned and executed a mission to capture Aideed. The Malaysians and the Pakistanis, despite their earlier experiences, still maintained the semblance of being engaged on a peacekeeping mission, including their being in regular contact with their capitals. They were not informed of the Rangers' operation and were totally unprepared to take part in the ensuing rescue mission. One American official commented that 'Unity of command is one of the principles of war. We complained when other units in the UN force referred orders back to their headquarters, but when it comes to unity of command, we are the worst.'[9] What was particularly unfortunate in the American case was that ten years previously, and to put down again some doctrinal markers, the lessons from the Lebanon following the loss of 241 American lives in a bomb attack were: be impartial, use minimum force and know your enemy. In the raid on the Bakhara Markets in Mogadishu, 18 Americans died and 77 were wounded. The Malaysians and the Pakistanis also suffered casualties. The International Committee of the Red Cross (ICRC) estimated that over 200 Somalis had died in the battle, with hundreds wounded. The Somalia experience had a dramatic effect upon the consideration of involvement in future operations (particularly in Rwanda) by the UN and the USA. This need not have been necessary since all that was required in the future was the avoidance of elementary and unforced errors of judgement.

The 1994 Rwanda crisis was unique, for in a country the size of Wales there were three separate, ongoing military operations. France took part unilaterally in what was, in effect, a Chapter VII operation. The US also entered the fray unilaterally, on a different, humanitarian mission. The UN did insert a force, the UN Assistance Mission in Rwanda (UNAMIR). A 400-strong Belgian Parachute Battalion that had been in a quiet area of Somalia on a Chapter VII mandate in 1993, found itself in 1994 in genocidal Kigali with a Chapter VI mandate. For the UN commander, the situation in Kigali was an impossible mission because he was unable to offer protection to the minority Tutsis if it depended upon the continuing consent and cooperation of the majority, belligerent Hutus. The UN military in Kigali had information of arms caches before the descent into mayhem and chaos and asked the UN for permission to seize them. 'They refused', said the commander in Kigali, 'because UNAMIR was deployed under a Chapter VI mandate – traditional peacekeeping. New York argued that a cordon and search was an offensive operation for which permission would not be granted.'[10] In the scale of activities, Rwanda was a 'grey-area' event for which there were no rules nor understanding because it had not been in the UN's interest to grasp that nettle. How, in the face of genocide in Rwanda, could the Belgians remain impartial, as was expected of them on this traditional peacekeeping mission? In fact, they became inextricably involved in the crisis when ten of their number were taken into captivity by the Hutus and brutally killed. The Hutu intention was to get the Belgians to leave Rwanda, a ploy that worked. For the UN, Rwanda was its most shameful experience.

Meanwhile, in Bosnia in 1993–95 there had been problems with the concept of safe areas. The Dutch had been the only Western UN state to offer troops in support of the Security Council's Safe Area Resolution. 'Peacekeeping', wrote Honig and Both,[11] 'was extremely popular in the Netherlands.' The Netherlands suffered the wellnigh universal problem of having traditional peacekeeping in mind when, in reality, pre-Dayton Bosnia was another vicious 'grey-area' environment. But the Dutch government had discovered in this post-Cold War period that military power could be used in support of foreign policy goals despite their own military advice that they should not get involved.

What happened is history, a testimony to muddled thinking and ignorance. A senior Bosnian Serb officer complained to the author that 'Serb territory was being attacked from the Safe Areas on a daily basis. Even before we liberated Srebrenica, terror groups entered our villages to burn them down. We asked UNPROFOR to control the situation, to disarm the Safe Areas, but they did not.' The Dutch government had gone out of its way to put a battalion into Srebrenica with its 40,000 Muslim population but, according to the former journalist Martin Bell,

They were from a conscript-based army, ill-prepared for the hardships of Srebrenica ... but there was also surely a loss of nerve which would not, or should not, have occurred in a professional battalion disciplined in the tradition of soldiering-on in adversity.[12]

What Bell is emphasising is the reality that there is no common military standard upon which to impose a detailed, universalist doctrine. When troops are put into a conflict environment it is wise to deploy them, if the option exists, according to the principle 'forces for courses'. More often than not, as was the case in Kigali, no such latitude exists. 'I found it utterly unacceptable that fifty per cent of the personnel in my command were non-operational.'[13] As the experienced UN peacekeeping General Gustav Hägglünd said, in differentiating between peacekeeping and the conflict environment such as in the 'grey area',

> It simply requires different forces and a completely different concept. An intention to deter and enforce requires forces that are as frightening as possible. For this kind of mission great-power battalions, professional soldiers and all the means at their disposal are preferable.

The Dutch had a totally inadequate mandate for the 18 months they were in Srebrenica before retreating in 'disarray and dishonour', leaving the Muslims to the attention of the vengeful Serbs.[14] It was for the UN their most humiliating experience in the Bosnian conflict.

Honig and Both point out the reality, that the Netherlands 'did not have the means, the wherewithal, or finally the will to make it [the Srebrenica Safe Area] work'. In addition, the

> second basic problem with the UN operation was that it relied on the cooperation and consent of the interested parties and that it was driven above all things by the desire to remain impartial. Very few politicians and soldiers ever questioned this premise of impartiality. But the fact is that relying on the cooperation and consent of the Bosnian Serbs meant that the eastern Safe Areas could not work.[15]

In 1996 the author received a first draft Army Field Manual entitled *Peace Support Operations*. It was fundamentally flawed in that it did not address the core issues arising from operations in Somalia, Rwanda and Bosnia. Nor did it 'probe into the viscera of living conflict', but rather it 'rattled the skeletons' of Wider Peacekeeping. *Peace Support Operations* is a utopian rather than realist statement. In this there is some semblance to what went on during the inter-war period, when some parties believed conflict could be legislated against. In 1939 E. H. Carr wrote in *The Twenty Years Crisis*:

> The advocate of a scheme for an international police force or for collective security or some other project for an international order generally replied to the criticism not by an argument to show how and why he thought his plan will work but by a statement that it must be made to work because the consequence of its failure to work would be so disastrous.[16]

The inappropriately described *Peace Support Operations*, not surprisingly, is divided into Peacekeeping and Peace Enforcement. It is an unashamed, second-generation version of Wider Peacekeeping and remains undiluted 'dangerous nonsense', failing to recognise adequately the limits of consent and impartiality and to reflect experience beyond a limited and distorted vision of events in Bosnia and Herzegovina. Institutional interests conspired to encourage the British doctrinal establishment to persist with flawed doctrine, lending credence to Liddell Hart's observation that one thing more difficult than getting new ideas into the military is getting old ones out. The litmus test of any doctrine is that it must be believed. The original mistake was, in effect, to suppress the debate on the initial concept of Wider Peacekeeping. The second mistake was to make insufficient intellectual investment in developing the doctrine. Furthermore, this process of doctrine formulation, and, more dangerously, of doctrine protection, appears to have developed an unstoppable momentum. By the process of changing the front cover, the Army Field Manual became a Joint Field Manual. How appropriate the quotation from Tacitus: 'The worst crime was dared by a few, willed by more and tolerated by all.' It is policy which protects and underwrites flawed doctrine which can foster irrelevant policy. As part of the research for this chapter, a view was presented to a departmental head at the FCO that we had the reality of a situation whereby there was a spectrum of military interventionist activity anchored at both ends by traditional Chapter VI peacekeeping and Chapter VII intervention, with a broad, grey, undefined area in between. He conceded that this was a correct interpretation but added, 'It is not policy'.

That we should be persisting in the maintenance of an irrelevant, status-quo policy without the benefit of political steering might appear curious. The reason we have seen no positive activity may have something to do with the fact that political life revolves around the avoidance of those debates the government does not want to discuss. In that respect, the UN and conflict is similar to European Monetary Union. What seems to worry and perplex our chattering classes is their discovery that their enemy's enemy may well *not* be their friend. Few of yesterday's past reassurances can be carried forward into today and tomorrow. Things are not as black and white nor as easily identifiable as they used to be, but have become diffused in a blanket of grey mist. Modern conflict is no exception, but its very nature demands an end to political prevarication. It would be nothing short of a military crime not to define the 'grey area' and what it involves. States no longer understand where they are in this new environment and understandably their ardour to support UN resolutions has cooled. It is undoubtedly a conflict environment where there is no peace to be kept. The military activity that takes place in the 'grey area' must not be described as peacekeeping – it is not. If remedial action is not taken to address that reality, then the lessons from Mogadishu, Kigali and Srebrenica will have been ignored. That is a political and military crime.

The requirement goes somewhat further than replacing the *Peace Support Operations* doctrine. The whole environment is in a state of flux and desperately needs assessment and definition as a total package. We talk of 'warfighting' when there has not been a declaration of war since 1945, but we cling to the vague concept of 'warfighting' because it is from this that the rationale for force structuring and equipment flows. However, the notion of preserving 'warfighting' is none the less valid, for in the range of military conflict it is true that the skills required by armed forces trained at the general global and regional levels of conflict do cascade down to lower levels, whereas the reverse is not true. This leads us to a real dichotomy because we talk of Operations Other than War in minimalist terms when in reality it is the only type of conflict our servicemen are likely to face for a very long while. We have in the past categorised conflict into levels of intensity. Mid-intensity conflict (MIC) differed from high-intensity conflict (HIC) principally because weapons of mass destruction did not feature as a consideration in the former. Today, it is possible that weapons of mass destruction could be introduced into what used to be described as low-intensity conflict (LIC). The understanding of what comprised low-intensity conflict became severely undermined when it was realised that Russia's bloody intervention in her neighbour in her 'near abroad', Chechnya, was categorised within the system as LIC.

There is also the consideration of what the North Atlantic Treaty Organisation's role is going to be in support of the UN as a sanctioned organisation. NATO has shown a propensity to utilise the non-autonomous air arm in conflict resolution because the political risks of putting infantry on the ground can be a tricky threshold to negotiate.

210

NATO's role has expanded since the July 1990 London Declaration to include not only collective defence but also collective security. The recent extension of NATO into Central and Eastern Europe, pushed through despite the considerable weight of informed protest, lends credence to the view that here we have an organisation still in search of a proper post-Cold War role. If it pushes too hard to become a global strike force it is likely to self-destruct. NATO's original intervention in the pre-Dayton 'grey area' of Bosnia was because of the UN's peacekeepers' failure to stop atrocities in Sarajevo, Srebrenica and Zepa. Not so long ago, it was thought unlikely that NATO would operate outside Europe on grey-area missions. At the December 1998 NATO Conference, Secretary of State Albright told the NATO allies that future NATO missions would take them further afield. It does promise to be an interesting exercise to see how effective the UN will be in future in controlling its surrogate once it is loosed from the trap. One worrying development within NATO is the serious suggestion emanating from some quarters that NATO should consider the option of operating above the law. The other consideration is America. NATO is increasingly likely to become the instrument for the exercise of American foreign policy in Europe and its immediate periphery, although America will continue to act unilaterally where it appears her own nationals are at risk – a *Civis Romanus Sum* game. Retribution and reprisal will invariably be in the form of air-delivered ordinance.

It behoves anyone who argues that a doctrine is irrelevant, poorly structured and too simple to recommend the manner in which it should be superseded. It has become apparent that there is a requirement for an overarching, general doctrine to bond all the components within a coalition operation. There is also a case for a specific, detailed, national doctrine which will relate the general doctrine to the participants' way of engaging in conflict, usually within operational boundaries. In outline, the new overarching doctrine will need to be in four parts. The first will establish principles, definitions, the structure under which the several levels of doctrine function, and the actors to be found in these environments (government organisations, agencies and non-governmental organisations). The remaining three parts apply doctrine top-down, as stand-alone entities, not envisaged as being of similar length, at the military strategic, the operational and the tactical doctrine levels. It might be appropriate to subdivide, or alternatively to produce separate documents which examine Chapter VI peacekeeping, the 'grey area', and Chapter VII military intervention. Of the three, it is the grey area which has to be addressed urgently, so that soldiers and civilians will no longer die because of the preservation of vested interests and ignorance. The time for someone to take charge of this process is long overdue. The recognition and the making available of some of the wherewithal to engage in expeditionary conflict is the beginning not the end of the process. The United Kingdom should resume the lead in developing a sensible and relevant doctrine as a framework of understanding of the approach to expeditionary conflict in order to provide the foundation for its practical application.

NOTES

1. J. F. C. Fuller to Liddell Hart, Liddell Hart Papers, 1/302/61.
2. J. F. C. Fuller, *The Generalship of Ulysses S. Grant* (London: Baltimore Press, 1929), p. ix.
3. There are three levels of doctrine: tactical, operational and military strategic. The last is the highest.
4. *Design for Military Operation: The British Military Doctrine* (Internal MoD publication, produced by Chief of the General Staff, 1989).
5. Boutros Boutros-Ghali, 'Empowering the United Nations', *Foreign Affairs* (Winter 1992–93), pp. 98–9.
6. Sir Brian Urquhart in an address to the New Dimensions of United Nations Peacekeeping Symposium, Tokyo, 19–20 January 1995.
7. Sir Brian Urquhart, interview with the author, The Hague, 22 March 1995.
8. Quoted in R. M. Connaughton, 'Military Support and Protection for Humanitarian Assistance. Rwanda, April–December 1994', *SCSI Occasional Paper*, No. 18 (1996), p. 11.
9. Quoted in *Independent on Sunday*, 17 October 1993.
10. Author's interview with Col. Marachal, Brussels, 30 March 1995.
11. J. W. Honig and N. Both, *Srebrenica, Record of a War Crime* (London, Penguin, 1996), p. 181.
12. Martin Bell, quoted in *The Times*, 2 November 1996.
13. Author's interview with Col. Marachal.
14. Honig and Both, *Srebrenica*, p. 181.
15. Ibid.
16. E. H. Carr, *The Twenty Years Crisis* (London: Penguin, 1939), p. 8.

A Recipe for Making Safe Areas Unsafe

STUART GORDON

INTRODUCTION

The collapse of the safe area of Srebrenica in 1995 represented far more than a brutal humanitarian catastrophe. It brought the credibility of both the United Nations and the North Atlantic Treaty Organisation (NATO) into question and precipitated the collapse of the already failing consent-based mandate of the UN Protection Force (UNPROFOR). However, ultimately it began a process which led to a peace agreement, initialled at Dayton, Ohio, which brought the Bosnian war to an end. This chapter explores the significance of the safe-areas regime to the several parties and endeavours to identify failures in the construction and implementation of the regime.

CREATION AND DISCORDANCE

During much of 1992 the Bosnian Serb Army (BSA) ethnically cleansed large swaths of northern, eastern and central Bosnia, driving 100,000 internally displaced civilians into enclaves centred upon the towns of Bihac, Cerska, Konjevic Polje, Srebrenica, Jajce, Zepa and Gorazde, as well as a swath of land in central Bosnia-Herzegovina (BH). By the time that Jajce fell in October 1992 the BSA had captured nearly 70 per cent of BH. This territorial distribution remained largely unchanged until the combined Croat–Federation offensive in late 1995.[1]

Throughout 1992 and 1993 the international community remained troubled by the plight of Sarajevo, besieged by BSA heavy artillery. The stricken town served the Bosnian Serbs as a diversion, drawing media attention away from the horrors taking place in other parts of Bosnia, and tying down the rudimentary Bosniac army in an attritional conflict. However, with secure confrontation lines in central Bosnia and international media attention focused elsewhere, the BSA turned upon the remaining eastern enclaves. First to fall was Cerska on 2 March 1993, closely followed by Konjevic Polje on 11 March. It became increasingly clear that Srebrenica would be next and there were clear strategic reasons why an assault was essential from the perspective of the BSA.

Bosnian Army (BiH) and Bosnian Croat forces (Hrvatsko Vijece Odbrane or HVO), increasingly outnumbered the BSA. By 1994 the Federation could muster over 120,000 troops, the BSA only 80,000. However, the BSA had inherited significant quantities of armour and artillery from the Yugoslav National Army and possessed formed manoeuvre units. In contrast, until late 1994 the BiH was lightly armed and possessed only a limited capacity for all-arms actions. It was therefore ill-equipped and -trained to confront BSA units in sustained engagements. Consequently, unless the terrain particularly suited small-unit infantry tactics[2] the BiH could not hold ground against a determined BSA assault. However, the BiH's capacity to hold territory was not conditioned by topography alone. Harsh Balkan winters and arctic conditions in mountainous areas favoured movement by infantry rather than by armoured and mechanised artillery units. Consequently, during the 1992/1993 winter BiH units made territorial gains around Srebrenica and used the same terror tactics against Serb civilians that had been used against them. However, as the thaw proceeded and the ground became more suited to the passage of armoured and mechanised artillery units, regular and militia Serb forces retook territory and, by March 1993, looked set to retake Srebrenica itself.

After considerable obstruction by the Serbs, the French Commander of UNPROFOR's Bosnia-Herzegovina Command (BHC) General Philippe Morillon arrived in Srebrenica. On 13 March, prevented from leaving the town by its besieged inhabitants, Morillon made an unscripted (and not authorised by the UN Security Council), televised pledge to protect the population. This encouraged non-aligned states on the Security Council to press for robust enforcement action. The British and the French, with troops deployed in areas that were potentially vulnerable to BSA retaliatory action,[3] and aware that deployments into safe areas would hinder the withdrawal of their own troops if the UNPROFOR mission collapsed entirely,[4] were fearful that the USA and non-aligned states would drive the UNPROFOR mandate into enforcement. They were, therefore, inclined to make some concessions in terms of the robustness of the mandate, particularly with respect to towns such as Srebrenica,

Sarajevo and Gorazde. It was expected that this would limit calls for broader and more intense enforcement options, which were viewed as ultimately self-defeating. However, events in theatre also caused the UNPROFOR mandate to evolve.

On 17–18 April a meeting of UNPROFOR, BSA and BiH commanders at Sarajevo airport concluded by agreeing to a ceasefire around Srebrenica town, its demilitarisation and the drawing up of a map defining its geographical extent. The commander of the BiH in Srebrenica Nasser Oric subsequently agreed either to remove the heavy weapons from the safe area or to place them under UN control. Similarly, BiH troops would be disarmed or withdrawn. This was generally adhered to for some six months, although unarmed BiH soldiers continued to enter the demilitarised zone in order to rest before resuming military operations. UNPROFOR later attempted to broker an agreement extending the demilitarised area to the confrontation line around Srebrenica. However, the failure of the BiH to demilitarise[5] caused the BSA to refuse to extend the concept.

Developed in isolation, the text of Security Council Resolution 819, declaring Srebrenica to be a safe area, arrived during the Sarajevo airport meeting. It made provision for an immediate ceasefire and demanded that the enclave be 'free from any armed attack or any other hostile act'. However, it provided little in the way of guidance either as to how UNPROFOR would implement the concept or to its standing in international law. Given that the airport negotiations had provided more detail on the implementation of a demilitarised zone than the Security Council resolution, resolution 819 was effectively ignored. At 2 am on 18 April Generals Mladic and Halilovic agreed on the principles of a ceasefire.[6]

In the absence of effective Security Council guidance on the methods of implementation, UNPROFOR commanders chose to adopt the concept of demilitarised areas contained in para. 3, Article 60, Protocol 1 of the Geneva Convention of August 1949.[7] As such, they envisaged that the area would be free of military equipment and combatants and would not be used by any belligerent parties to conduct military operations. However, in many ways the concepts of demilitarised zones as contained in the Geneva Conventions were entirely inappropriate for the circumstances of Srebrenica. The zones detailed in the Conventions are, in essence, a means for protecting civilian populations against the effects of war. They are not a means for maintaining the grip of one belligerent over territory it cannot maintain through force of arms. However, several states on the Security Council considered the Bosnian government to have a right of self-defence on its own territory, and non-aligned states such as Venezuela and Pakistan viewed the demilitarisation, not in terms of the creation of a humanitarian demilitarised zone, but of preventing a humiliating surrender by the legitimate Bosnian authorities. Thus the philosophical underpinnings of the concept were increasingly removed from the strategically neutral concept contained in the Geneva Conventions.

Understandably, such approaches were not universally popular with other Security Council members; several Western states, for example, privately rejected the idea of safe areas, fearful of the idea of authorising the UN Secretariat to create what were, potentially, a set of UN protectorates. Furthermore, the safe areas were likely to be exceptionally difficult to implement militarily without the consent of the BSA. However, overt rejection of such apparently humanitarian action was politically dangerous, running the risk of domestic unpopularity and stimulating more robust approaches from the USA and non-aligned members of the Security Council.

However, as the humanitarian situation throughout eastern Bosnia deteriorated, partly in response to continuing BiH military activity[8] within the enclaves, the Security Council passed two resolutions. The first of these, Resolution 824 (6 May 1993), extended the concept to Sarajevo, Zepa, Tuzla, Gorazde and Bihac. The second, Resolution 836, effectively ended all hope of reciprocal demilitarisation by extending UNPROFOR's mandate in order to 'promote the withdrawal of military or para-military units other than those of the Government of the Republic of Bosnia and Herzegovina'.[9] The debate in the Security Council[10] and the wording of the resolutions appeared extremely robust, with Resolution 836 containing the apparent possibility of robust air action in the event of obstruction on the part of the BSA. However, the UN Secretariat's Department of Peacekeeping Operations (DPKO), fearful of the conequences of enforcement action on the rest of the mandate, interpreted the meaning of the resolution as an increased reliance upon the presence of UNPROFOR troops deterring attacks upon themselves and only by extension the civilian population.[11] The result was, effectively, continued reliance upon a consent-based, safe-areas regime resulting in a less confrontational relationship with the BSA and a continuation of the humanitarian programmes of the UN High Commissioner for Refugees (UNHCR). As the safe areas were a temporary rather than a long-term expedient, this provided a means of stabilising rather than resolving the situation before a negotiated and overarching political settlement. The resolutions also represented a means of regaining the diplomatic initiative in the immediate aftermath of the Bosnian Serb Assembly's rejection of the Vance–Owen Peace Plan and European rejection of the US-sponsored Joint Action Plan at a point when the United Kingdom and France feared increasing calls in the US Congress for more robust air action against the BSA. As such, they promised a reinvigorated political process in the setting of an essentially consent-based UNPROFOR mandate. The gap between political rhetoric and mandate was therefore enormous.

'COVENANTS WITHOUT SWORDS BE BUT WORDS': [12] IMPLEMENTING THE SAFE AREAS

UNPROFOR commanders recommended that 34,000 troops[13] would be required to implement the safe-areas policy. The DPKO, convinced of troop-donating governments' unwillingness to provide such numbers[14] and fearful of the spiralling costs of such a policy, recommended a 'light option of 7,600',[15] a figure described by Lord Owen as the 'most irresponsible decision taken during my time as co-chairman',[16] changing, as it did, the nature of the force deployed within the safe areas.

The Secretary-General Boutros Boutros-Ghali had recognised that 7,600 troops could not themselves 'guarantee the defence of the safe areas, but would provide a basic level of deterrence, assuming the consent and cooperation of the parties'.[17] Given the apparently partial purpose of the safe-areas regime this assumption was likely to be challenged. The Security Council agreed to this figure in Resolution 844 (18 June 1993). However, by 10 March 1994 only 5,000 of the troops had arrived.[18]

The implications of adopting such a 'light option' were enormous. In the absence of robust and extensive ground forces air-power was to be used to offset the paucity of numbers and their inability to provide for their own defence.[19] Boutros-Ghali stated:

> since it is assumed that UNPROFOR ground troops will not be sufficient to resist a concentrated assault on any of the safe areas particular emphasis must be placed upon the availability of a credible air-strike capability provided by member states.[20]

Subsequently, the North Atlantic Council announced its willingness to offer 'protective air power in case of attack against UNPROFOR in the performance of its overall mandate if it so requests',[21] the key phrase in this being the overt linkage of air-power to the defence of UNPROFOR troops rather than the civilian populations. In effect, this eroded the apparent commitment to the use of air-power on the part of NATO members and diluted the humanitarian element of the safe-areas regime.

However, it was not entirely valueless. While an element of the military implementation plan conceived of a large trip-wire force deterring attacks by their presence, there was also an assumption that even a smaller, lightly armed force possessed the capacity to change the behaviour of the belligerent parties through persuasion. A 'presence' could therefore encourage compliance with Security Council resolutions without total reliance on the military capability of UNPROFOR. The question therefore became to what extent was it realistic to rely upon this persuasive element, rather than on the deterrent component, of the regime? Therefore, in the absence of a credible denial-based deterrent, the willingness of the parties to consent to the safe-areas regime, and therefore become amenable to persuasion, became critical. However, the Security Council's efforts to preserve the population of Srebrenica and the Council's apparent unwillingness to demilitarise the enclave tended to erode the BSA's commitment to the regime. For the Serbs, the Security Council appeared to offer a commitment to maintain territory in the hands of BiH forces. As such, the regime was different from that provided for by humanitarian law. Consequently, the concept increasingly became something that could only exist in so far as the BSA had no strategic imperative to assault the enclaves, or it was underwritten by a credible threat of NATO air action. In the event of the latter, this would require the threatened use of disproportionate force and 'escalation dominance' rather than the proportionate, essentially defensive use of close air support (CAS). However, the UN Secretariat and the Security Council remained wedded to the idea that the latter could not escalate the use of force for fear of the impact upon the other elements of its mandate. The Secretary-General stated that 'UNPROFOR's protection role is derived from its mere presence; UNPROFOR is neither structured nor equipped for combat and has never had sufficient resources, even with air support, to defend the safe areas against a deliberate attack'.[22] Furthermore, the very failure to demilitarise ensured that the BiH threat remained. Consequently the BSA was unable to remove its own forces from, particularly, the Srebrenica and the Gorazde areas; yet the reorganisation and arming of the Croatian and Bosnian Presidency forces in 1994 had considerably improved their effectiveness. Consequently, the BSA, overstretched by economic sanctions, extended confrontation lines and the impact of lessened support from Belgrade, had increasing cause to desire the neutralisation of the threat from the BiH garrisons in the major enclaves. Thus by 1995 the BSA had clear strategic imperatives for retaking some of the safe areas, particularly Srebrenica. Some senior BSA officers even privately admitted to UN officials as early as April 1995 that they would do so.

TECHNICAL CONSTRAINTS ON THE USE OF COERCIVE FORCE

The use of air-power in defence of UNPROFOR ground troops unable to withdraw or defend themselves through their own means entailed additional problems for the regime. Serb enhancements to regional and local surface-to-air missile systems (in 1994) increased the potential numbers of NATO aircrew casualties and therefore the political costs of using CAS. This increased risk to CAS aircraft also reduced the willingness to place UNPROFOR troops in places where recourse to CAS may have been required, thereby also further reducing the scope for UNPROFOR's freedom of action. Where air-strikes, even CAS, were deemed necessary, it increased the number of BSA targets that would need to be neutralised. It therefore became increasingly difficult to portray the use of CAS as a defensive rather than a retaliatory or punitive measure. This problem enhanced the possibility that CAS would precipitate an escalating conflict between the BSA and UNPROFOR/NATO. As this would potentially entail enormous costs for the rest of the mission, it further reduced UNPROFOR's willingness to countenance such action. The Secretary-General and the Secretary-General's Special Representative remained cognisant of the impact of escalation upon the primary humanitarian mission and the perception of UNPROFOR's impartiality that was necessary for the peacekeeping mission in places other than the safe areas. The use of air-power therefore became something of a victim to counter technology.

This issue became a critical concern for NATO after an American F16 aircraft was shot down on 2 June 1995. As a result of the increasing threat to NATO aircraft on combat air patrol (CAP), NATO and US guidelines required that aircraft on CAP were accompanied by aircraft capable of suppressing enemy air defences in order to minimise the risk of further casualties. This required additional reconnaissance, target-location and weapons-delivery aircraft. The relative paucity of such specialist aircraft, but particularly those capable of suppressing air defences, severely limited the numbers of NATO aircraft on CAP over Bosnia. This had obvious implications for the speed of air response[23] and gave the BSA the perception that it had driven NATO from the skies by simply shooting down one aircraft. Furthermore, the requirement to suppress air defences even before a CAS mission, in principle, generated a wider array of targets than assaults on BSA units directly targeting UNPROFOR troops. CAS therefore became an increasingly major undertaking rather than a surgical and limited response, and thus an important issue affecting the relationship between NATO and UNPROFOR in late 1994, with UNPROFOR staff officers increasingly drawing the conclusion that NATO was using the issue of the suppression of enemy air defences (SEAD) provision in order to increase the range of targets to facilitate an incremental shift toward an enforcement strategy.

This became particularly apparent in late 1994 after Croatian Serb aircraft had attacked Bosniac targets in the Bihac enclaves. NATO commanders placed considerable pressure on UNPROFOR to accept a broad package of air-strikes against the Croatian Serb base at Udbina and the Croatian Serb and Bosnian Serb regional air-defence systems. To UNPROFOR commanders the NATO target list, with targets as dispersed as Banja Luka, represented a disproportionate response to the Croatian Serb action and, as such, an escalatory and punitive response. UNPROFOR commanders ultimately secured a reduction in the numbers of targets, limiting them to those in proximity to the Udbina base.

The use of CAS and wider offensive air action also required both UNPROFOR and NATO agreement, a system known as the dual-key arrangement. This reflected both the requirement for UNPROFOR to have a veto over air action and target lists and the political requirement to prevent a US-dominated NATO structure taking robust enforcement action against the wishes of the main troop-donating governments. However, the dual-key system was both slow to authorise air action [24] and resented by NATO commanders and US politicians. It also signalled to the BSA a general reluctance to escalate the level of air threat, reducing the level of deterrence inherent within the Security Council mandate for UNPROFOR and weakening the link between BSA assaults on UN troops and responses by NATO. In effect, this changed the nature of NATO CAS from 'defensive' to 'delayed retaliation'.

The problem with command and control was compounded by technical difficulties arising from the operation of fast jet aircraft at low level in a mountainous environment and the fact that BSA targets were often located near to populated areas. This deliberate policy on the part of the BSA,[25] combined with the possibility of civilian casualties from inaccurately delivered or faulty weapons systems, served to limit the occasions upon which air-power could be risked. The result was to destroy the certainty of linkage between attacks on UNPROFOR and CAS responses. This weakened the deterrent effect of CAS further.

The technical limitations of the weaponry also served to place restrictions on the utility of air-power. Contrary to the apparent trend, there was a preference on the part of NATO headquarters to use 'dumb' bombs rather than precision-guided munitions (PGMs). The latter had upwards of a 5 per cent probability of technical malfunction, potentially causing them to hit civilian targets. The result was that the more predictable, but less accurate, unguided weapons were used in preference. However, the occasions upon which their inaccuracy (rather than their reliability) would potentially cause collateral civilian casualties acted to limit further the occasions upon which air-power could be used.

Air-power was further restricted by the strongly territorial nature of the fighting. Troops from one locality were frequently unwilling to fight in another. This had implications for the capacity of all sides, but particularly the numerically inferior BSA, to create the critical mass of troops necessary to facilitate major military successes on the ground. This had several implications. First, it reinforced the impact of the maintaining of garrisons around the safe areas, effectively compounding BSA overstretch. Second, it had implications for where air-strikes could be used. A Serb in Banja Luka, for example, was effectively fighting a localised war. As such, he would have difficulty in accepting being targeted by NATO aircraft in response to the actions of Pale Serbs. Thus, air action needed to be as localised as possible in order to maintain the link between the perpetrator of an offence requiring the use of NATO air-strikes and the action itself.

NATO rules of engagement also required what was termed 'constant visual guidance' by forward air control (FAC) officers. Restrictions on UNPROFOR freedom of movement served to limit the ability to deploy FAC parties, thereby also limiting the occasions upon which CAS could be used. For example, in April 1994, despite UNPROFOR requests for *more* air-strikes against leading BSA tanks, the paucity of FACs led Admiral Smith, the senior NATO operational commander, ultimately to restrict the use of air-power.

The principle of 'proportionality' (in terms of NATO air response), which underpinned the use of CAS, had both benefits and costs. While it appeared to some as an entirely defensive gesture, it also provided the BSA with the capacity to predict and circumvent the circumstances in which air-strikes could be authorised. It delivered the power of initiative to the BSA. For example, the BSA counterattacks into the Bihac enclave in late 1994 were spearheaded by rebel Muslim forces, loyal to Fikret Abdic, and dismounted BSA infantry. In such circumstances it proved technically difficult to use CAS against troops closely engaged against BiH and UNPROFOR targets and was politically difficult for the North Atlantic Council and the Security Council to authorise air-strikes against Muslims, even rebel ones, without adding an element of confusion which would fatally weaken domestic support in Western countries for the principle of air-strikes. Similarly the July 1995 BSA assault upon Srebrenica, bypassing UN blocking positions and giving the impression of geographically limited objectives,[26] minimised the chances of the UN authorising either CAS or the wider use of air-power.

MANDATE TO USE FORCE

The legitimacy of UNPROFOR's resort to force was also, perhaps surprisingly, ambiguous. For example, throughout much of UNPROFOR's existence it did not have a 'mandate to deter attacks from forces outside the Republic of Bosnia and Herzegovina and/or internal warring factions'.[27] Certainly until the passage of Security Council Resolution 900, UNPROFOR did not even 'enjoy the right to use close air support on Croatian territory in the event of such attacks'.[28] Similarly, several of the safe areas (Bihac, Tuzla and Gorazde) were not geographically defined either by Security Council resolution or agreement by the warring factions throughout much of their existence. Without clearly defined boundaries[29] and in the absence of unambiguously defined trigger events, the BSA was unlikely to take threats of retaliatory action to heart. The ambiguity of the deterrent was demonstrated clearly in Gorazde in April 1994. The BSA attacked the town essentially to encourage the Presidency's acceptance of an emerging peace plan; the BSA effectively negotiated the size of the 'safe area' down by capturing parts of it until it was a circle around the town with only a 3-km radius. Threats of widespread NATO air action were hardly heeded at all.

Similarly, the Bihac enclave was not geographically defined by the UN until May 1994. Then it was defined by UNPROFOR, rather than the Security Council, as the result of the possibility of its collapse. Following offensives by the BiH's 5th Corps, the BSA counterattacked into the enclave, threatening to take the safe area itself and recapturing all of the territory it had lost. Despite UNPROFOR forwarding a map of their definition of the safe area, the BSA overran large parts of this without incurring NATO air attacks.

DETERRENT OR HOSTAGE?

The paucity of UNPROFOR troops deployed in the safe areas and the inability of CAS to provide an effective deterrent created additional difficulties. The troops deployed within the enclaves were few in number and comparatively lightly armed.[30] Furthermore, their deployment patterns accentuated their vulnerability. For example, the Sarajevo and the Gorazde ceasefire agreement of January and April 1994, respectively, made provision for the creation of heavy weapons collection points and observation posts behind BSA lines, or between these and those of the BiH. Maintaining demilitarised zones, implementing demilitarisation agreements and simply resupplying UNPROFOR troops in the enclaves therefore placed UNPROFOR troops in positions where they could be taken hostage by the BSA and, ultimately, the BiH. Use of NATO aircraft in ways which the BSA perceived to be retaliatory and/or escalatory therefore precipitated hostage-taking.[31] This provided the BSA with the means of halting any escalatory use of air-power; a feature that Gow describes as a 'counter-coercive instrument'.[32] The BSA husbanded this capacity by forcing UNPROFOR to retain small numbers of lightly armed and lightly armoured troops within the enclaves. However, it was also aware that this did not provide it with complete freedom of action, as the indiscriminate precipitation of crises which generated a recourse to hostage-taking could ultimately harden international attitudes against the Bosnian Serbs and lead to NATO air action. There was, therefore, something of a self-limiting aspect to BSA actions.

However, UNPROFOR was not simply a passive victim of circumstance; it deployed troops into positions that would make the use of NATO air-strikes impossible. UNPROFOR's Bosnian headquarters, Bosnia-Herzegovina Command (BHC), deployed troops between and alongside both BiH and BSA forces on Mount Igman in 1993 and again in February 1994. These were ostensibly deployed as an interpositionary and observer force designed to facilitate the disengagement of the factions. However, it is clear that while these troops provided a means of defusing crises through their own agency, it was also apparent that their presence prevented escalatory NATO air action. Despite this, the intention underlying their deployment was not to prevent *all* NATO air action, only the threat of widespread enforcement action. Thus in early 1994 Swedish UNPROFOR troops, supported by NATO aircraft, advanced on BSA lines on Mount Igman in order to press them back as part of a disengagement initiative. CAS was threatened in the event of hostile actions on the part of the BSA against the Swedish force.[33]

General Rose, commander of BHC, attempted to address the vulnerability issue in mid-1994 by unofficially earmarking small 'enforcement units', known as a theatre reserve, which could provide a capability that would preclude immediate resort to CAS. While such a force potentially provided a means of reducing the vulnerability of UNPROFOR troops deployed in central Bosnia and Sarajevo, it was unlikely to be of use in the event of BSA action against UNPROFOR troops deployed in the other, far more isolated enclaves. Despite such limited utility, troop-donating governments resisted the creation of such a force on the grounds of both cost and of the danger of being drawn into an uncontrollable and escalating conflict. The vulnerability issue was not resolved until late 1995, in the aftermath of the 25 May 1995 round of UNPROFOR hostage-taking by the BSA. As a result of this action by the BSA, UNPROFOR troops were withdrawn to positions behind Federation frontlines. Furthermore, in order to retain control of the UNPROFOR mission while sending a strong political signal to the Serbs, the British and the French governments authorised (on their own initiative) the deployment of a brigade-sized rapid reaction force. This unit, replete with artillery and augmented by a force of British Warriors, provided a capability to fill the gap between UNPROFOR's use of small-calibre weapons and resort to CAS. It, in combination with the withdrawal of vulnerable UNPROFOR troops, reduced reliance upon CAS.

However, it did not return UNPROFOR's mission to the *status quo ante bellum*. The fall of Srebrenica and threats to Gorazde galvanised political will to attempt to construct a deterrent to further BSA attacks against the remaining enclaves. Enhanced NATO rules of engagement and reduced vulnerability to hostage-taking reduced the BSA's capacity to halt the escalatory use of air-power. Consequently, the explosion of a BSA mortar shell in Sarajevo's Mrkale market square triggered NATO air action, Operation Deliberate Force, which changed both the balance of military advantage and, ultimately, through the medium of a Croatian army assault into central Bosnia, the ethnic topography of Bosnia-Herze-govina. However, UNPROFOR's efforts to rationalise troop deployments by reducing the numbers of personnel deployed in exposed positions, while allowing a greater range of enforcement action, almost perversely may have precipitated the fall of Srebrenica. The act of signalling an UNPROFOR troop withdrawal from the eastern enclaves added to Bosnian Serb perceptions that the enclaves were of marginal importance to NATO.

A KALEIDOSCOPE OF SIGNIFICANCE

Despite its later actions, the BSA could have gained considerable advantages from the creation of demilitarised enclaves, particularly in eastern Bosnia. The UNPROFOR brokered ceasefire around Srebrenica and Zepa offered the BSA both the demilitarisation of the enclaves and UN supervision of the process. By early April 1993 Mladic's offensive against Srebrenica had secured and passed beyond the Zvornik to Milici Road, the BSA's main supply route in eastern Bosnia and arguably the primary physical objective of any Serb assault. Having achieved this, the BSA could potentially have benefited enormously from a ceasefire and subsequent demilitarisation agreement. Similarly, Milosevic, aware of the adverse political impact of the collapse of the towns and the potential inter-national willingness to take enforcement action in such an event, plus the potential for brutal Bosnian Serb retribution against BiH troops and civilians, would have perceived significant benefits from a negotiated solution.[34] Furthermore, ethnic cleansing was incomplete in parts of eastern Bosnia outside the enclaves. With attention focused elsewhere, this could be continued with relative impunity.[35] A form of UN protectorate over the safe areas prevented the need to assault an urban area and incur the heavy losses that would result. The JNA's experience in its assault on Vukovar (Croatia) in 1991 had starkly demonstrated the cost of such actions. Demilitarisation was, in contrast, far simpler and removed the risk of NATO enforcement action.

The policy also provided a solution to the dilemma of what the BSA could do with the tens of thousands of people who were now besieged in Zepa and Srebrenica. Lord Owen suggests that

> the ICFY [International Commission on the Former Yugoslavia] was doing everything possible to build up its moral authority to halt ethnic cleansing and we thought that to make it apparent that Muslims pushed out of their homes could go into safe areas would be to flash a green light to the Serbs that ethnic cleaning could go ahead.[36]

The emerging safe-area regime, therefore, provided a solution to a humanitarian problem which could potentially precipitate robust international intervention. However, without demilitarisation the enclaves increasingly represented a challenge to the Bosnian Serbs both politically and strategically. Bihac, for example, separated Croatian and Bosnian Serb territory and straddled a major communications route. The BiH 5th Corps, located in Bihac, presented a significant military threat to both Serb armies and also complicated any efforts to unite Serb territories in Croatia and Bosnia.

Srebrenica, Zepa and Gorazde represented similar difficulties, providing both a sizeable military threat tying down significant military resources and complicating the achievement of a mono-ethnic Serb statelet. Gorazde was also strategically located, sitting astride the primary road link between Belgrade and the coast, and the river Drina. Furthermore, the military threat from within the safe areas grew throughout 1994. BSA numerical inferiority was compounded by geography. BiH, HVO and Hrvatska Vojska (HV or Croatian Army) forces benefited from internal lines of communication, with the BSA having to police a long, 1,000-km plus, confrontation line with fewer troops and less operational-level mobility than its opponents. UNPROFOR estimates indicated that, as a result, the safe areas were a considerable drain on BSA troop strength. Four thousand Serb troops alone were tied down by Srebrenica and Zepa.[37] Improvements in the military capabilities of the BiH and the HV/HVO ensured that, increasingly, the initiative lay with the Federation rather than the BSA, otherwise outright winners in 1992. HV and BiH reorganisation created fewer territorially based structures and more mobile manoeuvre elements. The result was that both were increasingly able to take and to hold territory. The BiH assault on Kupres in late 1994 and the rash of attacks (Mount Vlasic, Brcko, Posavena, Sarajevo, for instance) in early 1995 hinted at a fundamentally changing balance of military advantage as well as a strategy on the part of the Federation of maintaining the fluidity of the confrontation lines in order to prevent their translation into political realities.

It also became increasingly apparent from 1993 that the Bosnian Serbs were unlikely to accept a peace plan that linked the eastern enclaves together and, therefore, cut off Bosnian Serb territory to the south of Gorazde. Small, besieged, unviable Muslim enclaves would be acceptable to the Bosnian Serbs, but a broad swath of linked territories centred on the enclaves and attached to central Bosnia threatened the creation of a Respublika Srpska. Consequently the Serbs rejected elements of the Union of Three Republics Plan, the European Union Action Plan and the July 1994 Contact Group Map as a result of plans to link several of the enclaves.[38] Almost perversely, the possible Bosnian Serb realisation that the final Contact Group plan (which did link the eastern enclaves) was unlikely to be abandoned lightly by the international community may have contributed to the decision to extinguish Zepa and Srebrenica, thereby removing the problem.

Then the failure of the BiH to demilitarise the enclaves ensured that the strategic rewards for the Serbs in retaking the enclaves remained if NATO air-strikes could be avoided. Once the 300 plus UNPROFOR hostages had been taken in May and June 1995, this course of action became increasingly possible. However, before this there were several other means to achieve the same result. Throughout its existence the BSA ensured that by limiting access to and freedom of movement within the enclaves they were economically and socially unviable in the long term. Humanitarian assistance was limited to food relief aid and winterisation materials while reconstruction and infrastructural repair assistance was routinely obstructed, particularly in the case of the Srebrenica, Zepa, Gorazde and Bihac enclaves.

For the humanitarian community, particularly the UN specialised agencies and UNHCR as lead agency, the safe areas represented enormous challenges. Individuals often remained within their own homes, presenting a set of complicating factors in terms of linking the humanitarian programmes (ideally, strategically 'neutral') with strategic consequences. The humanitarian effort, both in terms of the emergency relief and protection functions, became associated in the minds of Bosnian Serb commanders with maintaining the integrity of the safe areas' territory rather than insulating the non-combatant populations from the worst effects of warfare. To a large extent this was unavoidable given the nature of the BSA's ethnic-cleansing programme; however, it reduced the 'humanitarian space' and challenged the humanitarian integrity of such efforts in the enclaves. It also created unacceptable choices. For example, UNPROFOR's efforts in 1993 to exchange the Serb population of Tuzla for some of the worst affected people in Srebrenica could be viewed as assisting the BSA to cleanse ethnically the Srebrenica region. The alternative was to leave individuals in life-threatening circumstances.

UNPROFOR's air action, itself invariably precipitated by events concerning the safe areas, also impacted directly on UNHCR's activities. Sadako Ogata, in a letter to the UN Secretary-General (24 April 1994), stated that 'The use and threat of use of NATO air power in support of UNPROFOR has ... made the UNHCR in the eyes of the Bosnian Serbs a direct party to the conflict'. On average it took six weeks after air action before the Bosnian Serbs would allow humanitarian convoys into the eastern enclaves.

IMPARTIALITY AND THE NATURE OF BSA CONSENT

Maintaining UNPROFOR without recourse to enforcement required a return to traditional peacekeeping principles of consent, impartiality and the use of force in self-defence. There was a clear and implicit assumption that UNPROFOR impartiality would lead to consent. However, there were a number of problems with this. Impartiality may be perceived by warring factions as an active variant of neutrality. It is possible to apply impartially a set of criteria to any situation. However, where one party predominantly breaks the prevailing norms, the impartial but persistent application of punishment can lead to a perception of bias rather than neutrality on the part of the intervening organisation. The use of force in anything other than an obviously defensive way with regard to the safe areas therefore created among the Bosnian Serbs a perception of bias. This was exacerbated by the failure to demilitarise the enclaves themselves and the perception, among the BSA, that the safe areas protected territory rather than people.

UNPROFOR impartiality as a whole was prejudiced by the European Community's (EC) decision, on 16 September 1991, to recognise seceding Yugoslav Republics, without permission from Belgrade and without applying similar privileges to Serbs resident in Bosnia and Croatia. This not only made a new, international, legal precedent but brought into question, even before it was born, UNPROFOR's impartiality towards the Serb communities. Arguably this was the very issue that should *not* have been prejudged immediately before the UN assumed responsibility

227

for what turned out to be relatively protracted operations. In effect, UNPROFOR was deployed after the EC had recognised the very borders that were disputed and had created the conflict.

In a situation where consent was effectively compelled by forcing the BSA to have regard for the consequences of failing to comply with Security Council resolutions and where there were, increasingly, profound benefits to be gained from forcing the surrender of the enclaves, it is not surprising that the regime ultimately failed. Similarly, a regime dependent upon consent for implementation, where consent offers few benefits to one of the parties, is unlikely to be sustainable. However, the safe-area concept could conceivably have worked if it had been possible to effect reciprocal demilitarisation. This could potentially have allowed an extension of the concept to other towns, conceivably even those occupied by Bosnian Serbs. The possibility of this was raised by UNPROFOR's Sector North-East headquarters in a discussion paper which envisaged an extension of safe-area status to the Serb towns of Brcko, Doboj and Zvornick.[39] Similarly, the Contact Group's later plans envisaged extensions of the eastern enclaves. However, it was clear that the failure to demilitarise presented the Bosnian government with clear benefits, potentially enabling them to lure the BSA into a conflict with NATO. In such circumstances demilitarisation offered little benefit to them.

CONCLUSION

The Bosnian safe-areas concept clearly suffered from profound limitations, ultimately leading to the horrifying massacres of the male inhabitants of Srebrenica and the shameful capitulation of UNPROFOR. The failure to ensure a reciprocal demilitarisation, to draw distinctions between protecting people and territory, and the insufficient numbers of UNPROFOR troops combined with difficulties in constructing an effective deterrent regime to undermine its ultimately viability. It also had dire humanitarian consequences, allowing the Sarajevo government to adopt a strategy of detaining the civilian population and forcing them to remain in what were the most appalling circumstances. As a concrete expression of efforts to combine the UN's humanitarian, political and military activities the safe-areas regime at the very least was ultimately a failure.

NOTES

The opinions expressed here are those of the author alone and do not necessarily reflect those of the United Nations, the Ministry of Defence or RMA Sandhurst. Particular thanks are due to Col. Simon Shadbolt, Brig. Guy De Vere Hayes, Brig. Andrew Cuming, Maj. George Waters, Capt. Nick Illic, Amanda Gordon and Barbera Snook for their comments and advice.

1. There is some evidence to suggest that this offensive was little more than an advance to a line agreed by both the Croatian Army (HV) and the Serbs.
2. For example, heavily wooded, mountainous or urban territory.
3. At this stage French troops were vulnerable to the BSA in Sarajevo and British forces were in less vulnerable positions in Croat- and Muslim-controlled central Bosnia.
4. Until mid-1994 all major troop-contributing countries were conducting six-monthly reviews in order to determine whether withdrawal was the most effective course of action.
5. For a full discussion see UN Doc. S/1994/300, 16 March 1994, paras. 30–5.
6. A mission of the Security Council subsequently dispatched to the town of Srebrenica contended that, without the passage of Security Council Resolution 819, the demilitarisation agreement would not have been reached (see UN Doc. S/25700, 30 April 1993).
7. This was not an unreasonable assumption. Security Council Resolution 771, 13 August 1992, already required that all sides would be bound by the provisions of the Geneva Conventions and Additional Protocols.
8. UN Doc. S/1994/1389, 9 May 1994.
9. Security Council Resolution 836, 4 June 1993.
10. UN Doc. S/PV3228, 4 June 1993, p. 13.
11. Private interview with senior DPKO official.
12. Thomas Hobbes, *Leviathan* (London: Dent, 1983).
13. UN Doc. S/25939, para. 5, 14 June 1993.
14. Furthermore, no major troop-donating country was willing to provide troops with a mission that went beyond a 'presence' in the safe areas.
15. UN Doc. S/25939.
16. Lord Owen, *Balkan Odyssey* (London: Gollancz, 1995), p. 178.
17. UN Doc. S/1994/555, p. 2, 4 March 1994.
18. UN Doc. S/1994/300, 16 March 1994.
19. Private interview with UNPROFOR Chief of Staff.
20. UN Doc. S/25939, 14 June 1993.
21. *Atlantic News*, No. 2533, 11 June 1993; see also *Atlantic News*, No. 2534, 12 June 1993.
22. UN Doc. S/1994/555, 9 May 1994, para. 13.
23. It also ensured that from this point onwards NATO, in effect, retreated from enforcement of the no fly zone over Bosnia.
24. For example, on 12 March 1994 French troops deployed within the Bihac enclave requested CAS in order to extricate themselves from positions which were being shelled and shot at by the BSA. The request took three hours before it was approved and by this stage the targets had ceased firing and moved away; the air attacks were cancelled as a result. The speed of approval was generally a result of deliberations in the UN HQ in Zagreb and New

York rather than technical 'friction'.

25. This appeared to be common to all sides. For example, the main BiH mortar position in Sarajevo was located in the hospital compound.
26. That is, to retake the Jadar Valley in the south of the Srebrenica enclave.
27. UN Doc. S/1994/300, p. 11, para. 33a-b, 16 March 1994.
28. Ibid., p. 11, para. 33b.
29. UNPROFOR attempted to broker agreements delineating all of the safe areas. (See UN Doc. S/1994/555, 9 May 1994, para. 18.) However, to impose definitions of the extent of the safe areas ran the risk of prejudging the location of confrontation lines and the status of territories on the other side of the boundaries.
30. For example, no tracked armoured fighting vehicles such as Warrior were allowed into the enclaves.
31. The BSA had taken large numbers of UNPROFOR troops hostage during the Gorazde crisis in April 1994.
32. J. Gow, 'Coercive-Cadences', unpublished paper.
33. Despite this NATO had already rejected the concept of redefining 'self-defence' in such a way. In effect, air-power (CAS) was being used to pursue the mandate rather than simply to protect UNPROFOR troops.
34. At the very least such action could have precipitated an augmentation of the sanctions regime established under Security Council Resolutions 757 (20 May 1992) and 820 (17 April 1993).
35. Private interview with Larry Hollingworth, UNHCR.
36. Owen, *Balkan Odyssey*, p. 66.
37. Private interview with unnamed UNPROFOR battalion commander.
38. Owen, *Balkan Odyssey*, pp. 212, 241 and 284–5, respectively.
39. See Lt-Col. A. H. Le Hardy, Chief of Operations, HQ UNPROFOR Sector Northeast, *Interpreting the Safe Areas*, UNPROFOR Doc.

14

Civil Affairs: Soldiers Building Bridges

EDWARD FLINT

INTRODUCTION

Depictions of scenes of misery from such places as northern Iraq, Bosnia, Rwanda and Somalia have now become familiar features in the media and, together with factors described elsewhere in this book, have encouraged a more forthright international response to complex emergencies.[1] This response has seen a more extensive use of civilian as well as military agencies. The fact that there have been more peacekeeping operations since the end of the Cold War than during it is now familiar.[2] Moreover, militarily many of these operations are larger in terms of scope and size and much more complicated than the relatively straightforward, consent-based monitoring of Cold War peacekeeping. Peacekeeping in its contemporary form is, of course, a rather broad term and many would make distinctions between peacekeeping, peace-support operations, peace enforcement, humanitarian intervention, wider peacekeeping and so on. In such missions military forces are increasingly used in a variety of functions ranging from observation, liaison, protection of relief convoys and refugees, reconstruction, support to civilian agencies, and medical and humanitarian work through to actual combat. The net result is that military forces are now used in ways, numbers and for purposes that their Cold War equivalents would never have thought possible, and for which much adaptation has proved to be necessary.[3] This has included developments and improvements in the area of civil–military interaction, particularly in humanitarian support, coordination and consent-building activities.

CIVIL–MILITARY COOPERATION (CIMIC), CIVIL AFFAIRS, G5

> Civil Affairs operations encompass the relationship between military forces, civil authorities, and people in a friendly or occupied country or area. CA operations support national policy and implement US national objectives by coordinating with, influencing, developing, or controlling indigenous infrastructures in operational areas. CA commanders, staffs, units, and supporting CA elements secure local acceptance of, and support for US forces.[4]

The variety of terms adds an element of confusion to the subject matter, as there may be subtle yet critical differences between them, even if the net effect in the circumstances of a complex emergency is often the same. The policy of improving relations with groups of civilians, non-governmental agencies, communities and populations is increasingly referred to as civil–military cooperation (CIMIC), although the use of the terms civil affairs (the historical term[5] and the title given to specially trained military units) and G5 (the staff branch within military head-quarters tasked with identifying and planning civilian-orientated oper-ations) is not unusual. The use of the term CIMIC is closely associated with peace-support operations (PSOs) in complex emergencies and tends to suggest policies designed to enhance coordination between military and humanitarian activities at the tactical level as well as military involve-ment in building consent. Civil affairs, on the other hand, tends to imply a wider range of military capabilities outside of complex emergencies. It is important to distinguish between the headquarters process of identifi-cation and planning and actual activity by forces in the field. It is now a regular feature of most if not all complex emergency-based, peace-support operations to have a G5[6] section in all major headquarters.[7] Generally, the US Armed Forces are unique in staffing their G5 section with specially trained members of their civil affairs forces. In other armies, other cap badges[8] are posted into such work for a 'tour' of (typically) six months. In the field, tasks (either carrying out the work or facilitating contracts) may be conducted either by small teams of specialist civil affairs troops or general military units.

To put civil affairs peace-support operations activity into context, the wider range of roles associated with 'general war' and 'operations other than war' (OOTW) include for the US Armed Forces the following additional tasks: population-control measures; resource procurement and distribution; initiation of restorative measures for civilian government; enemy prisoner of war and civilian internees' programmes; domestic support operations; civil administration; non-combatant evacuation operations; insurgency; counter-insurgency; counter-drug; and counter-terrorism roles.[9] For peace-support operations civil affairs activities include foreign humanitarian assistance, humanitarian and civic assistance, support to displaced persons, developing stability and achieving the aims of a peace agreement. Moreover, civil affairs forces may help in staff planning by supplying information about the local culture, identifying third-party and target population, helping to avoid collateral damage, and assessing host-nation military and civilian capabilities and requirements.[10] As an example of a CIMIC plan, CIMIC troops deployed throughout Bosnia as part of NATO's Peace Implementation Force Bosnia (IFOR)[11] were tasked with conducting operations in support of the military implementation of the General Framework Agreement for Peace (GFAP), promoting cooperation and utilising the potential leverage provided by non-governmental organisations (NGOs), international organisations and governments, thereby helping to create a parallel civilian effort in support of the GFAP. Since the creation of IFOR and its subsequent evolution into the Stabilisation Force (SFOR), the focus of CIMIC has shifted[12] from a first phase of emergency humanitarian relief and prisoner release, to a second one of election and humanitarian support, reconstruction of infrastructure and longer-term programmes to a third phase of repatriation, reconstruction, capital investment, further election support and civil-institution building. CIMIC units have worked with NGOs, the World Bank, the United Nations mission in Bosnia, the Organisation for Security and Cooperation in Europe (OSCE) and the Joint Civilian Commission set up by the primary international civilian body in Bosnia, the Office of the High Representative (OHR).

The extent of the development of a civil affairs capability varies from army to army. Only the USA has a substantial, permanent and specially trained capability,[13] although the United Kingdom has recently formed a similar but smaller Civil Affairs Group.[14] Most armies do not have a separate organisation, preferring instead to second troops from other units where relevant specialisms exist (for instance, engineers, medics or logisticians).

It is important to note the difference between military and UN civil affairs. UN Civil Affairs Officers (CAO), formerly Political Affairs Officers, are civilians and work on autonomous political roles directed at local political processes as specified by a given UN mandate. These roles may include the supervision and running of elections, refugee-return programmes, the repeal of provocative laws, the suppression of intimidation, overseeing and running government departments, supervising the

233

release of political prisoners, the supervision of local media and local police, monitoring human rights and overseeing the tasks of and running the UN International Police Task Force.[15]

COMPLEX EMERGENCIES AND THE MILITARY

It has been suggested[16] that four issues in particular have caused military planners conceptual problems in terms of the shape and nature of the complex emergency or 'grey-area' environment they now have to deal with on a regular basis. Each of these has implications for civil–military interaction and thus CIMIC. First, consent is viewed by many PSO doctrines as the cornerstone of an operation. However, in a complex emergency contending sources of authority have in most cases replaced the sovereign state system of a single source of authority and each has to be won over. Moreover, the concept of state sovereignty is also being challenged in the face of gross and systematic abuses of human rights and of international humanitarian law. From the point of view of planning CIMIC, this may throw up a series of contradictory needs for which there may be little or no guidance from the international community. Second, even in situations where a state does remain it may only do so in certain areas. In areas where it has lost control there is likely to be a proliferation of groups and sub-groups each with its own agenda. This further adds to the problem of carefully and impartially relating to such groups in order to retain the consent necessary to carry out an effective humanitarian operation. Third, a large displaced population fleeing from conflict or famine may become the focus of attention for these groups – their control, division, relocation and extermination being a war aim. For the intervening force, this does not necessarily fit with the concepts and principles of war, thus providing a challenge. Add to this the possibility that the aiding of one community may lead warring factions to deem a humanitarian operation as partial, with the result that the security of an operation might be put into jeopardy. Fourth, unlike their own counterparts in a conventional conflict, military forces in a complex emergency do not necessarily act alone or first. Civilian agencies often arrive first, are more numerous, and have better local knowledge. In many complex emergencies military forces are likely to be working alongside a diverse range of NGOs and UN agencies. In particular, the proliferation of NGOs has challenged military bodies to develop means of forming useful relationships with such organisations. The numbers of such relationships may be enormous. It is estimated that in Bosnia during

IFOR's operations upwards of 400 NGOs have been active.[17] The diversity within such a large community, particularly in terms of operating principles and attitudes to risk, serves to complicate relationships with military formations.

MILITARY HUMANITARIANISM AND HUMANITARIAN SUPPORT

CIMIC is not simply about forming relationships. Military formations can be involved directly in the provision of humanitarian assistance. The nature of such involvement may vary enormously within a complex emergency. Some operations specifically call for military humanitarian activity, whereas others call for support (generally transport and security). In Operation Provide Comfort in northern Iraq, for example, 13,000 personnel moved 7,000 tons of supplies to 1.5 million Kurdish refugees. In Operation Sea Angel 8,000 troops provided 6,000 tons of aid to 1.7 million cyclone victims in Bangladesh.[18] In Rwanda in 1994 600 British troops from 5 Airborne Brigade were sent to assist in humanitarian support. Within the space of two months the 150-strong team from a British mobile field hospital had treated more than 82,000 people. Engineers had, among other tasks, restored the water supply to Ruhengeri (Rwanda's third largest town) and repaired a bridge on a major supply route.[19] However, the use of military forces for humanitarian work has not been without criticism. In particular, it has been argued that military structures cannot deal with the sheer numbers of people on the move in a complex emergency. In Rwanda an American military reverse-osmosis water purification system was unable to provide the quantity of water necessary for the tens of thousands of refugees and displaced persons.[20] The British military programme of immunisation at Gikongoro, while of benefit, did not stop rising death rates[21] because of poor water and sanitation conditions. Furthermore, the military response, digging latrines themselves, was futile. Later Médecins Sans Frontières (MSF) and Oxfam initiated a more successful and significantly larger self-help programme. It has been argued as a general point that military humanitarianism is inefficient, less effective and fails to build local capacity;[22] also the military may potentially overlook the impact of their actions on the wider population.[23]

Aid, in general, may act to further a war economy: developing the political economy of relief and the possible legitimisation of oppressive local leadership or social structures. Such events and processes may be overlooked by military planners, lacking experience of humanitarian issues, or simply restricted by the nature of an operation (mandate or time-scale). Then the economic and social impact of civil affairs work may also be in need of greater thought. In their search for interpreters, military units may pay a very advantageous wage. During the UN Transitional Authority in Cambodia (UNTAC) mission to Cambodia, for example, many medical workers, who were able as the result of their medical training to speak better than average English, were leaving the local medical services to work as interpreters. Naturally, this left large gaps in the provision of services in a system that was already overstretched. In a similar way, reconstruction projects may use foreign labour, military labour or at least labour-saving machines in an environment where jobs are few.[24] Such criticism may be unwarranted as increasingly overstretched military forces utilise local firms and labour for projects. In fact, many of the infrastructure repair tasks performed by the military are primitive and small-scale.[25] Larger and more complex reconstruction projects, in particular, are contracted to local firms. Indeed, the whole thrust of (particularly US) civil affairs doctrine, and the reason why forces are penny-packeted, is so that local groups can begin to develop local capacity. This, however, is often linked to political objectives. The possible frictions between the needs of short-term relief, long-term development and a tightly constrained military force continue to be apparent. Civil affairs units are thus caught between recognising the long-term needs and the constraints imposed upon the force commander. The priorities set by the force commander in ensuring the success of the military operation (in terms of compliance with his specific mandate) may mean that some badly needed infrastructure reconstruction (such as utilities, sewerage, refuse disposal) has to be either ignored by the military or put off until other more pressing military-oriented reconstruction is completed (such as bridges, roads, minefields).[26] The ability of a military organisation to adapt its priorities is also generally constrained by what could be described as the prevailing organisational architecture. For example, many of the major reconstruction programmes in Bosnia (from 1996 to 1998) were controlled by the International Management Group (IMG) with SFOR helping to coordinate activities. However, the ability of SFOR to co-ordinate is limited by the lack of coordination among the civilian agencies and the local practice (stemming from communist times) of referring all decisions upwards.[27] This helped to slow severely the 1998 reconstruction programme.

The presence of large numbers of troops can bring additional problems. It has often contributed to rising incidences of prostitution, the emergence of black economies and increasing crime – all of which may put even more pressures on the local health service, police and courts.

Here policy advice and training by civil affairs units can have some impact. During the Gulf War US civil affairs units conducted a wide-ranging cultural-awareness programme[28] and a similar one has been initiated in subsequent US operations, with mixed results.[29]

DIFFERENT DOCTRINES

The coordination of CIMIC activities by different nations involved in a PSO is not helped by the fact that very different approaches may be taken. In Bosnia it has been recognised that, as a result of frequent troop rotation, different approaches and inconsistency of service have led to a certain amount of local frustration with civil affairs projects.[30] These differences are compounded by differing national approaches in terms of objectives, interpretations of the aims, attitudes toward consent, impartiality and rules of engagement. Thus differences concerning civil affairs are only to be expected.

Clearly different national approaches can be identified both from recent operational experience and the focus of national military doctrine. Generally, Russia and the USA take a narrow approach, focusing purely on the benefit to the military operation, whereas France and Britain take a slightly wider approach, enabling both flexibility and the achievement of perhaps slightly wider policy aims. Moreover, Canada and the Nordic states probably take the broadest approach in order to encompass the strong humanitarian principles that these states wish to portray as national and foreign-policy characteristics.[31] The link between the wider doctrines of peacekeeping/PSOs and that of civil affairs/CIMIC is often critical to understanding the reasoning behind such different approaches.

The narrow approach adopted by Russia and the USA stems from the importance of such concepts as 'full-spectrum dominance'[32] which stresses the requirement to achieve victory. Thus the role of CIMIC is one of facilitating that aim. Moreover, the American approach has been referred to as passive in relation to civil–military cooperation activities.[33] The reasoning behind this tends to revolve around a number of issues, ranging from the need at all times to ensure the security of one's forces, to fears of allowing NGOs and other civilian organisations to become too dependent on military resources. Indeed, these issues have surfaced in recent US operations in Bosnia where, at least initially during the days of IFOR, the much-criticised policy of stationing CIMIC centres within US military bases was evident.[34] CIMIC activity was further hindered by the policy that all vehicle movements should be made in a minimum of a four-vehicle convoy, both difficult (when at short notice) and intimidating.[35] This level of security has created a reflex response from several NGOs and civil aid agencies who have felt that if the military needed such protection then so must they. This, of course, upsets attempts at reducing the dependency of NGOs on the military.

Dependency can be inadvertently created in other ways. In Somalia the attempt to control the proliferation of small arms resulted in a US policy of insisting on ID cards for all aid workers and the forbidding of the carrying of arms in port areas. This was perceived by many as increasing insecurity and leading to unfulfilled requirements for the increased provision of security. Many aid agencies understandably regretted the imposition of this policy and the resulting loss of security.[36] In some cases domestic political differences can have a major impact on the nature of the role played by a civil affairs unit. In the case of the US participation in Operation Support Hope in Rwanda, the State Department was not involved in the initial plan. This, together with reservations that were voiced by Congress, meant that severe limitations were placed upon the US armed forces. A natural US military fear of 'mission creep' resulted in an operation with extremely limited tasks and, once these had been achieved, US forces quickly returned home, much to the dismay of the aid community and the State Department.[37] Thus, even if the civil affairs units are able to identify needs their ability to develop a long-term strategy is frequently limited.

The French approach is to distinguish between three types of civil–military relationship.[38] French CIMIC focuses on preventing local civilian issues from interfering with the military operation, by, for example, controlling refugees or gathering information about civilian activities which might have a detrimental effect upon military activity. Military–civil affairs focuses on helping local institutions and services to return to normal, through infrastructure regeneration programmes. Military–civil relations encompasses activities which help to facilitate the military mission. By dividing activities into different areas, it is suggested that the French approach can more easily respond to changes in the military environment, the mandate of an operation and the supply of both human and financial resources.

The United Kingdom has, as mentioned above, recently developed a specialist Civil Affairs Group, although for most of the work continues to rely on conventional forces drafted into specific civil affairs duties. The UK PSO doctrine, rather like its predecessor Wider Peacekeeping, puts great emphasis on the concepts of consent, impartiality and minimum necessary force. In this respect, British CIMIC may be seen as a consent-promoting technique. Moreover, it has been recognised that a small specialist staff (G5) is of use to the commander in enhancing the prepared-ness and effectiveness of an operation by providing an assessment of local needs and resources. It is equally felt that a few civil affairs specialists on the ground can more easily deal with the problems faced in a complex emergency. In particular, it is felt that duties such as the handling of refugees, the facilitation of Department for International Development (DFID) projects and liaison with local civilian groups are much better handled by a single organisation where experience can be built up rather than a short-term, *ad hoc* solution.

Within NATO it has been recognised, as the result of the deployment of IFOR, that there was no common view of such issues as CIMIC capabilities, limitations, roles, missions or personnel.[39] Indeed, some suggest that more than 30 approaches were evident in Bosnia.[40] It was also noted that such NATO guidelines that existed were rather too restrictive and could, and must, allow for more expansive CIMIC activity.[41] As with a number of policies, much of IFOR's CIMIC plan was delegated by the force commander to the three individual divisional commanders (the UK, France and the USA). This resulted in diversity and inconsistency. The situation was not helped by the general lack of understanding or aware-ness of civil affairs issues among commanders or, indeed, the problem of having only one civil affairs officer involved in the planning of IFOR at AFCENT.[42] The lack of military coordination in Bosnia resulted in a command and control problem for the two units based in Sarajevo. Civil–Military Task Force (CMTF) was based in the city and sought to co-ordinate all theatre-wide CIMIC. Allied Rapid Reaction Corps (ARRC) Headquarters (acting as headquarters for IFOR) CIMIC had responsi-bility for activities in the city. The existence of two organisations for such a small area led to duplication and excessive spare capacity.[43] This situation arose because of the British and the French divisional areas' rejection of American civil affairs support and the significance of Sarajevo in media and political terms. Moreover, as the result of both organi-sations' desire to 'own' CIMIC a 'turf battle' broke out. Consequently, in a strange role-reversal CMTF became the practitioner while ARRC CIMIC became policy coordinator, but with little policy going beyond the city limits.[44] The need to anticipate different doctrines has been identified as an important area of development for US civil affairs forces and to some extent the problem has been eased both by such identi-fication, new doctrinal developments and by exchanges, seminars and training.[45] In the short term, the problem of harmonising different approaches as well as improving numbers of non-US civil affairs forces has been eased by the development of a NATO Pre-Employment Training CIMIC Course.[46] Furthermore, the need for a common NATO doctrine is currently being addressed and reviews of British and American civil affairs doctrine are taking this development into account.

WIDER CIVIL AFFAIRS TASKS

The focus of many armed forces on PSOs has, it might be suggested, resulted in other areas of military training, doctrinal development and general interest being neglected. It has been argued that in its focus on PSOs, emerging British civil affairs doctrine may be neglecting wider civil affairs duties.[47] While for those interested in complex emergencies this may seem of little interest, it has been pointed out that such general war tasks as the military administration of a region may be deemed necessary for an operation where the state has collapsed and a short-term fix is required. Indeed, in a more limited sense, American civil affairs units have been involved in the restoration and development of civil administration in Bosnia and Haiti, a capability the United Kingdom does not have. In Haiti 34 US civil affairs officers served as advisers to 12 ministries (education, public works, transport, commerce, public health, for instance), helping to create, often from scratch, institutional guidelines for emergencies and budgetary plans.[48] In Bosnia, US civil affairs troops have helped to reconstruct the judicial system.[49] From a practical point of view Britain is likely only ever to operate as part of a coalition in a PSO, and thus more specialist roles could be provided by another contributing armed force. However, this suggests, given the relative underdevelopment of civil affairs among many armies, that there would be continued dependency on American civil affairs officers, who may not always be willing or able to participate. Thus there is, perhaps, a need for a country like the United Kingdom to have a full spectrum of civil affairs capabilities.

NUMBERS

In Bosnia in the first two years of IFOR approximately 1,400 US civil affairs specialists were deployed, with 320 in theatre at any given time and with numbers coming mostly from the Reserve Component of the US Army.[50] While the average numbers in Bosnia have fallen since the shift from the Civil–Military Task Force (CMTF) to the CIMIC Task Force (CIMICTF) in December 1997,[51] a new problem emerged: that of increasing multinationality. Fifty per cent of the new task force was made up of non-US military. Therefore within NATO there is a requirement for a more substantial capability. With ever pressing financial expediency (together with different doctrinal approaches), it is to be expected that calls for vast numbers of civil affairs troops cannot be tolerated. Britain is thus unusual in taking the decision to develop a small reserve-based Civil Affairs Group, albeit without the range of capabilities available to US forces. However, in the quest for numbers Britain, like the USA, has the problem that much of its capability comes from reserve forces (96 per cent of US civil affairs capability comes from the Reserve Component). This presents a problem for operations short of war.[52] Early, or at least prompt, deployment is viewed as increasingly useful as civil affairs troops can prepare the way for the main force by coordinating with civil organisations and easing local concerns. In Bosnia, the late arrival of CIMIC units in theatre resulted in a number of missed opportunities in terms of coordinating policy with NGOs already on the ground.[53] However, it would seem that this is a lesson that has to be repeatedly learnt.[54] While the British Reserve Forces Act allows for a much greater flexibility in using reservists and the USA has been able to call up[55] compulsorily its civil affairs reservists, there is perhaps the wider question of whether such a balance is useful.

This is a difficult area as members of the Territorial Army and reserves often have civilian skills[56] which are more appropriate to the task at hand. Voluntary mobilisation, a practice used by both Britain and the USA, is seen by some as undermining the need to 'train as you fight'.[57] Moreover, it has also been suggested that the training and missions of the reserve component need to be brought more up to date and made relevant to operations focused not just on general war but also complex emergencies.[58] Some commentators have also suggested that the present doctrine is too abstract and needs to be made more practical.[59] One solution to the issue of numbers is to 'shadow-post' a regular member of the armed forces with a secondary war role.[60] Indeed, in the United Kingdom members of the Army's Educational and Training Services (ETS) have traditionally been given G5 staff work. Their use is not always appropriate since their familiarity with the wider army may be less. However, adequate training and the use of a more judicious and balanced mixture of cap badges can solve this shortcoming. Nevertheless, shadow-posting creates a more insoluble problem in that few military posts can easily or quickly be vacated without impacting negatively upon the rest of the army. This leads to the question of whether specialist civil affairs forces are required.

Members of the Royal Engineers set up many of the reconstruction contracts in Bosnia and many resource-control duties are conducted by members of the Royal Logistic Corps. Thus there may be profit in keeping British civil affairs small and focused more on staff planning and identification functions, and on developing consent through CIMIC.

Further to the issue of numbers, some commentators have suggested that civil affairs can, as the result of general military training, run into problems in terms of the ability to identify sex-related issues and the needs of vulnerable groups.[61] A suggestion is to recruit more women into the field of civil affairs. Yet this raises the general problem that civil affairs is not regarded as a mainstream activity.[62] Consequently, suitably qualified candidates, whether men or women, may avoid the job for fear of ending up in a career cul-de-sac.

COMMAND FUNCTION

Civil affairs is, as noted elsewhere, given the title G5 in a headquarters. Yet, given its critical role in helping to fine-tune the overall operational plan (as produced by the G3 (operations) branch), some have suggested that this division for complex emergencies is both unnecessary and may reinforce the idea that somehow the military and the civilian aspects of such an emergency are separable.[63] Thus the existence of a peacekeeping doctrine that regards military forces as being able to stand alone rather than existing as a part of an international, multifunctional force is compounded by a rather narrow view of the military's role in complex emergencies (dictated by a fear of 'mission creep'). Consequently, the success of a civil affairs mission may well be limited.[64] It has been suggested that in such grey-zone quagmires the military should be totally immersed in all areas so as to make more effective use of the resources they can bring to a complex emergency.[65]

ABILITY TO BUILD CONSENT

CIMIC operations and civil affairs forces have adopted consent building as one of their principal aims, albeit limited to in-theatre activities. The scope of consent building may vary from the local (dealing with a village's concerns over the extent of military traffic passing through) to the national (winning the consent of populations from one or more of the warring sides). Yet the ability of civil affairs forces to build consent may be undermined by a variety of factors.

At the operational level commanders may be ignorant of the possible value of civil affairs and thus underutilise the capability at their disposal.[66] Moreover, there is a tendency in both doctrinal and practical terms to lump civil affairs with the other so-called 'consent builders' such as media operations and, critically, psychological operations (PSYOPS). The latter has a (frequently misplaced) reputation for spreading propaganda. Thus attempts by civil affairs forces to disseminate practical information designed to win confidence[67] (such as health warnings) may be less effective if it is recognised by the target population that civil affairs and PSYOPS come from the same stable. As a result, some have called for a greater distance between PSYOPS and civil affairs.[68] Furthermore, the piecemeal approach of different styles of civil affairs, which are frequently compounded by the financial necessity of going for small, detached projects rather than an integrated approach, can undermine the macro benefits that could be developed.

'Honest broker' civil affairs activities are, however, relatively easy when compared with activities which attempt to persuade or compel local civilian and military authorities to adopt policies with which they have no sympathy. However, it has been almost impossible to use humanitarian assistance in such a conditional way because of NGO willingness to provide aid where it has been withheld by the international community. Such independent actions by NGOs in Bosnia have created inordinate amounts of work for former UNPROFOR commanders such as Generals Morillon and Cot.[69]

The ability to 'persuade' a warring faction may, indeed, come only when the intervening military forces can effectively dominate all the warring parties. In Bosnia this ability arrived only with IFOR. Its ability to compel any faction not considered to be making an 'effective effort' in mine clearance could be enforced by actions such as training and movement bans.[70] Yet to reach such a situation requires a single-minded willingness on the part of the international community. Thus, as some have suggested, ultimately consent is not generated by in-theatre activity but rather by international willingness to act.[71]

COORDINATION

If consent building is problematic then the ability to coordinate the activities of military forces and civilian agencies can be seen as relatively straightforward. Indeed, a number of structures have been developed or created at various levels to enhance cooperation between civilian bodies and military forces. Humanitarian Operations Centres (HOCs)[72] were developed to coordinate between national governments, UN agencies and the NGO community, and tend to be run by a designated UN-led agency. Their tasks have included the developing of a humanitarian assistance strategy, coordinating logistics support, arranging military support and monitoring progress. At other levels NGO coordination has been forthcoming through bodies such as the International Consortium of Voluntary Agencies (ICVA) and the NGO Coordinating Committee for Northern Iraq (NCCNI). Such bodies, although not without their faults, have helped CIMIC by providing one point of contact for areas of NGO military activity (such as the passing on of security information) rather than their having to talk to 300–400 NGO personnel separately.

At the military level, Civil–Military Operations Centres (CMOCs) have been a regular feature of complex emergencies since Operation Provide Comfort in northern Iraq during 1991. The purpose of a typical CMOC is to screen, validate and coordinate requests for military support, to explain military policies to other agencies and bodies (as well as acting as a conduit for civilian policies in reaching the force commander), to set up planning groups for large multi-agency programmes, to provide relevant security information to other agencies and to respond to emergencies. At a recent workshop[73] it was acknowledged that many NGOs and agencies found CMOCs of particular use in giving security briefs, staffing convoy security and emergency response, helping the planning and coordination process, providing technical help (communication support and repair) and allowing access to air and sea ports under military control.[74] It was further suggested that these relationships worked better when the CMOC was 'outside the wire' of a military base and when information was shared between CMOCs in real time thus avoiding the problem of different, confusing and even competitive policies emerging.[75] It has also become apparent that the more ambiguous the position of the CMOC, the greater the chances of successful civil–military relations developing. In Somalia the CMOC set up by US forces was technically under the command of Unified Task Force (UNITAF), but in reality it seconded itself to the UN humanitarian mission and became an integral part of the HOC.[76] Moreover, small, well-dispersed CMOCs had an added advantage of being on-site, less intimidating and less bureaucratically motivated. Yet problems continue to exist. For example, in Bosnia the CIMIC centre in the American sector was plagued by inadequate resources: it lacked a telephone, fax and e-mail facilities for significant periods.[77]

One of the problems facing any response to a complex emergency is that of gathering pertinent information that will help to govern both the scale and the type of response at the strategic level. Information gathered by both military and civilian organisations, when fused, will contribute, potentially, toward the formulation of a more coherent response. It is surprising therefore that such information exchanges are at best patchy and, despite the improvements outlined above, there is a need for further developments to overcome the rather *ad hoc* nature of existing relationships. The need for cooperation as early as possible is seen as essential, even to the extent of early warning programmes to highlight potential risk areas. NGOs, aid agencies and military units will all tend to notice different signals of a pending problem and thus information needs to be shared.[78] However, there are issues that will have to be dealt with, such as a more open planning process and the scepticism of many civilian bodies as to whether their information will actually be used.

Not all of the problems faced in coordinating civil–military relations are the result of military shortcomings. In Bosnia, as an example, many of the civilian coordinating bodies were late in starting up as the result primarily of funding and staff shortfalls. Consequently, much pressure was placed on IFOR CIMIC to fill the gaps, particularly as regards electricity, water and gas infrastructure repair. From a military point of view this verged on the edges of 'mission creep'. Moreover, once the primary civilian body, the OHR, was created, its loose structure (that it, it lacked any formal and permanent controlling committee) created significant problems in coordinating activity between it and the North Atlantic Council of NATO, which provided the political steerage for IFOR policy.[79]

Yet despite new structures, problems remain in terms of general civil–military coordination. Foremost among these are the different objectives and perspectives of the military and civilian bodies alluded to in other parts of this chapter. Several additional points may, however, be summarised.[80] First, while both want to generate stability there is often a difference in terms of how and when. In terms of the 'how' aid agencies are naturally focused on the provision of relief while military forces are focused on the need to provide security, which may mean that support to the relief effort may not be forthcoming. In terms of 'when' it has perhaps until recently become the norm for a force commander to think in terms of an 'end date' which is motivated either by the nature of a mandate or by the doctrine-driven planning process of developing an 'exit strategy'. Aid agencies often think in terms of an 'end state' which tends to raise the possibility of a long-term effort, and thus see the military effort as a short-term palliative rather than a real solution.[81] Yet thinking may be changing in this regard as the staff of the present SFOR operation now talk increasingly in terms of a defined end state.[82]

Many force commanders and civilian agencies face coordination problems because of differing interpretations of what is meant by the term security. To the force commander security cannot in most cases be provided to everyone all the time, yet this is often just what civilian agencies demand. In Somalia the inability of the force commander to provide such ubiquitous support resulted in the continued use of local security firms (whose ill-discipline and lack of training frequently left much to be desired). Although the issues may be resolved by moving the CMOC in with the civilian agencies, as happened to some extent in Somalia,[83] this difference in the perception of the use of force will continue to occur. Moreover, this difference is not helped by the view among some armies that civilian agencies should not become too dependent on their forces.

It has been suggested that four areas in particular cause frustration between the military and NGOs.[84] First, a number of commentators[85] have noted that, while in many ways military and civilian aid practitioners are surprisingly similar in motivation, the values of each are rather different. NGOs are generally regarded as more adaptable to 'grey-area' issues in that, unlike the military, they do not seek to identify an enemy and they tend to engage those around them in a more participatory fashion. Second, the organisational structures and motivations of NGOs are different from those of the military, who like hierarchy, discipline, strong leadership and clearly focused control and task execution. Thus inevitably many force commanders may become frustrated with what they regard, sometimes incorrectly, as ill-disciplined, unfocused, poorly led and inefficient NGOs. NGOs generally rely on donated funds (either from official bodies or private individuals) to carry out their work; thus at headquarters level they tend to respond to the needs of donors, budget limitations and the public relations consequences of taking or not taking a particular action. The focus therefore of an NGO may shift without warning, thus confirming the views held by many military staff that NGOs are inefficient or without effective leadership. Third, the decision-making processes of each are different. The military has a highly centralised, hierarchical and task-driven decision-making process, whereas NGOs tend to delegate, to take bigger decisions at lower levels and to be reactive to individual events and needs. Finally, the military may view NGO actions as both inefficient and damaging to the process of consent building at higher levels. This may result from a needs-based approach impacting negatively upon perceptions of impartiality. Consequently, Western militaries have often called for enhanced coordination arrangements for NGOs in complex emergencies.

The problem of ignorance by both soldier and civilian worker can be a major handicap as the one tends to know very little about the other's work. This can be reinforced by a series of entrenched prejudices. Many force commanders are unaware that, unlike the military, who, regardless of accuracy, have a self-image of flexibility and a perceived ability to shift easily from one task to another, civilian agency projects are less flexible. To move from relief to development-oriented projects can take time and resources to retool.

Furthermore, many aid agency staff are concerned that the military will tread on their toes by being too assertive,[86] imposing conditions and upsetting links with local communities. Better civil–military relations tend to occur where there is greater clarity of mission, particularly in defining areas of functional responsibility,[87] and relations work best where the military operation is viewed at a local level as legitimate and successful. Where the military operation is seen to be failing, aid agencies may do all they can to loosen ties with the military so as to enable work to carry on after the departure of an operation.[88]

To overcome the misperceptions of each other much work has been and continues to be done, ranging from conferences, workshops, training exercises,[89] formal publications, databases,[90] temporary military second-ments to civilian agencies, the exchanging of after-action reports,[91] and, of course, developing the CIMIC process and civil affairs units so that these issues become less of an obstacle.[92] In particular, the UN High Commissioner for Refugees (UNHCR) has published guidelines for enhancing civil–military cooperation entitled 'Working with the Military' and 'A UNHCR Handbook for the Military on Humanitarian Operations'. These guides put forward a ten-step process for more productive and effective coordination.[93] There is a fear, however, that much of this improvement is personality-based and that as new personnel engage one another in a new complex emergency the painful process has to start all over again.[94]

CONCLUSION: MEASURING SUCCESS

Working in the field of civil affairs has been acknowledged to be a difficult job in that, unlike an infantry attack or, indeed, care work in a refugee camp, there are few tangible measures of success, and even if these are apparent they may take months or years to bear fruit. It may also be a thankless task in that good news does not sell[95] and many achievements may be short-lived before they are plundered. It has been noted of civil affairs by one official of the US Agency for International Development (USAID) that in Haiti special force units with civil affairs troops attached were more effective at achieving the aims of that agency.[96] However, such evidence is anecdotal. Holmes has described civil affairs troops as 'invaluable diplomacy multipliers', useful in the early-warning and planning capabilities. Yet such comments, although heartfelt, have as we have seen many practical limitations. Perhaps the most telling comment is the view that, in reality, civil affairs is too broad a concept to be of practical use as a cover-all term. In its ability to smooth relations between locals at the tactical level and the military it has been shown that civil affairs can have a positive impact, even if the lessons have to be relearnt all too frequently, and that institutional relationships are excessively based upon personal chemistry. Yet at the level of gaining operational consent, civil affairs is beholden to the cohesiveness and policies of the international systems rather than the ability of the well-meaning, but ultimately limited civil affairs units.

NOTES

The opinions expressed here are those of the author and do not necessarily reflect those of either the Ministry of Defence or RMA Sandhurst.

1. In 1986 the US Office of Foreign Disaster Assistance (OFDA) classified three situations as complex emergencies; in 1995 the figure had risen to 26. Moreover, Operation Provide Comfort (northern Iraq, 1991) is widely regarded as a watershed in military participation in complex emergencies. See L. W. Davidson, R. E. Hayes and J. J. Landon, *Humanitarian and Peace Operations: NGOs and the Military in the Interagency Process*, Institute for National Strategic Studies (December 1996), National Defense University website.
2. In its first 43 years, the UN authorised 13 peacekeeping operations; in the 43 months from 1988 to 1992 13 additional ones were authorised. J. J. Landon and R. E. Hayes, *National Approaches to Civil–Military Coordination in Peace and Humanitarian Operations*, Evidence Based Research Inc., C4ISR Cooperative Research Program website.
3. J. Mackinlay, 'Peace Support Operations Doctrine', *British Army Review*, No. 113, August 1996, pp. 5–14.
4. US Army Field Manual FM 41-10, 'Civil Affairs Activities'. This may be found at the Joint Staff website.
5. Civil affairs history can be traced back over a century, although it was only during World War II that it developed into a substantial and purposeful military activity. Much of the early civil affairs work was concerned with the military administration of liberated/captured areas, although a limited humanitarian angle had been developed as a result of both the wide adoption by states of the 1907 Hague Conventions and the operational needs to prevent refugees from impinging upon military operations. 'Civic action' was used to help build 'hearts and minds' in the Vietnam War, but generally civil affairs, as a discrete activity, faded away after 1945 outside the US Armed Forces.
6. In some armies G5 goes by such titles as J5 or CJ9.
7. What qualifies as a G5 activity can vary from army to army. In some, for instance, resource control operations (effectively, local procurement) is the task of the G4 (Logistics) section.
8. In the British Army members of the Educational and Training Services (ETS) branch of the Adjutant-General's Corps have traditionally filled G5 posts.
9. US Armed Forces Joint Publication 3-57, 'Doctrine for Joint Civil Affairs'.
10. Ibid. and J. F. Powers and T. G. Knight, 'Civil Affairs, A Command Function',

Military Review (September–October 1995), p. 65.

11. J. J. Landon, 'CIMIC: Civil–Military Cooperation', in L. Wentz (ed.), *Lessons From Bosnia: The IFOR Experience*, Centre for Army Lessons Learnt website.

12. W. R. Phillips, 'Civil–Military Cooperation: Vital to Peace Implementation in Bosnia', *NATO Review*, No. 1 (Spring 1998), pp. 22–3.

13. The US Civil Affairs force structure consists of three US Army Reserve (USAR) CA Commands, nine USAR CA brigades, 24 USAR CA battalions, and one regular active duty CA battalion, as well as smaller civil affairs capabilities in the US Marine Corps and the US Navy. US civil affairs skills included public administration, public safety, public health, legal advice, manpower, public welfare, public finance, public education, civil defence, civilian supply (both to and from), food, agriculture, economics, commerce, property control, public works, public communications, public transportation, civil information, arts and monuments, cultural affairs and helping dislocated civilians.

14. The CA Group is made up of predominantly Territorial Army (TA) and is set to reach a target of 250 personnel.

15. C. Thornberry, 'Civil Affairs in the Development of UN Peacekeeping', *International Peacekeeping*, 1, 4 (Winter 1994), pp. 473–4.

16. J. Mackinlay and R. Kent, 'Complex Emergencies Doctrine, The British Are Still the Best', *RUSI Journal* (April 1997), p. 40.

17. As an indication of growth, in northern Iraq an estimated 28 NGOs were involved. By the time that a UN force was deployed to Somalia the figure had grown to 78. The UN Assistance Mission for Rwanda (UNAMIR) encountered 170, in Haiti (UNMIH) and the Implementation Force (IFOR) in Bosnia over 400 each. See L. W. Davidson *et al.*, *Humanitarian and Peace Operations*.

18. T. G. Weiss and K. M. Campbell, 'Military Humanitarianism', *Survival*, 33, 4 (September/October 1991), p. 451.

19. S. Kenny, 'British Army Brings Much-needed Help to Rwanda', *Army Quarterly and Defence Journal*, 124, 4 (October 1994), pp. 397–9.

20. A retired Los Angeles fireman saved the day with a converted fire tender. See N. Stockton, 'The Role of the Military in Humanitarian Emergencies: Reflections', *Refugee Participation Network (RPN)* 23, January–April 1997, RPN website.

21. Ibid. The death rates reached an estimated eight per 10,000 per day.

22. S. Sessions, '"Civic Action": Towards Best Practice in Humanitarian Interventions', *British Army Review*, No. 119 (August 1998), p. 57.

23. Ibid.

24. Ibid.

25. N. A. Sutherland, 'Reconstruction in Bosnia – Winning the Peace', *British Army Review*, No. 120 (December 1998), p. 22.

26. During IFOR's existence 62 bridges were repaired helping to produce a 300 per cent increase in civil traffic and an unknown increase in economic activity. Ibid., p 23.

27. Ibid.

28. Final Report to Congress, *Conduct of the Persian Gulf War* (Washington, DC: US Government Printing Office, 1992), p. 539.

29. Cultural training in Somalia as to the sensitivity of the Somalis' seeing the

soles of people's feet did not stop US soldiers from flying them as passengers in helicopters with their legs dangling out of the doorway. Interview with former UN Operation in Somalia (UNOSOM) staff officer.

30. N. A. Sutherland, 'Reconstruction in Bosnia', p. 19.
31. J. J. Landon and R. E. Hayes, *National Approaches to Civil–Military Coordination in Peace and Humanitarian Operations*.
32. The dominance of a military force over its adversary in every aspect of its operations.
33. J. J. Landon and R. E. Hayes, *National Approaches to Civil–Military Co-ordination*.
34. Most NGOs were at least 20 minutes' drive from the Civil Military Operations Centre (CMOC), ibid.
35. Ibid.
36. K. M. Kennedy, 'The Relationship between the Military and Humanitarian Organizations in Operation Restore Hope', *International Peacekeeping*, 3, 1 (Spring 1996), pp. 105–7.
37. J. E. Lange 'Civilian–Military Cooperation and Humanitarian Assistance: Lessons from Rwanda', *Parameters* (Summer 1998), pp. 106–14.
38. J. J. Landon, 'CIMIC: Civil–Military Cooperation'.
39. Ibid.
40. Ibid.
41. H. A. Holmes, 'Civil Affairs Soldiers are Confronted with a Rapidly Changing World and Vast Uncertainties', *Defense Issues*, 11, 60, Defenselink website (comments from 1996 Worldwide Civil Affairs Conference, by H. Allen Holmes, Assistant US Secretary of Defense).
42. J. J. Landon, 'CIMIC: Civil–Military Cooperation'.
43. Ibid.; 308 civil affairs personnel.
44. NGOs brief on the new limits of IFOR CIMIC action took place only in Sarajevo, ibid.
45. The John F. Kennedy Special Warfare Center and School, Fort Bragg, has hosted a number of visits, training programmes and exchanges. H. A. Holmes, 'Civil Affairs: Reflections of the Future', *Defense Issues*, 12, 32, Defenselink website (comments from 1997 Worldwide Civil Affairs Conference, by H. Allen Holmes).
46. W. R. Phillips, 'Civil–Military Cooperation', pp. 24–5.
47. C. G. Nobbs, 'G5/Civil Affairs: A Short Term Fix or a Long Term Necessity?', *British Army Review*, No. 115 (April 1997), pp. 54–5.
48. H. A. Holmes, 'Civil Affairs Soldiers'.
49. J. J. Tuozzolo, 'The Challenge of Civil–Military Operations', *Joint Forces Quarterly* (web edition), Summer 1997, US Joint Chiefs of Staff website.
50. W. R. Phillips, 'Civil–Military Cooperation'.
51. This was to help to overcome the belief that the US was trying to dominate CIMIC in Bosnia. J. J. Landon, 'CIMIC: Civil–Military Cooperation'.
52. British reserve forces traditionally need either an act of war or time-consuming Parliamentary agreement in order to be mobilised.
53. In particular, IFOR wanted to reduce the dependency of NGOs on the military that had grown up during the UNPROFOR mission. J. J. Landon, 'CIMIC: Civil–Military Cooperation'.
54. It has been acknowledged that on several occasions civil affairs forces have arrived late. During the Gulf War many civil affairs units arrived just as their

host units were moving up to engage the Iraqis (Final Report to Congress, *Conduct of the Persian Gulf War*, p. 540). In Bosnia, IFOR civil affairs units arrived on D-Day, not the planned D-13 (Landon, 'CIMIC: Civil–Military Cooperation' and Holmes, 'Civil Affairs Soldiers'). In the case of Bosnia, however, civil affairs units were not as late as the OHR in deploying. Civil affairs units also arrived late in US operations in Grenada and Panama (W. E. Wright and R. L. Fiegle, 'Civil Affairs Support in Operations Other than War', *Military Review* (October 1993), p. 28.

55. W. R. Phillips, 'Civil–Military Cooperation', p. 24.
56. W. E. Wright and R. L. Fiegle, 'Civil Affairs Support', pp. 28–9.
57. Ibid., p. 28.
58. Ibid., p. 32.
59. For example, J. A. Jacobs, 'Civil Affairs in the Assault', *Military Review* (September–October 1996), pp. 66–7.
60. G. C. Swan, 'Bridging the Nongovernmental Organization–Military Gap', *Military Review* (September–October 1996), p. 33.
61. For example, S. Sessions, '"Civic Action": Towards Best Practice in Humanitarian Interventions', p. 57.
62. Ibid., p. 57 and J. Mackinlay (ed.), *A Guide to Peace Support Operations* (Providence, RI: T. J. Watson Institute for International Studies, Brown University, 1996). Web edition available at *Journal of Humanitarian Assistance* website.
63. J. Mackinlay, *A Guide to Peace Support Operations*.
64. Ibid., p. 11.
65. Ibid., p. 12.
66. J. J. Landon, 'CIMIC: Civil–Military Cooperation'.
67. P. C. Siegel, 'Target Bosnia: Integrating Information Activities in Peace Operations, NATO-led Operations in Bosnia-Herzegovina, December 1995–1997', Centre for Army Lessons Learnt website.
68. C. Nobbs, 'G5/Civil Affairs', p. 55.
69. M. Clarke, 'The Lessons of Bosnia for the British Military', *Brassey's Defence Yearbook* (London, 1995), p. 50.
70. N. A. Sutherland, 'Reconstruction in Bosnia', p. 21.
71. J. Mackinlay, *A Guide to Peace Support Operations*, p. 12.
72. HOC was first used in Somalia, since when similar bodies such as On-Site Operations Coordination Centre (OSOCC, Rwanda) and Humanitarian Affairs Centre (HAC, Haiti) have developed.
73. 'Humanitarian and Peace Operations: The NGO/Interagency Interface', Workshop sponsored by the Institute for National Strategic Studies, US National Defense University; a report may be found at the NDU website.
74. L. W. Davidson *et al.*, *Humanitarian and Peace Operations*.
75. Ibid.
76. K. M. Kennedy, 'The Relationship', p. 96.
77. J. J. Landon, 'CIMIC: Civil–Military Cooperation'.
78. G. C. Swan, 'Bridging the Nongovernmental', p. 34.
79. J. J. Landon, 'CIMIC: Civil–Military Cooperation'.
80. G. C. Swan, 'Bridging the Nongovernmental', pp. 30–33.
81. H. Slim, 'The Stretcher and the Drum: Civil–Military Relations in Peace Support Operations', *International Peacekeeping*, 3, 2 (Summer 1996), p. 131 and K. M. Kennedy, 'The Relationship', pp. 102–4.

82. M. Rogers, 'NATO Agrees Plans to Extend Bosnian Force', *Jane's Defence Weekly*, 13 May 1998, p. 3.
83. K. M. Kennedy, 'The Relationship', pp. 100–1.
84. G. C. Swan, 'Bridging the Nongovernmental', pp. 30–3.
85. For example, H. Slim, 'The Stretcher and the Drum'.
86. Ibid., pp. 133–4.
87. K. M. Kennedy, 'The Relationship', pp. 108–9.
88. H. Slim, 'The Stretcher and the Drum', p. 133.
89. There is, however, the question of who pays and do the aid agencies have anybody available to attend? L. W. Davidson *et al.*, *Humanitarian and Peace Operations*.
90. Reliefweb and InterAction have websites.
91. G. C. Swan, 'Bridging the Nongovernmental', pp. 33–4. The same article also suggests the creation of NGO chairs at military colleges and the hiring of former military personnel by NGOs.
92. The CMOC in Somalia had inclusiveness, information sharing and responsiveness as its principal aims. K. M. Kennedy, 'The Relationship', p. 100.
93. Central coordination, early agreement on responsibilities, common areas of responsibility, compatible communications, collocation, liaison officers, interagency meetings, routine contacts, CMOCs and pre-mission reconnaissance.
94. J. Mackinlay, 'NGOs and Military Peacekeepers: Friends or Foes?', *International Defence Review* (August 1997), p. 53.
95. P. C. Siegel, 'Target Bosnia'.
96. H. A. Holmes, 'Civil Affairs Soldiers'.

15

Warlordism, Complex Emergencies and the Search for a Doctrine of Humanitarian Intervention

PAUL B. RICH

The period since the end of the Cold War has seen a growing interest in the phenomenon of 'warlords' and 'warlordism' in international politics. Warlords have come to be seen as one of the main obstacles to the entrenchment of stable structures of liberal democracy, especially in the developing world. Warlordism challenges the basic precepts of Western liberalism since its authority is seen to depend on armed force and the usurpation of the rule of law while its income and revenue may be derived from the forcible taxing of a subject population or even the use of forced labour, as well as dealings in narcotics and small arms.[1] Some military analysts have depicted warlords as part of a new 'warrior class' that threatens the stability of international relations as state structures become undermined by 'erratic primitives of shifting allegiance, habituated to violence, with no stake in civil order'.[2] Much of the emphasis of this discussion has been on Africa where a number of weak states have collapsed with the end of the Cold War and the demise of the external superpower patronage that in many cases propped up weak and highly corrupt regimes.

Warlordism is thus depicted in much of the recent scholarly literature as a malaise in international politics which, if unchecked, threatens to spread a new Hobbesian anarchy in parts of the developing world and quite possibly to some parts of the developed world as well.[3] The phenomenon represents in effect the logical opposite of the growth of international civil society and the promotion of increasingly powerful structures and mechanisms for conflict resolution. However, as this chapter will seek to argue, it would be a fallacy to fit all 'warlords' into a single template:

this would end by pandering to the trend visible in many of the Western media to homogenise conflicts in the developing world and to link them to a single process of state 'failure' or breakdown.[4]

Warlordism is a compact form of social militarisation that takes a variety of forms. In broad terms it may be seen as one of the manifestations of a new global 'underclass' of marginal and dispossessed peoples, especially in the developing world, with little or no stake in conventional political activity through the structures of conventional states. Warlordism degrades and undermines the discourse and activity of conventional politics and marks, in form at least, a return to more primitive forms of political authority. However, this 'precolonial' interpretation is too simple since it fails to account for the manner in which warlords also reflect the increased globalisation of international politics in the course of the twentieth century.[5]

This chapter is divided into three sections. The first examines the nature of warlordism and seeks to develop an analytical definition of it; the second examines warlordism in relation to current concepts of warfare while the final one discusses warlordism in relation to contemporary debates on peacekeeping and humanitarian intervention in 'complex emergencies'.

CONCEPTUALISING WARLORDISM

A clear and workable definition of warlordism is not easy given that it has emerged in a variety of forms. The growth in warlordism in contemporary international politics has tended to undermine some of the dominant assumptions behind the notion of 'praetorianism' in Western social science. 'Praetorianism' refers to the intervention of the military in politics and the breakdown of civil–military relations. As Huntington has pointed out, a praetorian society can exist with varying degrees of political participation, though the most stable would be praetorian oligarchies where politics would be dominated by rival families and cliques. The greater the degree of mass involvement the less stable the system would be, resulting in either the capture of power by a 'totalitarian' party or else a resort to authoritarian rule. Huntington recognised that in societies with only poor development of political institutions 'the end result of social and economic modernisation' would be 'political chaos'.[6]

It is in the societies without effective political institutions that there has been a resurgence of warlordism. The phenomenon is not entirely new. Some of the best recent analysis of warlordism has been in the arena of Chinese politics following the collapse of the Manchu dynasty in 1911 and the failure to establish a coherent republican regime. The death in 1916 of Yuan Shih Kai, the one obvious claimant to national leadership in China, ushered in a period of political chaos.[7] This continued throughout the early 1920s until Chiang Kai Shek began to restore some form of order in 1927 following the crushing of the Communists in Shanghai. Many Western analysts in the period following the 1949 revolution have seen this period as inextricably linked with the political weakness and corruption, though some, such as C. P. Fitzgerald, have also seen the warlords performing a constructive role in hastening the destruction of the old imperial civil service and the withdrawal of the scholar class into the universities.[8] More recently, the debate over the warlords has taken a new turn as the question of federalism and local versus central power has re-emerged in Chinese politics, given the upsurge of pressures for democratisation and devolution of power on federal lines.[9]

The negative associations of the term warlord from the 1916–27 period in China has led some scholars to avoid using the word altogether in favour of other terms such as 'militarism' or 'praetorianism'. The term for warlord in Chinese – *junfa* – has strongly pejorative associations and in the period following 1949 it was widely assumed that warlordism had been effectively banished from Chinese politics. Waldron has shown that the *junfa* concept is not, in fact, Chinese in origin since it is an importation from Europe. Chinese military theorists did not celebrate the employment of military force and warlord figures were rare in Chinese history. The concept of the warlord only really came into prominence following the collapse of the Manchu dynasty in 1911. It was then that Chinese military commanders acquired the title *dujun* or 'supervisor of military affairs'.

The notion of *dujun* began to be replaced by the early 1920s by the more negative term of *junfa* or warlord, since it conjured up the idea of military activity that was oriented to no specific political purpose. The negative connotation was largely due to the general distinction that developed among radical and left-wing intellectuals in Europe after World War I between violence that could be meaningless, as in trench warfare, or redemptive, revolutionary violence as in the case of the Russian revolution of 1917. The term *junfa* particularly conjured up the idea of military commanders engaged in meaningless militarism. It is in this sense that it came to be used by nationalists such as Sun Yat-sen as well as Mao Zedong, who employed it to denounce the Kuomintang after the crushing of the Communists in Shanghai in 1927. In this usage the KMT warlords were the expression of a comprador class in league with Western imperialism.[10]

The concept of the *junfa* became closely linked to either weakness or the complete breakdown of central political authority at the national level and a high degree of political autonomy for local military commanders. It meant in effect the fissuring of the Chinese military elite and the creation of a number of rival military commanders eager to gain access to political power. To this extent, warlordism represented what McCord has termed a 'fragmented praetorianism' or 'fragmented militarism' in which there was no longer a single and cohesive military class capable of governing the country.[11]

It is evident from the Chinese example that rival warlords can differ considerably in their level of power and authority. Lucien Pye has classified the warlords who emerged in the 1920s in the power vacuum at the centre of Chinese politics into three distinct types: field commanders at the local level with only a limited following; more prominent military commanders known as *tuchuns* who were active in politics; and a third group of national political figures with a military following. Each group mobilised a following around the loyalty of subordinate officers and troops rather than on the basis of ideological appeals. One of the strongest forms of loyalty was family loyalty, though this was usually not an important factor in the loyalty of subordinates to the *tuchuns*. Where family connections did come into play the *tuchun* was given added influence, as in the case of Chang Tso-lin and his two sons, who were divisional commanders in the Fengtien army.[12]

The Chinese model of warlordism, however, has rather limited applicability to other situations in the post-1945 period. In comparison with inter-war China, the emergence of more recent cases of warlord conflict in Sub-Saharan Africa has been a result of weak statehood and strongly ethnic, 'tribal' and clan attachments. Unlike the Chinese case, where warlords owed much of their following to the prestige that had been previously derived from the Chinese imperial army, military commanders in post-colonial African states have tended to derive their support from more localised followings, despite the hopes of some Africanists that the post-colonial military regimes in Africa could enhance the state-building process as they facilitated the emergence of a new, professional, military class that could break with the previous 'warrior' stage in African state building.[13] This latter view invested heavily in the idea of the professionalisation of African armies, though it was undoubtedly seriously distorted by the external intervention by the rival superpowers into African intra-state politics during the Cold War.

This is particularly well exemplified by the case of Somalia, where the military build-up occurred under the dictatorship of Siad Barre after 1969, first with the support of the Soviet Union and then, after the Soviet Union switched sides to support the rival Marxist regime of the Dergue in

Ethiopia (following the military revolution that overthrew and murdered Haile Selassie in 1977), with the support of the West. Under Barre there was a massive military build-up in the 1970s and the 1980s that helped to consolidate the regime at the centre. However, clan affiliations were never completely eclipsed. Popular attachments were traditionally centred around six dominant, unranked clan families: the Hawiye, Darod, Isaaq, Dir and Digil/Mirifle. These clan affiliations have ensured that the clan leaders have considerable leeway to mobilise their clans for either constructive or destructive political ends. This situation helped to create some of the features of a warrior society, where those groups, such as the castes along the Red Sea coast engaged in trades such as toolmaking and haircutting, became marginalised from the general thrust of the society's politics. By contrast, those mobilised into clans have been able to use them as a simple form of trade unionism in which clan consciousness became a means of securing collective economic and social goals.[14]

Clan consciousness though has by no means been a 'primordial' feature of Somali society, since it has tended to rise and fall in accordance with the wider patterns of national politics. Under the autocratic regime of Siad Barre after 1969 there was a marked diminution in clan identification as the regime strongly discouraged rural clan warfare and introduced rural self-help projects and rural and urban literacy campaigns. This had a considerable impact until the 1977–78 Ogaden war with Ethiopia, which did much to upset the balance of the clans in Somalia as a group of discontented officers from the Majerteyn (Darod) sub-clan attempted a coup. This led the ruling regime to protect itself by mobilising clan support and creating a counter-insurgency force centred on the Marehan clan which, with refugees from the Ogaden, increased the army's size from 37,000 in 1977 to 120,000 in 1982. In a situation of rapid militarisation, the opposition became mobilised around the leader of the coup attempt Colonel Abdullahi Yusuf, who organised in exile in Ethiopia the Somali Salvation Democratic Front (SSDF). This soon lost momentum but it opened up political space for other guerrilla formations to emerge, such as the Somali National Movement (SNM), first formed in 1981 and based on the Isaaq clan in the north of the country. The repressive response from the regime included Latin American-style death squads and led to some 50,000 casualties. In the north something like a point of no return was reached as Barre's army carried out reprisals on the Isaaq clan, devastating the main city Buroa and forcing a large part of the population to flee to Ethiopia.[15] The carnage and destruction resulted in a cut in foreign aid which further compounded the country's economic crisis and exacerbated clan identifications.[16]

It was in this situation of mounting crisis that warlordism emerged, beginning with the establishment in 1989 of the United Somali Congress (USC) by Hawiye dissidents under the civilian leadership of a businessman Ali Mahdi Mohamed. The USC had a military wing under the leadership of General Farah Mohamed Aidid, who gained the support of the SNM while in exile in Ethiopia. However, as he moved into the country he turned against the Hawiye and initiated a Darod-Hawiye clan war. In this situation of mounting chaos further militarised factions emerged, such as the USC in the central part of the country based on the Hawiye and the Somali Patriotic Movement (SPM) in the south based on the Ogadenis who are part of the Darod group. The USC, the SPM and the SNM formed a loose coalition and eventually secured the overthrow of Siad Barre, who fled the country in January 1991. Ali Mohamed declared himself interim president and gained external support from the Italians, the Egyptians and the United Nations, despite opposition from the other internal Somali opposition factions. It had been Aidid's forces though which had secured Barre's removal from power and Aidid believed he should be involved in the government. The stage was thus set for a new round of clan warfare which led to the division of the country into 12 zones of control and the destruction of most of the infrastructure, prompting the eventual UN intervention in the form of the UN Operation in Somalia (UNOSOM) following the UN-brokered ceasefire of 3 March 1992.[17]

The more recent manifestations of warlordism in the developing world, such as the case of Somalia, indicate that the Chinese model derived from the inter-war period may be simply at one end of a continuum linked to state disintegration and collapse. As Zartman has pointed out, state collapse is the extreme end of a process of a crisis in governance which is not necessarily irretrievable. Many states pass through a process of governmental overload and crisis but manage to restore governmental authority, while other states prove incapable of doing this and sink into a state of complete collapse. The exact reasons for this are a matter for extensive further research since as yet we have no convincing typology which can enable both analysts and policymakers to predict state collapse.[18] Much indeed appears to depend upon situational and tangential factors, driven by the role and the capacity of individual political leaderships and personalities.

The example of inter-war Chinese warlordism is interesting for the manner in which it defined a period of crisis in central government before a degree of restoration of authority at the centre was secured by Chiang Kai Shek in the late 1920s. In Somalia, by contrast, no such central government restoration proved to be possible after the débâcle of 1991–92, as a weak state was effectively pushed over the brink into complete collapse, in part through the badly managed, UN-brokered ceasefire of

March 1992 which – in the absence at this stage of a peacekeeping force – had the effect of escalating tensions between rival clans as well as of undermining the position of those clans that had hitherto managed to remain neutral.[19]

It has been in the latter instance of state breakdown that warlordism has acquired its particular reputation in post-Cold War politics in which no effective state authority exists. We can thus classify warlordist behaviour along a continuum stretching from extensive regional followings for a military commander on the basis of his personal prestige and ability to secure benefits for his followers, to more limited types of militarised ethnic and clan formations mobilised behind a local strongman. There is also a strong leadership dimension to the warlordist phenomenon which has been underplayed in recent analyses of Third World politics, especially those of Sub-Saharan Africa. As Njuguna Ng'ethe has pointed out, the control of the state by strongmen such as Siad Barre in Somalia or Samuel Doe in Liberia has been an important factor in state collapse. The rule of such strongmen has tended to inhibit the emergence of any sort of resilient civil society which could help to facilitate the re-establishment of the state once it had entered a crisis of legitimacy.[20] In a broader sense too it is possible to see warlordism as in some senses an emulation at the local and the regional level of the previous structure of strongman rule at the centre – though this is a phenomenon that requires more comparative research.

This continuum of warlordism also fits into a wider series of classifications of conflict. At the most developed end it blurs into a regional or secessionist movement that may be able to develop nationalist or proto-nationalist political aspirations. At the lower end of the continuum it blurs into a variety of forms of low-intensity conflict, such as organised gangsterism and brigandage. It is also possible that we are seeing the beginnings of a new phase of warlordism on a transnational plane with the development of terrorist operations such as those of Osama Bin Laden, the Saudi Arabian dissident currently based in Afghanistan, with followers in a number of other countries such as Sudan.

THE WARLORD AND THE THEORY OF MODERN WARFARE

The growing significance of the warlord in international politics compels a reassessment of theories of modern warfare. Warlord conflict is a good example of what Holsti has termed 'wars of the third kind' in the twentieth century. Coming in the wake of 'institutionalised warfare' of the eighteenth and the nineteenth century and 'total warfare' in the first half of the twentieth century, 'wars of the third kind' are characterised by an absence of fixed territorial boundaries, elaborate institutionalised military rituals, major fronts and military campaigns.[21] As with various forms of guerrilla warfare, warlordism reflects a growing breakdown of professional military activity in favour of more informal forms of military conduct in which military authority and discipline become personalised around a single political leader.

The power of the warlord is highly militarised. There is a strong tendency in such situations for terror to be also employed to buttress the leadership of the warlord, leading to what Walter, in a pioneering study in the uses of political terror among the Zulu in nineteenth-century South Africa, has termed a 'regime of terror', where systematic violence works to maintain power relations.[22] Such a model of militarised and despotic power hardly resembles that of 'people's war' which Holsti has seen as a dominant feature of 'wars of the third kind'. Warlordism tends to be derived more from models of autocratic tribal rule or large-scale gangster-ism than revolutionary wars of national liberation in which the main basis of support lies in the general civilian population.[23] Its structures of hier-archical power – where leadership is based on various forms of patronage, nepotism and political clientelism – bears little resemblance to doctrines of popular mobilisation, even though these features have on occasions been exhibited by anti-colonial national liberation movements in the post-1945 era.

Warlordism increasingly came into prominence in the wake of the main period of revolutionary wars of national liberation against European colonial rule. This period may be broadly characterised as running from 1945 up to the early 1980s. It contained a number of notable examples of guerrilla movements that succeeded in fighting European colonial regimes to a military stalemate, leading in turn to a negotiated process of decolonisation. Examples of such movements are the Front de Libéra-tion's (FLN) bitter, seven-year war against the French in Algeria between 1954 and 1962, the Frente de Libertação de Moçambique's (FRELIMO) struggle against Portuguese colonial rule in Mozambique between 1964 and 1975, and the long war of the Vietnamese National Liberation Front (NLF) against first French and then American power in Vietnam between 1945 and 1975. One of the last major examples of such anti-colonial guerrilla insurgencies was the campaign of the Zimbabwe African National Union-Patriotic Front (ZANU-PF) against the Smith regime in Rhodesia in the 1970s leading to a negotiated transfer of power in 1979–80 under British auspices and the creation of the new state of Zimbabwe. Thereafter the impact of such insurgencies has progressively declined, since by the 1980s most European colonial dependencies had been relinquished. The ending of the Cold War in the late 1980s also deprived any remaining movements of effective superpower patronage, especially after the demise of the Soviet Union in 1991. The collapse of such external supports was undoubtedly a major reason why one of the last major, anti-colonial, insurgent movements, the African National Congress (ANC) in South Africa, was driven by 1990 to abandon 'armed struggle' against the white minority regime in Pretoria in favour of a negotiated transfer of power.

The emergence of warlordism as an increasingly important factor in international relations really dates from the end of this post-war phase of anti-colonial insurgency. It reflects the decline of ideological appeals to 'national liberation' in Third World politics since the early 1980s and the fracturing of a number of post-colonial 'quasi states' that had enjoyed only juridical rather than empirical legitimacy.[24] There was an element of mythology in any case at the heart of the national liberation ideal. In Algeria, for instance, the lack of any strong ideological cohesion in the FLN during its war against the French rather undermined the precept of Frantz Fanon that anti-colonial revolution necessitated complete unity among the colonised to secure the removal of colonial rule.[25]

The FLN, in fact, remained until the late 1950s a coalition of agitators and organisers with relatively few intellectuals or administrators, and even this coalition was maintained only with considerable difficulty. It was initially based on an alliance of nine loosely based chieftains called the Revolutionary Committee of Unity and Action (CRUA). This established an underground network of commandos organised into five separate military zones or *wilayas*. The *wilayas* were forced to rely upon their own resources as the French military tightened the frontiers with Tunisia and Morocco and cut off external sources of supply and resembled in many ways warlord-type military formations. By the late 1950s the FLN insurgency inside Algeria was isolated from its external wing. This weakness encouraged it to persist with the strategy of terrorism rather than trying to build up its internal political organisation. Its French enemy, on the other hand, proved to be increasingly vulnerable to the growing anti-colonial international mood, and terrorism enabled it to achieve a high degree of publicity for its cause with relatively limited organisational resources.[26] It was largely for political rather than military reasons that the Gaullist state in France finally opted to negotiate an exit from Algeria in 1962.

The Algerian state did not fracture into warlord factions after independence as it came under a firm praetorian regime after a military coup overthrew the FLN regime of Ahmed Ben Bella in 1965.[27] In other cases of Third World decolonisation the experiment with national liberation was followed by political fracturing and the emergence of warlordism.

The triumph of the Marxist-Leninist FRELIMO liberation movement in Mozambique, for instance, proved to be short-lived. After removing Portuguese colonial rule in 1975, FRELIMO embarked in the late 1970s on radical policies of land reform and the collectivisation of peasant production, which alienated some sections of the peasantry and rural chiefs who drifted towards opposition factions centred on the Mozambique Resistance Movement or Resistância Nacional Moçambicana (RENAMO) which had initially been established by the Smith regime in Rhodesia, but was taken over by the South African government in Pretoria following the 1980 transfer of power to the ZANU-PF regime of Robert Mugabe. By the early 1980s the FRELIMO government was thrust on to the defensive as its neighbour South Africa began a war of destabilisation in southern Africa and military and political support for RENAMO guerrillas in Mozambique.

The South African destabilisation campaign led to the destruction by RENAMO of much of the basic infrastructure in Mozambique in the early 1980s and effectively forced the FRELIMO government to enter into negotiations with the South Africans. In 1984 it signed the Nkomati Accord with the government of P. W. Botha and the same year applied to join the World Bank. RENAMO's success, though, was not due entirely to South African backing since it had been able to pick up support from a number of social groups inside Mozambique, such as chiefs, witchdoctors, church and religious sects and cadres of young men known as *mujibas*. These groups had been alienated from the FRELIMO government's land-reform programme and provided a basic organisational base to RENAMO, which was not just a collection of motley 'bandits' as FRELIMO propaganda tried to maintain. The basic operational unit consisted of 150 men which was in frequent radio contact with RENAMO headquarters. The organisational structure was strictly hierarchical and in a number of cases younger *mujibas* were press-ganged into the movement and terrorised into staying on through fear of murder or mutilation if they tried to desert. The organisation was not an entirely random one since there was a clear command structure and a number of military rituals were followed such as saluting.[28] While ultimate authority was personalised around a figurehead such as Afonso Dhlakama, at the local level the organisation allied itself to local cults such as Shona spirit mediums. RENAMO's first military commander, Andre Matsangaissa, died in 1979 when trying to retake Gorongosa after being assured of victory by a Shona medium.

The wanton destruction of RENAMO suggests that it was in some respects the logical opposite of a 'nation building' movement such as FRELIMO. However, the local dynamics of the movement indicate that it was more than just a group of bandits as local chiefs helped to recruit a corps of local police to collect taxes and recruit *mujibas*. Much of this support was secured on an ethnic basis: in its most successful province Zambezia it managed to establish a food-production system through local chiefs, though in Gaza, by contrast, it was generally unsuccessful in gaining much of a following as it was viewed as a mainly Ndau movement.[29]

The ethnic base to warlordism is repeated throughout much of Sub-Saharan Africa. In Liberia the original opposition by Charles Taylor's National Patriotic Front of Liberia (NPFL) to the largely Krahn-based regime of Samuel Doe was centred on the Gio and the Mano ethnic groupings. Outside Africa, too, the main basis for warlord activity has often been ethnic. In Afghanistan the warlord groupings have been largely ethnically based: Abdul Rashid Dostum has led a mainly Uzbek group in the north while Ahmad Shah Massou and Burhanuddin Rabbani have commanded Tajik groups in alliance with other ethnic groupings in the north-east. The Taliban movement, by contrast, was established with Pakistani backing by privately educated *ulama* from the Pushtun groupings in the South.[30]

Overall, therefore, warlordism represents a rather more profound break with conventional military doctrine than guerrilla warfare and insurgency. Military strategists since Clausewitz have recognised that guerrilla warfare marks only a partial break with conventional military campaigning, since it is ultimately pivoted around the need to foster the state as the most civilised form of political conduct. Guerrilla theorists in the twentieth century, such as Mao Zedong and Giap, built on this and argued that the guerrilla phase is the precursor of a more conventional phase in the evolution of revolutionary 'people's war' in which the enemy is finally defeated.[31] Compared with this, warlordism veers towards a total combination of military and political means. Warfare in effect becomes politics and politics warfare in a permanently militarised, anarchical society where the authority of an effective central state no longer prevails.

There has been a tendency for analysts to misunderstand those aspects of warlordism that distinguish it from orthodox insurgent movements. Clapham, in a recent important survey of Africa, has termed such movements 'warlord insurgencies', characterised by personal leadership, weak organisational structures, weak or opportunistic ideologies and a general failure to establish durable governmental structures.[32]

A similar misperception tends to pervade the current conceptualisation behind peacekeeping operations which have been largely premised upon policing strategies. These in turn assume that the 'insurgent' warlord factions can be ultimately driven into accepting a peace settlement in which the *status quo ante bellum* can be restored and the old nation state resurrected and put back together again. However, there is considerable evidence to suggest that this is a difficult and protracted task, given that peacekeeping forces are limited in the range and extent of their mission and prevented from becoming a semi-permanent occupying force with the capacity to install a new and durable regime. Certainly such a force may be necessary in order to conduct full-scale policing so that individual warlords could be prosecuted before war crimes tribunals and barred from standing in elections.[33]

In the case of Liberia, for instance, the morale of the regional peace-keeping force sent by the Economic Community of West African States (ECOWAS) and known as the Economic Community of West African States Monitoring Group (ECOMOG) plummeted when it was necessary to fire in self-defence against the child soldiers used by the Independent Patriotic Front of Liberia (IPFL) of Charles Taylor. Conventional counter-insurgency methods are not especially effective in such a situation either since there was no clear political alternative to offer to the supporters of the rival factions. Limited by resources and political infighting, ECOMOG frequently had to make deals with some of the warlord leaders such as the Armed Forces of Liberia (AFL) and the Independent National Patriotic Front of Liberia (INPFL) of Prince Johnson.[34]

The growth of warlordist activity can in a number of instances be seen as part of a wider 'insecurity dilemma' among developing states. This stems from the fact that many of them are, in practice, state-nations with multiple ethnic communities residing inside their territorial boundaries while their governing structures command only a low level of domestic political legitimacy. Clearly not all such state-nations fragment into war-ring factions. Some analysts have seen this issue in cultural rather than military terms. John Glenn, for instance, has pointed to the invention of national myths in the fostering of a sense of national cohesion. This dimension of ethnic identity, though, may well extend beyond questions of cultural symbolism. The role of warlord leaders signifies an additional military variable which has been generally neglected by analysts of ethnicity.[35]

WARLORDISM AND PEACEKEEPING

From the previous discussion it is evident that warlordism is likely to be an increasingly important dimension in low-intensity conflict in the post-Cold War era. In a few scattered theatres, such as Kosovo and East Timor, guerrilla conflicts of a fairly classical vintage may continue for a number of years since they are linked to unresolved issues of ethnic and national self-determination.[36] However, in a variety of other cases there are signs that there is a progressive undermining of the conventional Western model of the sovereign state in a number of regions of the developing world (particularly Sub-Saharan Africa) where states with little or no distinct national identity, civic culture or cohesive political institutions have effectively 'failed'. In such states it is difficult to forge an inclusive nationalism that can build upon Western notions of popular sovereignty and sustain effective sovereign statehood. The nationalism that does implant itself in these societies has tended to be more of an ethno-nationalism which has taken on an increasingly exclusive form, leading in extreme cases such as Rwanda to ethnic genocide.[37] This has, significantly, not occurred in all cases of state breakdown. In Somalia the absence of a central state has not prevented the flourishing of a market economy which has capitalised on the collapse of many of the companies nationalised under the Barre regime. Markets can in fact develop in a situation of statelessness.[38]

Nevertheless, warlordism has in the post-Cold War period largely superseded earlier forms of national liberation struggles in the developing world, reflecting the declining appeal of global ideology in Third World military conflict. Warlordism is generally based on more local and particularistic appeals, anchored around a familiar and trusted local strongman capable of delivering benefits and advantages to his followers (warlords tend to be mainly patriarchal social formations). The bases of this trust and loyalty are diverse and each warlord situation tends to be different. This makes the task of formulating coherent military doctrine when dealing with warlords as part of a strategy of humanitarian intervention particularly difficult. Warlord formations and militias tend to be highly decentralised and with limited command structures. It is not easy to predict their capacity to mobilise support (which may extend to involving the use of child soldiers) and this compounds the difficulties of an external military force that is seeking to disarm the general population and re-establish national government in the former loci of power. With protracted civilian resistance, it becomes more or less inevitable that the intervening force has to involve itself in some form of dialogue with some of the warlord formations. This threatens to undermine the authority of the force if it is intervening for humanitarian reasons and politicises its involvement.[39]

There is thus no easily recognisable military doctrine for dealing with warlords in 'complex emergencies'. This may, in part, be explained by the fact that it is hard for states to know what their real interests necessarily are in situations of post-national liberation conflict where warlord formations command no large-scale followings on the basis of a coherent ideological appeal. As one American military analyst has observed, 'victory by non-proselytizing insurgents, even those ideologically hostile to the United States, is unlikely to threaten our interests'.[40] This was well exemplified by the reluctance of the USA to be dragged into the Liberian civil war after the invasion of the country in 1989 by the NPFL led by Charles Taylor. Despite distaste for the brutality of the regime of Samuel Doe, Liberia had served as a valuable military staging and intelligence post during the 1980s. There seemed to be a lingering Cold War-inspired interest to maintain as far as possible the political status quo. Moreover, the US government was worried that sending in the Marines might encourage Liberians to emulate Haitians and rush to seek asylum at the US Embassy. This indecision though helped to prolong the conflict since it polarised ethnic antagonism as Doe's largely Krahn-based army proceeded to wreak havoc in Nimba County, which backed Taylor. Moreover when ECOMOG was finally sent in at the end of 1990 it too helped to sustain the conflict by preventing Taylor from swiftly taking Monrovia and so ending the war.[41]

Lack of decision can exacerbate some conflicts as much as a precipitate decision to intervene, as in the case of Somalia in the form of the UN Operation Restore Hope. Warlordism poses a considerable challenge to strategic thinking, given the way that warlord-based conflict dissolves the Clausewitzean distinction between politics and war, though it is important to note that this is by no means an entirely new dilemma of the post-Cold War world. American strategic theorists had to a considerable degree abandoned conventional counter-insurgency doctrine as far back as the middle 1970s as it became evident in the wake of the Vietnam débâcle that counter-insurgent operations by no means uniformly sustain nation-building programmes.[42]

However, modern forms of warlordism present a series of new and acute dilemmas to strategic theorists, following the demise of superpower conflict and the growing saliency of 'complex emergencies' and the need to promote coherent programmes of 'humanitarian intervention' in the post-Cold War international order. Conventional military operations have been distinguished by a separation between a strategic level of command dealing with overall political objectives and the actual execution of these tasks. In complex emergencies, however, political objectives intrude into the actual military operations themselves and politicise the functions of junior and middle-ranking officers.[43]

Humanitarian operations by bodies such as the UN are continually prone to the dangers of 'mission creep' and the continuous expansion of their perceived tasks. This is especially likely in situations where there is no easily understood limit to military action in terms recognised by the original drafters of the UN Charter. In the relatively simpler world of the

1940s the Charter sought 'collective security' through military force to restrain and halt the actions of a recalcitrant member of the international society of states. As part of this objective it was intended that force should be used that was proportional to the original violation and no more than was operationally necessary.[44] In the more complex cases presented by 'failed states' it is by no means clear whether the objective should be one of 'peacekeeping' or 'peace enforcement' and this became a dangerously divisive issue in the case of the UN operation in Somalia.

In the greyer world of warlordism it is hard to know in advance what sort of force is needed commensurate to the original violation. The original UN intervention into Somalia in the form of UNOSOM I in March 1992, for instance, occurred during a period of truce between the warring factions in the country. It consisted of a mere 500 troops operating in a supportive role behind a massive humanitarian operation consisting 30 non-governmental organisations (NGOs). The inability to establish any form of order in the country led to a situation where most of the food intended to reach the victims of starvation was looted on the docks by armed gangs. By December 1992 the Security Council authorised the use of force under Chapter VI rather than Chapter VII and this led to the formation of the Unified Task Force (UNITAF) consisting of 37,000 troops occupying 40 per cent of the country.[45]

The humanitarian operation tended to contain its own internal dynamic towards greater military intervention, though with the withdrawal of the bulk of US forces in 1993 a new UN mission was established in May 1993 in the form of the Second United Nations Operation in Somalia (UNOSOM II). This consisted of a force of 28,000 troops of whom 5,000 were from the USA. Unlike UNOSOM I, this was concerned with 'peace enforcement', though the precise objectives were not clearly spelt out. The idea of 'peace enforcement', derived largely from Boutros Ghali's proposal in *An Agenda for Peace* in 1992 for 'peace enforcement units' operating under Article 40 of the Charter, which would be distinguishable from forces operating under Article 43, in response to international aggression.[46] The notion of 'peace enforcement' was intended to occupy a middle ground between the conventional UN notion of peacekeeping and the large-scale terrain of enforcement as in Korea and the Gulf War. However, the concept remained a vague one and failed to transform itself into a credible military doctrine by the time the USA was entrusted with the control of UNOSOM II.

It was evident in the Somali case that most UN officials in the field still thought in terms of conventional peacekeeping, with civilian staff operating in a non-military context.[47] However, UNOSOM II was given a mandate covering the whole of Somalia and was directed to act against ceasefire violations and to disarm the several factions. Following the death of 25 Pakistani peacekeepers on 5 June 1993, the force targeted the faction of General Aideed and this led to the débâcle of 3 October when two US helicopters were shot down and the body of a dead US serviceman was dragged through the streets of Mogadishu. This humiliating spectacle was enough to force a change in US policy and US forces were withdrawn from Somalia by March 1994, while a UN Commission of Inquiry recommended no further enforcement within internal conflicts of states.[48] The UN force was finally withdrawn in March 1995. Somalia remains a fractured or 'failed' state in which there is no common government and, indeed, the northern part of Somaliland has effectively seceded as an autonomous *de facto* state of the Isaaq clans.

The Somali case has raised major questions about the whole notion of 'peace enforcement', with the implication that the central military tasks of an intervening force should be the restoration of order and the rebuilding of structures of governmental authority, including those of the police and the military. How far in pursuit of this goal should the intervening force side with one or more of the warlord factions? If it does this it risks putting the legitimacy of the whole operation under threat unless it can at the same time form secure links with either influential sections of the remaining civil society or the major international aid agencies and NGOs engaged in the task of rebuilding the society once the internal conflict has ended.

The successful resolution of complex emergencies will increasingly depend upon the close integration of military 'peacekeeping' or 'peace enforcement' tasks with those of humanitarian relief as well as longer-term, post-conflict development. The management of such integration will in many cases be a complex task, given the wide diversity of the groups involved. In some instances the activities of these groups may run in contradiction with each other, especially if the NGOs engage in supplying emergency aid to those warlord factions that are not encompassed by the intervening force. It may well also be the case that one of the warlord factions will emerge as a the *de facto* government of the country with which states, NGOs and international financial institutions will eventually be forced to deal, despite the fact that the faction's human rights record may be grim.

A credible military doctrine for dealing with warlordism will be based on the increased political and diplomatic role of an intervention force, which may need to assist in various forms of humanitarian aid as part of a general strategy of establishing order and rebuilding stable military and police formations. Much will depend upon the degree of common under-standing worked out in advance between the military organisations and the relief agencies involved, which may in turn be assisted by joint training

268

programmes. When these are properly coordinated it may be possible to exert considerable diplomatic pressure in a complicated or confused situation. The military may be used to secure the increased participation of relief organisations, while the relief organisations may in turn use greater or lesser degrees of military back-up to facilitate the effectiveness of their service programmes.[49]

Professional militaries, with negative experiences of working with civilian agencies, may well resist efforts by politicians to promote the national interest through humanitarian support operations. Coordination can be secured on an *ad hoc* basis, but in the longer term the future of international peacekeeping is likely to depend upon the creation of new multinational and even supranational force structures. A doctrine for dealing with warlord-based conflicts in the longer term will, in all probability, entail a revised notion of the military professional involved in humanitarian interventions. As Alfred Stepan has noted, the last major revision of military professionalism in Western armies occurred in the context of threats from insurgent and guerrilla movements in the 1950s and the 1960s. These movements threatened a revolutionary overthrow of state power and the establishment of Marxist-Leninist regimes on the Vietnamese or the Chinese model. In response, there emerged the doctrine of the national security state and a revised notion of military professionalism which no longer rested on the challenge of inter-state conflict but one of 'internal security and national development'.[50] This professional ethic entailed a new class of military bureaucrats steering armies away from conventional notions of war into strategies to contain revolutionary warfare. The parameters of this new professionalism were still largely those of the nation state, though national security regimes, such as Brazil, Argentina and Chile, might swap intelligence and emulate each other's domestic counter-insurgency programmes.

This 'new' professionalism looks increasingly outmoded in the context of post-Cold War warlordist conflict in which counter-insurgency and nation-building methods may not easily work in a failed state with no easily recognisable locus of central political authority. 'Second-generation' peacekeeping after the Cold War needs to be put on a different sort of footing, involving a rapid deployment force which could amount to a UN reserve force operating under Chapter VII of the Charter and made up from designated national units.[51] So far this proposal has not met with any widespread enthusiasm, even from those 19 UN member states which had pledged units for such a force. When the UN, for instance, requested 5,500 troops for an intervention force in Rwanda in 1994 all 19 states declined. It may be that such a force will need to be organised more on a regional basis, and both Britain and France have suggested in the African context the creation of a Multi National African Rapid Deployment Peace Force (MARDPF), while the then US Secretary of State Warren Christopher proposed in 1996 an African Crisis Response Force (ACRF). For these proposals to work with any sort of political authority the Organisation of Africa Unity (OAU) might need to be involved, though this also runs the risk of doctrinal confusion if there may is no common agreement on the purposes of such a force.[52] One potential way out is the Canadian proposal that the UN should provide a vanguard force which could lead to further engagement from other states on a regional peace-keeping basis. Such a force though would still depend on a standby force of some form organised through the UN.[53]

Moreover, the creation of permanent peace-enforcement units indicates that a new form of professionalism will be needed which rather blurs conventional distinctions between military and civilian actors. Such a professional code will be one that is geared to the re-establishment of order and a coherent structure of political authority, but at the same time devolves responsibility to individual field commanders for liaison with the civilian aid agencies and relief organisations. This suggests a growing class of professional 'military humanitarians' who may on occasions be more successful at up-staging the media profile of conventional humanitarian organisations and relief agencies. They will be bound to abide by the policies of their national governments and to some degree earn credit for their country's ruling politicians.

In this changing setting the success of peace-enforcement operations in warlord-based conflicts will increasingly depend upon the managerial and negotiating skills of middle-ranking officers. An overly rigid military hierarchy is likely to inhibit the flexibility needed to cope with the volatile and unpredictable nature of contemporary warlordist conflict. The management of such operations follows in a broad sense similar trends in other areas of 'new public management' involving the devolution of decision-making to lower tiers.

At present warlord-type formations tend to be perceived through a stereotype of criminality exemplified by the UNOSOM II operation against General Aideed. With a greater knowledge of the internal structure and economic base of warlord formations it should be possible to develop a typology of warlords, ranging from those that are effectively large-scale criminal gangs to those that resemble insurgent and national liberation movements with claims towards being treated as legitimate political actors. This in turn will act as a major determinant on policies of military and humanitarian intervention, as well as indicating that warlords cannot be treated as entirely passive and static entities but active participants of policy-making in fractured or fracturing states.

NOTES

1. See Neil Cooper, 'The Arms Trade and Militarised Actors in Internal Conflict' and Glen Segell, 'Warlordism and Drug Trafficking from South-East Asia to Sub-Saharan Africa', in Paul B. Rich (ed.), *Warlords in International Relations* (Basingstoke: Macmillan, 1999).
2. Ralph Peters, 'The New Warrior Class', *Parameters* (Summer 1994), p. 16. See also David Tucker, 'Fighting Barbarians', ibid. (Summer 1994), pp. 69–79.
3. Robert Kaplan, 'The Coming Anarchy', *Atlantic Monthly* (February 1994).
4. Don Redding, 'Time For Scrutiny', paper presented to a conference at Church House, London, 28 May 1998; http://alertnet.org/alertnet.nsf/5314
5. See P. B. Rich, *Warlords in International Relations*.
6. Samuel Huntington, *Political Order in Changing Societies* (New Haven, CT and London: Yale University Press, 1971), p. 198.
7. Yuan himself had national claims and was not really a proto-warlord. His Peiyang army was developed through the manipulation of the central government bureaucracy and was not based on regional support. Stephen R. Mackinnon, 'The Peiyang Army, Yuan Shih-k'ai, and the Origins of Modern Chinese Warlordism', *Journal of Asian Studies*, 32, 3 (May 1973), pp. 405–23.
8. C. P. Fitzgerald, *The Birth of Communist China* (Harmondsworth: Penguin, 1970), p. 52.
9. Arthur Waldron, 'Warlordism versus Federalism: The Revival of a Debate?', *China Quarterly*, 121 (March 1990), pp. 116–28.
10. Arthur Waldron, 'The Warlord: Twentieth Century Chinese Understanding of Violence, Militarism and Imperialism', *American Historical Review*, 96, 4 (October 1996), pp. 1073–100.
11. Edward A. McCord, *The Power of the Gun: The Emergence of Modern Chinese Warlordism* (Berkeley, CA: University of California Press, 1992), p. 4. Lucien Pye detected a virtue in this feature of Chinese warlordism since he considered it contained at least the foundations for a pluralistic society, something that was wiped out by the communist regime in China after the revolution of 1949. Lucien W. Pye, *Warlord Politics: Conflict and Coalition in the Modernization of Republican China* (New York, NY: Praeger, 1971).
12. L. W. Pye, *Warlord Politics*, pp. 41–5.
13. See, for instance, Ali A. Mazrui, 'The Lumpen Proletariat and the Lumpen Militariat: African Soldiers as a New Political Class', *Political Studies*, 21, 1, pp. 1–12.
14. Hussein M. Adam, 'Somalia: Militarism, Warlordism or Democracy?', *Review of African Political Economy*, 54 (1992), p. 13; Hussein M. Adam, 'Class Conflicts and Democratization in Somalia', in Harvey Glickman (ed.), *Ethnic Conflict and Democratization in Africa* (Atlanta, GA: African Studies Association Press, 1995), pp. 197–226.
15. Richard Dowden, 'Skeletons Mark the Death of a Country', http://www.users.interport.net/-mmaren/dowden.html
16. H. M. Adam, 'Somalia: Militarism, Warlordism or Democracy?', *Review of African Political Economy*, 54 (1992), p. 13; Hussein M. Adam, 'Class Conflicts and Democratization in Somalia'; Richard H. Schultz, 'State Disintegration and Ethnic Conflict: A Framework for Analysis', *Annals, AAPSS*, 541 (September 1995), pp. 84–5.

17. Jeffrey Clark, 'Debacle in Somalia', *Foreign Affairs*, 72, 1 (1992/93), p. 112.
18. I. William Zartman, 'Introduction: Posing the Problem of State Collapse', in H. Glickman (ed.), *Ethnic Conflict and Democratization*, p. 8.
19. J. Clark, 'Debacle in Somalia', p. 115.
20. Njuguna Ng'ethe, 'Strongmen, State Formation, Collapse and Reconstruction in Africa', in H. Glickman (ed.), *Ethnic Conflict and Democratization*, pp. 251–64.
21. K. J. Holsti, *The State, War and the State of War* (Cambridge: Cambridge University Press, 1996), p. 34.
22. E. V. Walter, *Terror and Resistance: A Study of Political Violence* (London: Oxford University Press, 1969), p. 291.
23. Ibid., p. 39.
24. Robert Jackson, *Quasi States, Sovereignty, International and the Third World* (Cambridge: Cambridge University Press, 1990).
25. William B. Quandt, *Revolution and Political Leadership: Algeria, 1954–1968* (Cambridge, MA and London: MIT Press, 1969), pp. 10–15; John Talbott, *The War Without a Name: France in Algeria, 1954–1962* (London and Boston, MA: Faber, 1981), pp. 83–9.
26. For details see Martha Crenshaw Hutchinson, *Revolutionary Terrorism: The French in Algeria, 1954–1962* (Stanford, CA: Hoover Institution Press, 1978).
27. Though this in turn has given vent to a new civil war in the 1990s between a secular regime and a radical Islamist opposition that has many of the features of a vicious counter-insurgency war.
28. Tom Young, 'RENAMO and Counter Revolutionary Insurgency', in Paul B. Rich (ed.), *The Dynamics of Change in Southern Africa* (Basingstoke: Macmillan, 1994), pp. 149–69.
29. Ibid., pp. 140–1.
30. Barnett R. Rubin, *The Search for Peace in Afghanistan: From Buffer State to Failed State* (New Haven, CT and London: Yale University Press, 1995), p. 139.
31. Geoffrey Fairbairn, *Revolutionary Guerrilla Warfare* (Harmondsworth: Penguin, 1974), pp. 41–4. See also Walter Laqueur, 'The Origins of Guerrilla Doctrine', *Journal of Contemporary History*, 10, 3 (July 1975), pp. 341–78; for Clausewitz's conceptions of statehood see Peter Paret, *Clausewitz and the State* (Oxford: Oxford University Press, 1976). Some critics have pointed out that Paret rather underplays the moral dimension that Clausewitz attributes to the state as a civilised political form. See Azar Gat, 'Clausewitz's Political and Ethical World View', *Political Studies*, 37 (1989), pp. 97–106.
32. Christopher Clapham, Africa and the International System (Cambridge, Cambridge University Press, 1998), p. 212.
33. Claudia McElroy, 'Now or Never for Liberia's Untrustworthy Warlords', *Guardian*, 29 November 1996.
34. Herbert Howe, 'Lessons of Liberia: ECOMOG and Regional Peacekeeping', *International Security*, 21, 3 (Winter 1996/97), pp. 145–76.
35. John Glenn, 'The Interregnum: the South's Insecurity Dilemma', *Nations and Nationalism*, 3, 1 (1997), pp. 45–63.
36. Robert H. Jackson and Alan James, 'The Character of Independent Statehood', in Robert H. Jackson and Alan James (eds), *States in a Changing World* (Oxford: Clarendon Press, 1993), pp. 6–7.

37. Richard H. Schultz, 'State Disintegration and Ethnic Conflict: A Framework for Analysis', *Annals, AAPSS*, 541 (September 1995), pp. 75–88.
38. Ilene R. Prusher, 'Post US, Somalia Finds Many Cash in on Chaos', *Christian Science Monitor*, 20 October 1997.
39. John Mackinlay, 'Beyond the Logjam: A Doctrine for Complex Emergencies', in Max G. Manwaring and John T. Fishel (eds), *Toward Responsibility in the New World Disorder* (London: Frank Cass, 1998), p. 121.
40. Steven Metz, 'A Flame Kept Burning: Counterinsurgency after the Cold War', *Parameters* (Autumn 1995), p. 35.
41. Reed Kramer, 'Liberia: A Casualty of the Cold War's End', http://www.africanews.org/usaf/liberia.html
42. Lawrence E. Grinter, 'Nation Building, Counter Insurgency and Military Intervention', in Ellen P. Stern (ed.), *The Limits of Military Intervention* (Beverley Hills, CA and London: Sage, 1977), pp. 237–52.
43. Fishel, *Towards Responsibility* (London: Frank Cass, 1998), p. 126.
44. See Jarat Chopra *et al.*, *Fighting for Hope in Somalia*, Norwegian Institute of International Affairs, Peacekeeping and Multinational Operations, No. 6, 1995, p. 6; http://131.111.106.147/Articles/A007A.Htm.
45. Thomas R. Mockaitis, 'Peacekeeping in Intra State Conflict', *Small Wars and Insurgencies*, 6, 1 (Spring 1995), p. 117.
46. J. Chopra *et al.*, *Fighting for Hope in Somalia*, p. 8.
47. Ibid., p. 10.
48. T. R. Mockaitis, 'Peacekeeping in Intra State Conflict', p. 116.
49. John E. Lange, 'Civilian–Military Cooperation and Humanitarian Assistance: Lessons from Rwanda', *Parameters* (Summer 1998), pp. 106–22.
50. Alfred Stepan, 'The New Professionalism of Internal Warfare and Military Role Expansion', in Alfred Stepan (ed.), *Authoritarian Brazil: Origins, Politics and Future* (New Haven, CT and London: Yale University Press, 1973), pp. 47–65.
51. T. R. Mockaitis, 'Peacekeeping in Intra State Conflict', pp. 121–2.
52. M. Malan, 'Towards Sounder Investments in Developing African Peace Operations Capabilities', *African Security Review*, 6, 1 (1997).
53. Nicholas Stockton, 'The Role of the military in Humanitarian Emergencies', RPN 23 January–April 1997, p. 4; http://www.qeh.ox.ac.uk/rsp/rpn234.htm

Index

Please note that any references to footnotes contain the page number followed by 'n' and footnote number, while references to tables are in italics.

Index

285

of, 116, 118; relief, protection of, 8;
UNITAF, and, 206; warlordism,
258, 267–8, *see also* Somalia
UNPREDEP (United Nations Preventive
Deployment Force), 190
UNPROFOR (United Nations
Protection Force, Bosnia and
Herzegovina-Herzegovina): armed
protection, 171; belligerents, and,
xxiv; command and control
difficulties, 21; 'Dobbie doctrine',
185; DPKO, and, 27; establishment,
30; failures, perceived, 56;
humanitarian aid, delivery of, 7–8;
humanitarian operations, evolution,
116; joint battalions, 68; Kosovo
crisis, 51–2; operational
commanders, 33; safe areas, and,
214–27; safety zones, 9; Saravejo,
security provision 124n4; Security
Council, and, xxiii; SFOR, and, 42;
Wider Peacekeeping doctrine,
xxv–xxvi
UNSAS (United Nations Standby
Arrangement System), 30, 31,
205
UNTAC (United Nations Transitional
Authority in Cambodia), 30, 115,
116, 236
UNTAG (United Nations Transition
Assistance Group), 30, 115
Urquhart, Sir Brian, 3, 14, 15, 204
USA *see* United States (USA)
USAID (US Agency for International
Development), 247
USAR (United States Army Reserve)
249n13
USC (United Somali Congress), 258

Van Brabant, Koenraad, 141–62,
163–78
Vance-Owen Peace Plan (VOPP), 216

vertical integration, 25
Vietnam 248n5, 260

Waldron, Arthur, 255
Walter, E.V., 260
War Colleges, 199
war, humanitarian values, 125–40;
humanity, minimal, 129–31;
impartiality, 134–5; morale,
personal, 137–8; neutrality,
abandoning, 131–4; organisational
positioning, 137–8; solidarity,
135–7; third parties, 127–9
warfare, levels of 40n18
warfighting, 210
warlordism, 253–73; conceptualising,
254–9; modern warfare, theory of,
259–64; peacekeeping, and, 264–70
WEU (Western European Union) 46,
48, 57n7, 74, 186
WFP (World Food Programme), 36, 110
'white helmets', 14
Whitman, Jim, 101–14
Wider Peacekeeping ('Dobbie')
doctrine, xxv–xxvi, 50, 182–6, 203,
208, 209
wilayas (military zones), 261
World Bank, 26, 94, 233, 262
World Food Programme (WFP), 36, 110

Yellowstone Park, 105–6
Yorke, Edmund, 78–98
Yuan Shih Kai, 255
Yugoslavia, Former (FRY), 23, 42–59

Zaire, 10, 12, 14, 16, 111, 120
ZANU-PF (Zimbabwe African National
Union-Patriotic Front), 260
Zartman, I.W., 258
Zepa, 10
Zimbabwe, 260
ZNA (Zimbabwe National Army), 87